COMPUTER BOOK SERIES FROM IDG

Excel 5 For Macs

Sheet

Mac Shortcut Keys in Excel 5.0

Keystroke	What it does
⌘ +A	Selects entire worksheet
⌘+Shift+B	Turns bold on and off
⌘ +C	Copies the selection to the Clipboard
⌘+Shift+D	Turns font outline style on and off
⌘+Shift+I	Turns italics on and off
⌘ +L	Displays the Define Name dialog box
⌘ +N	Creates new workbook
⌘ +O	Opens workbook
⌘ +P	Prints
⌘ +R	Fills right
⌘ +S	Saves
⌘ +T	Changes selected cell reference from relative to absolute, absolute to mixed, and mixed to relative
⌘ +U	Activates Edit mode in cell and formula bar
⌘+Shift+U	Turns underline on and off
⌘ +V	Pastes
⌘ +X	Cuts the selection
⌘ +Z	Undoes last action

IDG BOOKS

Cheat Sheet $2.95 value. Item 186-8

For more information about IDG Books, call 1-800-434-3422 or 415-312-0650

. . . For Dummies: #1 Computer Book Series for Beginners

Excel 5.0 Function Key Template — ©1994 IDG Books Worldwide

	F1	F2	F3	F4	F5	F6	F7	F8	F9	F10	F11	F12
⌘+Shift			Create command			Previous window					[illegible]	[illegible]
⌘		Info window	Define command	Close window	Restore windowsize	Next window					Exc Ma [illegible]	[illegible]
Shift	Contextual Help	Note Command	Function Wizard			Previous pane		Add On/Off	Calculate active wksht.	Shortcut menu	Ins wo [illegible]	[illegible]
Alone	Undoes last action	Cut	Copy	Paste	Go To	Next pane	Spelling	Extend On/Off	Calculate all sheets	Menu bar	Insert new chart sheet	Save as

Excel 5 For Macs For Dummies

COMPUTER BOOK SERIES FROM IDG

Cheat Sheet

More Cool Mac Shortcut Keys in Excel 5.0

Shortcut keys*	What it does
⌘ +; (semicolon)	Enters the time
⌘ +- (hyphen)	Enters date
⌘ +Shift+_(underscore)	Applies or removes strikethrough
Control+9	Hides rows
Control+Shift+9	Unhides rows
Control+0 (zero)	Hides columns
Control+Shift+0 (zero)	Unhides columns
Control+Shift+~	General number format
Control+Shift+$	Currency number format
Control+Shift+%	Percentage number format
Control+Shift+#	Date format with day, month, and year
Control+Shift+@	Time with hour, minute, and AM or PM
Control+Shift+!	Comma number format
⌘ +Option+0 (zero)	Outline border
⌘ +Option+- (hyphen)	Removes all borders

Excel 5.0 Function Key Template — © 1994 IDG Books Worldwide

	⌘+Shift	⌘	Shift	Alone
Home	Select to beg. of wksht.	Beginning of worksheet	Select to beg. of current row	Beginning of row
End	Select to end of worksheet	Go to last cell of worksheet		End mode
Page Up		Go to next sheet	Select to beginning of column	One screen up
Page Down		Go to prev. sheet	Select to end of Screen Vw.	One screen down
◆			Select one cell left	Move left one cell
∅			Select one cell right	Move right one cell
↑		Go to top of column	Select one cell up	Move up one cell
↓	Select to btm. of sheet	Go to bottom of column	Select one cell down	Move down one cell

IDG BOOKS

Cheat Sheet $2.95 value. Item 186-8
For more information about IDG Books, call 1-800-434-3422 or 415-312-0650

. . . For Dummies: #1 Computer Book Series for Beginners

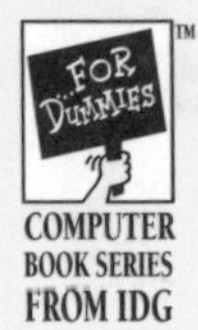

COMPUTER BOOK SERIES FROM IDG

Excel 5 For Macs For Dummies

Cheat Sheet

Mac Shortcut Keys in Excel 5.0

Keystroke	*What it does*
⌘ +A	Selects entire worksheet
⌘+Shift+B	Turns bold on and off
⌘ +C	Copies the selection to the Clipboard
⌘+Shift+D	Turns font outline style on and off
⌘+Shift+I	Turns italics on and off
⌘ +L	Displays the Define Name dialog box
⌘ +N	Creates new workbook
⌘ +O	Opens workbook
⌘ +P	Prints
⌘ +R	Fills right
⌘ +S	Saves
⌘ +T	Changes selected cell reference from relative to absolute, absolute to mixed, and mixed to relative
⌘ +U	Activates Edit mode in cell and formula bar
⌘+Shift+U	Turns underline on and off
⌘ +V	Pastes
⌘ +X	Cuts the selection
⌘ +Z	Undoes last action

Excel 5.0 Function Key Template — ©1994 IDG Books Worldwide

	F1	F2	F3	F4	F5	F6	F7	F8	F9	F10	F11	F12
⌘+Shift			Create command			Previous window						Print
⌘		Info window	Define command	Close window	Restore windowsize	Next window					Excel 4.0 Macro sheet	Open
Shift	Contextual Help	Note Command	Function Wizard			Previous pane		Add On/Off	Calculate active wksht.	Shortcut menu	Insert new worksheet	Save
Alone	Undoes last action	Cut	Copy	Paste	Go To	Next pane	Spelling	Extend On/Off	Calculate all sheets	Menu bar	Insert new chart sheet	Save as

IDG BOOKS

Cheat Sheet $2.95 value. Item 186-8
For more information about IDG Books, call
1-800-434-3422 or 415-312-0650

. . . For Dummies: #1 Computer Book Series for Beginners

Excel 5 For Macs For Dummies

Cheat Sheet

More Cool Mac Shortcut Keys in Excel 5.0

Shortcut keys*	***What it does***
⌘ +; (semicolon)	Enters the time
⌘ +- (hyphen)	Enters date
⌘ +Shift+_(underscore)	Applies or removes strikethrough
Control+9	Hides rows
Control+Shift+9	Unhides rows
Control+0 (zero)	Hides columns
Control+Shift+0 (zero)	Unhides columns
Control+Shift+~	General number format
Control+Shift+$	Currency number format
Control+Shift+%	Percentage number format
Control+Shift+#	Date format with day, month, and year
Control+Shift+@	Time with hour, minute, and AM or PM
Control+Shift+!	Comma number format
⌘ +Option+0 (zero)	Outline border
⌘ +Option+- (hyphen)	Removes all borders

Excel 5.0 Function Key Template — ©1994 IDG Books Worldwide

	Alone	**Shift**	⌘	⌘+Shift
Home	Beginning of row	Select to beg. of current row	Beginning of worksheet	Select to beg. of wksht.
End	End mode		Go to last cell of worksheet	Select to end of worksheet
Page Up	One screen up	Select to beginning of column	Go to next sheet	
Page Down	One screen down	Select to end of Screen Vw.	Go to prev. sheet	
◆	Move left one cell	Select one cell left		
∅	Move right one cell	Select one cell right		
→	Move up one cell	Select one cell up	Go to top of column	
⌐	Move down one cell	Select one cell down	Go to bottom of column	Select to btm. of sheet

IDG BOOKS

Cheat Sheet $2.95 value. Item 186-8
For more information about IDG Books, call 1-800-434-3422 or 415-312-0650

. . . For Dummies: #1 Computer Book Series for Beginners

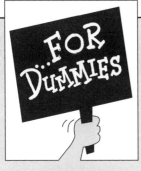

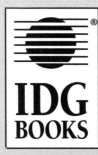

EXCEL 5 FOR MACS FOR DUMMIES™

EXCEL 5 FOR MACS FOR DUMMIES™

by Greg Harvey

IDG Books Worldwide, Inc.
An International Data Group Company

San Mateo, California ♦ Indianapolis, Indiana ♦ Boston, Massachusetts

Excel 5 For Macs For Dummies

Published by
IDG Books Worldwide, Inc.
An International Data Group Company
155 Bovet Road, Suite 610
San Mateo, CA 94402

Library of Congress Catalog Card No.: 94-77628

ISBN 1-56884-186-8

Printed in the United States of America

10 9 8 7 6 5 4 3 2 1

1D/QY/RY/ZU

Distributed in the United States by IDG Books Worldwide, Inc.

Distributed in Canada by Macmillan of Canada, a Division of Canada Publishing Corporation; by Computer and Technical Books in Miami, Florida, for South America and the Caribbean; by Longman Singapore in Singapore, Malaysia, Thailand, and Korea; by Toppan Co. Ltd. in Australia and New Zealand; and by Transworld Publishers Ltd. in the U.K. and Ireland.

For general information on IDG Books in the U.S., including information on discounts and premiums, contact IDG Books 800-434-3422 or 415-312-0650.

For information on where to purchase IDG Books outside the U.S., contact Christina Turner at 415-312-0633.

For information on translations, contact Marc Jeffrey Mikulich, Foreign Rights Manager, at IDG Books Worldwide. FAX 415-286-2747.

For sales inquiries and special prices for bulk quantities, write to the address above or call IDG Books Worldwide at 415-312-0650.

For information on using IDG Books in the classroom, or ordering examination copies, contact Jim Kelly at 800-434-2086

The text in this book is printed on recycled paper.

About the Author

Greg Harvey is a product of the great American Midwest. Born in the Chicago area in 1949 (thus his saying, "I'm only as old as China" — Red China, that is) in the dark ages of the Cold War, before the age of McDonald's, MTV, and, certainly, personal computers. On the shores of Lake Michigan, he learned his letters and numbers and showed great promise in the world of academia (quickly achieving Red Bird reading status after being put back as a Yellow Bird, due to an unforeseen bout of chickenpox at the start of the school year). After earning many gold stars along with a few red, he graduated from Roosevelt School (named for Teddy, not that socialist Delano) in 1963.

During his stint at Thornridge High School in the perfectly boring Chicago suburb of Dolton, Illinois, he found great solace in Motown music (thanks Phil!) and the drama department (to this day, he can recite every line from the play *Auntie Mame* — verbatim). Bored with what passed for academic studies, he went through high school in three years. Looking back on these formative years, Greg was sure thankful for the great tunes and Auntie's philosophy, "Life's a banquet, kid, and some poor suckers are starving."

In 1966 (ah, the Sixties), he entered the University of Illinois at Urbana, Illinois, where he was greatly influenced by such deep philosophers as Abby Hoffman and Mahatma Gandhi. In the summer of 1968, he purchased his first pair of handmade sandals (from Glen, a hippie sandal maker who'd just returned from the Summer of Love in San Francisco).

During his college years, he became quite political. He holds the distinction of being one of a handful of men and women to attend the "camp-out" protest against women's dorm curfews (back then, not only were dorms not sexually integrated, but women were locked up at 11 PM on weeknights, 1 AM on weekends) and the last one to leave after all others went back to their dorms. During his subsequent college years, he became a regular at the Red Herring coffee house, the veritable den of SDS activity on campus.

In addition to antiwar protests, Greg attended various and sundry classes in the Liberal Arts (such as they were in the last half of the 20th century). In the end, he took a major in Classical studies (Ancient Greek and Latin) and a split minor in American History and French. (Greg showed a facility for foreign language, probably stemming from the fact that he's always had a big mouth.) In the course of his Classical studies, he was introduced to his first computer-based training, learning basic Latin with a CAI program called what else but PLATO!

At the beginning of 1971 (January 12, in fact), Greg migrated West from Chicago to San Francisco (with flowers in his hair). Deciding it was high time to get a skill so that he could find a real job, he enrolled in the Drafting and Design program at Laney College in Oakland. After that, he spent nine years working over a hot drafting table, drawing (by hand, mind you) orthographic and perspective plans for various and sundry engineering projects. During his last engineering gig, he worked with a proprietary CAD software package developed by Bechtel Engineering that not only generated the drawings but kept track of the materials actually needed to create the stuff.

In 1981, following his engineering career, Greg went back to school at San Francisco State University, this time to earn his secondary teaching credentials. Upon completion of his teacher training, he bought one of the very first IBM personal computers (with 16K and a single 160K floppy disk!) to help with lesson preparation and student bookkeeping. He still vividly remembers poring over the premier issue of *PC World* for every piece of information that could teach him how to make peace with his blankety blankety personal computer.

Instead of landing a teaching job at the high school or community college (since there weren't any at the time), Greg got a job with a small software outfit, ITM, that was creating an on-line database of software information (well ahead of its time). As part of his duties, Greg reviewed new computer programs (like Microsoft Word 1.0 and Lotus 1-2-3 Release 1) and wrote articles for business users.

After being laid off from this job right after the Christmas party in 1983 (the first of several layoffs from high-tech startups), Greg wrote his first computer book on word processing software for Hayden Books (as a result of a proposal he helped to write while still employed full-time at ITM). After that, Greg worked in various software evaluation and training jobs. After a few more high-tech, software testing, and evaluation jobs in Silicon Valley, Greg turned to software training to get, as he put it, "the perspective of the poor schmoe at the end of the terminal." During the next three years, Greg gave training in a whole plethora of programs to business users of all skill levels for several major independent software training companies in the San Francisco Bay area.

In the Fall of 1986, he hooked up with Sybex, a local computer book publisher, for whom he wrote his second computer training book, *Mastering SuperCalc*. And the rest, as they say, is history. To date, Greg is the author of more than 30 books on using computer software, with the titles created under the ...*For Dummies* aegis for IDG being among his all-time favorites.

In mid-1993, Greg started a new multimedia publishing venture, Media of the Minds. As a multimedia developer, he hopes to enliven his future computer books by making them into true interactive learning experiences that will vastly enrich and improve the training of users of all skill levels.

ABOUT IDG BOOKS WORLDWIDE

Welcome to the world of IDG Books Worldwide.

IDG Books Worldwide, Inc., is a subsidiary of International Data Group, the world's largest publisher of business and computer-related information and the leading global provider of information services on information technology. IDG was founded more than 25 years ago and now employs more than 5,700 people worldwide. IDG publishes more than 200 computer publications in 63 countries (see listing below). Forty million people read one or more IDG publications each month.

Launched in 1990, IDG Books is today the fastest-growing publisher of computer and business books in the United States. We are proud to have received 3 awards from the Computer Press Association in recognition of editorial excellence, and our best-selling ...*For Dummies* series has more than 7 million copies in print with translations in more than 20 languages. IDG Books, through a recent joint venture with IDG's Hi-Tech Beijing, became the first U.S. publisher to publish a computer book in the People's Republic of China. In record time, IDG Books has become the first choice for millions of readers around the world who want to learn how to better manage their businesses.

WINNER
Eighth Annual Computer Press Awards 1992

Our mission is simple: Every IDG book is designed to bring extra value and skill-building instructions to the reader. Our books are written by experts who understand and care about our readers. The knowledge base of our editorial staff comes from years of experience in publishing, education, and journalism — experience which we use to produce books for the '90s. In short, we care about books, so we attract the best people. We devote special attention to details such as audience, interior design, use of icons, and illustrations. And because we use an efficient process of authoring, editing, and desktop publishing our books electronically, we can spend more time ensuring superior content and spend less time on the technicalities of making books.

You can count on our commitment to deliver high-quality books at competitive prices on topics customers want to read about. At IDG, we value quality, and we have been delivering quality for more than 25 years. You'll find no better book on a subject than an IDG book.

John Kilcullen
President and CEO
IDG Books Worldwide, Inc.

WINNER
Ninth Annual Computer Press Awards 1993

IDG Books Worldwide, Inc., is a subsidiary of International Data Group. The officers are Patrick J. McGovern, Founder and Board Chairman; Walter Boyd, President. International Data Group's publications include: **ARGENTINA'S** Computerworld Argentina, Infoworld Argentina; **AUSTRALIA'S** Computerworld Australia, Australian PC World, Australian Macworld, Network World, Mobile Business Australia, Reseller, IDG Sources; **AUSTRIA'S** Computerwelt Oesterreich, PC Test; **BRAZIL'S** Computerworld, Gamepro, Game Power, Mundo IBM, Mundo Unix, PC World, Super Game; **BELGIUM'S** Data News (CW) **BULGARIA'S** Computerworld Bulgaria, Ediworld, PC & Mac World Bulgaria, Network World Bulgaria; **CANADA'S** CIO Canada, Computerworld Canada, Graduate Computerworld, InfoCanada, Network World Canada; **CHILE'S** Computerworld Chile, Informatica; **COLOMBIA'S** Computerworld Colombia, PC World; **CZECH REPUBLIC'S** Computerworld, Elektronika, PC World; **DENMARK'S** Communications World, Computerworld Danmark, Macintosh Produktkatalog, Macworld Danmark, PC World Danmark, PC World Produktguide, Tech World, Windows World; **ECUADOR'S** PC World Ecuador; **EGYPT'S** Computerworld (CW) Middle East, PC World Middle East; **FINLAND'S** MikroPC, Tietoviikko, Tietoverkko; **FRANCE'S** Distributique, GOLDEN MAC, InfoPC, Languages & Systems, Le Guide du Monde Informatique, Le Monde Informatique, Telecoms & Reseaux; **GERMANY'S** Computerwoche, Computerwoche Focus, Computerwoche Extra, Computerwoche Karriere, Information Management, Macwelt, Netzwelt, PC Welt, PC Woche, Publish, Unit; **GREECE'S** Infoworld, PC Games; **HUNGARY'S** Computerworld SZT, PC World; **HONG KONG'S** Computerworld Hong Kong, PC World Hong Kong; **INDIA'S** Computers & Communications; **IRELAND'S** ComputerScope; **ISRAEL'S** Computerworld Israel, PC World Israel; **ITALY'S** Computerworld Italia, Lotus Magazine, Macworld Italia, Networking Italia, PC Shopping, PC World Italia; **JAPAN'S** Computerworld Today, Information Systems World, Macworld Japan, Nikkei Personal Computing, SunWorld Japan, Windows World; **KENYA'S** East African Computer News; **KOREA'S** Computerworld Korea, Macworld Korea, PC World Korea; **MEXICO'S** Compu Edicion, Compu Manufactura, Computacion/Punto de Venta, Computerworld Mexico, MacWorld, Mundo Unix, PC World, Windows; **THE NETHERLANDS'** Computer! Totaal, Computable (CW), LAN Magazine, MacWorld, Totaal "Windows"; **NEW ZEALAND'S** Computer Listings, Computerworld New Zealand, New Zealand PC World, Network World; **NIGERIA'S** PC World Africa; **NORWAY'S** Computerworld Norge, C/World, Lotusworld Norge, Macworld Norge, Networld, PC World Ekspress, PC World Norge, PC World's Produktguide, Publish& Multimedia World, Student Data, Unix World, Windowsworld; IDG Direct Response; **PAKISTAN'S** PC World Pakistan; **PANAMA'S** PC World Panama; **PERU'S** Computerworld Peru, PC World; **PEOPLE'S REPUBLIC OF CHINA'S** China Computerworld, China Infoworld, Electronics Today/Multimedia World, Electronics International, Electronic Product World, China Network World, PC and Communications Magazine, PC World China, Software World Magazine, Telecom Product World; IDG HIGH TECH BEIJING'S New Product World; IDG SHENZHEN'S Computer News Digest; **PHILIPPINES'** Computerworld Philippines, PC Digest (PCW); **POLAND'S** Computerworld Poland, PC World/Komputer; **PORTUGAL'S** Cerebro/PC World, Correio Informatico/Computerworld, Informatica & Comunicacoes Catalogo, MacIn, Nacional de Produtos; **ROMANIA'S** Computerworld, PC World; **RUSSIA'S** Computerworld-Moscow, Mir - PC, Sety; **SINGAPORE'S** Computerworld Southeast Asia, PC World Singapore; **SLOVENIA'S** Monitor Magazine; **SOUTH AFRICA'S** Computer Mail (CIO),Computing S.A.,Network World S.A., Software World; **SPAIN'S** Advanced Systems, Amiga World, Computerworld Espana, Communicaciones World, Macworld Espana, NeXTWORLD, Super Juegos Magazine (GamePro), PC World Espana, Publish; **SWEDEN'S** Attack, ComputerSweden, Corporate Computing, Natverk & Kommunikation, Macworld, Mikrodatorn, PC World, Publishing & Design (CAP), Datalngenjoren, Maxi Data,Windows World; **SWITZERLAND'S** Computerworld Schweiz, Macworld Schweiz, PC Tip; **TAIWAN'S** Computerworld Taiwan, PC World Taiwan; **THAILAND'S** Thai Computerworld; **TURKEY'S** Computerworld Monitor, Macworld Turkiye, PC World Turkiye; **UKRAINE'S** Computerworld; **UNITED KINGDOM'S** Computing /Computerworld, Connexion/Network World, Lotus Magazine, Macworld, Open Computing/Sunworld; **UNITED STATES'** Advanced Systems, AmigaWorld, Cable in the Classroom, CD Review, CIO, Computerworld, Digital Video, DOS Resource Guide, Electronic Entertainment Magazine, Federal Computer Week, Federal Integrator, GamePro, IDG Books, Infoworld, Infoworld Direct, Laser Event, Macworld, Multimedia World, Network World, PC Letter, PC World, PlayRight, Power PC World, Publish, SWATPro, Video Event; **VENEZUELA'S** Computerworld Venezuela, PC World; **VIETNAM'S** PC World Vietnam

Dedication

To all our Mac friends: This one's for you!

Acknowledgments

Let me take this opportunity to thank all the folks at IDG Books Worldwide and at Harvey & Associates, whose dedication and talent combined to make this book so successful.

At IDG Books, I want thank Janna Custer and Megg Bonar in San Mateo, David Solomon (for seeing the wisdom of creating a separate Mac Excel Dummies book), Corbin Collins (you're the best), Linda Boyer, Mary Breindenbach, Kent Gish, Angela F. Hunckler, Patricia R. Reynolds, Gina Scott, and last and never least, Greg Robertson (ever the comic) in Chicago.

At Harvey & Associates, many thanks to Shane Gearing and Jane Vait. To Shane fell the great task of making the earlier Windows incarnation of this book true to the Macintosh both in spirit and form. This also meant overseeing the entire update of the book as well as doing the "author" review. (Shane, you did one hell of a job!) To Jane fell the unenviable task of taking screen shots of the Excel program (beta, mind you) to provide the figures for this book. (Jane, you're a saint!) Thanks to you, the Macintosh users of Excel now have a *Dummies* book of their very own!

Credits

Publisher
David Solomon

Managing Editor
Mary Bednarek

Acquisitions Editor
Janna Custer

Production Director
Beth Jenkins

Senior Editors
Sandra Blackthorn
Diane Graves Steele
Tracy L. Barr

Production Coordinator
Cindy L. Phipps

Associate Aquisitions Editor
Megg Bonar

Production Quality Control
Steve Peake

Editorial Assistant
Rebecca Forrest

Project Editor
Gregory R. Robertson

Technical Reviewer
Michael Partington

Production Staff
Linda Boyer
Mary Breidenbach
J. Tyler Connor
Kent Gish
Angela F. Hunckler
Patricia R. Reynolds
Gina Scott

Proofreading
Carol Micheli

Indexer
Nancy Anderman Guenther

Book Design
University Graphics

Cover Design
Kavish + Kavish

Contents at a Glance

Cartoons at a Glance

By Rich Tennant

page 77

page 257

page 293

page 145

page 193

page 317

page 7

Table of Contents

Introduction

Welcome to *Excel 5 For Macs For Dummies*, the definitive work on Excel for those of you who have no intention of ever becoming a spreadsheet guru — brought up-to-date with Excel 5. In this book, you'll find all the information you need to keep your head above water as you accomplish the everyday tasks that normal people do with Excel. The intention here is to keep things simple and not bore you with a lot of technical details that you neither need nor care anything about. As much as possible, this book attempts to cut to the chase by telling you in plain terms just what you need to do to get a particular thing done with Excel.

Excel 5 For Macs For Dummies covers all the fundamental techniques you need to create, edit, format, and print your own worksheets. This book covers the basics in Excel and, although the screen shots used in this book cover Excel 5, users of earlier versions should have no trouble using them. In addition to learning your way around the worksheet, you are exposed to the basics of charting and creating databases. Keep in mind that this book just touches on the easiest ways to get a few things done with these features — I make no attempt to cover charting and databases in anything approaching a definitive way (I know you're relieved to hear that). In the main, this book concentrates on the *worksheet,* because this is the part of the program you probably work with most often.

About This Book

This book is not meant to be read from cover to cover. Although the chapters are loosely organized in a logical order, progressing as you might when learning Excel in a classroom situation, each topic covered in a chapter is really meant to stand on its own.

Each discussion of a topic briefly addresses the question of what a particular feature is good for before launching into how to use it. In Excel, as in most other sophisticated programs, there is usually more than one way to do a task. For the sake of your sanity, I have deliberately limited the choices by giving you only the most efficient way to do a particular task. Later on — if you're so tempted — you can experiment with alternative ways of doing something. For now, just concentrate on learning how to perform the task as described.

As much as possible, I've tried to make it unnecessary for you to remember things covered in another section of the book in order to get something to work in the section you're currently reading. From time to time, however, you'll encounter a cross-reference to another section or chapter in the book. For the most part, such cross-references are meant to help you get more complete information on a subject, should you have the time and interest. If you have neither, no problem. Just ignore the cross-references as if they never existed.

How to Use This Book

This book is like a reference in which you start out by looking up the topic you need information on (either in the table of contents or the index) and then refer directly to the section of interest. Most topics are explained conversationally (as though you were sitting in the back of a classroom, where you could safely nap). Sometimes, though, my regiment-commander mentality takes over, and I list the steps you need to take to get a particular task accomplished in a particular section.

What You Can Safely Ignore

When you come across a section that contains steps you take to get something done, the important stuff is in bold type. You can safely ignore all text accompanying the steps that *isn't* in bold if you have neither the time nor the inclination to wade through more material.

Whenever possible, I have also tried to separate background or footnote-type information from the essential facts by exiling that kind of junk to Technical Stuff sections flagged by an icon. You can easily disregard text marked this way. Note also that the information you find flagged with a Tip icon, although designed to help you become more efficient with the program, is also extraneous and can be safely skipped over until you're ready for it.

When you see the bomb that signifies the Warning icon, however, it may be a good idea to linger a while and take some time to read about what could happen if you do something bad.

Foolish Assumptions

I'm going to make only one assumption about you (let's see how close I get): You have access to a Mac at least some of the time that has some version of the Macintosh Finder and Microsoft Excel installed on it. I also assume that you have no previous experience using Excel.

But wait! Maybe I've overlooked some things. Some of you may have upgraded to the latest version: Excel 5.0. Some of you may still be using Excel 4.0 (you ought to upgrade soon — I promise that you'll be happy you did).

This book is targeted primarily toward new users of Excel 5.0 for Macintosh, but there's still plenty of handy information for users of Excel versions prior to 5.0. Keep in mind, however, that Excel 5.0 uses a different pull-down menu system and toolbar arrangement than did 4.0 and earlier versions. For that reason, you may find it very confusing (if not down right impossible) to learn Excel 4.0 from this book. Either get your hands on the first edition of *Excel For Dummies* or, — better yet — upgrade to Excel 5.0.

For those of you who've had some exposure to Excel 4.0, I've marked the brand new features that have never before been seen with the icon that appears next to this paragraph.

Don't worry if you don't have much experience with the Mac, either, or if you don't really have a clear idea of what Excel can do for you. If I think that you need some additional Mac information that I can't provide within the framework of the book, I'll let you know when it's time to get out another book, such as *Macs For Dummies* or *Macworld Guide to System 7.1* or *Macworld Complete Mac Handbook Plus CD* (all books published by IDG Books Worldwide).

If *Excel For Dummies* piques your interest, and you think you're ready for the big time, you can find in-depth information about Excel in two other books published by IDG Books Worldwide: *More Excel for Dummies* by Greg Harvey, and *Macworld Guide to Excel* by David Maguiness. My *More Excel for Dummies* is targeted to Windows users; however both versions of Excel 5 are very similar, much more even than earlier versions of Excel. Just remember that at least you are free to ignore DOS and Windows limitations. Isn't that great?

How This Book Is Organized

This book is organized into seven parts, each of which starts off with one of those great Rich Tennant cartoons! Each part contains two or more chapters (to keep the editors happy) that more or less go together. Each chapter is divided into loosely related sections that cover the basics of the topic at hand. But you shouldn't get too hung up about following along with the structure of the book — ultimately, it doesn't matter at all whether you first learn how to edit the worksheet or how to format it, or whether you learn printing before you learn editing. The important things are that you find the information when you need to do any of these things and that you understand it when you find it.

Just in case you're interested, a brief synopsis of what is in each part follows.

Part I: The Absolute Basics

As the name implies, Part I covers fundamentals such as how to start the program, identify the parts of the screen, enter information in the worksheet, save a document, and so on. If you're starting with absolutely *no* background in using spreadsheets, you should for sure glance at Chapter 1 to learn what this program is good for before you move on to how to create new worksheets in Chapter 2.

Part II: The More Things Change . . .

Part II gives you the skinny on how to make worksheets look good as well as how to make major editing changes to them without courting disaster. Refer to Chapter 3 when you need information on changing the way the information appears in the worksheet. Refer to Chapter 4 when you need information on rearranging, deleting, or inserting new information in the worksheet.

Part III: Ferreting Out the Information

Part III lets you know what to do with the information in a worksheet after it's in there. Chapter 5 is full of good ideas on how to keep track of the whereabouts of the information in a worksheet. Chapter 6 gives you the ins and outs of getting the information down on paper.

Part IV: Amazing Things You Can Do with Excel (for Fun and Profit)

Part IV explores some of the other aspects of Excel besides the worksheet. In Chapter 7, you find out just how ridiculously easy it is to create a chart using the data in a worksheet. In Chapter 8, you learn how useful Excel's database capabilities can be when you have to track and organize a large amount of information. In Chapter 9, you discover how make to your work in Excel a little more interesting by spreading it out into more than one worksheet in a single workbook.

Part V: Excel — Have It Your Way

Part V gives you ideas about how to customize the way you work with Excel. In Chapter 10, you learn how to change the display options in Excel and how to record and play back macros to automate tasks. In Chapter 11, you learn how to customize the built-in toolbars and create new toolbars of your own.

Part VI: Excel Function Reference (for Real People)

Part VI gives you information on using specific Excel functions. Chapter 12 covers everyday functions such as SUM, AVERAGE, and ROUND. Chapter 13 gets more adventurous and covers more sophisticated functions, like the financial functions PV and PMT and the text functions PROPER, UPPER, and LOWER.

Part VII: The Part of Tens

As the tradition goes in these . . . *For Dummies* books, the last part contains lists of useful and useless facts, tips, and suggestions. So don't worry. You don't have to read ten more chapters if you get this far.

Conventions Used in This Book

The following information gives you the lowdown on how things look in this book. Publishers call these the book's *conventions* — no campaigning, flag-waving, name-calling, or finger-pointing is involved, however.

Keyboard and mouse

Excel is a sophisticated program with lots of fancy boxes, plenty of bars, and more menus than you can count. In Chapter 1, I explain all about these features and how to use them. Be sure to review Chapter 1 if you have any questions about how to get around in the program.

Although you use the mouse and keyboard-shortcut keys to move your way in, out, and around the Excel worksheet, you do have to take some time to enter in the data so that you can eventually mouse around with it. Therefore, I occasionally encourage you to type a specific something into a specific place in the worksheet. Of course, you can always choose not to follow the instructions, but you'll see what they look like anyway. For example, when I tell you to enter a specific function, what you are to type appears like this:

```
=PROPER(this_is_it)
```

When stuff appears on a screened line like this, you type exactly what you see: = (an equal sign), the word **PROPER**, a left parenthesis, the text **this_is_it** (complete with underscores), and a right parenthesis. Of course, you have to press Return after all that to make the entry stick.

When I ask you to type something that's just right there in the paragraph, it is formatted in **bold** type.

When Excel isn't talking to you by popping up message boxes, it displays highly informative messages in the status bar at the bottom of the screen. This book renders any messages in a special typeface, like this: `Ready`. (That's the highly informative status message I mentioned.) This special typeface always identifies any on-screen information or messages.

Special icons

The following icons are strategically placed in the margins to point out stuff you may or may not want to read.

This icon alerts you to nerdy discussions that you well may want to skip (or read when no one else is around).

This icon alerts you to shortcuts or other valuable hints related to the topic at hand.

This icon alerts you to information to keep in mind if you want to meet with a modicum of success.

This icon alerts you to information to keep in mind if you want to avert complete disaster.

This icon alerts you to brand new features never seen before Excel 5.0.

Where to Go from Here

If you've never worked with a computer spreadsheet, I suggest you go first to Chapter 1 to find out what you're dealing with. If you're already familiar with the ins and outs of electronic spreadsheets but don't know anything about creating worksheets with Excel, jump into Chapter 2, where you find out how to start entering data and formulas. Then, as specific needs arise (like "How do I copy a formula?" or "How do I print just a particular section of my worksheet?"), you can go to the table of contents or the index to find the appropriate section and go right to that section for answers.

Part I

The Absolute Basics

The part in which . . .

You discover that a spreadsheet program is not just a word processor with braces (formed by column and row gridlines). You find out that Excel exhibits some real smarts that can help you get your work done without involving you in deep understanding of what's going on — a dream come true!

In this part, you learn how to get in and out of Excel without doing you or your computer irreparable harm. And you embark on your first solo mission: getting information into an Excel document and making sure it stays there.

Chapter 1

Now, Just What Have You Gotten Yourself Into?

In This Chapter

- How Excel 5.0 is so special
- How to start Excel 5.0
- How to open the workbook you want to work on at the same time you start Excel 5.0
- How Excel uses the mouse
- How to move around the workbook
- How to select commands from the various menus on the menu bar
- How to use the shortcut menus
- How to make your selections in a dialog box
- How to get on-line help anytime you need it
- How to quit Excel

As Alice found out in Wonderland, "It's always best to begin at the beginning." Chapter 1 of this book, therefore, takes the Excel program from the top. This chapter acquaints you with the awesome nature of the spreadsheet beast that you are about to use before going on to teach you how to start the darn thing. (Actually, Excel is rather more *beauty* than *beast*.)

Because I'm arming you with the knowledge of how to get yourself in trouble by starting Excel, it's only fair to let you know how to bail out of the program as well as how to follow proper etiquette during your stay. While dispensing this wisdom, I protect your inalienable right *not* to know and at the same time make sure you have all the information you need to keep your head above water.

Who Put the "Work" in Workbook?

In the olden days, humankind crunched numbers with primitive tools such as pencils, paper, and handheld calculators — not with their trusty computers and sophisticated electronic spreadsheet programs like Excel. So it was that our ancestors actually did financial planning by writing the numbers that they punched up on their calculators onto long green sheets of paper (by hand, mind you)!

These green sheets, because they were much wider than they were tall, became known as *spreadsheets*. The spreadsheet used fine gridlines to divide the large sheet into a series of columns and rows. The number cruncher would then pencil in the calculated figures in the spaces created at the intersection of column and row gridlines. The gridlines helped to line up the numbers in the spreadsheet so that other people could tell whether the numbers referred to widgets, wodgets, or gadgets.

An electronic spreadsheet program like Excel pays homage to this glorious past by presenting you with a facsimile of the old green sheet on your computer screen in the workbook that appears when you start the program. (This workbook, named Workbook1, actually contains 16 blank spreadsheets that you can use.) In keeping with its paper spreadsheet tradition, each electronic spreadsheet uses fine gridlines to divide the sheet into a series of columns and rows into which you enter your text and numbers, as illustrated in Figure 1-1.

You should note that spreadsheet programs, Excel included, are more apt to refer to their electronic sheets as *worksheets* rather than spreadsheets. You should also note that although it is perfectly acceptable (even preferable) to call one of Excel's electronic spreadsheets a worksheet, you should never *ever* refer to Excel as a worksheet program — you should always refer to Excel as a spreadsheet program (go figure — it's just the way it is).

Semantics aside, the electronic worksheet differs from the traditional paper spreadsheet in another significant way: The worksheet contains a frame used to label the columns and rows. As you can see in Figure 1-1, columns are labeled with letters of the alphabet, and the rows are labeled with numbers. The columns and rows are labeled because the Excel worksheet is humongous. (Figure 1-1 shows only a tiny part of the total worksheet.) The column and row labels act like street signs in a city — the labels can help you identify your current location (even when they fail to prevent you from becoming lost).

So, how big is it?

Measuring 256 columns by 16,384 rows, each of the 16 *worksheets* in an Excel workbook dwarfs the largest paper spreadsheet. If you were to produce the entire worksheet grid on paper, you would need a sheet approximately 21 feet wide by 341 feet long!

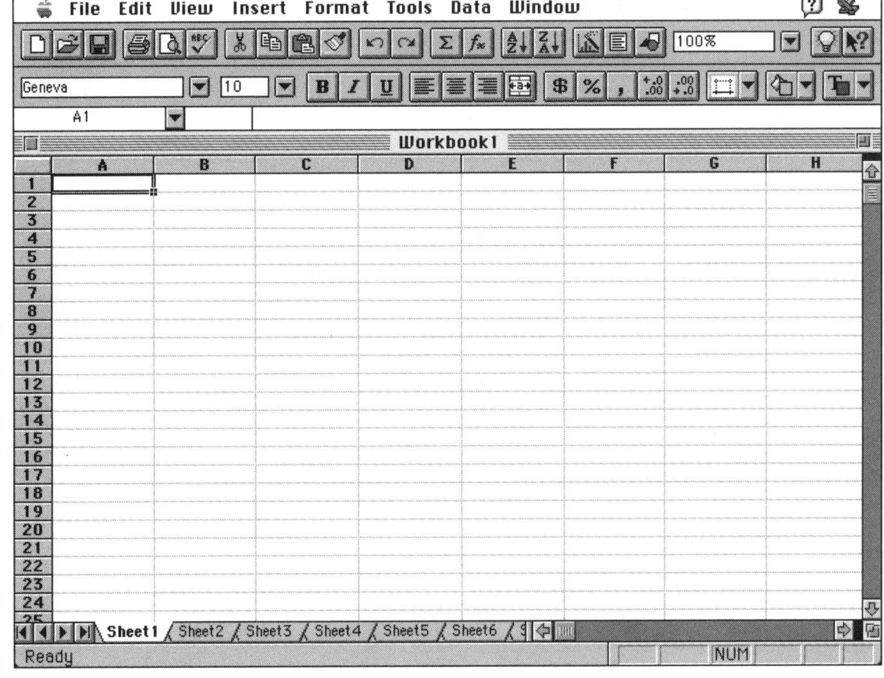

Figure 1-1: Each worksheet in an Excel workbook divides the work area into columns and rows.

On a 13-inch monitor, you can normally see no more than 9 complete columns and 18 complete rows of the entire worksheet. With columns at around 1 inch wide and rows approximately 1/4 inch high, 9 columns represent a scant 4 percent of the total width of the worksheet, whereas 18 rows are only about 1/10 of 1 percent of its total length. These figures should give you some idea of how little of the total worksheet area is viewable on-screen, as well as how much total area is available.

Meet me at F and 15th Streets

I bring up the facts and figures on the worksheet size not to intimidate you but to make you aware of how important it is that the Excel worksheet has a good reference system. Excel keeps you informed at all times of your exact position in each worksheet of your workbook. Because each worksheet offers you so much room for expansion, if you didn't know where you were placing particular information, you could easily lose track of it.

To help you identify the location of entries and find them again, Excel not only displays a frame around the worksheet that shows you column letters and row numbers, but the program also uses these column and row references to keep you continually informed of your current location.

Figure 1-2 shows you how the labeling system works. In this figure, the current location is the intersection of column F and row 15 on Sheet 1. (The sheet number is indicated by the active tab — that is, the one that appears as part of the bottom of the worksheet you're looking at.)

The current location is indicated in two ways. First, in the worksheet itself, this area is highlighted with a heavy outline called the *cell pointer*. Second, the column letter and row number appear at the beginning of the bar directly above the one containing the column letters. This bar is identified as the *formula bar* in Figure 1-2.

In this particular example, because the cell pointer occupies the space at the intersection of column F and row 15, F15 appears in the formula bar. F15 identifies your location in the worksheet, just like saying "I'm at the intersection of F and 15th Streets" pinpoints your location in town. The cell address in the formula bar gives you the current address of the cell pointer relative to the starting point of the worksheet (A and 1st Streets, called A1 in Excel).

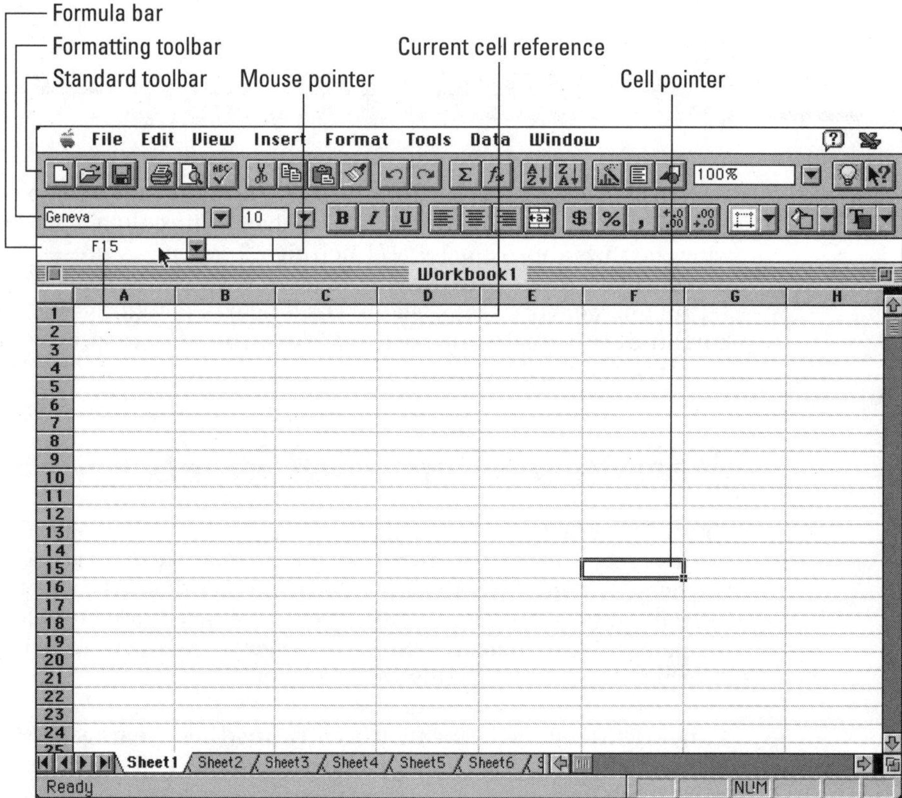

Figure 1-2: Excel displays the current column and row reference on the formula bar.

Excel supports a really weird alternate system of cell references called the *R1C1 cell reference system.* In this system, both the columns and rows in the worksheet are numbered, and the row number precedes the column number. For example, cell A1 is called R1C1 (row 1, column 1), cell A2 is R2C1 (row 2, column 1), and cell B1 is R1C2 (row 1, column 2). To find out how to switch to this cell reference system, see Chapter 10.

Cellmates

The space identified by the column letter and row number on the formula bar is called a *cell.* The cell pointer actually outlines the borders of the current cell. The worksheet cell works somewhat like a prison cell, at least in the sense that any information you put into the cell of the worksheet remains imprisoned there until the warden (you) either clears out the information or moves it to another cell. However, quite unlike cells in an actual prison, a worksheet cell only supports one inmate at a time (a normal prison cell may house dozens). If you try to put new information in a cell that is already occupied, Excel replaces the old cell inmate with the new one.

I've forgotten what comes after Z

Our alphabet, with its mere 26 letters, is certainly insufficient to label the 256 consecutive columns in the Excel worksheet. To make up the difference, Excel doubles up the cell letters in the column reference so that column AA immediately follows column Z. Column AA is followed by column AB, AC, and so on to AZ. After column AZ, you find column BA, BB, BC, and so on. According to this system for doubling the column letters, the 256th and last column of the worksheet is column IV. The very last cell of the worksheet has the cell reference IV16384!

What's this thing good for anyway?

So far, you know the following information about Excel:

- Excel uses a workbook made up of 16 enormous electronic worksheets, all modeled after a paper spreadsheet.
- Each of the 16 worksheets in a workbook is divided into columns and rows and contains a frame that labels the columns with letters and the rows with numbers.
- You enter all your information in the itty-bitty compartments (called *cells*) that are formed by the intersection of each column and row.
- Excel is more humane than most prison systems because it allows only one inmate in each cell at one time.

Armed with this information alone, however, you could easily get the mistaken idea that Excel is little more than a quirky word processor with gridlock that forces you to enter your information in tiny, individual cells rather than offering you the spaciousness of full pages.

Well, I'm here to say that Bill Gates didn't become a billionaire several times over by selling a quirky word processor. (All you Microsoft Word users out there, please hold your tongues!) The big difference between the cell of a worksheet and the pages of a word processor is that each cell offers computing power along with text editing and formatting capabilities. This computing power takes the form of *formulas* that you create in various cells of the worksheet.

Quite unlike a paper spreadsheet, which contains only values computed somewhere else, an electronic worksheet can store both the formulas and the computed *values* returned by these formulas. Even better, your formulas can use values stored in other cells of the worksheet, and (as you'll see shortly) Excel automatically updates the computed answer returned by such a formula anytime you change these values in the worksheet.

Excel's computational capabilities, combined with its editing and formatting capabilities, make the program perfect for generating any kind of document that uses text and numeric entries and requires you to perform calculations on the values. Because you can make your formulas dynamic — so that their calculations are automatically updated when you change referenced values stored in other cells of the worksheet — you will find it much easier to keep the calculated values in a worksheet document both current and correct.

Ladies and Gentlemen, Start Your Spreadsheets

You can start Excel with several different methods. To start Excel 5.0, you need to find the Microsoft Excel folder. After you locate (and open, if necessary) the Microsoft Excel folder, you can start the program: Position the mouse pointer (the arrowhead) on the Microsoft Excel icon, as illustrated in Figure 1-3, and *double-click* the mouse button. If double-clicking doesn't work for you, you can just click on the icon to select it (selection is indicated by a highlighted icon and name) and then press ⌘+O.

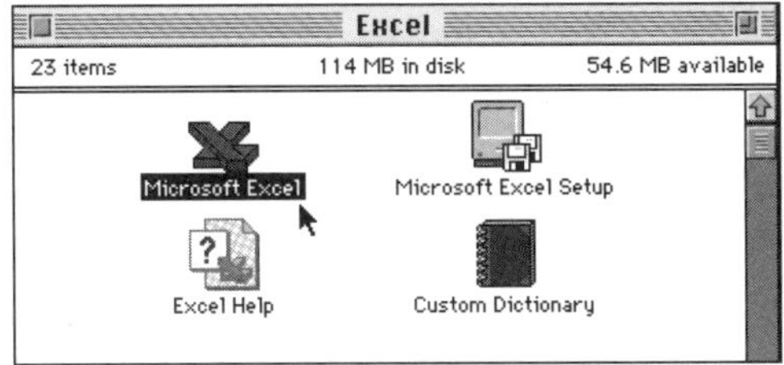

Figure 1-3: Macintosh Finder shows the Microsoft Excel folder containing the Microsoft Excel icon.

Opening a document when starting Excel

You may have times when you want to get right down to work on a particular workbook the moment Excel starts. For these times, you can open the workbook and start Excel at the same time. The easiest way to do this procedure is to locate the Excel document that you want to work on, and then position the mouse pointer on the document icon and *double-click* the mouse button, as shown in Figure 1-4. (Alternatively, you can click on the document name once and then press ⌘+O.) Because the Macintosh Finder knows that Excel documents are created by Excel, Finder starts Excel, and then Excel automatically opens the document you have selected!

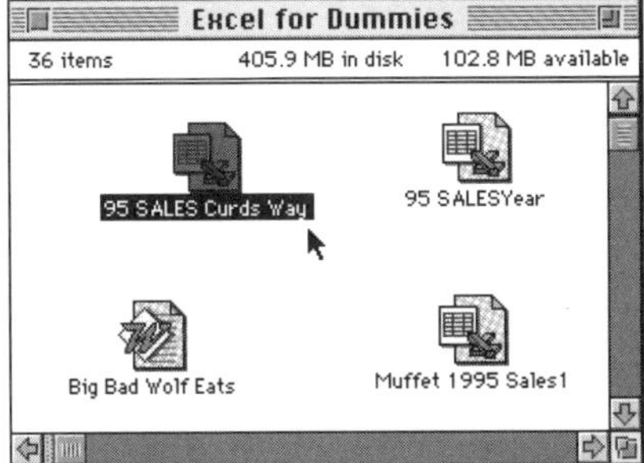

Figure 1-4: Finder displays the Microsoft Excel document icon before selection.

What Happens if I Press This Button?

Figure 1-5 identifies the different parts of the Excel program window that appears when you first start the program (assuming that you haven't selected an existing workbook to open at the same time the program starts). As you can see, the Excel window is full of all kinds of useful but potentially confusing stuff.

The menu bar

The first bar in the Excel window is the menu bar. This bar contains the Excel pull-down menus that you use to select various Excel commands you need to use. (Jump ahead to the section "Menurama: Pull-Down versus Shortcut" for more information on how to select commands.)

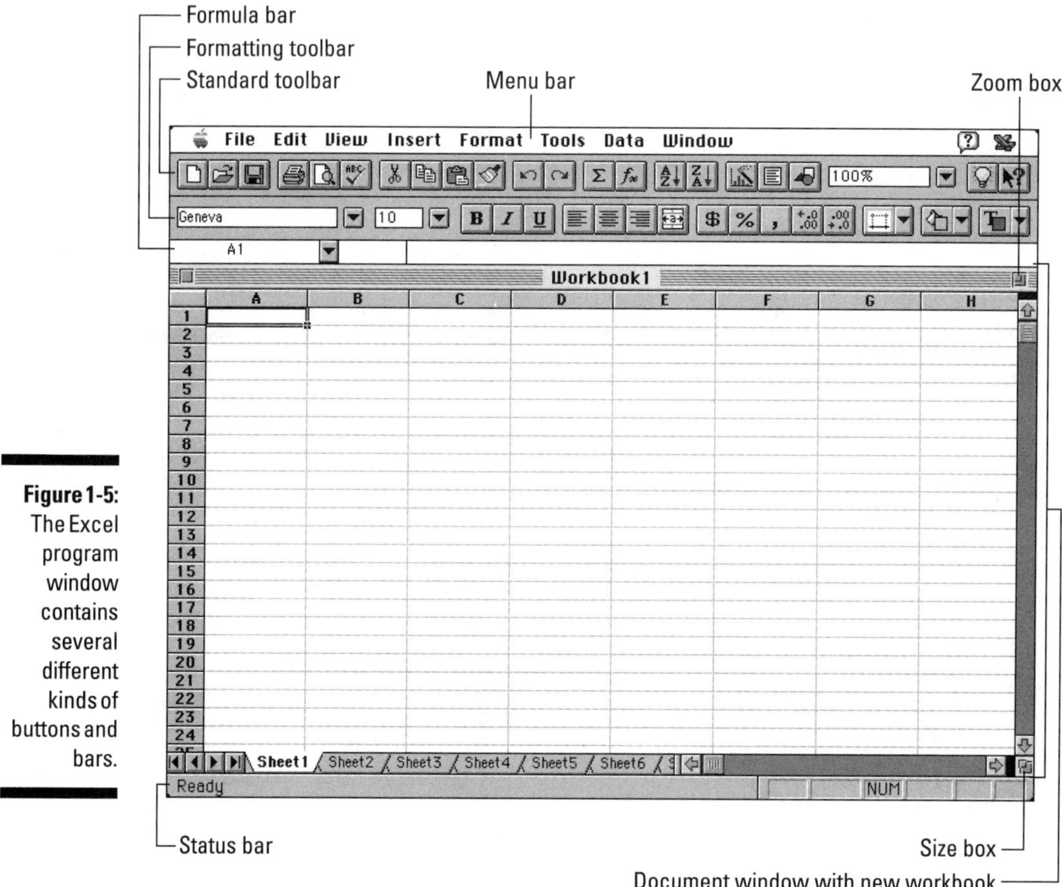

Figure 1-5: The Excel program window contains several different kinds of buttons and bars.

The Standard toolbar

The Standard toolbar occupies the second bar of the Excel window. Each button, more commonly called a *tool,* in this bar performs a particular function when you click on it with the mouse. For example, you can use the first tool to open a new workbook, the second tool to open an existing workbook file, the third tool to save the current workbook, and the fourth tool to print the workbook. Table 1-1 shows you the name and function of each tool on the Standard toolbar. Rest assured, you will come to know each tool intimately as your experience with Excel grows.

To display the name of a tool on any toolbar shown on-screen, simply position the mouse pointer on the tool, and Excel displays the name of the tool in a little box below the pointer. (Microsoft refers to this kind of help as *Tooltips* — don't blame me, I don't make these things up!)

Table 1-1 The Cool Tools on the Standard Toolbar

Tool	*Tool Name*	*What the Tool Does When You Click on It*
	New Workbook	Opens a new workbook with 16 blank worksheets
	Open	Lets you open an existing Excel workbook
	Save	Saves changes in the active workbook
	Print	Prints the workbook
	Print Preview	Lets you preview how the worksheet will appear when printed
	Spelling	Checks the spelling of text in your worksheet
	Cut	Cuts the current selection to the Clipboard
	Copy	Copies the current selection to the Clipboard
	Paste	Pastes the contents of the Clipboard in the current worksheet
	Format Painter	Lets you apply all the formatting used in the current cell to any cell selection you choose
	Undo	Undoes your last action
	Repeat	Repeats your last action
	AutoSum	Sums a list of values with the SUM function
	Function Wizard	Steps you through creating a formula by using one of Excel's many built-in functions (see Chapter 2)
	Sort Ascending	Sorts data in a cell selection in alphabetical order and/or numerical order, depending on the type of data in cells

(continued)

Table 1-1 *(continued)*

Tool	*Tool Name*	*What the Tool Does When You Click on It*
	Sort Descending	Sorts data in a cell selection in reverse alphabetical order and/or numerical order, depending on the type of data in cells
	ChartWizard	Steps you through the creation of a new chart in the active worksheet (see Chapter 7)
	Text Box	Creates a text box that you can use to add notes to a worksheet (see Chapter 7)
	Drawing	Displays the Drawing toolbar, which enables you to draw various shapes and arrows (see Chapter 7)
100%	Zoom Control	Lets you change the screen magnification to zoom in or out on your worksheet data
	TipWizard	Gives you tips on how to do things faster and quicker in Excel, based on whatever actions you've just been performing. You know that Excel has some tips for you when the light bulb icon used by the TipWizard turns yellow (instead of white). Click on the TipWizard tool to display a box containing numbered tips and scroll arrows beneath the Formatting toolbar at the top of the screen. To get rid of the tips after reading them, just click on the TipWizard tool a second time.
	Help	Gives you help information on the command or region of the screen that you click on with the question-mark pointer

The Formatting toolbar

Beneath the Standard toolbar you see the Formatting toolbar, so-called because its buttons are mainly used to format cells in your worksheet. Table 1-2 shows you the name of each tool on this toolbar along with a brief description of its function.

Table 1-2 The Cool Tools on the Formatting Toolbar

Tool	*Tool Name*	*What the Tool Does When You Click on It*
Arial	Font	Applies a new font to the entries in the cell selection
10	Font Size	Applies a new font size to the entries in the cell selection
B	Bold	Applies bold to the cell selection
I	Italic	Applies italics to the cell selection
U	Underline	Underlines the *entries* in the cell selection, not the cells. (If the entries are already underlined, clicking on this tool removes the underlining.)
	Align Left	Left aligns the entries in the cell selection
	Center	Centers the entries in the cell selection
	Align Right	Right aligns the entries in the cell selection
a	Center Across Columns	Centers the entry in the active cell across selected columns
$	Currency Style	Applies a Currency number format to the cell selection to display all values with a dollar sign, commas between thousands, and two decimal places
%	Percent Style	Applies a Percentage number format to the cell selection by multiplying the values by 100 and displaying with a percent sign and no decimal places
,	Comma Style	Applies a Comma number format to the cell selection to display commas separating thousands and two decimal places
+.0 .00	Increase Decimal	Adds one decimal place to the number format in the cell selection each time you click on the tool. (Reverses direction and reduces the number of decimal places when you hold down the shift key as you click on this tool.)
.00 +.0	Decrease Decimal	Reduces one decimal place from the number format in the cell selection each time you click on the tool. (Reverses direction and adds one decimal place when you hold down the Shift key as you click on this tool.)

(continued)

Table 1-2 *(continued)*

Tool	*Tool Name*	*What the Tool Does When You Click on It*
	Border	Lets you select a border for the cell selection from the pop-up palette of border styles
	Color	Lets you select a new color for the background of the cells in the cell selection from the pop-up color palette
	Font Color	Lets you select a new color for the text in the cells in the cell selection from the pop-up color palette

The Standard and Formatting toolbars contain the most commonly used tools and are the ones that are automatically displayed in the Excel window when you first start the program. Excel does, however, include several other toolbars that you can display as your work requires their special tools. As you soon discover, Excel's toolbars are a real boon to productivity because they make the program's standard routines so much more accessible than the pull-down menus.

The formula bar

The formula bar displays the cell address and the contents of the current cell. This bar is divided into three sections by two vertical lines. If the current cell is empty (as is cell A1 in Figure 1-5), the third section of the formula bar is blank. After you begin typing an entry or building a worksheet formula, the second and third sections of the formula bar come alive. After you press a key, a pop-up list button (designed to show you a list of range names that you've created for the workbook) and the Cancel, Enter, and Function Wizard buttons appear in the second section. (See Chapter 5 for details on using range names, and Chapter 2 to learn how to use the special buttons.) Following this string of buttons and in the third section of the formula bar, you see the character that you've typed, mirroring the character that appears in the worksheet cell itself. After you complete the entry in the cell (either by clicking on the Return button on the formula bar or by pressing Return or an arrow key), Excel displays the entire entry or formula in the formula bar, and the string of buttons disappears from the center section of the formula bar. The content of that cell thereafter appears in the formula bar whenever that cell contains the cell pointer.

The document window

A blank Excel workbook appears in a new document window right below the formula bar after you first start the program. As you can see in Figure 1-6, this new document window displays the worksheet number as a temporary workbook name (Workbook1 when you first start Excel, Workbook2 when you open your next new worksheet document window, and so on). At the bottom of the document window, you see tab-scrolling buttons, the tabs for activating the various worksheets in your workbook (16 new sheets to start), followed by the horizontal scroll bar that brings new columns of the current worksheet into view. On the right-hand side of the document window, you see a vertical scroll bar that brings new rows of the current worksheet into view (keep in mind that you are only viewing at any time a small percentage of the total columns and rows in each worksheet). At the intersection of the horizontal and vertical scroll bars, in the lower right-hand corner, you find a size box that modifies the size and shape of the document window.

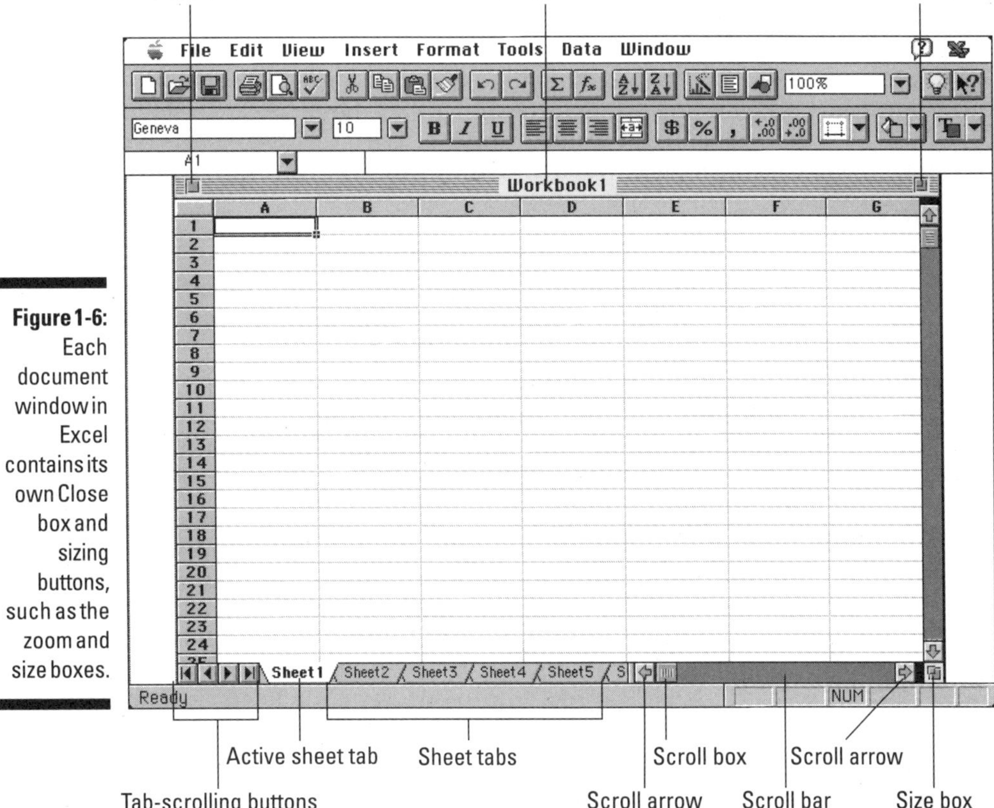

Figure 1-6: Each document window in Excel contains its own Close box and sizing buttons, such as the zoom and size boxes.

As soon as you start Excel, you can immediately begin creating a new worksheet in Sheet1 of the Workbook1 workbook that appears in the document window.

Other types of Excel documents

Worksheets are not the only type of document that Excel uses. In addition to worksheet documents, you can have charts and macro sheets open in the Excel program window. Each of these different types of Excel documents is contained in its own document window. (See Chapters 7 and 10 for more on charts and macro sheets.)

Sizing and moving document windows

You can use the Close box or the Zoom box found on the title bar of the document window to automatically change the size of the active document. In addition to these buttons, which are also found on the title bar of the Excel window, each document window contains a Size box, located in the lower right-hand corner that you can use to manually control the Size of the window (see Figure 1-6).

To change the size of a document window, you simply position the mouse pointer on this Size box. After the mouse pointer changes shape to an arrow, click and hold down the mouse button, drag the mouse as needed to adjust the size of the side(s) of the window, and release the mouse button. While the pointer is positioned within the Size box, the pointer retains its arrowhead shape.

- If you position the pointer on the bottom side of the window and drag the pointer straight up, the window becomes shorter. If you drag straight down, the window becomes longer. Whether you make it shorter or longer, the width remains the same.
- If you position the pointer on the right side of the window and drag the pointer straight to the left, the window becomes narrower. If you drag straight to the right, the window becomes wider. The height remains the same in either case.
- If you position the pointer on the lower right-hand corner of the window and drag the pointer diagonally toward the upper left-hand corner, the window becomes both shorter and narrower. If you drag diagonally away from the upper left-hand corner, the window becomes longer and wider.

After the outline of the window reaches the desired size, you then release the mouse button, and Excel redraws the document window to your new size.

After changing the size of a document window with the Size box, you can either use the Size box again if you want to restore the window to its original dimensions, or you can use the Zoom box to maximize or minimize the window.

Besides resizing document windows, you also can reposition them in the Excel window.

1. **To move a document window, simply pick it up and move it by the scruff of its neck, which in this case corresponds to the window's title bar.**
2. **After you've got it by the title bar, drag the window to the desired position and release the mouse button.**

Maximizing a document window

When you click on the Zoom box in the upper right-hand corner of a document window, Excel enlarges the document window so that it takes up all the space between the formula bar and the last bar in the window. Click on this button again to restore the document window to its previous size. As shown in Figure 1-7, Excel tacks the name of the document window onto the Excel title bar.

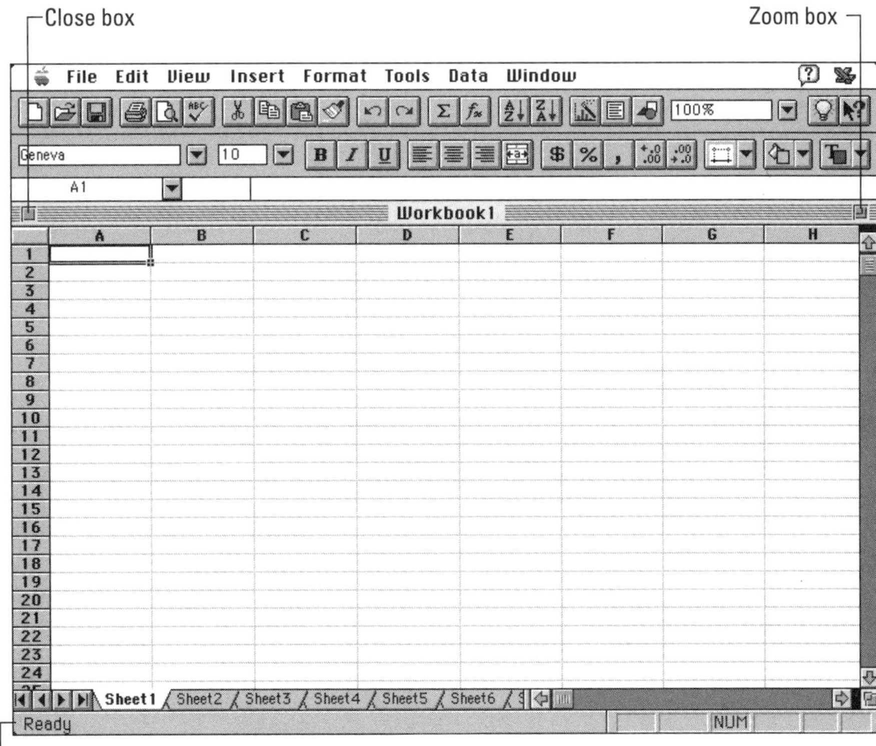

Figure 1-7: The Sheet1 document window after it's maximized.

Going from sheet to sheet

At the very bottom of the Excel document window containing a blank workbook, you see the tab-scrolling buttons and tabs for the first six worksheets in the workbook. Excel indicates which worksheet is active by displaying its tab in white, as though it were part of the displayed worksheet (rather than belonging to unseen worksheets below). To activate a new worksheet (thus bringing it to the top and displaying its information in the document window), you click on its tab.

If the tab for the worksheet you want to work with is not displayed, you can use the tab scrolling buttons to bring the worksheet into view. Click on the buttons with the triangles pointing left and right (the two triangle buttons in the middle of the four) to scroll one worksheet at a time in either direction (left to scroll left, and right to scroll right). Click on the buttons with the triangles pointing toward the vertical lines (the two triangle buttons at the extreme left and right of the four) to scroll the sheets so that the tabs for the very first or very last worksheets are displayed at the bottom.

The status bar

The bar at the very bottom of the Excel program window is called the status bar because it displays information that keeps you informed of the current state of Excel. The left part of the status bar displays messages indicating the current activity you're undertaking or the current command you've selected from the Excel menu bar. After you first start Excel, the message `Ready` is displayed in this area (as shown in Figure 1-7), telling you that the program is ready to accept your next entry or command.

The right side of the status bar contains various boxes that display different indicators. These indicators tell you when you've placed Excel in a particular state that somehow affects how you work with the program. For example, after you first start Excel, the `NUM` indicator, which indicates that you can use the numbers on the numeric keypad to enter values in the worksheet, appears in this part of the status bar.

Making the Mouse Less of a Drag

Like it or not, the mouse is one of the more challenging computer tools. Let's face it, the little rats demand a level of hand-eye coordination that makes touch typing on the keyboard seem like a walk in the park. In large part, this difficulty exists because your brain has to learn how to correlate the movement of the mouse pointer across a slightly curved vertical plane (your monitor) with the smaller movements you make with the mouse on a flat horizontal plane (your desk). Then again, we may have difficulty because most of us are klutzes.

Whatever the reason, you'll probably find mastering Excel mouse techniques to be some kind of fun. Keep in mind that using the mouse requires different muscles than using the keyboard does, and therefore you may experience some initial discomfort in your upper back and shoulders (keep that Ben Gay handy!). However, I'm quite sure that with just a modicum of mouse experience under your belt, you, too, will be double-clicking with the best of them in no time.

The many ways of using the mouse

Although you can access most of Excel's wonders by using the keyboard, the mouse is the most efficient way to select a command or perform a particular procedure. For this reason alone, if you need to use Excel regularly to get your work done, it is well worth your time to master the program's various mouse techniques.

Windows programs (like Excel) use three basic mouse techniques to select and manipulate various objects in the program and document windows:

- *Clicking on an object.* Position the pointer on an object and then press and immediately release the mouse button.
- *Double-clicking on an object.* Position the pointer on an object and then press and immediately release the mouse button rapidly twice in a row (click-click).
- *Dragging an object.* Position the pointer on an object and then press and hold down the mouse button as you move the mouse in the direction you want to drag the object. After you have positioned the object in the desired position on-screen, release the mouse button to place the object.

When clicking on an object to select it, make sure that the point of the arrowhead is touching the object you want to select before you click. To avoid moving the pointer slightly before you click, grasp the sides of the mouse between your thumb and your ring and pinkie fingers and then click the button with your index finger. If you run out of room on your desktop for moving the mouse, just pick up the mouse and reposition it on the desk. (This action does not move the pointer.)

Learning the mouse by your lonesome

One of the best (and most fun) ways to master the basic mouse techniques is to play the Puzzle game included in the Apple system, located in the Apple pull-down menu at the upper left hand corner of your screen. In this computer version of the popular game, you click on the pieces of the puzzle next to the open space to rearrange them to solve the puzzle. The latest version of Puzzle forms the Rainbow Apple logo on color Macs. Playing Puzzle enables you to practice basic mouse techniques in a relaxed setting; the game is the ideal tool for practicing and gaining mastery of the mouse.

The many faces of the mouse pointer

The shape of the mouse pointer is anything but static in the Excel program. As you move the mouse pointer to different parts of the Excel screen, the pointer changes shape to indicate a change in function. Table 1-3 shows you the various faces of the mouse pointer as well as the use of each shape.

Don't confuse the cell pointer with the mouse pointer. The mouse pointer changes shape as you move it around the screen. The cell pointer always maintains its shape as an outline around the current cell or cell selection (where it expands to include all the selected cells). The mouse pointer responds to any movement of your mouse on the desk and always moves independently of the cell pointer. You can use the mouse pointer to reposition the cell pointer, however, by positioning the thick white cross pointer in the cell that will hold the cell pointer and then clicking the primary mouse button.

You Gotta Get Me out of This Cell!

Excel provides several methods for getting around each of the huge worksheets in your workbook. One the easiest ways is to click on the tab for the sheet you want to work with and then to use the scroll bars in the document window to bring new parts of this worksheet into view. In addition, the program provides a wide range of keystrokes that you can use not only to move a new part of the worksheet into view but also to make a new cell active by placing the cell pointer in it.

Table 1-3 The Many Mouse Pointer Shapes in Excel

Mouse Pointer Shape	*What It Means*
✣	The thick white cross pointer appears as you move the pointer around the cells of the current worksheet. Use this pointer to select the cells you need to work with.
+	The fill handle (thin black cross) appears only when you position the pointer on the lower right-hand corner of the cell that contains the cell pointer. Use this pointer to create a sequential series of entries in a block or to copy an entry or formula in a block of cells.
↖	The arrowhead pointer appears when you position the pointer on the toolbar, the Excel menu bar, or on one of the edges of the block of cells you've selected. Use this pointer to choose Excel commands or to move or copy a cell selection with the drag-and-drop technique.
I	The I-beam pointer appears when you click on the entry in the formula bar, double-click on a cell, or press F2 to edit a cell entry. Use this pointer to locate your place when you edit a cell entry in the cell itself or on the formula bar.
↖?	The help pointer appears when you click on the Help tool in the Standard toolbar. Use this pointer to click on the menu command or tool on a toolbar for which you want help information.

Scrolling away

To understand how scrolling works in Excel, imagine the worksheet as a gigantic papyrus scroll attached to rollers on the left and right. To bring into view a new section of a papyrus worksheet that is hidden on the right, you crank the left roller until the section with the cells you want to see appears. Likewise, to scroll into view a new section of the worksheet that is hidden on the left, you crank the right roller until the section of cells appears.

Back and forth with the horizontal scroll bar

To do this type of left/right scrolling to the worksheet in Excel, you use the horizontal scroll bar at the bottom of the document window. On the scroll bar, the left and right scroll arrows play the part of the rollers. Now, here's the tricky part: The Excel software engineers arranged the scroll arrows in just the opposite way that their roller counterparts function. In other words, the left scroll arrow plays the part of the right roller, and the right scroll arrow plays the part of the left roller!

- Clicking on the *left* scroll arrow in the scroll bar is like turning the right roller on the papyrus scroll — the worksheet moves slightly to the *right,* bringing a new column, previously hidden on the left, into view.
- Clicking on the *right* scroll arrow is like turning the left roller on the papyrus scroll — the worksheet moves slightly to the *left,* bringing a new column, previously hidden on the right, into view.

Up and down with the vertical scroll bar

To visualize scrolling the worksheet up and down with the vertical scroll bar, you have to think of the papyrus worksheet as being suspended vertically between two rollers, with one roller above and the other below. To scroll up the papyrus worksheet to uncover rows that were otherwise hidden at the bottom, you crank the top roller until the cells you want to see appear. To scroll down the papyrus worksheet so that you can see rows that were otherwise hidden at the top, you crank the bottom roller.

The vertical scroll bar at the right edge of the document window contains the up and down scroll arrows. As with the horizontal scroll arrows, you need to think of the vertical scroll arrows as being put on backwards to the rollers on a vertical papyrus scroll.

- To scroll *up* the worksheet, bringing into view the next hidden row at the bottom, click on the *down* scroll arrow.
- To scroll *down* the worksheet, bringing into view the next hidden row at the top, click on the *up* scroll arrow.

Scrolling screens

You also can use the scroll bar to scroll larger sections at a time than a column or row. To scroll the worksheet a screenful at a time, click anywhere on the gray area of the scroll bar between the scroll box and the scroll arrows.

- To scroll the sheet up or down by a screenful, click on the vertical scroll bar. Click above the scroll box to scroll up, click below it to scroll down.
- To scroll the sheet left or right by a screenful, click on the horizontal scroll bar. Click on the left of the scroll box to scroll left, click on the right to scroll right.

You can drag the scroll box in one direction or the other to scroll larger sections of the worksheet. The position of the scroll box in its scroll bar reflects its relative position in the *active area* of the worksheet — roughly equivalent to the cells in the worksheet that currently have entries. (See the sidebar "Getting involved with the active area" if you're just dying to know the precise definition!)

Keystrokes for moving the pointer

The one disadvantage to using the scroll bars to move around is that the scrolls only bring new parts of the worksheet into view — they don't actually change the position of the cell pointer. If you want to start making entries in the cells in a new area of the worksheet, you still have to remember to select the cell or group of cells where you want the data before you begin entering the data.

Excel offers a wide variety of keystrokes for moving the cell pointer to a new cell. When you use one of these keystrokes, the program automatically scrolls a new part of the worksheet into view if this is required in moving the cell pointer. Table 1-4 summarizes these keystrokes and how far each moves the cell pointer from its starting position. (Chapter 9, "Coping with More than One Worksheet at a Time," provides additional navigation tips.)

Experienced Mac wizards will prefer using the ⌘ key rather the Control key made popular on that *other* computer platform; however, the keys are interchangeable in Excel for the Mac.

When reading Table 1-4, keep in mind that you use ⌘ and an arrow key to move from edge to edge in a table or between tables in a worksheet. Hold down ⌘ as you press one of the four arrow keys (indicated by the + symbol in keystrokes, such as ⌘ +→).

Table 1-4 Keystrokes for Moving the Cell Pointer

Keystroke	*Where the Cell Pointer Moves To*
→ or Tab	Cell to the immediate right
← or Shift+Tab	Cell to the immediate left
↑	Cell up one row
↓	Cell down one row
Home	Cell in column A of the current row
⌘ +Home	First cell (A1) of the worksheet
⌘ +End or End, Home	Cell in the lower right-hand corner of the active area in the worksheet
Page Up	Cell one screenful up in the same column
Page Down	Cell one screenful down in the same column
⌘ +Page Up	Cell last selected in next worksheet of current workbook
⌘ +Page Down	Cell last selected in previous worksheet of current workbook

(continued)

Table 1-4 (continued)

Keystroke	*Where the Cell Pointer Moves To*
⌘ + → or End, →	First occupied cell to the right in the same row that is either preceded or followed by a blank cell
⌘+← or End, ←	First occupied cell to the left in the same row that is either followed or preceded by a blank cell
⌘ +↑ or End, ↑	First occupied cell above in the same column that is either followed or preceded by a blank cell
⌘ +↓ or End, ↓	First occupied cell below in the same column that is either preceded or followed by a blank cell

Getting involved with the active area

The last cell in the active area of the worksheet is the one located at the intersection of the last occupied column and row in the worksheet. The active area then encompasses all the cells between A1 and the last cell in the active area. You can move the pointer to this last active cell by pressing Control + End or ⌘+End.

The size of the active area determines how much of the worksheet you scroll when you drag the scroll box to a new position in its scroll bar. For example, if the active area extends to row 100 of the worksheet and you drag the scroll box to the middle of the vertical scroll bar, row 50 will be the first row that appears in the document window. But if the active area extends to row 200, row 100 will then be the first visible row.

Moving from block to block

The keystrokes that combine the ⌘, Control, or End key with an arrow key are among the most helpful for moving quickly from one edge to the other in large tables of cell entries or in moving from table to table in a section of the worksheet that contains many blocks of cells.

Table is used in spreadsheet program jargon to refer to groups of related data; *blocks* are somewhat equivalent terms. Tables are contiguous blocks of data.

- If the cell pointer is positioned on a blank cell somewhere to the left of a table of cell entries that you want to view, pressing ⌘+← moves the cell pointer to the first cell entry at the leftmost edge of the table (in the same row, of course).

- When you then press ⌘+→, the cell pointer moves to the last cell entry at the rightmost edge (assuming that you have no blank cells in that row of the table).
- If you then switch direction and press ⌘+↓, Excel moves to the last cell entry at the bottom edge of the table (again assuming that you have no blank cells below in that column of the table).
- If, when the cell pointer is at the bottom of the table, you press ⌘+↓ again, Excel moves the pointer to the first entry at the top of the next table located below (assuming that you have no other cell entries above this table in the same column).

If you press the ⌘, Control, or End and arrow key combinations and you have no more occupied cells in the direction of the arrow key you selected, Excel advances the cell pointer directly to the cell at the very edge of the worksheet in that direction.

- If the cell pointer is located in cell C15 and you have no more occupied cells in row 15, when you press ⌘+→, Excel moves the cell pointer to cell IV at the rightmost edge of the worksheet.
- If you are in cell C15 and you have no more entries below in column C, when you press ⌘+↓, Excel moves the pointer to cell C16384 at the very bottom edge of the worksheet.

When you use ⌘ and an arrow key to move from edge to edge in a table or between tables in a worksheet, hold down ⌘ as you press one of the four arrow keys (indicated by the + symbol in keystrokes, such as ⌘+→).

When you use End and an arrow key alternative, you must press and then release the End key before you press the arrow key (indicated by the comma in keystrokes, such as End, →). Pressing and releasing the End key causes the END indicator to appear on the status bar, which is your sign that Excel is ready for you to press one of the four arrow keys.

Because you can keep the ⌘ or Control key pressed down while you press the different arrow keys you need to use, the ⌘ or Control +arrow-key method provides a more fluid means for navigating blocks of cells than the End, arrow key method.

Moving the cell pointer with the Goto feature

Excel's Goto feature provides an easy method for moving directly to a distant cell in the worksheet. To make this move, you display the Go To dialog box by choosing Go To on the Edit pull-down menu or by pressing F5. To move the cell pointer, type the address of the cell you want to go to in the Reference text box and then select OK or press Return. Note that when you type the cell address in the Reference text box, you can type column letters in upper- or lowercase letters.

When you use the Goto feature to move the cell pointer, Excel remembers the references of the last four cells you visited. These cell references appear in the Go To list box. Notice that the address of the last cell you went to is also listed in the Reference text box. This address makes it possible to move quickly from your present location to your preceding location in a worksheet by pressing F5 and then Return (provided that you used the Goto feature to move to your present position).

Menurama: Pull-Down versus Shortcut

For those occasions when the Excel toolbars don't provide you with a ready-made tool for getting a particular task done, you have to turn to its system of menu commands. Excel exhibits a little bit of menu overkill: In addition to the regular pull-down menus found in virtually all Macintosh applications, the program also offers a secondary system of *shortcut menus.*

Shortcut menus are so called because they offer faster access to the often-used menu commands. Shortcut menus are attached to a particular screen object (such as a toolbar, document window, or worksheet cell) and contain only the commands that pertain to that object. As a result, shortcut menus often bring together commands that are otherwise found on several individual pull-down menus on the menu bar.

May I take your order, Ma'am?

Macintosh users will probably choose to stick with their handy mouse as the way to select commands from the pull-down menu bars. However, recent converts to the Mac coming from the DOS or Windows universes may be faster selecting menu commands with the keyboard.

- To open a pull-down menu with the mouse, you simply click on the menu name on the menu bar and then drag down the pointer through the open menu until you highlight the desired command. Then you release the mouse button.

- Alternatively, you can press and release F10 or / (forward slash key to the immediate left of the right shift key) to activate the menu bar and then press → until you highlight the menu you want to open. Then, to open the menu, you press ↓ until you highlight the desired command. Believe it or not, many PC users prefer this method of repeated key tapping for selecting commands after years of practice.

Many commands on the pull-down menus lead to the display of a dialog box that contains further commands and options (see "How to Have an Intelligent Conversation with a Dialog Box" later in this chapter). You can tell which commands on a pull-down menu lead to dialog boxes because the command name is followed by three periods (. . .) known as an *ellipsis.* For example, you know that selecting the Save As command on the File menu opens a dialog box because the command is listed as Save As . . . on the File menu.

Also, note that pull-down menu commands are not always available to you. You can tell when a command is not currently available because the command name appears in light gray (*dimmed*) on the pull-down menu. A command on a pull-down menu remains dimmed until the conditions under which it operates exist in your document. For example, the Paste command on the Edit menu remains dimmed as long as the Clipboard is empty. But as soon as you move or copy some information into the Clipboard with the Cut or Copy commands on the Edit menu, the Paste option is no longer dimmed and appears in normal bold type when you open the Edit menu — indicating, of course, that this command is now available for your use.

PC keyboard weenies take note

Windows and DOS users will not be able to use their trusted Alt key on the Mac. You can use F10 to enable the stationary pull-down menus you are familiar with. The key letter of the menu and commands will be underlined. By typing this letter or combination of letters, the command is selected. For example, to close a worksheet, you can press F10 and then F to open the File pull-down menu, and then press C to select the Close command. The pull-down menu stays down until you have completed your selection. If you had used the mouse to select the pull-down menu, the menu only stays selected as long as you press the mouse button.

For 1-2-3 refugees only

If you have ever used (or tried to use) Lotus 1-2-3 for DOS, you may remember that you press / (the forward slash key — the key that does double duty with the ?) to activate the 1-2-3 menus. In deference to the millions of diehard 1-2-3 users out there, Excel also recognizes and responds appropriately (that is, it activates the menu bar) when you press the / key. It is only right that Excel borrows this keystroke from Lotus 1-2-3, because 1-2-3 borrowed the key from its predecessor, VisiCalc, which actually originated its usage.

Because the slash key activates the menus, you can combine its use with the command letters when you want to select Excel commands with the keyboard. For example, to save changes to the active document, you can just as well press /FS.

- You can make it so that when you select the 1-2-3 command, Excel tells you what menu and menu commands you use to do the same thing in Excel (kinda like saying something in English and having your computer display the French equivalent).
- Or you can have it so that when you select the 1-2-3 command, Excel *demonstrates* what menu and menu commands you choose to do the same thing in Excel (kinda like saying something in English and having your computer actually *say* it in French).

To set up Excel so that the program shows or tells you what to do in Excel via the 1-2-3 equivalents, follow these steps:

1. **Choose Options from the Tools menu to open the Options dialog box.**
2. **Click on the Transition tab in the Options dialog box to display the options for changing the Transition settings.**

After switching from the default Microsoft Excel Menus setting to Lotus 1-2-3 Help in the Options dialog box, when you type the almighty / key, rather than activating the Excel menu bar, the program displays the Help for Lotus 1-2-3 Users dialog box. This dialog box contains a Menu list box that shows all the old familiar 1-2-3 menus (from Worksheet through Quit).

Although Excel *prefers* that you press = (equal sign) to start a formula, the program does accept the + (plus sign) used in 1-2-3. Similarly, although Excel does not require anything other than = (equal sign) followed by the function name when you use a built-in function, the program does accept the @ ("at" symbol) that 1-2-3 requires. For example, Excel accepts @SUM but converts it to the preferred =SUM. Finally, although Excel uses a colon between the first and last cell address when designating a cell range, the program accepts the 1-2-3 method of placing two periods between the cell addresses. (Excel accepts the range address A1..A4 but converts it to the preferred A1:A4.)

Making short work of shortcut menus

Unlike the pull-down menus, which you can access either with the mouse or the keyboard, you *must* use the mouse to open shortcut menus and select their commands. Because shortcut menus are attached to particular objects on-screen, such as document windows, toolbars, or worksheet cells, Excel uses the mouse button to open shortcut menus. To display an Excel shortcut menu on the Macintosh, you hold down the Control key as you click on the screen object. (If your keyboard doesn't have a Control key, you need to press both the ⌘ and Option keys while you click on the screen object).

Figure 1-8 shows you the shortcut menu attached to the Excel toolbars. To open this menu, position the mouse pointer somewhere on the toolbar and press ⌘+ Option + click (or press Control + click).

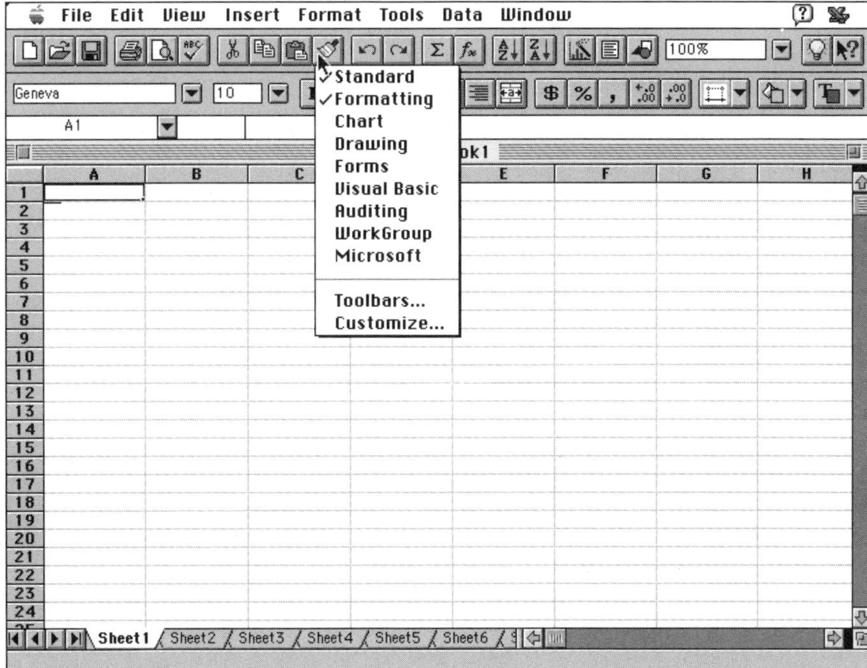

Figure 1-8: The toolbar shortcut menu.

After you open the toolbar shortcut menu, you can use its commands to display or hide any of the built-in toolbars or to customize the toolbars (see Chapter 11 for details).

Figure 1-9 shows you the shortcut menu attached to any of the cells in a worksheet. To open this shortcut menu, position the pointer on any one of the cells, press and hold down the Control key (or the ⌘+Option keys), and click the mouse button. Note that you also can open this shortcut menu and apply its commands to a group of cells you have selected. (You learn how to make cell selections in Chapter 2.)

The commands on shortcut menus do not contain command letters (although some of them do display shortcut keystrokes). To select one of their commands, drag until the desired command is highlighted, and then release the mouse button.

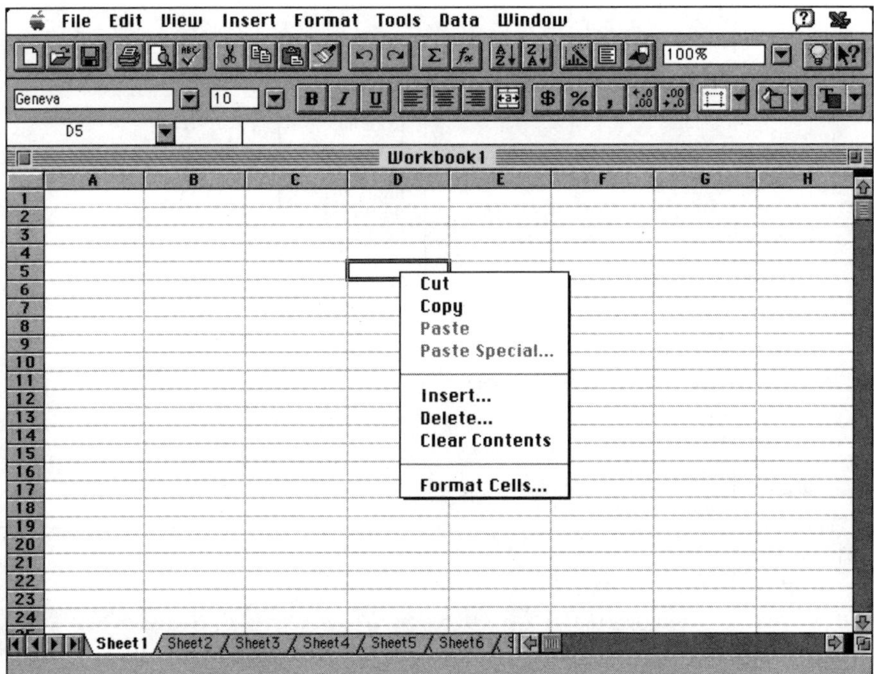

Figure 1-9: A worksheet cell shortcut menu.

How to Have an Intelligent Conversation with a Dialog Box

As mentioned earlier, many an Excel command is attached to a dialog box that presents you with a variety of options that you can apply to the command. Figures 1-10 and 1-11 show you the Save As and Options dialog boxes, respectively. Between these two dialog boxes, you see all the different types of buttons, tabs, and boxes used by Excel. Table 1-5 catalogs the parts of a dialog box.

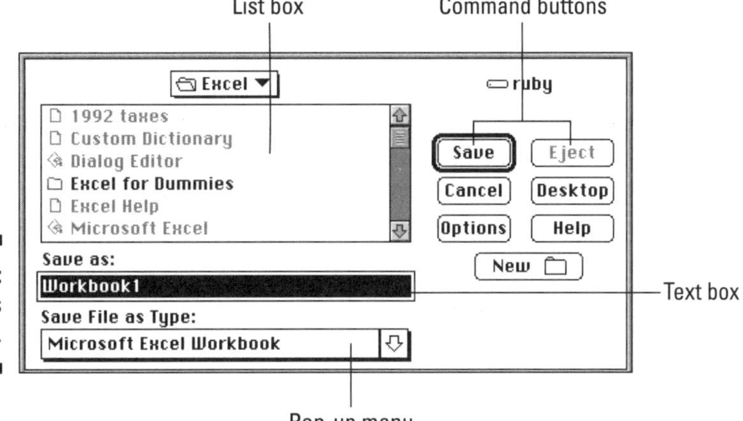

Figure 1-10: The Save As dialog box.

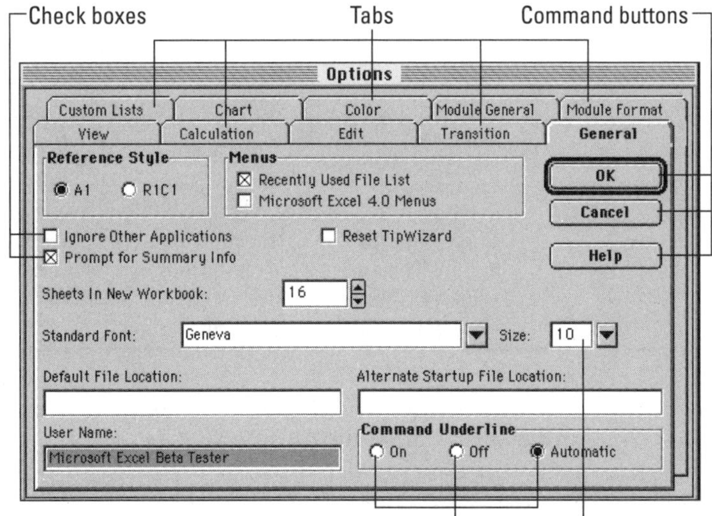

Figure 1-11: The Options dialog box.

Table 1-5 The Parts of a Dialog Box

Button or Box	*What It's Good For*
Tab	Provides a means for displaying a certain set of options in a complex dialog box that brings together many different types of program settings that you can change.
Text box	Provides a place for typing a new entry. Many text boxes contain default entries that you can edit or replace.
List box	Provides a list of options from which you choose. If the list box contains more options than can be displayed in its box, the list box contains a scroll bar that you can use to bring new options into view. Some list boxes are attached to a text box, allowing you to make a new entry in the text box either by typing the entry or by selecting it in the related list box.
Pop-up menu	Provides a condensed version of a standard list box that, instead of displaying several options in its list, shows only the current option (which originally is also the default option). To open the pop-up menu and display the other options, you click on the pop-up button (the arrow) that accompanies the box. After the list is displayed, you can select a new option from the list, as you would in any standard list box.
Check box	Presents an option that you can turn on or off. When the check box contains an X, you know that its option is selected. When a check box is blank, you know that its option is not selected.
Radio button	Presents items that have mutually exclusive options. The button consists of a circle followed by the name of the option. Radio buttons are always arranged in groups, and only one of the options in the group can be selected at one time. Excel lets you know which option is currently selected by placing a dot in the middle of its circle. (When an option button is selected, it works like a station button on an old-fashioned car radio, thus the name *radio button.*)
Command button	Initiates an action. The command button is rectangular in shape, and the name of the command is displayed within the button. If a name in a command button is followed by an ellipsis (. . .), Excel displays another dialog box containing even more options after you select the button.

You can move a dialog box within the active document window by dragging its title bar. You can close the dialog box by pressing the Esc key.

Note: Although you can move a dialog box out of the way of some data in your worksheet, you cannot change the box's size or shape — these dimensions are permanently fixed by the program.

Many dialog boxes contain default options or entries that are automatically selected unless you make new choices before you close the dialog box.

- To close a dialog box and put your selections into effect, choose the OK button or the Close button. (Some boxes lack an OK button.)
- If the OK button is surrounded by a dark border, which is very often the case, you also can press the Enter key or Return key to put your selections into effect.
- To close a dialog box without putting your selections into effect, you can select the Cancel or Close button in the dialog box, or — more simply — press Esc.

Most dialog boxes group related options together as an item, often by placing a box around the options. When using the mouse to make selections in a dialog box, simply click on the selection you want to use, or, in the case of text entries, click the pointer in the entry to set the insertion point, and then modify the entry.

The Mac, of course, doesn't have an Alt key (at least not the last time I looked). If you are keyboard-minded (as more and more Mac-heads are becoming), you can activate the menu bar and have Excel display the command letters on the Macintosh pull-down menus by typing / (forward slash), located on the same key as the question mark, or you can press the F10 function key. (Yes, Virginia, the Macintosh *does* have command letters.) Then you can select the commands by typing the underlined command letters on the Mac Excel menus to your heart's content.

When making selections with the keyboard, however, you sometimes must first activate the item before you can select any of its options.

- Press Tab until you activate one of the options in the item. (Pressing Shift+Tab activates the preceding item.)
- When you press Tab (or Shift+Tab), Excel indicates which option is activated by highlighting the default entry.

You also can select a list box option by typing the first few characters of its name. As soon as you begin typing, Excel opens a text box to contain your characters and jumps to the first option in the list box with the name that begins with the characters you enter.

In addition to the more elaborate dialog boxes shown in Figures 1-10 and 1-11, you also will encounter a simpler type of dialog box, known appropriately as the *alert box,* that displays messages and warnings. Many dialog boxes of this type contain only an OK button that you must select to close the dialog box after reading the message.

Help Is on the Way

You can get on-line help with Excel at any time you need it while using the program. The only problem with the help system is that it is really only truly helpful when you are familiar with the Excel jargon. If you don't know what Excel calls a particular feature, you will certainly have trouble locating it in the help topics — like trying use a dictionary to look up a word that you have no idea how to spell.

The easiest way to avoid this dilemma is to use the Help tool on the Standard toolbar to get help information specific to the particular command that you want to use. When you click on the Help tool, Excel changes the mouse pointer shape by adding a question mark to it (see Figure 1-12). To get help on a particular command or a part of the Excel window, you use this question mark pointer to select the command.

Suppose that you want to refresh your memory on how to use the AutoSum tool on the Standard toolbar to total a column of numbers. You simply click on the Help tool and then click on the AutoSum tool (the one with the Σ) with the arrowhead/question mark pointer. The program displays the Microsoft Excel Help window, which displays a brief paragraph of information about using the AutoSum feature.

You also can use the Help tool to get information about any of the commands on the pull-down menus. Suppose that you are curious about the purpose of the Full Screen command on the View pull-down menu. To obtain information on what this command does and how you use it, you click on the Help tool and then click on the View menu with the arrowhead/question mark pointer. After this menu is open, drag down to select the Full Screen command, which opens the Microsoft Excel Help window that has a screenful of information on displaying the maximum number of worksheet cells on-screen.

When reading a help topic in the Microsoft Help system, you may notice that certain terms are underlined (and in a different color on a color monitor).

- A term that is underlined with a solid underline is called a *jump* term because after you click on it, the Help system immediately "jumps" you to a related help topic. (This is also known as *hypertext.*)
- A term that is underlined with a dotted line is a *glossary term* because it is attached to a brief definition. After you click on a glossary term, the Help system displays the definition in a small pop-up dialog box for as long as you hold down the mouse button.

If you happen upon a help topic that you would like to print out, you can print it by selecting the Print Topic command on the File menu. First, be sure that your printer is turned on and that you select the File menu in the Microsoft Excel

Help window on the right, not the Excel window underneath. If you are in Excel Help, you can always print the topic by pressing ⌘+P rather than using the mouse.

If you don't want to use the arrowhead/question mark method of selecting specific help topics, there are three other, more or less useful, means of accessing general help. First is the shortcut key method, which you access by pressing ⌘+/, which brings up the full range of topics. The second method for accessing the Microsoft Help window is to use the question mark pull-down menu at the top right of the screen. This is equivalent to the ⌘+/ shortcut. The last help method is available with System 7 and later only, and is called Balloon Help; you also select it from the question mark pull-down menu. It usually gets on your nerves, and most people turn it off to prevent premature senility. Figure 1-12 shows two means of getting help.

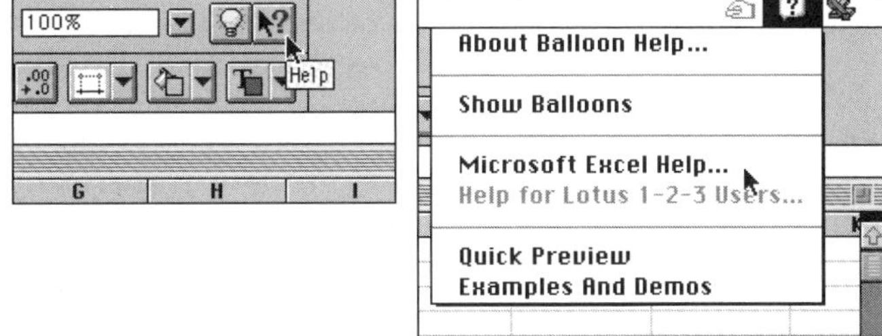

Figure 1-12: The Help keys.

You also can copy information from an Excel help topic to your word processor or even to an Excel document. To copy help information, choose the Copy command on the Edit menu (in the Microsoft Excel Help window). The Help system displays a Copy dialog box where you can select as much of the text as you want to copy. Drag the I-beam cursor through the text you want to copy (or hold down the Shift key as you press the arrow keys) and then select the Copy command button, or you click and drag with the mouse button to make a selection and then press ⌘+C.

After you've copied the selected information in this manner, you can copy the help information into a word-processing document or worksheet by starting the program, opening the document (if necessary), and then choosing the Paste command on the program's Edit menu, or you can copy it more easily by pressing ⌘+V. All Mac programs use the Clipboard in the Macintosh Finder to temporarily store cut or copied selections for possible pasting. The contents of the Clipboard are emptied or deleted when a new selection is cut or copied, because it contains only one selection at a time. The Clipboard can hold one letter or number, or it can hold whole worksheets or chapters. The Clipboard also can contain graphics, Quicktime movies, and photos.

If you are experiencing problems with the software or are suffering some sort of software/hardware incompatibilities that are driving you nuts, select the Technical Support command on the Help pull-down menu. Then select Microsoft Excel Help; at the end of the list is the Technical Support jump term. This takes you to a help topic that explains the product support policies and contains the on-line support telephone number.

When It's Quitting Time

When you're ready to call it a day and quit Excel, you have several choices for shutting down the program. One way to quit Excel is by choosing the Quit command on the File menu. You can accomplish the same thing by pressing ⌘+Q.

If you try to quit Excel after working on a workbook and you haven't saved your latest changes, the program thoughtfully beeps at you and displays an alert box asking whether you want to save your changes. To save your changes before quitting, choose Yes. (For detailed information on saving documents, see Chapter 2.) If you've just been playing around in the worksheet and don't want to save your changes, you can abandon the document by choosing No.

Chapter 2

Concocting Your First Workbook

In This Chapter

- How to start a new workbook
- How to enter different types of information in a workbook
- How to create simple formulas
- How to correct mistakes you make when entering information
- How to enter information in a group of cells
- How to repeat an entry in a group of cells
- How to use the AutoFill feature to extend a series of entries
- How to enter built-in functions with the Function Wizard
- How to save a workbook

Now that you know how to get into Excel and display that great big workbook with all its blank worksheets on the screen, I think it's high time you learned what to do with it. So, this chapter focuses on the ins and outs of getting information into a worksheet.

After you learn how to fill up a worksheet with the requisite raw data and formulas, you learn what has to be the most important lesson of all: how to save all the information on disk so that you don't ever have to enter the stuff again!

Where Do I Begin?

When you start Excel without specifying a document to open, you see a blank workbook in a new document window (temporarily named Workbook1). This workbook contains 16 blank worksheets (Sheet1 through Sheet16). To begin your work, you simply start entering information in the first sheet of the Workbook1 document window.

Here are a few simple guidelines to keep in mind when you start working in Sheet1:

- Whenever you can, organize your information in tables of data that use adjacent (neighboring) columns and rows. Start the tables in the upper left-hand corner of the worksheet and work your way down the sheet rather than across the sheet, whenever possible. When it's practical, separate each table by no more than a single column or row.
- When you set up these tables, don't skip columns and rows just to "space out" the information. In Chapter 3, you learn how to place as much white space as you want between information in adjacent columns and rows by widening columns, heightening rows, and changing the alignment.
- Reserve a single column at the left edge of the table for the table's row headings.
- Reserve a single row at the top of the table for the table's column headings.
- If your table requires a title, put the title in the row above the column headings. Put the title in the same column as the row headings. You learn how to center this title across the columns of the entire table in Chapter 3.

You may wonder why, after the big deal about the size of the worksheets included in each Excel workbook in Chapter 1, the emphasis in these guidelines is on keeping information as close together as possible in each one. After all, given the vast amount of wide open space in an Excel worksheet, it seems natural that space conservation would be one of your lowest priorities when setting out your information.

You would be right, except that space conservation in the worksheet equals memory conservation. You see, as the table grows and expands into new areas of the worksheet, Excel decides on a certain amount of computer memory to hold open for the cell entries. If you skip columns and rows that you really don't need to skip, you waste computer memory that could otherwise be used to store more information in the worksheet.

Keep in mind that it's the amount of computer memory available to Excel that determines the ultimate size of the worksheet, not the total number of cells in the blank worksheet. When you run out of memory, you've effectively run out of space — no matter how many columns and rows are still left to fill. To maximize the information you can get into a worksheet, always adopt this "covered wagon" approach to worksheet design.

To check out how much computer memory is available to Excel at any given time, you must switch to the Macintosh Finder. You do not need to quit Excel; you can switch between any program and the Finder by selecting the Excel icon at the top right of your screen; this is known as the Application menu in System

7 (and later versions). If you have sufficient memory, you may have several programs open at the same time. After selecting the Finder on the Application menu, you need to select the Apple menu at the top left of your screen. Select About This Macintosh at the top of the Apple menu. You see how much memory each of the open programs is using, including the system software. The available system memory is shown along with the total Macintosh memory (RAM). If you want to change the memory Excel (or any Mac program) can use, then you must quit Excel and select the Excel program icon by clicking on it once with the mouse. Then press ⌘+I. You see a special dialog box that displays the Excel icon at the top and the Memory Requirements box at the lower right-hand side (see Figure 2-1). You can increase both (or either) the Minimum Size and Preferred Size by selecting the contents and entering new amounts of memory available to Excel. Sorry, no magic allowed: You cannot cheat and enter more memory than you have available in your Mac.

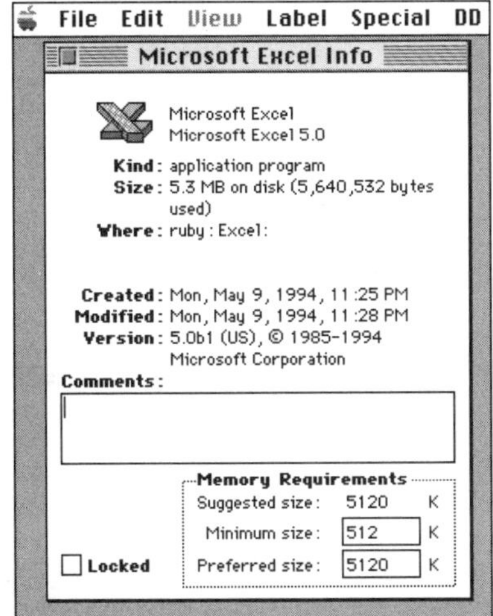

Figure 2-1: Excel Info dialog box.

The ABCs of Data Entry

To enter information in a new worksheet, just select the cell (click on it) where you want the information to appear, and begin typing. As soon as you begin typing, the characters you type appear both in the selected cell and in the formula bar above.

When you activate the formula bar in this manner, Excel displays the Cancel, Return, and Function Wizard (marked with `fx`) boxes, followed by the characters you typed and the insertion point (the flashing vertical bar) on the right. As you continue to type, Excel displays your progress both on the formula bar and in the active cell in the worksheet (see Figure 2-2).

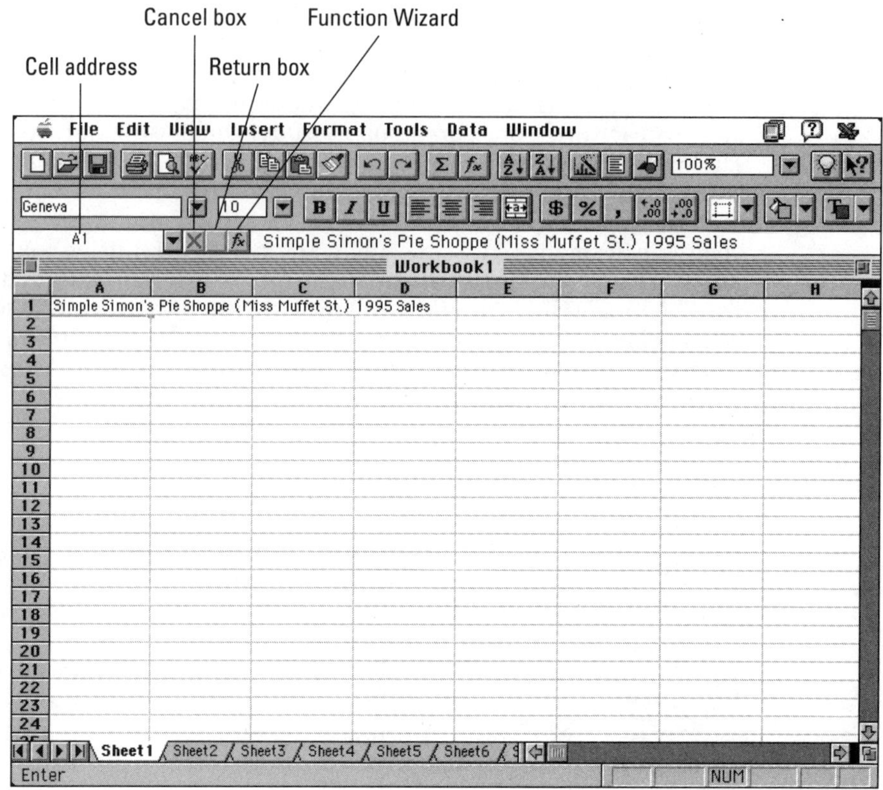

Figure 2-2: Entering information in a blank worksheet cell.

After you finish typing an entry, you still have to enter it in the active cell by clicking on the Return box (the one with the check mark in it) on the formula bar, pressing the Return key, or pressing one of the direction keys, such as ↓ or →.

Please take note:

- If you click on the Return box in the formula bar, Excel leaves the cell pointer in the cell that contains the newly typed entry.
- If you press the Return key (or press the ↓ key, of course), Excel completes the cell entry and selects the next cell down.

On the Macintosh, you can complete an entry by pressing either the Return key or the Enter key (located on the numeric keypad on the extended keyboard). If you press the Enter key, Excel enters the information and moves the cell pointer down one row. If you press the Return key, Excel enters the information without moving the cell pointer.

As soon as you complete your entry in the active cell, Excel deactivates the formula bar by removing the Cancel, Return, and Function Wizard boxes. The information you entered continues to appear in the cell in the worksheet. Every time you put the cell pointer into that particular cell, the cell entry reappears on the formula bar.

If you realize that you're just about to put information in the wrong cell, you can clear and deactivate the formula bar before you complete the entry by clicking on the Cancel box (the one with the X in it) or by pressing Esc.

Excel automatically advances the cell pointer to the next cell down in the column every time you press the Return key to complete the cell entry. If you want to customize Excel so that pressing Return *doesn't* move the cell pointer as the program enters your data, choose Tools ⇨ Options ⇨ Edit tab, and then click on the Move Selection after Return option in the Settings section to remove the X from its check box. Then choose OK or press Return.

Is the Data Your Type?

Excel checks each entry you make to see whether you've entered a formula that should be calculated. Excel performs the check to classify the entry as one of three different types of data: *text, value,* or *formula.*

If Excel finds that the entry is a formula, the program calculates the formula and displays the computed result in the worksheet cell (you continue to see the formula itself, however, on the formula bar). If Excel is satisfied that the entry does not qualify as a formula (the qualifications for a bona fide formula appear later in this chapter), the program then determines whether the entry should be classified as text or as a value.

Note that Excel must make this determination so that it knows how to align the entry (text goes to the left, values to the right). Also, most formulas work properly only when they are fed values. You can foul up formulas if you enter text in a cell where a value ought to be.

In contrast to formulas, text and values are considered *constants.* They are constants because they only change when you edit or replace them in their cells. Formulas, on the other hand, update their computed values as soon as you modify any of the values they use.

Text (neither fish nor fowl)

Excel reads as text any entry that doesn't shake out as either a formula or a value — making text the catch-all category of Excel entries. Most text entries (also known as *labels*) consist of a combination of letters and punctuation, or letters and numbers used for titles and headings in the worksheet.

You can tell right away that Excel has accepted a cell entry as text because a text entry is automatically aligned at the left edge of its cell. If the text entry is wider than the cell can display, the display of the entry spills over into the neighboring cell or cells on the right, provided that the next cell is blank (see Figure 2-3).

If, sometime later, you enter information in the cell next door, Excel cuts off the spillover of the long text entry (see Figure 2-4). Not to worry: Excel doesn't actually lop these characters off the cell entry — it simply shaves the display to make room for the new entry. If you feel separation anxiety for your "missing" text, just widen the column for the cell that contains the missing characters (to learn how to widen a column, skip ahead to Chapter 3).

A space, although undetectable to the eye, is considered to be as much a text character as the letter A or Z. If you introduce a space into an otherwise completely numeric entry, Excel categorizes the entry as text (indicated by its alignment at the left edge of the cell). If you feed that entry into a formula, the text classification completely throws off the answer, because a text entry is treated as a 0 (zero) in a formula.

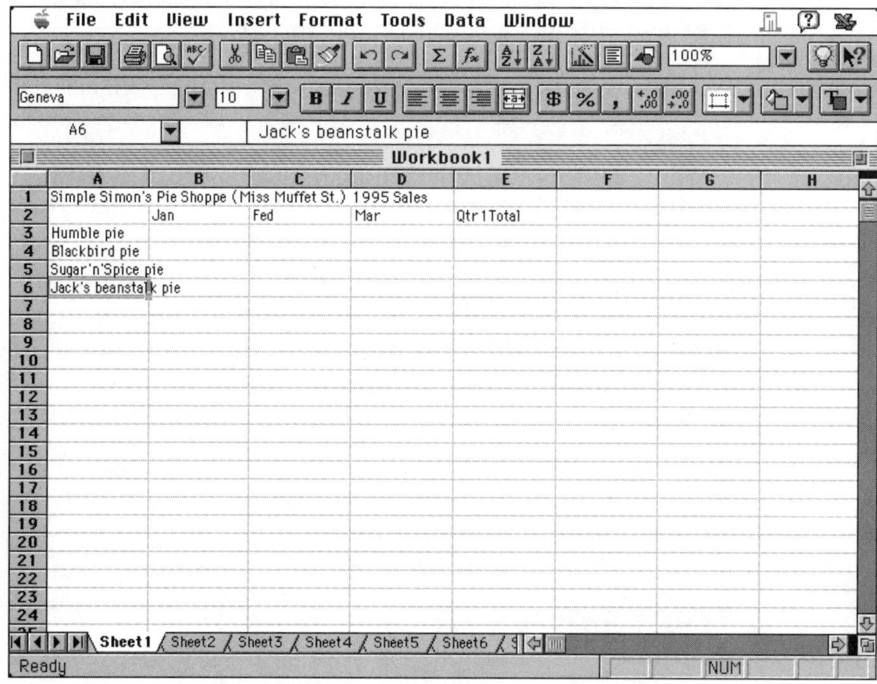

Figure 2-3: Long text entries spill over into neighboring blank cells.

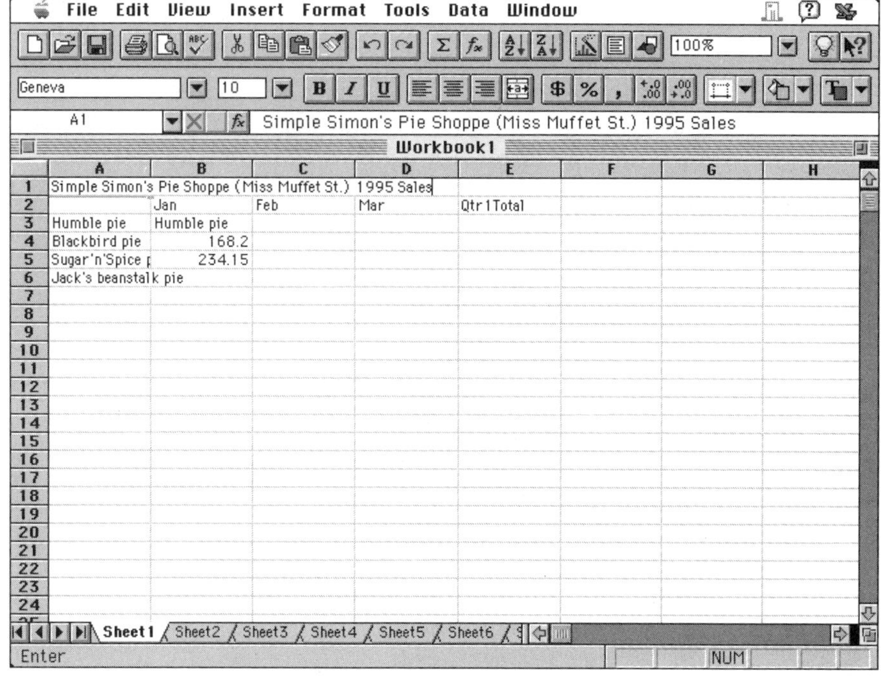

Figure 2-4: Cell entries in the cells to the right cut off the spillover text.

Values to the right of me

Values in Excel can be of two kinds: numbers that represent quantities (such as 10 stores or 100,000 dollars) and numbers that represent dates (such as January 11, 1995) or times (such as 11:59 AM).

You can tell when Excel has accepted a cell entry as a value, because numeric entries are automatically aligned at the right edge of their cells. If the value is wider than the column containing the cell can display, Excel automatically converts the value to (of all things) *scientific notation*. For example, 6E+08 indicates that the 6 is followed by eight zeros, for a grand total of 600,000,000! To restore a value that's been converted into that weird scientific notation stuff back into a regular number, simply widen the column for that cell (see Chapter 3).

Number, please!

To enter a numeric value, select a cell and type the number. To enter negative values in a cell, begin the number with the minus sign or hyphen (–): for example, **–175**. Alternatively, enclose the number in parentheses: **(175)**. If you use parentheses, Excel automatically converts the numeric value to one with a minus sign; for example, if you enter **(5.75)** in a cell, Excel changes it to **–5.75** as soon as you complete the entry.

With numeric values, you can include dollar signs ($) and commas (,) just as they appear in the printed or handwritten numbers you are working from. Just be aware that when you enter a number with commas, Excel assigns a number format to the value that matches your use of commas (for more information on number formats and how they are used, see Chapter 3). Likewise, when you preface a financial figure with a dollar sign, Excel assigns an appropriate dollar number format to the value (one that automatically inserts commas between the thousands).

When a numeric value uses decimal places, use the period as the decimal point. When you enter decimal values, the program automatically adds a zero before the decimal point (Excel inserts 0.34 in a cell when you enter **.34**) and drops trailing zeros entered after the decimal point (Excel inserts 12.5 in a cell when you enter **12.50**).

If you don't know the decimal equivalent for a value, you can enter the value as a fraction. For example, enter **2 3/16** (with a space between the **2** and **3**) instead of **2.1875**. When you enter the fractional form of a decimal number, Excel inputs the decimal equivalent in the formula bar, although it displays the fraction in the cell by assigning it a special fractional number format. When you enter simple fractions such as **3/4** or **5/8**, you must enter them as a mixed number preceded by zero; for example, enter **0 3/4** or **0 5/8** (be sure to include a space between the zero and the fraction — here is the one place where a space is OK within a numeric entry).

When entering a numeric value in a cell that represents a percentage, you have two choices: You can either divide the number by 100 and enter the decimal equivalent (by moving the decimal point two places to the left, just as your teacher taught you — for example, enter **.12** for 12 percent) or you can enter the number with the percent sign (for example, enter **12%**). Either way, Excel stores the decimal value in the worksheet and displays it in the formula bar (0.12 in this example). If you use the percent sign, Excel assigns a percentage number format to the value in the worksheet so that it appears as `12%` in the cell.

Let's make it a date!

It may strike you as odd that dates and times are entered as values in the cells of a worksheet rather than as text. The only reason dates and times are entered as values is so that they can be used in formulas.

Although you can enter dates as text without anything bad happening to you or the worksheet, you won't be able to use such dates in calculations performed by formulas. For example, if you enter two dates as values, you then can set up a formula that subtracts the more recent date from the older date and returns the number of days between them. If you enter the two dates as text entries, Excel cannot calculate the difference between them with a formula.

Dates are stored as serial numbers that indicate how many days have elapsed from a starting date; times are stored as decimal fractions that indicate the elapsed part of the 24-hour period. Excel supports two date systems: the 1900 date system used by Excel for Windows, where January 1, 1900, is the starting date (serial number 1) and the 1904 system used by Excel for the Macintosh, where January 2, 1904, is the starting date.

Excel determines whether the date or time you type is entered as a value or as text by the format you follow. If you follow one of Excel's built-in date and time formats, the program recognizes the date or time as a value. If you don't follow one of the built-in formats, the program enters the date or time as a text entry — it's as simple as that.

Excel recognizes the following time formats:

3:21 PM

3:21:04 PM

15:21

15:21:04

Excel knows the following date formats:

October 25, 1995

10/25/95 or 10-25-95

25-Oct-95

10-Oct

Oct-95

Oh, please fix my decimal places!

If you find that you need to enter a whole slew of numbers that use the same number of decimal places, you can turn on Excel's Fixed Decimal setting and have the program enter the decimals for you. This feature really comes in handy when you have to enter hundreds of financial figures that all use two decimal places for the number of cents.

To *fix* the number of decimal places in a numeric entry, follow these steps:

1. **Choose Tools ⇨ Options.**

   The Options dialog box appears.

2. **Choose the Edit tab.**
3. **Choose Fixed Decimal in the Settings section to place an X in its check box.**

   By default, Excel fixes the decimal place two places to the left of the last number you type.

4. **To change the default setting, type a new number in the Places text box.**

   For example, type **3** in the Places text box to enter numbers with the following decimal placement: 00.000.

5. **Choose OK or press Return.**

   Excel displays the FIX status indicator on the status bar to let you know that the Fixed Decimal feature is active.

After fixing the decimal place in numeric values, Excel automatically adds the decimal point to any numeric value you enter — all you do is type the digits and complete the entry in the cell. For example, to enter the numeric value 100.99 in a cell after fixing the decimal point at 2 places, type the digits **10099**. When you click on the Return box, press Return, or press an arrow key to complete the cell entry, Excel inputs the value 100.99 in the cell.

Remember that while the Fixed Decimal setting is turned on, Excel adds a decimal point to all the numeric values you enter. If you want to enter a number without a decimal point or one with a decimal point in a position different from the one called for by this feature, type the decimal point (period) yourself. For example, to enter the number 1099 instead of 10.99 when the decimal point is fixed at 2 places, type **1099.** in the cell.

When you're ready to return to normal data entry for numerical values (where you enter any decimal points yourself), open the Options dialog box, choose the Edit tab again, deselect the Fixed Decimal check box, and then choose OK or press Return. Excel removes the FIX indicator from the status bar.

Formulas equal to the task

As entries go in Excel, formulas are the real workhorses of the worksheet. If you set up a formula properly, the formula computes the right answer when you first enter it into a cell and from then on keeps itself up to date, recalculating the results whenever you change any of the values the formula uses.

You inform Excel that you are entering a formula in the current cell rather than some text or a value by starting the formula with = (equal sign). Most simple formulas follow the equal sign with a built-in *function* such as SUM or AVERAGE (see "Having Fun with the Function Wizard" later in this chapter for more information on using functions in formulas). Other simple formulas use a series of values or cell references (that contain values) separated by one or more of the following mathematical operators:

+ (plus sign) for addition

– (minus sign or hyphen) for subtraction

* (asterisk) for multiplication

/ (slash) for division

^ (caret) for raising a number to a power

For example, to create a formula in cell C2 that multiplies a value entered in cell A2 by the value in cell B2, enter the following formula in cell C2:

=A2*B2

To enter this formula in cell C2, follow these steps:

1. **Select cell C2.**
2. **Type the entire formula** =A2*B2 **in the cell.**

Alternatively, you can follow these steps:

1. **Select cell C2.**
2. **Type** = **(equal sign).**
3. **Select cell A2 in the worksheet by using the mouse or the keyboard.**

   This action places the cell reference A2 in the formula in the cell (as shown in Figure 2-5).

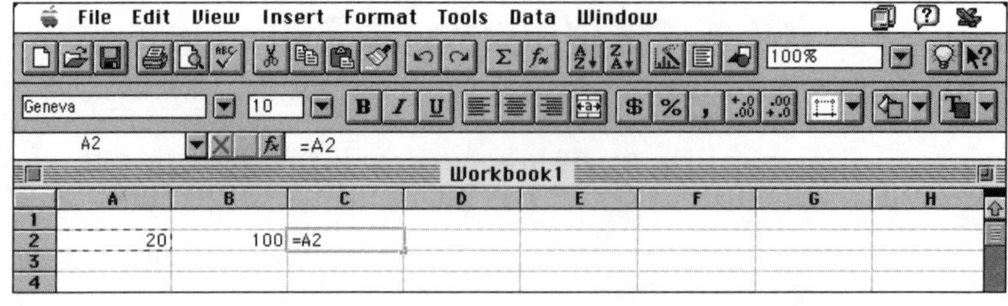

Figure 2-5: To start the formula, type = and then select cell A2.

4. **Type * (asterisk).**

   The asterisk is used for multiplication rather than the *x* you used in school.

5. **Select cell B2 in the worksheet.**

   This action places the cell reference B2 in the formula (as shown in Figure 2-6).

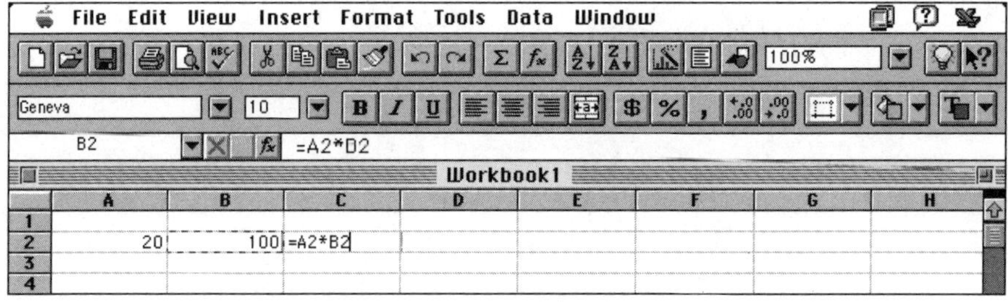

Figure 2-6: To complete the second part of the formula, type * and select cell B2.

6. **Click on the Return box or press Return.**

   Excel displays the calculated answer in cell C2 and the formula =A2*B2 in the formula bar (as shown in Figure 2-7).

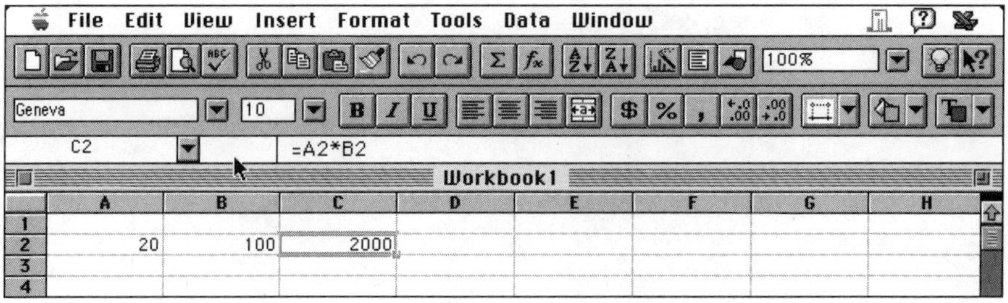

Figure 2-7: Click on the Return box to display the answer in cell C2.

When you complete entry of the formula **=A2*B2** in cell C2 of the worksheet, Excel displays the calculated result depending on the values currently entered in cells A2 and B2. The major strength of the electronic spreadsheet is the capability of formulas to automatically change their calculated results to match changes in the cells referenced by the formulas.

Here are some examples of how changes to cell values affect the calculated result:

- When cell A2 contains the value 20, and cell B2 contains 100, the program displays the result 2000 in cell C2 of the worksheet.
- If you change the value in cell A2 from 20 to 10, the calculated value in cell C2 immediately changes to 1000.
- If you clear cell B2 of its entry without replacing it with a new one, the calculated value in cell C2 changes to 0.

Empty cells carry a 0 (zero) value; the formula A2*B2 is equivalent to 20*0 when you clear cell B2.

Will you be so kind as to point it out?

The method of selecting the cells you use in a formula, rather than typing their cell references, is known as *pointing*. Pointing is not only quicker than typing cell references, it also reduces the risk that you may type the wrong cell reference. When you type a cell reference, you can easily type the wrong column letter or row number and not realize your mistake just by looking at the calculated result returned in the cell.

If you select the cell you want to use in a formula either by clicking on it or by moving the cell pointer to it, the chance of entering the wrong cell reference is reduced.

Following the pecking order

Many formulas that you create perform more than one mathematical operation. Excel performs each operation in the left-to-right direction, according to a pecking order (order of operations) that says multiplication and division pull more weight than addition and subtraction and are therefore performed first.

Consider the series of operations in the following formula:

=A2+B2*C2

If cell A2 contains 5, B2 contains 10, and C2 contains 2, Excel evaluates the following formula:

=5+10*2

In this formula, Excel multiplies 10 times 2 to equal 20 and then adds this result to 5 to produce the result 25.

If you want Excel to perform the addition between the values in cells A2 and B2 *before* the program multiples the result by the value in cell C2, enclose the addition operation in parentheses, as follows:

=(A2+B2)*C2

The parentheses around the addition portion tell Excel that you want this operation performed before the multiplication. If cell A2 contains 5, B2 contains 10, and C2 contains 2, Excel adds 5 and 10 to equal 15 and then multiplies this result by 2 to produce the result 30.

In fancier formulas, you may need to add more than one set of parentheses, one within another (like those Russian *matrushka* dolls that nest within each other) to indicate the order in which you want the calculations to take place. When *nesting* parentheses, Excel first performs the calculation contained in the most inside pair of parentheses, and then uses that result in further calculations as the program works its way outward. For example, consider the following formula:

=(A4+(B4–C4))*D4

Excel first subtracts the value in cell C4 from the value in cell B4, adds the difference to the value in cell A4, and finally multiplies that sum by the value in D4.

Without the additions of the two sets of nested parentheses, Excel, left to its own devices, would first multiply the value in cell C4 by that in D4, add the value in A4 to that in B4, and then perform the subtraction.

When nesting parentheses in a formula, pair them properly so that you have a right parenthesis for every left parenthesis in the formula. If you do not include a right parenthesis for every left one, Excel displays an alert dialog box with the message `Parentheses do not match` when you try to enter the formula. After you close this dialog box, Excel goes right back to the formula in the cell, where you can insert the missing parenthesis and press Return to correct the unbalanced condition. By the way, Excel always highlights matched parentheses.

When a formula freaks

Under certain circumstances, even the best formulas can freak out in a worksheet. You can tell right away that a formula's gone haywire because instead of the nice, calculated value you expect when you enter the formula, you get this strange, incomprehensible message in all uppercase letters, beginning with the number sign (#) and ending with an exclamation point or — in one case — a question mark. This weirdness is known in the parlance of spreadsheets as an *error value*. Its purpose is to let you know that some element, either in the formula itself or in a cell referred to by the formula, is preventing Excel from returning the anticipated calculated value.

The worst thing about error values is that they can contaminate other formulas in the worksheet. If a formula returns an error value to a cell, and a second formula in another cell refers to the value calculated by the first formula, the second formula returns the same error value.

After an error value shows up in a cell, you have to discover what caused the error and edit the worksheet. Table 2-1 lists the error values you may run into in a worksheet and explains the most common causes.

Table 2-1 Error Values That Can Be Returned by Formulas

What Shows Up in the Cell	*What's Going On Here?*
#DIV/0!	Appears when the formula calls for division by a cell that either contains the value 0 or, as is more often the case, is empty. Division by zero is a no-no according to the rules of math.
#NAME?	Appears when the formula refers to a range name (see Chapter 5 for info on naming ranges) that doesn't exist in the worksheet. This error value appears when you type the wrong range name or fail to enclose in quotation marks some text used in the formula, causing Excel to think that the text refers to a range name (see Chapter 13 for info on quotation marks).
#NULL!	Appears most often when you insert a space where you should have used a comma to separate cell references used as arguments for functions (see "Becoming Fully Functional" later in this chapter).

(continued)

Table 2-1 *(continued)*

What Shows Up in the Cell	*What's Going On Here?*
#NUM!	Appears when Excel encounters a problem with a number in the formula, such as the wrong type of argument in an Excel function or a calculation that produces a number too large or too small to be represented in the worksheet.
#REF!	Appears when Excel encounters an invalid cell reference, such as when you delete a cell referred to in a formula or paste cells over cells referred to in a formula.
#VALUE!	Appears when you use the wrong type of argument in a function, the wrong type of operator, or when you call for a mathematical operation that refers to cells that contain text entries.

Correcting Those Nasty Little Typos

Excel 5 gives you the choice of editing cell contents in the formula bar as in previous versions, or in the cell itself. When you double-click on a cell, or if after selecting a cell, you press ⌘+U, you see the insertion point within the cell. If you want to use the formula bar, you must use the mouse to position the insertion point on the formula bar.

When you enter information in a cell, it's quite easy to make a mistake — but the only time a mistake matters is when you don't catch it! You make and notice your mistakes at different times in the process of entering information in cells. Use the following list to apply the appropriate first aid:

- To edit an entry in a cell in Excel for the Macintosh so that the program positions the insertion point at the end of the entry and then allows you to edit it, press ⌘+U.
- If you catch the mistake before you complete the entry, you can delete it by pressing Delete until you remove all the incorrect characters from the cell. Then you can retype the rest of the entry or formula before you complete the entry in the cell.
- If you don't discover the mistake until after you've completed the cell entry, you can either replace the entry in its entirety or just edit the incorrect parts. To replace a cell entry, select the cell and type the replacement.

- You have the opportunity to restore the current entry if you discover you are about to replace the wrong cell. Although Excel appears to wipe out the current cell entry from the formula bar the moment you begin typing, the program doesn't actually replace the current information with the new entry until you complete the entry by clicking on the Return box, pressing Return, or pressing one of the arrow keys. To clear the formula bar of what you've just typed and restore the current entry, click on the Cancel box (the one with the X) or press Esc.

- If the error in an entry is relatively easy to fix, and the entry is long, you probably will want to edit the cell entry rather than replace it. To edit the entry in the cell, simply double-click on the cell. Excel displays the Return, Cancel, and Function Wizard boxes on the formula bar and places the insertion point at the end of the cell entry in the worksheet cell (see Figure 2-8). You then can use the mouse or the arrow keys to position the insertion point at the place in the cell entry that needs fixing.
- To edit the formula on the formula bar rather than in the cell itself (sometimes this is easier when you're dealing with a really long entry), position the mouse pointer on the formula bar at the first character in the entry that needs editing and click the mouse button to place the insertion point in front of that character. When you position the mouse pointer in the formula bar area, the pointer changes from the arrowhead to an I-beam. Place the I-beam between two characters on the formula bar and click the mouse button to place the insertion point between the characters (see Figure 2-9).

Table 2-2 lists the keystrokes you can use to reposition the insertion point in the cell entry and delete unwanted characters. If you want to insert new characters at the insertion point, simply start typing.

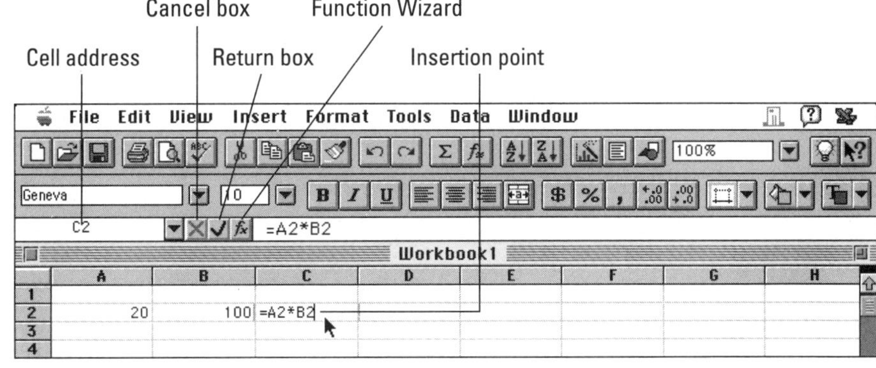

Figure 2-8: Editing cell contents within a cell.

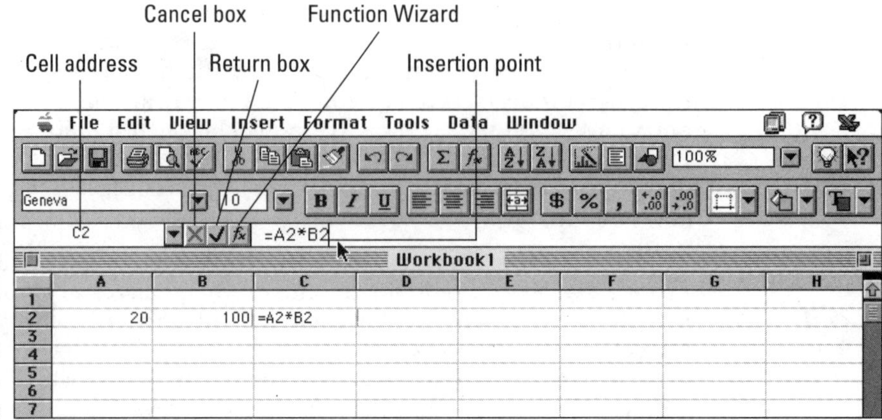

Figure 2-9: Editing cell contents on the formula bar.

EXCEL 5.0

You can reenter the edited cell contents by clicking on the Return box or by pressing the Return key, but *not* by using the arrow keys if you are editing cell contents in Excel 5 on the formula bar. The arrow keys and other keys listed in Table 2-2 only work when editing cell contents while in the cell. Previous versions of Excel for the Mac required you to edit contents on the formula bar only. When you are editing a cell entry, the arrow keys only move the insertion point through the entry and the cell will not be edited if you decided to edit the contents from the formula bar. When a formula in a cell is long and you've selected it for editing, the contents may appear to be on several lines. Please note the difference between ⌘+Home and Home in the table.

Table 2-2 Keystrokes for Editing Cell Entries In the Cell

Keystroke	*What the Keystroke Does*
Delete	Deletes the character in front (or to the left) of the insertion point
→	Positions the insertion point one character to the right
←	Positions the insertion point one character to the left
↑	Positions the insertion point, when it is at the end of the cell entry, to its preceding position to the left
Home	Moves the insertion point in front of the first character of the line in the cell entry
End	Moves the insertion point after the last character of the line in the cell entry
⌘+Home	Moves the insertion point in front of the first character of the first cell entry of the worksheet

(continued)

Keystroke	What the Keystroke Does
⌘+End	Moves the insertion point after the last character of the line in the cell entry
⌘+→	Positions the insertion point in front of the next word in the cell entry
⌘+←	Positions the insertion point in front of the preceding word in the cell entry
Forward Delete	Deletes the character following (or to the right of) the insertion point (Extended keyboard only)

Take Me Out to the Data Range

When you want to enter a table of information in a new worksheet, you can simplify the job of entering the data by selecting all the empty cells in which you want to make entries before you begin entering any information. Just position the cell pointer in the first cell of what is to become the data table and then select all the cells in the subsequent columns and rows (for information on how to select a range of cells, see Chapter 3). After you select the block of cells, you can begin entering the first entry.

When you select a block of cells — also known as a *range* — before you start entering information, Excel restricts data entry to that range, as follows:

- The program automatically advances the cell pointer to the next cell in the range when you click on the Return box or press Return to complete each cell entry.
- In a cell range that contains several different rows and columns, Excel advances the cell pointer down each row of the column as you make your entries. When the cell pointer reaches the cell in the last row of the column, the cell pointer advances to the first selected row in the next column to the right. If the cell range uses only one row, Excel advances the cell pointer from left to right across the row.
- When you finish entering information in the last cell in the selected range, Excel positions the cell pointer in the first cell of the now-completed data table. To deselect the cell range, click the mouse pointer on one of the cells in the worksheet (inside or outside the selected range — it doesn't matter) or press one of the arrow keys.

Be sure that you don't press one of the arrow keys to complete a cell entry within a preselected cell range instead of clicking on the Return box or pressing Return. Pressing an arrow key deselects the range of cells when Excel moves the cell pointer. To move the cell pointer around a cell range without deselecting the range, try these methods:

- Press Return to advance to the next cell down each row and then across each column in the range. Press Shift+Tab to move up to the preceding cell.
- Press Tab to advance to the next cell in the column to the right and then down each row of the range. Press Shift+Return to move back to the preceding cell.
- Press ⌘+. (period) to move from one corner of the range to another.

When You AutoFill It Up

Many of the worksheets you create with Excel require the entry of a series of sequential dates or numbers. For example, a worksheet may require you to title the columns with the 12 months from January through December or to number the rows from 1 to 100.

Excel's AutoFill feature makes short work of this kind of repetitive task. All you have to enter are the starting values for the series. In most cases, AutoFill is smart enough to figure out how to extend the series for you when you drag the fill handle to the right (to take the series across columns to the right) or down (to extend the series to the rows below).

Remember that the AutoFill handle, also known as the *fill* handle, looks like a little black cross (see Figure 2-10 to see an example of it) and appears only when you position the mouse pointer on the lower right-hand corner of the cell or on the last cell of a selected block of cells. Keep in mind that if you drag a cell selection with the white cross mouse pointer rather than the AutoFill handle, Excel simply extends the cell selection to the cells you drag through — see "Cell selections à la mouse" in Chapter 3 for more. If you drag a cell selection with the arrowhead pointer, Excel moves the cell selection (see "Drag until You Drop" in Chapter 4 for more).

When creating a series with the fill handle, you can drag only in one direction at a time. For example, you can extend the series or fill the range to the left or right of the cell range that contains the initial values, or you can extend the series or fill the range above or below the cell range that contains the initial values. However, you cannot extend the series or fill the range in two directions at the same time (such as down and to the right by dragging the fill handle diagonally).

When you release the mouse button after extending the range with the fill handle, Excel either creates a series (if it knows that a value starts a series) in all the cells you selected or fills the entire range with the initial value (if it doesn't recognize it as starting a series).

Figures 2-10 and 2-11 illustrate how to use AutoFill to create a row of months, starting with January in cell B2 and ending with June in cell G2. To create the row, you enter **January** in cell B2, position the mouse pointer on the fill handle in the lower right-hand corner of this cell, and then drag through to cell G2 on the right (see Figure 2-10). When you release the mouse button, Excel fills in the names of the rest of the months (February through June) in the selected cells (see Figure 2-11). Note that Excel keeps the cells with the series of months selected, giving you another chance to modify the series. If you went too far, you can drag the fill handle to the left to cut back on the list of months; if you didn't go far enough, you can drag the fill handle to the right to extend the list of months farther.

Table 2-3 shows some of the different initial values that AutoFill can use and the types of series that Excel can create from them.

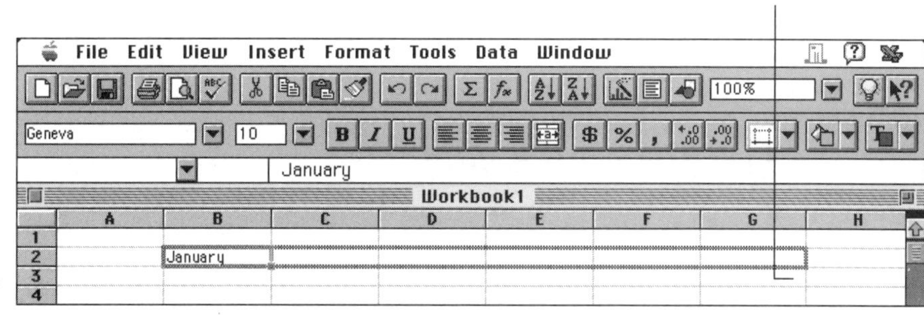

Figure 2-10: Use the AutoFill handle to select the range of cells where the rest of the months will appear.

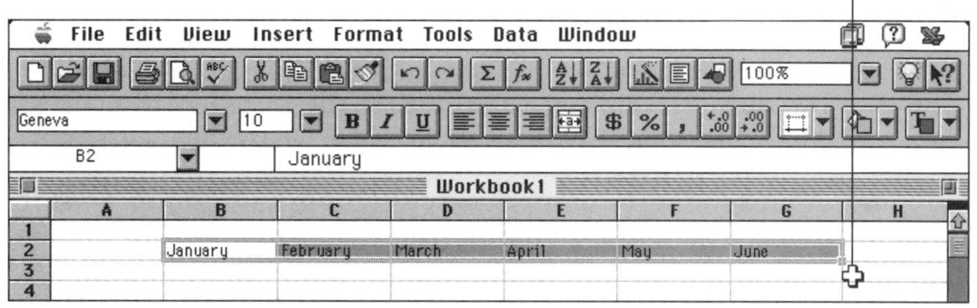

Figure 2-11: When you release the mouse button, Excel fills in the rest of the months.

Table 2-3 Examples of Series You Can Create with AutoFill

Value Entered in First Cell	*Series AutoFill Creates in the Next Three Cells*
June	July, August, September
Jun	Jul, Aug, Sep
Tuesday	Wednesday, Thursday, Friday
Tue	Wed, Thu, Fri
4/1/95	4/2/95, 4/3/95, 4/4/95
Jan-95	Feb-95, Mar-95, Apr-95
15-Feb	16-Feb, 17-Feb, 18-Feb
10:00 PM	11:00 PM, 12:00 AM, 1:00 AM
8:01	9:01, 10:01, 11:01
Quarter 1	Quarter 2, Quarter 3, Quarter 4
Qtr2	Qtr3, Qtr4, Qtr1
Q3	Q4, Q1, Q2
Product 1	Product 2, Product 3, Product 4
1st Product	2nd Product, 3rd Product, 4th Product

Spacing out a series

AutoFill uses the initial value you select (date, time, day, year, and so on) to *design* the series. All the sample series shown in Table 2-3 change by a factor of 1 (one day, one month, or one number). To tell AutoFill to create a series that changes by some other value, enter two sample values in neighboring cells that show the amount of change you want between each value in the series. Then make these two values the initial selection that you extend with the fill handle.

For example, to start a series with Saturday and enter every other day across a row, enter **Saturday** in the first cell and **Monday** in the cell next door. After selecting both cells, drag the fill handle across the cells to the right as far you need to extend the series. When you release the mouse button, Excel follows the example set in the first two cells by entering every other day (Wednesday to the right of Monday, Friday to the right of Wednesday, and so on).

You can *fill* a cell range with AutoFill (rather than create a series) by copying one entry to all the cells of the range, or even just formats or formulas. To fill a cell range, press and hold down the Control key, click the thin black cross pointer (+) on the lower right-hand corner of the cell, and then drag the fill handle. When you hold the Control key, a special AutoFill shortcut menu appears, as shown in Figure 2-12. This menu enables you to select how the contents of the cell or range of cells should be filled.

Designer series

In addition to varying the increment of change in a series created with AutoFill, you also can create your own custom series. For example, in the Simple Simon Pie Shoppes, you can choose from the following list of scrumptious pies:

- Humble pie (the one I end up eating most often)
- Blackbird pie
- Sugar'n'spice pie
- Jack's beanstalk pie

Rather than having to type this list in the cells of each new worksheet (or even copy them from an existing worksheet), you can create a custom series to produce the whole list of pies simply by entering **Humble pie** in the first cell and then dragging the fill handle to the blank cells where the rest of the pies should appear.

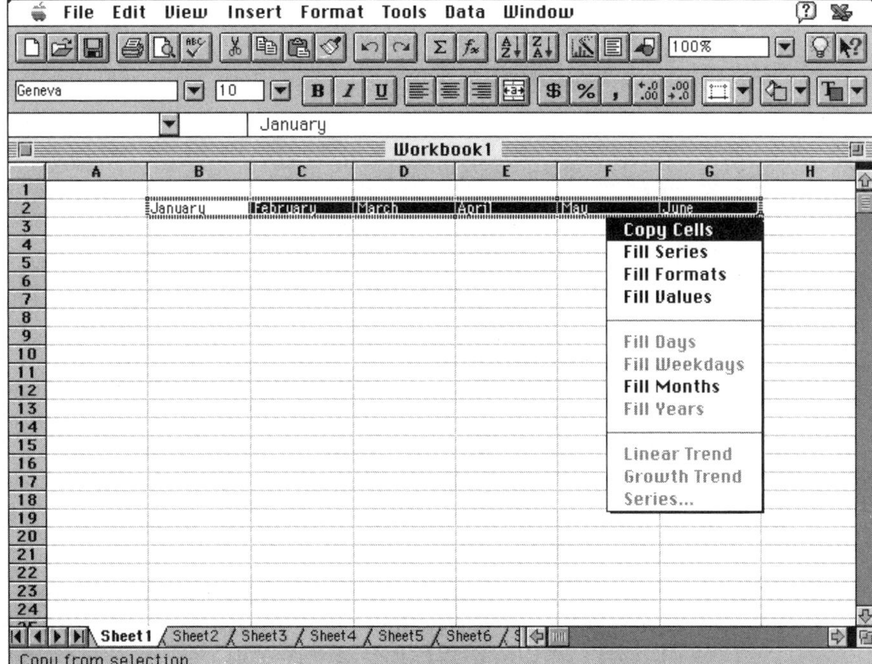

Figure 2-12: The AutoFill shortcut menu also allows you to copy contents and formulas.

To create this kind of custom series, follow these steps:

1. **Choose Tools ⇨ Options to open the Options dialog box.**
2. **Choose the Custom Lists tab to display the Custom Lists and List Entries list boxes.**
3. **If you've already gone to the time and trouble of typing the custom list in a range of cells, choose the Import List from Cells option, drag the dialog box out the way so that you can see your list, and then select the range of cells. (See Chapter 3 for details.)**

   After you select the cells, choose the Import button to copy this list into the List Entries list box.

   If you haven't yet typed the series in an open worksheet, choose instead the List Entries list box, and then type each entry (in the desired order). You can press Return after typing each one or add a comma after each entry.
4. **When all the entries in the custom list appear in the List Entries list box in the order you want, select the Add button to add the list of entries to the Custom Lists list box.**
5. **When you finish creating all the custom lists you need, choose OK or press Return to close the Options dialog box and return to the current worksheet in the active workbook.**

After you add a custom list to Excel, from then on you have only to enter the first entry in a cell and then use the fill handle to extend it to the cells below or to the right.

Double Your Data Entry, Double Your Fun!

You can save a lot of time and energy when you want the same entry (text, value, or formula) to appear in many cells of the worksheet — you can enter it in all the cells in one operation, as follows:

1. **Select the cell ranges that are to hold the information.**

   Excel lets you to select more than one cell range for this kind of thing (see Chapter 3 for details).
2. **Construct the entry on the formula bar.**
3. **Press Control+Return to get the entry into all the selected cell ranges.**

The key to making this operation a success is to hold down the Control key as you press Return — that way, Excel inserts the entry on the formula bar into all the selected cells. If you forget to hold down Control and you just press Return, Excel places the entry only in the first cell of the selected cell range.

Figure 2-13 is a sample worksheet that illustrates how to enter *Total* as the column heading in cell E3 and as the row heading in cell A7. To make this entry in both cells in one operation, select both cells before entering **Total** on the formula bar. When you press Control+Return, Excel inserts the entry in both cells E3 and A7.

If you are fortunate enough to have a Mac keyboard that has a Control key, you can repeat an entry by pressing Control+Return (not Control+Enter). Also, in this operation, the ⌘ key will not substitute for the Control key as it usually does in Excel for the Mac. Unfortunately, if you don't have the extended keyboard equipped with Control keys, this nifty feature is off-limits to you.

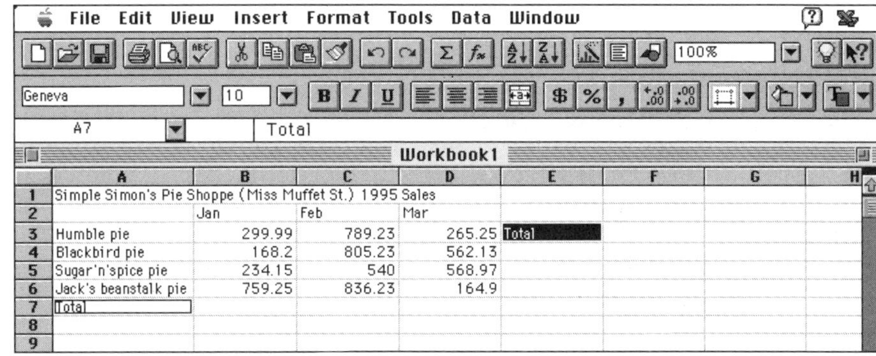

Figure 2-13: Entering the same value in more than one cell.

Becoming Fully Functional

Earlier in this chapter, you learned how to create formulas that perform a series of simple mathematical operations, such as addition, subtraction, multiplication, and division. Instead of creating more complex formulas from scratch out of an intricate combination of these operations, you can find an Excel *function* to get the job done.

A function is a predefined formula that performs a particular type of computation. All you have to do to use a function is supply the values that the function uses when performing its calculations (in the parlance of the Spreadsheet Guru, such values are known as the *arguments* of the function). As with simple formulas, you can enter an argument for most functions either as a numerical value (for example, **22** or **–4.56**) or, more commonly, as a cell reference (for example, **B10**) or cell range (for example, **C3:F3**).

As with a formula that you build yourself, each function you use must start with = (equal sign) so that Excel knows to enter the function as a formula instead of as text. After the =, you enter the name of the function in uppercase or lowercase letters (it doesn't matter as long as you don't misspell the name). Following the name of the function, you enter the arguments required to perform the calculations. All function arguments are enclosed in a pair of parentheses.

If you type the function directly in a cell, remember to not insert spaces between the equal sign, function name, and the arguments enclosed in parentheses. Some functions use more than one value when performing their designated calculations. When this is the case, you separate each function with a comma (not a space).

After you type = (equal sign), the function name, and **(** — left parenthesis, which marks the beginning of the argument of the function — you can point to any cell or cell range you want to use as the first argument instead of having to type the cell references. When the function uses more than one argument, you can point to the cells or cell ranges you want to use for the second argument right after you press **,** (comma) to complete the first argument.

After you finish entering the last argument, press **)** — right parenthesis, which marks the end of the argument list — and then click on the Return box or press Return or an arrow key to insert the function in the cell. Excel calculates the answer.

Having fun with the Function Wizard

Although you can enter a function by typing it directly into a cell, Excel provides a Function Wizard that you can use not only to select the function but also to specify the function arguments. The Function Wizard is a real boon when you're fooling with an unfamiliar function or one that's kinda complex (some of these puppies can be really hairy). The Function Wizard keeps track of all the arguments you need to use and sees to it that you don't mess up the parentheses or commas in the argument list.

To dial up the Function Wizard after selecting the cell that needs the formula, click on the Function Wizard button (next to the Σ button) on the Standard toolbar. Or, if you've already pressed =, you can click on the Function Wizard button on the formula bar right next to the Return button. When you click this button, the Function Wizard — Step 1 of 2 dialog box appears (similar to the one shown in Figure 2-14).

The Function Wizard — Step 1 of 2 dialog box contains two list boxes: Function Category and Function Name. When you open this dialog box, Excel automatically selects Most Recently Used as the category in the Function Category list box and displays the functions you usually use in the Function Name list box.

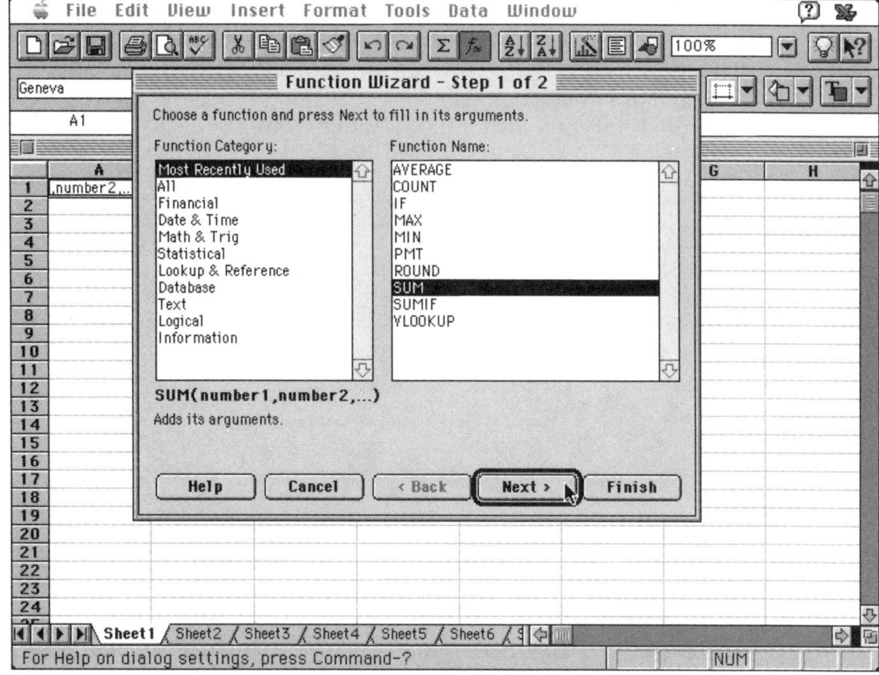

Figure 2-14: Select the function to use in the Function Wizard — Step 1 of 2 dialog box.

If your function isn't among the most recently used, you then must select the appropriate category of function in the Function Category list box (if you don't know the category, choose All). After that, of course, you still need to choose the particular function in the Function Name list box.

When you select a function in the Function Name list box, Excel displays the required arguments for the function at the bottom of the dialog box and inserts the function name along with the obligatory parentheses in the current cell. Suppose that you select the SUM function (the *crown jewel* of the Most Recently Used function category) in the Function Name list box. As soon as you select it, the program puts

```
=SUM()
```

in the cell (and on the formula bar) and shows the arguments as

```
SUM(number1,number2,...)
```

at the bottom of the Function Wizard — Step 1 of 2 dialog box.

To continue and fill in the number arguments for the SUM function, you then select the Next button in the Function Wizard — Step 1 of 2 dialog box. Selecting the Next button takes you (surprise, surprise) to the Function Wizard — Step 2 of 2 dialog box (similar to the one shown in Figure 2-15), where you can add the arguments for the SUM function.

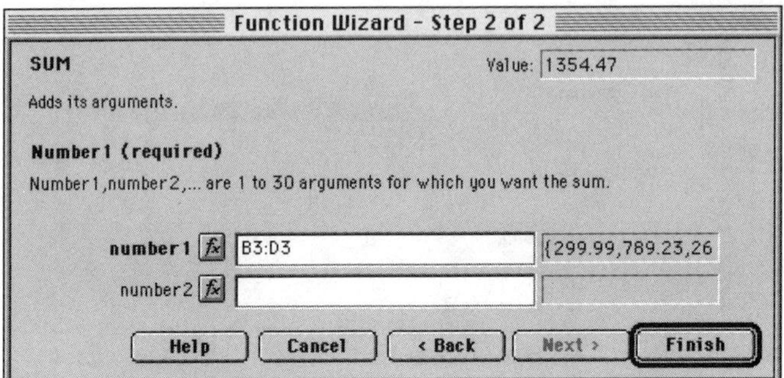

Figure 2-15: Specify the arguments to use in the Function Wizard — Step 2 of 2 dialog box.

As this second Function Wizard dialog box points out, you can select up to 30 numbers to be summed. What it doesn't tell you, however (there's always a trick, right?), is that these numbers don't have to be in single cells. In fact, most of the time you want to select a whole slew of numbers in nearby cells (in a multiple cell selection — that range thing) that you want to total. To select your first number argument in the Function Wizard — Step 2 of 2 dialog box, you click on the cell (or drag through the block of cells) in the worksheet beneath the dialog box while the insertion point is in the number1 text box. Excel then displays the cell address (or range address) in the number1 text box while at the same time showing the value in the cell (or values if you've selected a bunch of cells) in the box to the right and the total so far in the Value text box at the top.

If you're totaling more than one cell (or bunch of cells) in a worksheet, you then press Tab or click on the number 2 text box to move the insertion point there. (Excel responds by extending the argument list with a number 3 text box — as shown in Figure 2-16.) In the number 2 text box, you specify the second cell (or cell range) that is to be added to the one now showing in the number 1 text box. After you click on the cell (or drag through the second cell range), the program displays the cell address(es), with the numbers in the cell(s) to the right, and the running total in the Value text box.

When you've finished pointing out the cells or bunches of cells to be summed, click on the Finish button to close the second Function Wizard dialog box and to put the SUM function in the current cell.

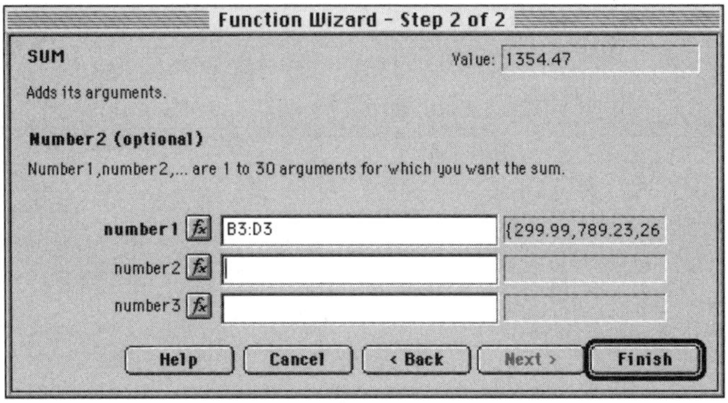

Figure 2-16: To specify additional arguments for a function, press Tab to extend the argument list.

I really AutoSum those numbers!

Before leaving this fascinating discussion on entering functions, I want you to be aware of the AutoSum tool on the Standard toolbar (the one with the Greek letter Σ that looks like a sorority pin). This little tool is worth its weight in gold — check out the following tasks that it can perform:

- Use the AutoSum tool to insert the SUM function in the formula bar (for more information on using SUM and other prominent functions, jump to Chapters 12 and 13).
- Use the AutoSum tool to tell Excel to select the cell range containing the values you want totaled. Nine times out of ten, Excel highlights the correct cell range. For that tenth case, you can correct the range by simply dragging the cell pointer through the correct range of cells.
- Use the AutoSum tool to total a list of numbers: Select the cell in which you want the sum to appear and click on the tool.
- Use the AutoSum tool to sum a list of values entered in a column.

Figure 2-17 shows how to use the AutoSum tool to total the sales of Humble pies in row 3. To total the sales in this row, position the cell pointer in cell E3, where the first-quarter total is to appear, and click on the AutoSum tool. Excel inserts the SUM function (equal sign and all) in the formula bar, places a *marquee* (the moving dotted line) around the cells B3, C3, and D3, and uses the cell range B3:D3 as the argument of the SUM function.

Figure 2-18 shows the worksheet after you insert the function in cell E3. The calculated total appears in cell E3 while the following SUM formula appears in the formula bar:

```
=SUM(B3:D3)
```

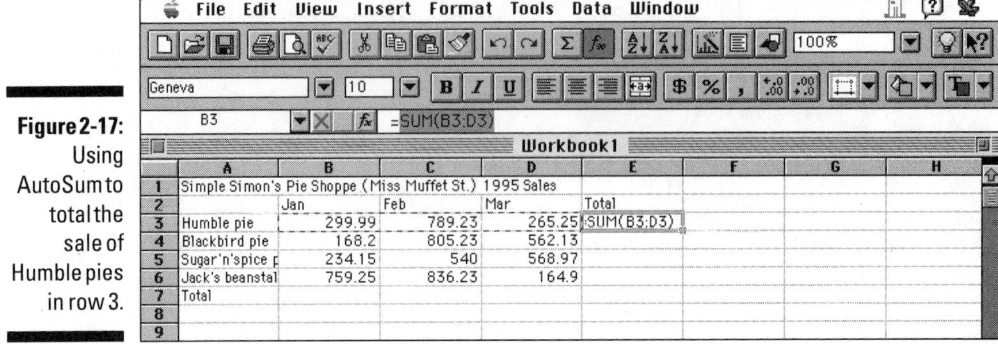

Figure 2-17: Using AutoSum to total the sale of Humble pies in row 3.

E3 =SUM(B3:D3)

Workbook1

	A	B	C	D	E	F	G	H
1	Simple Simon's Pie Shoppe (Miss Muffet St.) 1995 Sales							
2		Jan	Feb	Mar	Total			
3	Humble pie	299.99	789.23	265.25	1354.47			
4	Blackbird pie	168.2	805.23	562.13				
5	Sugar'n'spice p	234.15	540	568.97				
6	Jack's beanstal	759.25	836.23	164.9				
7	Total							
8								
9								

Figure 2-18: The worksheet with the first quarter total for Humble pies.

After entering the function to total the sales of Humble pies, you can copy this formula to total sales for the rest of the pies by dragging the fill handle down column E until the cell range E4:E6 is highlighted.

Figure 2-19 illustrates how you can use the AutoSum tool to total the January pie sales in column B. Position the cell pointer in cell B7, where you want the total to appear. When you click on the AutoSum tool, Excel places the marquee around cells B3, B4, B5, and B6 and correctly enters the cell range B3:B6 as the argument of the SUM function.

Figure 2-20 shows the worksheet after inserting the function in cell B7 and using the AutoFill feature to copy the formula to cells C7, D7, and E7. To use AutoFill to copy the formula, drag the fill handle through the cells to the right until you reach cell E7 and then release the mouse button.

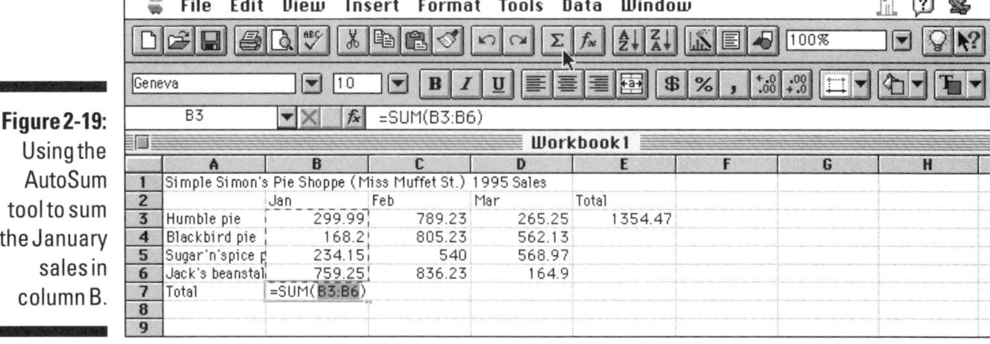

Figure 2-19: Using the AutoSum tool to sum the January sales in column B.

File Edit View Insert Format Tools Data Window

B7 =SUM(B3:B6)

Workbook1

	A	B	C	D	E	F	G	H
1	Simple Simon's Pie Shoppe (Miss Muffet St.) 1995 Sales							
2		Jan	Feb	Mar	Total			
3	Humble pie	299.99	789.23	265.25	1354.47			
4	Blackbird pie	168.2	805.23	562.13	1535.56			
5	Sugar'n'spice p	234.15	540	568.97	1343.12			
6	Jack's beanstal	759.25	836.23	164.9	1760.38			
7	Total	1461.59	2970.69	1561.25	5993.53			
8								
9								

Figure 2-20: The worksheet after copying the Sum formula.

Saving the Evidence

All the work you do in a worksheet is at risk until you save the document onto disk. If you lose power or if your computer crashes for any reason before you save the document, you're out of luck. You have to recreate each and every keystroke — a painful task, made all the worse because it's so unnecessary. To avoid this unpleasantness altogether, adopt this rule of thumb: Save your worksheet any time you've entered more information than you could possibly bear to lose.

To encourage frequent saving on your part, Excel even provides you with a Save tool on the Standard toolbar (the one with the picture of the disk, third from the left). You don't even have to take the time and trouble to choose File and then Save (or even to press ⌘+S) — you can simply click on this tool whenever you want to save new work on disk.

The first time you click on the Save tool, Excel displays the Save As dialog box (similar to the one shown in Figure 2-21). You can use this dialog box to replace the temporary document name (Workbook1, Workbook2, and the like) with a more descriptive filename and to select a new drive and directory before you save the file. It's just this easy:

- To change the drive where the file is to be saved, click on the Desktop pop-up list button and select the appropriate drive in the list box, or navigate the hierarchy of folders by clicking the pull-down menu at the top left of the dialog box. It is usually quicker to use the Desktop button if you want to save to a floppy disk or a second hard disk.
- To change the directory where you want the file stored, click on the appropriate folder in the Directories list box or use the top pull-down menu, which will have the current folder selection.
- To rename the document, type the filename in the Save As text box. When you first open the Save As dialog box, the suggested filename is selected — you can just start typing the new filename to replace it.

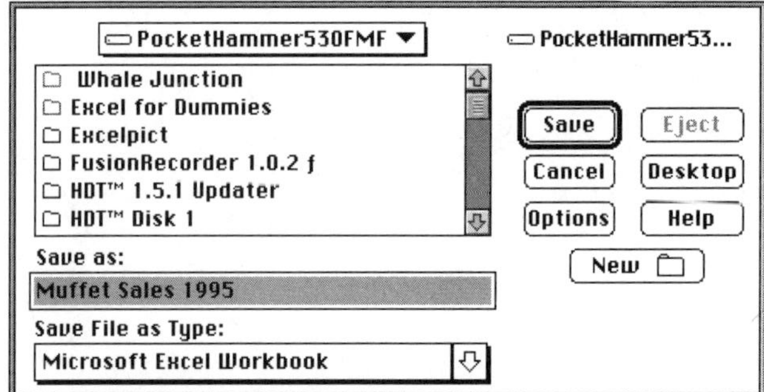

Figure 2-21: The Save As dialog box.

As a Mac user, you can give worksheet files descriptive names up to 32 characters long, adding spaces as necessary to separate the words.

When you finish making changes in the Save As dialog box, choose Save or press Return. Excel then displays the Summary Info dialog box (like the one shown in Figure 2-22), where you can add information that may help you locate this file later on down the line when you can't for the life of you tell what kind of a data you've stored under a cryptic filename!

Summary Info

File Name: 3
Directory: PocketHammer530FMF
Title: Simple Simons Pie Shoppe
Subject: 1995 Sales
Author: Greg Harvey
Keywords: 1st quarter sales, Miss Muffet
Comments:

OK
Cancel
Help

Figure 2-22: The Summary Info dialog box.

When filling out the Summary Info (which you can skip, of course, if you're in a hurry and are sure you'll never, ever forget what kinda stuff you put in the workbook file), you can specify the Title, Subject, Author, Keywords, and Comments about the worksheet.

Just keep in mind that later on you'll be able to search for this file by the information entered into any of the text boxes in the Summary Info dialog box (except for the Comments box — that's just for notes to yourself). For example, to later find the workbook being saved in Figures 2-21 and 2-22, you can search for all files that have 1995 Sales as the Subject in the Summary Info and Miss Muffet as the Keywords, which should narrow it down quite a bit (see Chapter 4 for information about finding files).

After filling in the Summary Info (or just moving on if you think it best), choose OK or press Return to save the workbook file (with all its worksheets) on disk. After saving a workbook the first time, Excel displays the filename you assigned in the document title bar. You can save all subsequent changes to the worksheet by clicking on the Save tool. You'll never be bothered by the Summary Info dialog box again unless you deliberately choose File and then Summary Info.

You don't have to fool with the Save As dialog box again unless you want to rename the workbook or save a copy of it in a different directory. If you want to do either of these things, you must choose the Save As command from the File menu rather than click on the Save tool or use ⌘+S.

Part II

The More Things Change. . .

The 5th Wave By Rich Tennant

"For further thoughts on that subject, I'm going to down-load Leviticus and go through the menu to Job, chapter 2, verse 6, file 'J,' it reads..."

The part in which . . .

You learn how to put some sizzle into your worksheet by dressing up the lackluster facts and figures you've entered. Here you learn how to outfit your worksheet data in new fonts and styles at the click of a tool. You also learn how to accentuate the positive by rearranging entries in their cells, changing the width of columns and rows, and adding pizzazz with new borders, rows, and patterns.

After learning how to show off your information to its best advantage, you learn how to cope with those inevitable and seemingly unending changes that need to be made to a worksheet. After you get through this part, you can undo your boo-boos and copy and move information to new places in the worksheet. You learn how to add new sections to the worksheet and how to remove those you want to abandon — all without hopelessly messing up the structure of the original document.

Chapter 3

Fancying Up the Figures

In This Chapter

- How to select ranges of cells with the mouse and the keyboard
- How to use the AutoFormat feature to spruce up a table of figures
- How to apply built-in number formats to a cell selection
- How to create custom formats
- How to change the widths of certain columns in the worksheet
- How to adjust the height of certain rows in the worksheet
- How to hide columns and rows in the worksheet
- How to assign a new font and font size to a cell selection
- How to change the alignment of the entries in a cell selection
- How to change the way entries are justified in a cell selection
- How to apply borders, shading, or colors to a cell selection
- How to use styles to format a cell selection

Now that you know how to get information into a worksheet and how to get it to stay there, you're ready to learn about all the ways you can pretty it up. In spreadsheet programs such as Excel, you normally don't worry about formatting the information until after you enter all the data in the worksheet.

After you decide on the formatting you want to apply to a portion of the worksheet, you select all the cells to be beautified and then click on the appropriate tool or choose the menu command to apply that formatting. Thus, before you learn about all the fabulous formatting features you can use to dress up cells, you first need to know how to pick out the group of cells that you want to format.

Entering information into a cell and formatting that information are two distinct procedures in Excel. When you change the entry in a formatted cell, the new entry assumes the cell's formatting. Therefore, you can format blank cells in a worksheet, and then when you make entries in those cells, the entries are displayed with that particular formatting.

Selectively Yours

Given the extremely rectangular nature of the worksheet and its components, you shouldn't be surprised to find that all the cell selections you make in the worksheet have the same kind of Mondrian-like feel: They are all basically just cell blocks made up of different numbers and arrangements of cells.

A *cell selection* (also known as a *cell range*) is whatever collection of neighboring cells you pick out for formatting or editing in some way. The smallest possible cell selection in a worksheet is just one cell, the so-called *active cell* — the cell with the cell pointer is really just a single cell selection. The largest possible cell selection in a worksheet is all the cells in that worksheet (the whole enchilada, so to speak). Most of the cell selections you need for formatting a worksheet fall probably somewhere in between, consisting of cells in several adjacent columns and rows.

Excel shows a cell selection in the worksheet by highlighting the block. Figure 3-1 shows several cell selections of different sizes and shapes.

In Excel, you can select more than one cell range at a time (a selection somewhat ingloriously called a *discontinuous* or *nonadjacent selection*). In fact, although I billed Figure 3-1 as having several cell selections, it is really just one, big, discontinuous selection.

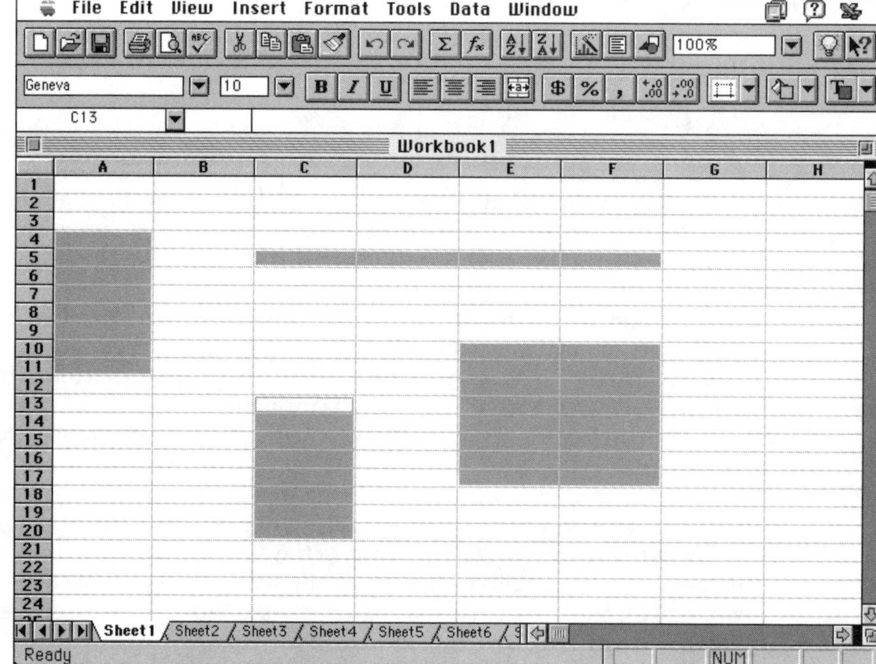

Figure 3-1: Several cell selections of various shapes and sizes.

Cell selections à la mouse

The mouse is a natural for selecting a range of cells. Just position the mouse pointer (in its fat white cross form) on the first cell, press and hold down the mouse button, and drag in the direction you want to extend the selection. When you've selected the entire range you want, release the mouse button.

- To extend the cell selection to columns to the right, drag right, highlighting neighboring cells as you go.
- To extend the selection to rows below, drag down.
- To extend the selection down and to the right at the same time, drag diagonally towards the cell in the lower right-hand corner of the block you are highlighting.

To speed up the selection procedure, you can use the old Shift+click method, which goes as follows:

1. **Click on the first cell in the selection to establish the cell pointer.**
2. **Position the mouse pointer in the last cell you want to include in the range.**
3. **Press and hold down the Shift key as you click the mouse button again.**

When you click the mouse button the second time, Excel selects all the cells in the columns and rows between the first cell and second cell.

The Shift key works with the mouse like an *extend* key to extend a selection from the first object you select through, to, and including the second object. Shift enables you to select the first and last cell, as well as all the intervening cells in a worksheet or all the document names in a dialog list box.

If, when you are making a cell selection with the mouse, you notice that you have included the wrong cells before you release the mouse button, you can deselect the cells and resize the selection by moving the pointer in the opposite direction. If you've already released the mouse button, click on the first cell in the highlighted range to select just that cell (and deselect all the others) and then start the whole selection process again.

Making a discontinuous selection

To select more than one range at the same time, highlight the first cell range and then hold down the ⌘ key as you click on the first cell of the second range and drag the pointer through the cells in this range. As long as you hold down ⌘ as you select the subsequent ranges, Excel doesn't deselect the first range.

The ⌘ key works with the mouse like an *add* key to include non-neighboring objects in Excel. With ⌘, you can add to the selection of cells in a worksheet or to the document names in a dialog list box without having to deselect those already selected.

Selecting entire columns and rows

You can use the worksheet frame to select entire columns and rows.

- To select every cell in a particular column, click on that column's letter on the frame at the top of the workbook window.
- To select every cell in a particular row, click on that row's number on the frame at the left edge of the workbook window.
- To select a range of entire columns or rows, drag through the column letters or row numbers on the frame surrounding the workbook window.
- To select entire columns or rows that are not right next to each other (that old discontinuous stuff again), press and hold down ⌘ while you click on the column letters or row numbers of the columns and rows you want to add to the selection.
- To select each and every cell in the worksheet, click on the "blank" button in the upper left-hand corner of the frame (at the intersection of the row of column letters and the column of row numbers).

You really AutoSelect me

Excel provides a really quick way (called AutoSelect) to select all the cells in a table of data entered as a block. (***Note:*** Don't try AutoSelect when you need to select empty cells.) To use AutoSelect, click on one of the cells in any of the four corners of the table to select it, hold down the Shift key, and then double-click on the edge of the active cell in the direction in which you want to expand the selection.

- Double-click on the top of the active cell to select cells in rows above.
- Double-click on the right edge of the cell to select cells in columns to the right.
- Double-click on the bottom edge of the cell to select cells in rows below.
- Double-click on the left edge of the cell to select cells in columns to the left.

Before you double-click on the edge of the cell, be sure that the mouse pointer changes from the thick white cross shape to its arrowhead guise.

After expanding the cell selection by double-clicking on one edge of the first cell, you can expand that cell selection in a second direction by double-clicking on one of its edges with the arrowhead pointer.

For example, to select a large table of data with AutoSelect, click on the first cell in the table (the cell in the upper left-hand corner), press and hold down the Shift key, and double-click on the right edge of that cell to expand the selection to the last column of the table. Then double-click on the bottom edge of the selection to extend the selection down to the last row of the table.

Note: You can just as easily extend the cell selection down and then to the right by first holding down the Shift key and double-clicking on the bottom of the first cell before double-clicking on the right edge of the selection.

Cell selections — keyboard style

If you're not really keen on using the mouse, you can use the keyboard to select the cells you want to use. In keeping with the Shift+click method of selecting cells, the easiest way to select cells with the keyboard is to combine the Shift key with other keystrokes that move the cell pointer (see Chapter 21 for a list of these keystrokes).

Start by positioning the cell pointer in the first cell of the selection, hold down the Shift key, and then press the appropriate direction keys, which include the arrow keys (↑, ←, ↓, →), Page Up, Page Down, ⌘+Page Up, or ⌘+Page Down. Excel anchors the selection on the current cell, moves the cell pointer as usual, and highlights the cells as it goes.

When making a cell selection with the keyboard, you can continue to alter the size and shape of the cell range with the direction keys as long as you don't release the Shift key. After you release the Shift key, pressing any of the direction keys immediately collapses the selection and reduces it to just the cell with the cell pointer.

If you find that holding down the Shift key while moving the cell pointer is too tiring, you can place Excel in *extend* mode by pressing (and promptly releasing) F8 before you press any direction keys. Excel displays the EXT (for *extend*) indicator on the status bar — your sign that the program will select all the cells that you move the cell pointer through. After you've highlighted all the cells you want to highlight in the cell range, press F8 again to turn off extend mode.

The keyboard equivalent of AutoSelect

When you're in a hurry to select a block of cell entries in a worksheet, you can combine F8 (or Shift) with the ⌘+arrow keys or End+arrow keys to zip the cell pointer from one end of a block to the other. Voilà! You have the keyboard equivalent of AutoSelect.

To select an entire table of data, follow these steps:

1. **Position the cell pointer in the first cell (the cell in the upper left-hand corner of the table).**
2. **Press F8 (or hold down Shift) and then press ⌘+→ (or End+→ if you prefer) to extend the cell selection to the cells in the columns to the right.**
3. **Press ⌘+↓ (or End+↓) to extend the selection to the cells in the rows below.**

Again, the order of the directions is arbitrary — you can just as well press ⌘+↓ (or End+↓) before you press ⌘+→ (or End+→). If you're using Shift rather than F8, be sure that you don't release the Shift key until after you finish performing the two directional maneuvers.

Discontinuous keyboard selections

Selecting more than one cell range is a little more complicated with the keyboard than it is with mouse. When using the keyboard, you have to do the following: Anchor the cell pointer, move the cell pointer to select the cell range, unanchor the cell pointer, and reposition it at the beginning of the next range. To unanchor the cell pointer so that you can move it into position for selecting another range, press Shift+F8. Now you are in *add* mode, in which you move to the first cell of the next range without selecting any more cells. Excel lets you know that the cell pointer is unanchored by displaying the `ADD` indicator on the status bar.

To select more than one cell range with the keyboard, follow these steps:

1. **Move the cell pointer to the first cell of the first cell range you want to select.**
2. **Press F8 to get into extend mode.**

   Move the cell pointer to select all the cells in the first cell range. Alternatively, hold down Shift as you move the cell pointer.
3. **Press Shift+F8 to switch to add mode.**

   The `ADD` indicator appears in the status bar.
4. **Move the cell pointer to the first cell of the next nonadjacent range you want to select.**
5. **Press F8 to get back into select mode and then move the cell pointer to select all the cells in this new range.**
6. **If you still have other nonadjacent ranges to select, repeat Steps 3 through 5 until you have selected and added all the cell ranges you want to use.**

I'm sure you'd rather use a mouse. I know I do!

Selecting cells with the Goto feature

If you want to select a really big cell range that would take a long time to select by pressing various direction (cell-pointer movement) keys, use the Goto feature to extend the range to a far-distant cell. Follow these steps:

1. **Position the cell pointer in the first cell of the range and then press F8 to anchor the cell pointer.**
2. **Press F5 to open the Go To dialog box, type the address of the last cell in the range (the cell catty-corner from the first cell if you're selecting more than one adjacent row or column), and then press Return.**

   Because Excel is in extend mode, the program not only moves the cell pointer to the designated cell address but selects all the intervening cells as well.

AutoFormat to the Rescue

Now that you know all about selecting the cells you want to format, you're going to learn about a formatting technique that doesn't require any kind of cell selection (kinda figures, doesn't it?). In fact, the AutoFormat feature is so automatic that to use it you only need to have the cell pointer somewhere within the table of data you want to format when you select Format ➪ AutoFormat.

As soon as you select Format ➪ AutoFormat to open the AutoFormat dialog box, Excel automatically selects all the cells in the table. (You get a rude message in an alert box if you choose the command when the cell pointer isn't within the confines of the table or in one of the cells directly bordering the table.)

After you open the AutoFormat dialog box, you can make short work of formatting the selected table. Choose one of the 17 built-in table formats by doing the following:

1. **Click on a format in the Table Format list box.**

   This step gives you an idea of what kind of formatting is included in a particular table format and how it makes the table look. Excel applies the formatting to a sample table of data in the Sample area of the AutoFormat dialog box. (Unfortunately, Excel cannot display a miniature of your own table in the Sample area.)
2. **Continue previewing formats from the list box in this manner to find the one you want to use.**

3. **After you find the table format you want, click OK to close the AutoFormat dialog box and apply the selected format to the table.**

   After you're familiar enough with the table formats to know which one you want to use, you can save time by double-clicking on the desired format in the Table Format list box. Double-clicking on the format closes the dialog box and applies the formatting to the selected table.

If you ever goof up and select a table format that you just absolutely hate after you see it in the worksheet, choose Edit ⇨ Undo AutoFormat (or press ⌘+Z) before you do anything else. Excel restores the table to its previous state. (For more on getting yourself out of a jam with the Undo feature, see Chapter 4.)

Each of the 17 built-in table formats offered by AutoFormat is nothing more than a particular combination of various kinds of cell and data formatting that Excel applies to the cell selection in a single operation. (Boy, does this feature save time!) Each table format enhances the headings and values in the table in a slightly different way.

Figure 3-2 shows the first quarter sales table for the Miss Muffet Street Simple Simon's Pie Shoppe (introduced in Chapter 2) just before I selected the Simple (what else!) table format from the AutoFormat dialog box.

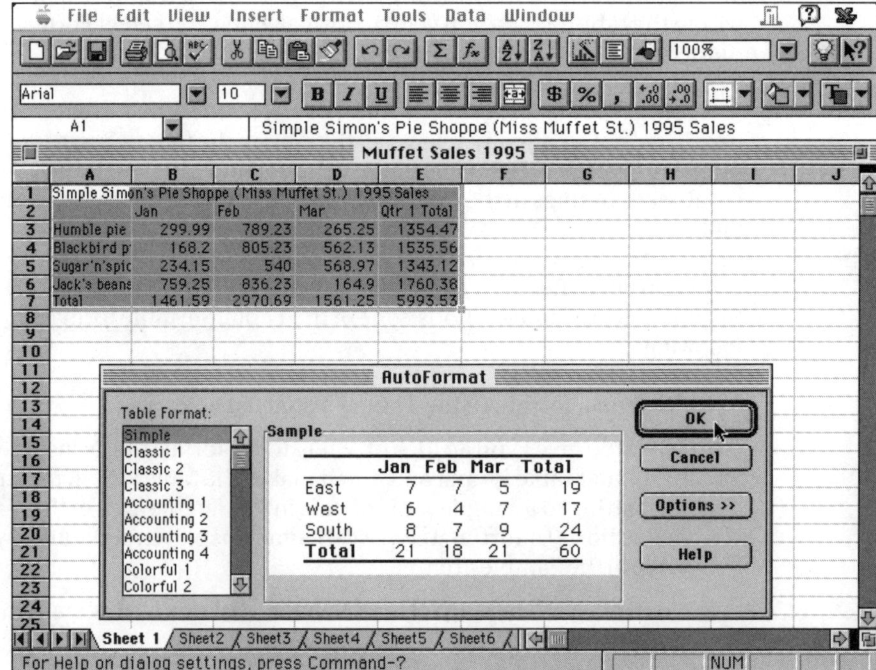

Figure 3-2: Using AutoFormat to select the Simple table format.

Figure 3-3 shows the sales table after I applied the Simple table format. Excel added bold formatting to the title and headings found in rows 1 and 2 and drew border lines to separate the headings from the rest of the data. Excel also tried (unsuccessfully) to center the title `Simple Simon's Pie Shoppe (Miss Muffet St.) 1995 Sales` over columns A through E. Unfortunately, the darned title is too long with its new formatting to center over these five columns — so the program shoved the first part of the title back under the frame.

To rectify the problem with the title, you must return the title to its natural state of left justification (so that the text overhangs the table and slops over into the blank columns in row 1). The easiest way to return the title to left justification is (with the cell selected) to click on the Align Left tool (the one with the text lined up left) on the Formatting toolbar. (For more information on aligning left, see "Line 'Em Up" later in this chapter.)

Figure 3-4 shows the table after I removed the Simple AutoFormat (courtesy of ⌘+Z) and then applied the 3D Effects 2 AutoFormat to the same cell range. Excel increased the width of column A to contain the entire worksheet title in cell A1. This kind of column sizing is known as *best fit* (obviously misapplied in this case) and is accomplished with the AutoFit feature.

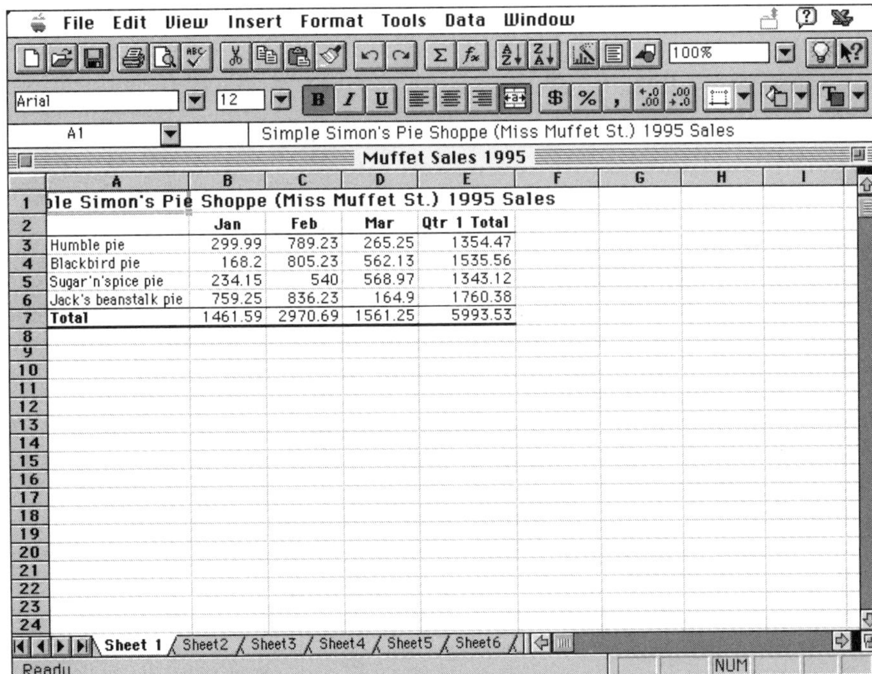

Figure 3-3: The Simple Simon's Pie Shoppe table in the Simple table format.

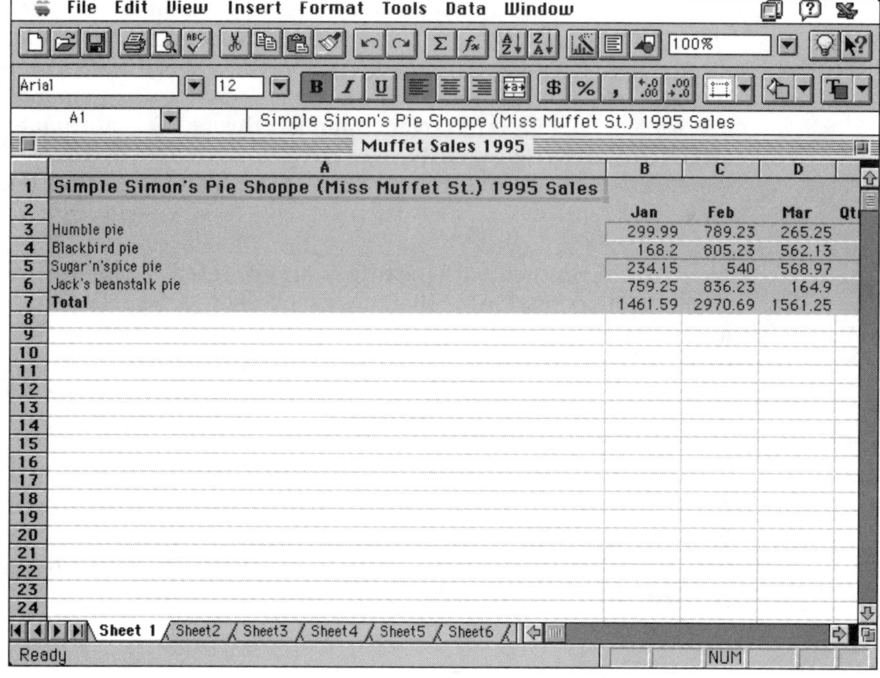

Figure 3-4: Simple Simon's Pie Shoppe table in the 3D Effects 2 table format.

If you want to extend the title over several columns rather than putting it all in column A, you simply reduce the width of column A until it's just wide enough to accommodate all the pie names in rows 3 through 6 (to find out how to widen and narrow columns, see "If the Column Fits…" later in this chapter). Then you can let the worksheet title in cell A1 once again overhang columns B through E as it naturally wants to do.

The 3D Effects 2 AutoFormat is not the only table format that uses AutoFit to apply best fit to all selected columns (and can give you a really wide first column if your table has a long title in the first cell — as in Figure 3-4). You also get this best-fit-but-not-really situation if you choose the Classic 2; Accounting 1, 2, or 3; Colorful 3; List 1 or 2; and 3D Effects 1 or 2 table formats. All the other formats prefer to center long titles in the first row across all the columns in the table, which can then give you the problem illustrated in Figure 3-3 — you can't win!

Formats at the Click of a Tool

Some worksheets require a lighter touch than that offered by AutoFormat. For example, you may have a table where the only emphasis you want to add is to make the column headings bold at the top of the table and to underline the row of totals at the bottom by drawing a border line along the bottom of the cells.

With the formatting tools on the Formatting toolbar, which appears right below the Standard toolbar, you can accomplish most data and cell formatting without ever venturing into the shortcut menus, let alone (heaven forbid!) opening up the pull-down menus.

You can use the tools on the Formatting toolbar to assign new fonts and number formats to cells, change the alignment of their contents, and add borders, patterns, and colors to them. (See Table 1-2 in Chapter 1 for a complete rundown on the use of each of the tools.)

Musical toolbars

Normally, the Standard and Formatting toolbars appear at the top of the Excel program window, right below the menu bar, in a stationary position (politely referred to as the *docked* position — *beached* is more like it). Although Excel automatically docks these toolbars at the top of the screen, you are free to move them (and any other toolbars that you open) around by dragging them, kicking and screaming, into new positions. (See Chapter 11 for details on using and customizing other toolbars.)

When you drag the Standard or Formatting toolbar down from its docked perch and into the work area containing the open workbook, the toolbar appears in a separate little window, such as the window containing the Formatting toolbar shown in Figure 3-5. Such a toolbar-in-a-window is called a *floating toolbar* because it floats like a cloud above the open workbook below (how poetic!). And you can not only move these little dears, you can resize them as well.

- You can move a floating toolbar into new positions over the worksheet document by dragging it by its tiny title bar.
- You can resize a floating toolbar by dragging the Size box. Position the mouse pointer over the Size box in the lower right corner of the Formatting tool box, and then start dragging.
- As you drag a side, the outline of the toolbar assumes a new shape to accommodate the tools in a prescribed tool arrangement. After the toolbar outline assumes the shape you want, release the mouse button, and Excel redraws the toolbar.

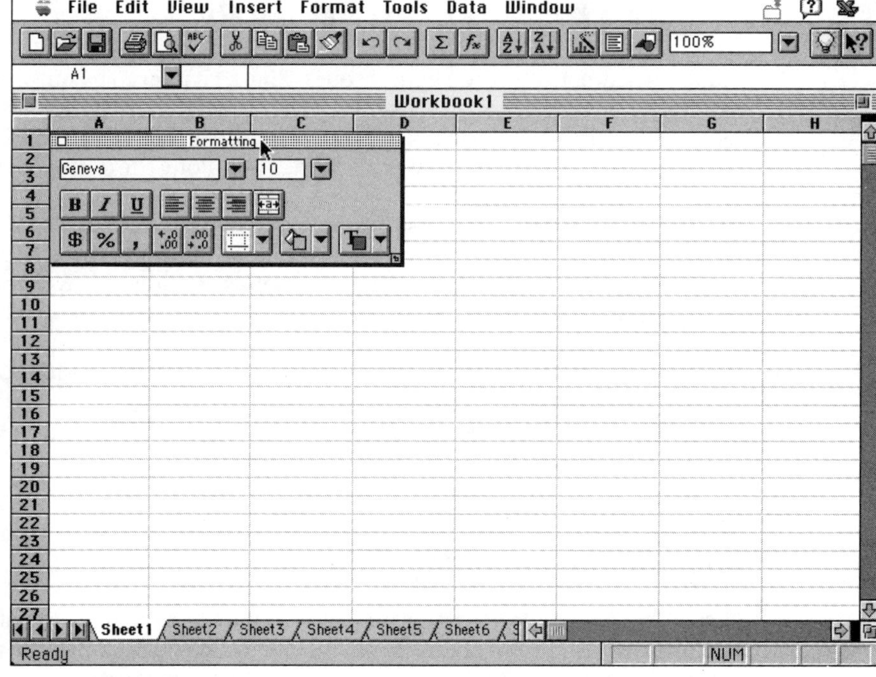

Figure 3-5: The Formatting toolbar floats above the workbook.

- To close a floating toolbar when you no longer want it in the document window, click on the Close box (the small box with the file handle in the upper left-hand corner of the toolbar window).

Any port in a storm

Let's face it: Sometimes a floating toolbar can be a real pain because you constantly have to move it out of the way as you add to and edit your worksheet data. To get a floating toolbar out of the way so that it no longer obscures any of the worksheet cells, you can simply dock it.

You can dock the toolbar at either of two docking stations, which correspond to the top and bottom of the Excel program window. Figure 3-6 shows the Formatting toolbar after it's docked at the bottom of the work area. When you dock a toolbar at the bottom of the screen, the toolbar appears right above the status bar.

To dock a floating toolbar in one of these areas, drag it as far to the side of the window as possible and release the mouse button after the outline of the bar assumes a shape that accommodates a single column.

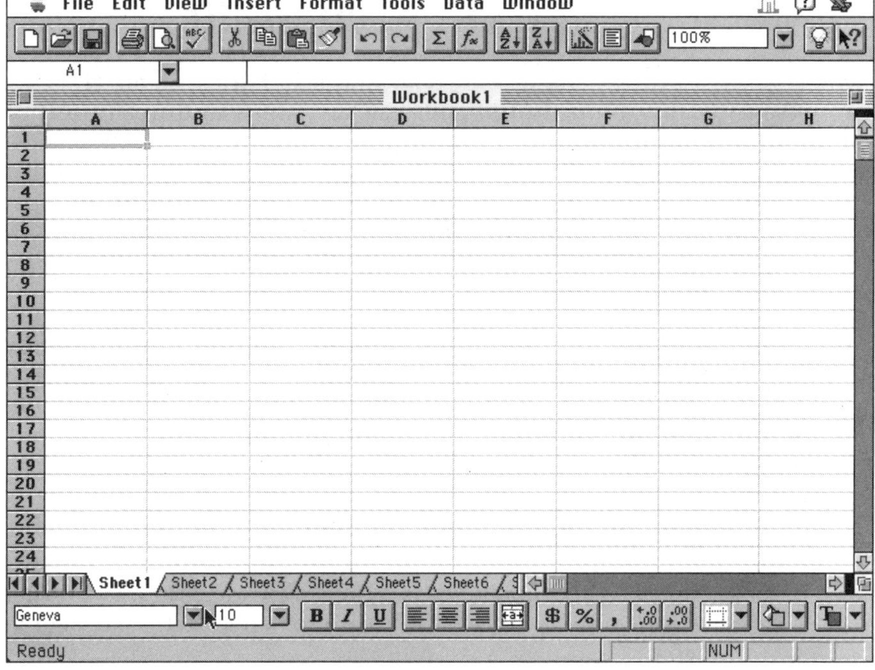

Fligure 3-6: The Formatting toolbar docked at the bottom of the work area.

Sometimes after docking a toolbar, the active document window loses one or the other of the scroll bars. To get back the missing scroll bar, click on the Zoom box in the upper right-hand corner of the document window to max out the current document. If you're working with an empty workbook (such as Workbook1), you can properly size the document window and restore the scroll bars by closing the workbook with the Close command on the File menu and then opening a new workbook in its place. Open the new workbook by clicking on the New tool (the very first tool) on the Standard toolbar. After Excel opens the new workbook (Workbook2), the document window fits nicely with all the scroll bars intact and with your current toolbar-docking arrangement.

When a toolbar refuses to dock on the left or right

Excel won't let you dock the Standard or Formatting toolbar on the left or right side of the screen because both of these toolbars contain a pop-up menu box that can't be reoriented with the toolbar. (The pop-up menu box can't pop out to the left or right of the toolbar.) This restriction on docking on the left or right side of the screen also applies to the Drawing, Chart, and WorkGroup toolbars because of their pop-up menu boxes.

Formatting Cells in a Nutshell

With Excel 5.0's new Cells command on the Format menu (⌘+1), you easily can apply a whole rash of different kinds of formatting to a cell selection. The Format Cells dialog box, which this command calls up, contains six tabs: Number, Alignment, Font, Border, Patterns, and Protection. In this chapter, you learn how to use the first five of these tabs to assign new number formats and fonts to your cells as well as change their alignment, borders, and patterns. (For information on how and when to use the options on the other tab, the Protection tab, see "Protect Yourself!" in Chapter 5.)

⌘+1, the keystroke shortcut that opens the Format Cells dialog box, is worth learning because you will be doing almost as much formatting as data entry in a worksheet. Just keep in mind that the shortcut uses ⌘ with the number 1 key, *not* the F1 function key.

Number formats fit for any value

As explained in Chapter 2, the way you enter values into a worksheet determines the type of number format the values get. Take a look at some examples:

- If you enter a financial value, complete with $ and two decimal places, Excel assigns a Currency number format to the cell along with the entry.
- If you enter a value representing a percentage as a whole number followed by the percent sign without any decimal places, Excel assigns to the cell the Percentage number format that follows this pattern along with the entry.
- If you enter a date — remember that dates are values, too — that follows one of the built-in Excel number formats, such as **02/19/95** or **19-Feb-95**, the program assigns a Date number format that follows the pattern of the date along with a special value representing the date.

Although it's fine to format values as you go in this manner, you don't *have* to format them in this way. You can always assign a number format to a group of values after you enter them. In fact, formatting numbers after the fact is often the most efficient way to go, because it's just a two-step procedure:

1. **Select all the cells containing the values that need dressing up.**
2. **Select the number format you want to use.**

   Many times you can use one of the tools on the Formatting toolbar — if not, you can select a number format from the Number tab in the Format Cells dialog box (⌘+1).

Even if you're a crack typist and prefer to enter each value thank-you-very-much *exactly* as you want it to appear in the worksheet, you still have to resort to using number formats when you want the values you enter to match those calculated by Excel.

You see, Excel applies a comprehensive number format to all the values it calculates (as well as any you enter that don't exactly follow one of the other Excel formats). As luck would have it, the numbers Excel puts into this format usually don't match the ones you format yourself — a situation that can really mess up the look of the worksheet.

Excel formats all calculated values and values that don't follow the pattern of a predefined number format with a general-purpose format called, appropriately enough, the General format. The problem with the General format is that it has a nasty habit of dropping all leading and trailing zeros from the entries, making it very difficult to line up numbers in a column on their decimal points. (Now you can see why Excel also has number formats.)

Figure 3-7 shows the sad state of affairs for the first-quarter sales figures before any of the values have been formatted with anything other than Excel's General number format. Notice how the columns of figures zig and zag. The only cure is to format the values with another, more uniform number format.

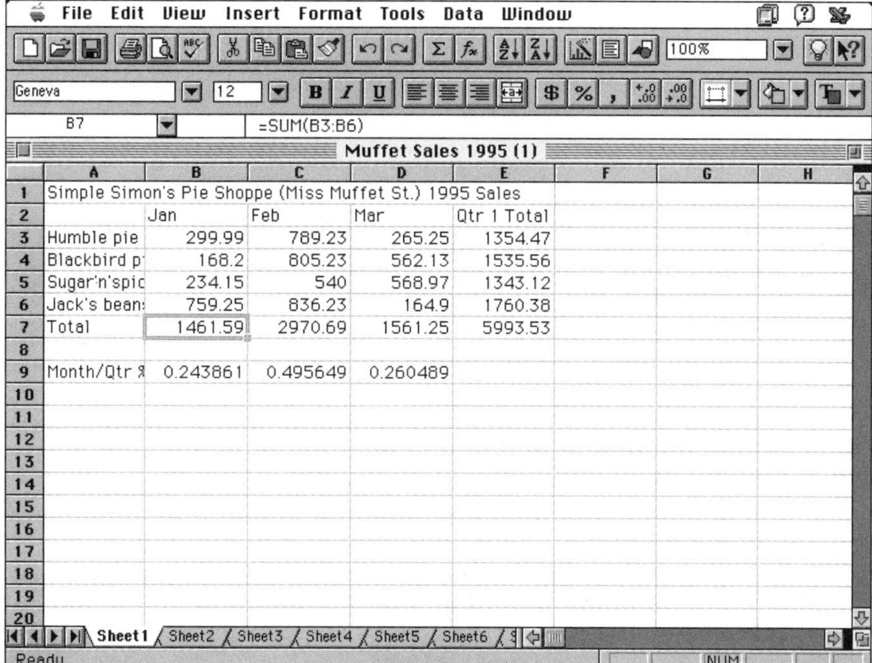

Figure 3-7: First-quarter sales, zigging and zagging.

Money, money, money

Given the financial nature of most worksheets, you probably use the Currency format more than any other. The Currency format is a very easy format to apply because the Formatting toolbar contains a Currency Style tool that adds a dollar sign, commas between thousands of dollars, and two decimal places to any values in a selected range. If any of the values in the cell selection are negative numbers, the Currency format displays them in parentheses (the way accountants like them) and displays them in red on a color monitor (the way governments like them).

In Figure 3-8, I selected only the cells containing totals (cell ranges E3:E7 and B7:D7). I then formatted this cell selection with the Currency format by simply clicking on the Currency Style tool on the Formatting toolbar (the one with the $).

Note: Although you can put all the figures in the table into the Currency format to line up the decimal points, this would result in a superabundance of dollar signs in a fairly small table. In this example, I've decided that only the totals will be formatted à la Currency.

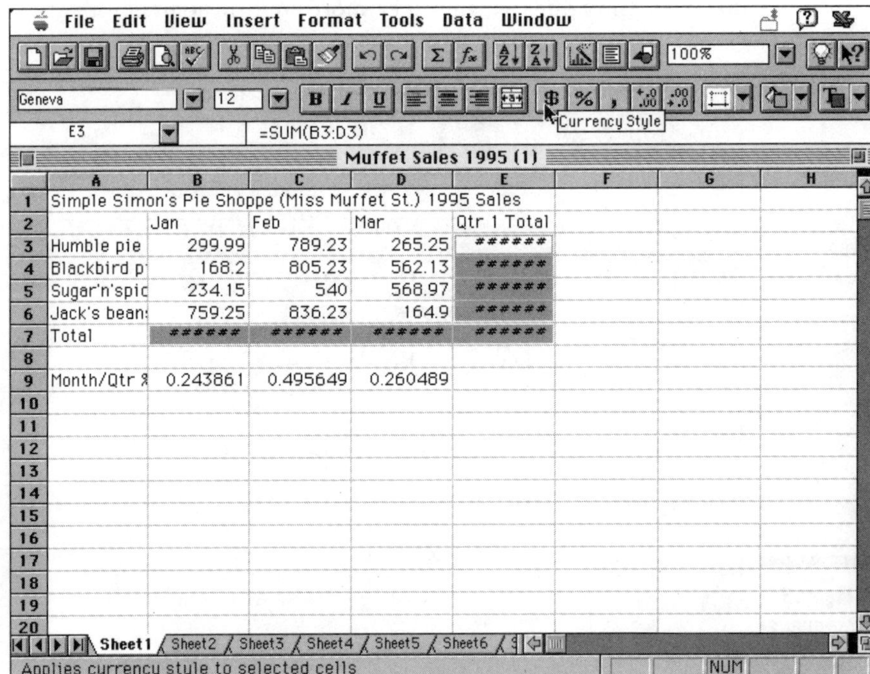

Figure 3-8: The totals in the sales table after clicking on the Currency Style tool.

Just too ####### much to show

You may be wondering whether I've lost it altogether, whether Excel has lost it altogether, or whether a combination of the two has occurred. Somehow, we must have a failure to communicate (maybe just a bum screen shot) because there's no way that the #######s showing in cell ranges E3:E7 and B7:D7 in Figure 3-8 come *close* to resembling the numbers that ought to be showing!

Well, if you carefully reread the caption for Figure 3-8, you see that all I'm claiming is that the figure represents how the totals appear in the table after clicking on the Currency Style tool on the Formatting toolbar. In fact, the appearance of the pound signs — rather than nicely formatted dollar totals — indicates that applying the Currency format adds so much to the display of the values that Excel can no longer display them within the current column widths.

These blasted #######s appear in cells whenever any number format you use (not just the Currency format) adds more junk to the values than can be displayed within the current column width. Be aware that these #######s replace perfectly fine-looking formatted numbers if the columns are too narrow.

To get rid of the pound signs and bring back the prettied-up values, simply widen the columns. Figure 3-9 shows you the Miss Muffet Street sales table after widening columns A through E (to find out how to widen columns, jump ahead to "If the Column Fits…" later in this chapter). As you can see, not only are the numbers all there now, but they're all sporting dollar signs, commas, and two decimal places.

Let's all remain comma

The Comma format offers a good alternative to the Currency format. Like the Currency format, the Comma format inserts commas in larger numbers to separate thousands, hundreds of thousands, millions — you get the idea.

The Comma format also displays two decimal places and puts negative values in parentheses and in red (on a color monitor). What the Comma format *doesn't* display is dollar signs, which makes it perfect for formatting tables that obviously deal with dollars and cents (hence no need to show the $) or for formatting larger values that have nothing to do with money.

The Comma format also works well for the bulk of the values in the sample first-quarter sales worksheet. Figure 3-10 shows this table after the 12 cells containing the monthly sales for each type of pie were formatted with the Comma format. To format these cells, I selected the cell range B3:D6 and clicked on the Comma Style tool on the Formatting toolbar. This tool is — you guessed it — the one with the little comma right next to the tool with the percent sign.

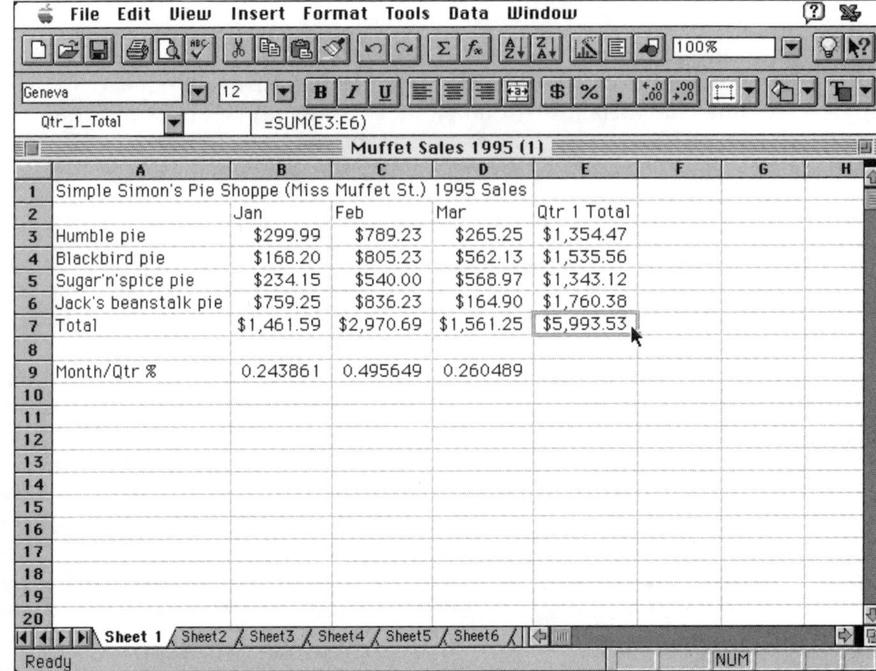

	A	B	C	D	E
1	Simple Simon's Pie Shoppe (Miss Muffet St.) 1995 Sales				
2		Jan	Feb	Mar	Qtr 1 Total
3	Humble pie	$299.99	$789.23	$265.25	$1,354.47
4	Blackbird pie	$168.20	$805.23	$562.13	$1,535.56
5	Sugar'n'spice pie	$234.15	$540.00	$568.97	$1,343.12
6	Jack's beanstalk pie	$759.25	$836.23	$164.90	$1,760.38
7	Total	$1,461.59	$2,970.69	$1,561.25	$5,993.53
8					
9	Month/Qtr %	0.243861	0.495649	0.260489	

Figure 3-9: The totals formatted as currency after widening columns A through E.

Figure 3-10 shows how the Comma format takes care of the earlier alignment problem in the quarterly sales figures. Moreover, notice how the Comma-formatted monthly sales figures align perfectly with the Currency-formatted monthly totals in row 7. If you look closely (you may need a magnifying glass for this one), you see that these formatted values no longer abut the right edges of their cells — they've moved slightly to the left. The gap on the right between the last digit and the cell border is there to accommodate the right parenthesis in negative values, ensuring that they also align precisely on the decimal point.

Playing the percentages

Many worksheets use percentages in the form of interest rates, growth rates, inflation rates, and so on. To insert a percentage in a cell, place the percent sign (%) after the number. To indicate an interest rate of 12 percent, for example, you enter **12%** in the cell. Excel then assigns a Percent number format and, at the same time, divides the value by 100 (making it a percentage) and places the result in the cell (0.12 in this example).

Not all percentages in a worksheet are entered by hand in this manner. Some percentages may be calculated by a formula and returned to their cells as raw decimal values. In such cases, you should add a Percent format to convert the calculated decimal values to percentages (by multiplying the decimal value by 100 and adding a percent sign).

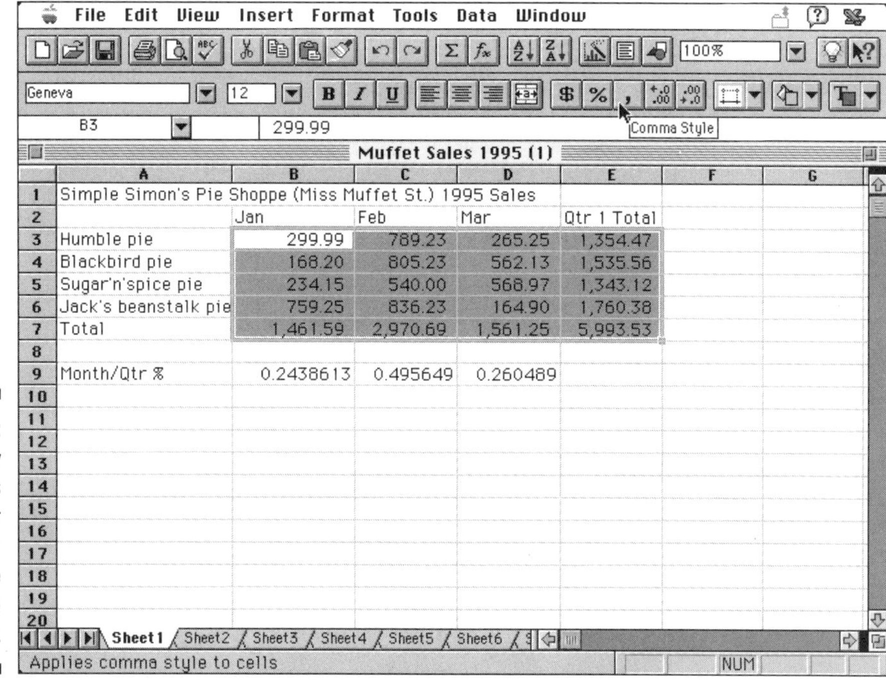

Figure 3-10: The monthly sales figures after formatting with the Comma format.

The sample first-quarter sales worksheet just happens to have some percentages calculated by formulas that need formatting in row 9. (These formulas indicate what percentage of the first-quarter total each monthly total is.) Figure 3-11 shows these values after being formatted with the Percent format. To format such percentages, simply select the cells and click on the Percent Style tool on the Formatting toolbar. (Need I point out that it's the tool with the percent sign?)

Decimal wheeling and dealing

You can increase or decrease the number of decimal places used in a value entered with the Currency style, Comma style, or Percent style tools on the Formatting toolbar. Simply select the cells and click on the Increase Decimal tool or the Decrease Decimal tool also located on the Formatting toolbar (to the immediate right of the Comma style tool). Remember: The cell range must be selected when you click on these tools for them to do any good.

Each time you click on the Increase Decimal tool, Excel adds another decimal place to the number format you applied. Figure 3-12 shows percentages in the cell range B9:D9 after I increased the number of decimal places in the Percent format from none to one (the Percent style doesn't use any decimal places). Simply click on the Increase Decimal tool once.

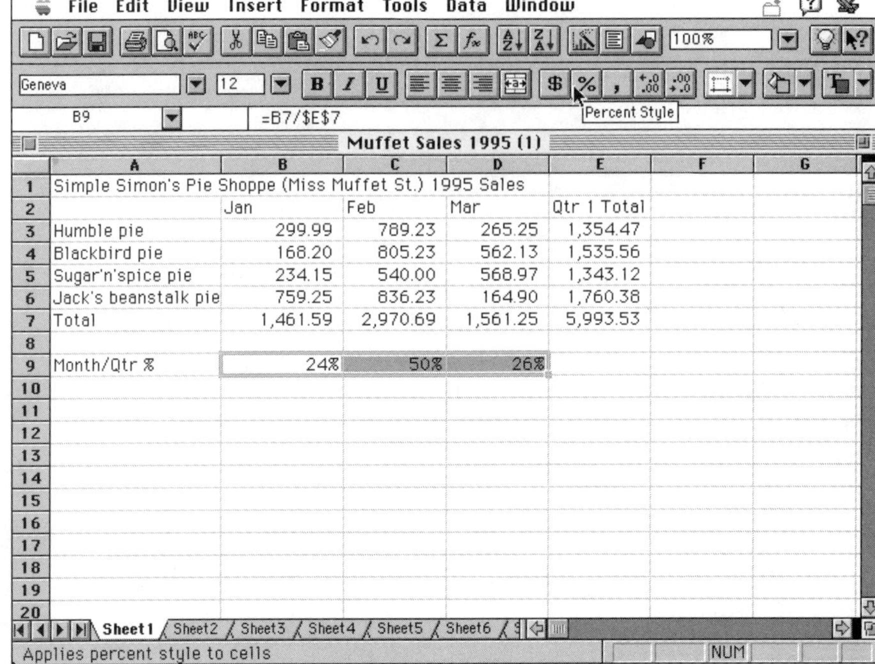

Figure 3-11: Monthly-to-quarterly sale percentages formatted with the Percent format.

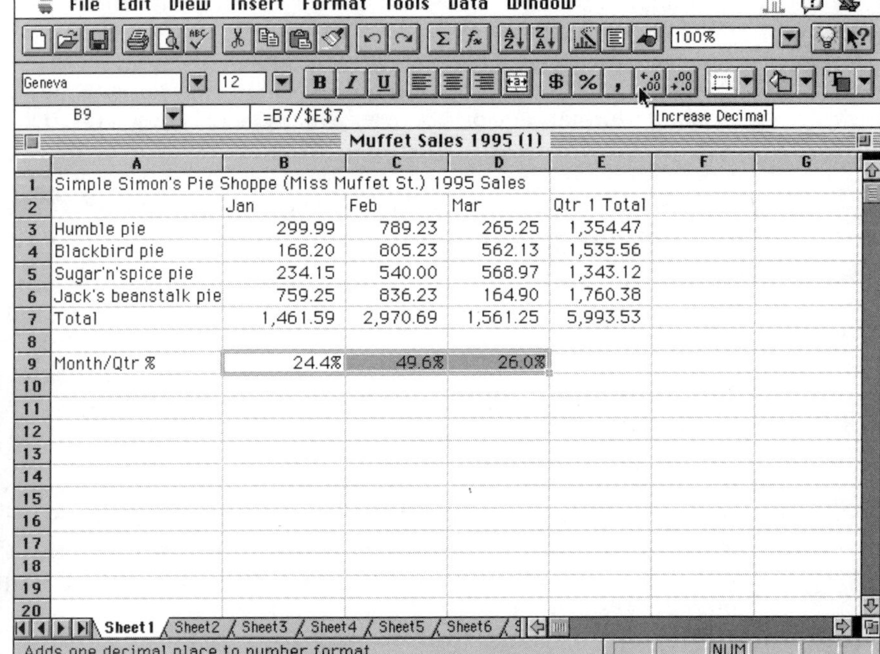

Figure 3-12: The monthly to quarterly sale percentages after adding one decimal place.

What you see is not always what you get

Make no mistake about it: All these fancy number formats do is spiff up the presentation of the values in the worksheet. Like a good illusionist, a particular number format sometimes appears to magically transform some entries, but in reality the entries are the same old numbers you started with. For example, suppose that a formula returns the following value:

```
25.6456
```

Now, suppose that you format the cell containing this value with the Currency Style tool. The value now appears as follows:

```
$25.65
```

This change may lead you to believe that Excel has rounded up the value to two decimal places. But in fact, the program has rounded up only the *display* of the calculated value — the cell still contains the same old value: 25.6456. If you use this cell in another worksheet formula, keep in mind that Excel uses the behind-the-scenes value in its calculation, not the spiffed-up one shown in the cell.

But what if you *want* the values to match their formatted appearance in the worksheet? Well, Excel can adjust the values in a single step. Be forewarned, however: This adjustment is a one-way trip. You can convert all underlying values to the way they are displayed by selecting a single check box, but you *cannot* return the values to their previous state by deselecting the check box.

Because you insist on knowing the little trick of converting the underlying values to the way they are displayed, here goes — just don't write to tell me that you weren't warned:

1. **Before you convert the precision of all values in the worksheet to their displayed form, be sure that the values are all formatted with the correct number of decimal places.**
2. **Select Tools ⇨ Options to open the Options dialog box.**
3. **Click on the Calculation tab to bring up the calculation options.**
4. **Choose the Precision as Displayed option under the Workbook Options to put an `X` in its check box, and then click on OK.**

   Excel displays the `Data will permanently lose accuracy` alert dialog box.
5. **Go ahead and live dangerously — click on OK or press Return to convert all values to match their display.**

Number formats made to order

Excel supports a whole bunch of other number formats that you'll seldom, if ever, use. To use the other formats, select the cell range (or ranges) to be formatted and then select the Format Cells command on the cell shortcut menu (by clicking the mouse button somewhere in the cell selection). Or choose the Cells command on the Format menu (⌘+1) to open the Format Cells dialog box. Then choose the Number tab and select the desired format from the Format Codes list box.

You'll discover only one problem with this technique: Excel isn't lying when it calls them format *codes.* All you see in the Format Codes list box is a bunch of weird-looking codes composed of a great many #, *0*, *?*, *D*, *M*, and *Y* characters. Rather than work yourself into a lather or (heaven forbid!) do something nerdy such as try to decipher this gibberish, make life easier for yourself by focusing your attention on the Sample area at the very bottom of the Number tab in the Format Cells dialog box. In the Sample area, you can select various formats from the Format Codes list box. Excel shows you how the value in the active cell of the selected range will look in the selected format. As soon as you see what you like, go for it by clicking on OK or pressing Return.

In addition to choosing built-in formats from the Number Format dialog box, you also can build number formats of your own. Although you do have to use codes (ugh), you really don't have to be a rocket scientist to figure out how to create the formats — but being a rocket scientist wouldn't hurt.

Rather than bore you with a bunch of examples of custom formats that would only prove how smart (nerdy) I am, I just want to introduce you to two custom formats that you may actually find quite handy in your worksheets: One formats dates in full (as in *February 15, 1996*), and the other hides entries in their cells. These formats aren't that complex, and besides, they work even if you don't understand their codes.

Number formats for the overly curious

If you just *have* to know what some of these number format codes mean, here goes. Each number format can control how positive numbers, negative numbers, and everything else looks. These number categories are divided by semicolons (any format not so divided covers all the other types of entries). The *0* is a placeholder for a digit and is filled by a zero if the value lacks a digit in that place. The *#* sign is a placeholder for a digit not to be filled if the value lacks a digit for that place. The *M* is used for *months* in dates or *minutes* in time. *D* is for *days, Y* for *years, H* for *hours,* and *S* for *seconds.*

To build a custom number format, click on the Code text box in the Number tab of the Format Cells dialog box and replace whatever is currently in the box with (you guessed it) the codes for your made-up format. For the full-month codes, enter the following in the box:

```
mmmm dd, yyyy
```

The *mmmm* tells Excel to spell out the full name of the month; the *dd* says to display the date (including a leading zero, as in *03*); the comma after the *dd* says to insert a comma after the date; the space after the comma says to insert a space after the comma; and the *yyyy* says to use all four digits of the year.

The second custom format is even easier to enter in the Code text box (although it is stranger-looking). To create a format that blanks out the display of any cell entry, just enter three semicolons in a row in the Code text box, with no spaces or anything in between, just like this:

```
;;;
```

This format says to display nothing for positive values, nothing for negative values, and while you're at it, nothing for anything else in the cell!

After you apply this hidden format to cells, the cell display disappears in the worksheet (although the contents still show up on the formula bar when you select the cell). This format is most useful when you want to remove certain information from a printed report without deleting it from the worksheet. To make hidden entries reappear, simply apply one of the visible number formats (the General format, for example) to the cells.

After entering the codes in the Code text box, click on OK to apply the custom format to the current cell selection. Custom formats are saved as part of the worksheet the next time you save the document. Remember, don't neglect that Save tool on the Standard toolbar!

To use a custom format on a cell selection, open the Format Cells dialog box (⌘+1). Select the Number tab and choose Custom in the Category list box. Excel lists all the custom number formats that you've created in the Format Codes list box, from which you can select the one you want to apply to selected cells.

If the Column Fits . . .

Adjusting column widths is one of those never-ending worksheet chores, akin to housekeeping chores like dusting or washing dishes. No sooner do you finish putting all the columns in order than you have to make a change to the worksheet, such as formatting a table of figures, that requires new column-width adjustments.

Fortunately, Excel makes changing the column widths a breeze. The easiest way to adjust a column is to do a *best fit* using AutoFit. With this method, Excel automatically determines how much to widen or narrow the column to fit the longest entry currently in the column.

Follow these steps to use AutoFit to get the best fit for a column:

1. **Position the mouse pointer on the column frame (the letter at the top of the column), along the right-hand border of the column that needs adjusting.**

   The mouse pointer changes to a double-headed arrow pointing left and right.

2. **Double-click the mouse button.**

   Excel widens or narrows the column width to suit the longest entry.

You can do a best fit for more than one column at a time. Simply select all the columns that need adjusting. If the columns are adjacent, drag through the column letters on the frame; if they are not adjacent, hold down ⌘ as you click on the individual column letters. After the columns are selected, double-click on any of the right borders on the frame.

As pointed out earlier in this chapter, best fit à la AutoFit doesn't always produce the expected results. All you have to do is AutoFit a column with a table title to become acquainted with this phenomenon (like the 3D Effects 2 table format did in Figure 3-4). A long title that spills into several columns to the right produces an awfully wide column when you use best fit. To be reminded of this fact, just look at what happened to the width of column A in Figure 3-13 when best fit was used to size the column.

When AutoFit's best fit doesn't look right, on the frame, *drag* the column's right-hand border, rather than double-clicking on it, until the column is the size you need. Figure 3-13 illustrates how the table looks as I drag the right border to the left, making the column just wide enough to accommodate the labels in column A. When I release the mouse button, the table settles into its new column sizes, as illustrated in Figure 3-14. This manual technique also works when you select more than one column — just be aware that *all* selected columns assume whatever size you make the one you're actually dragging.

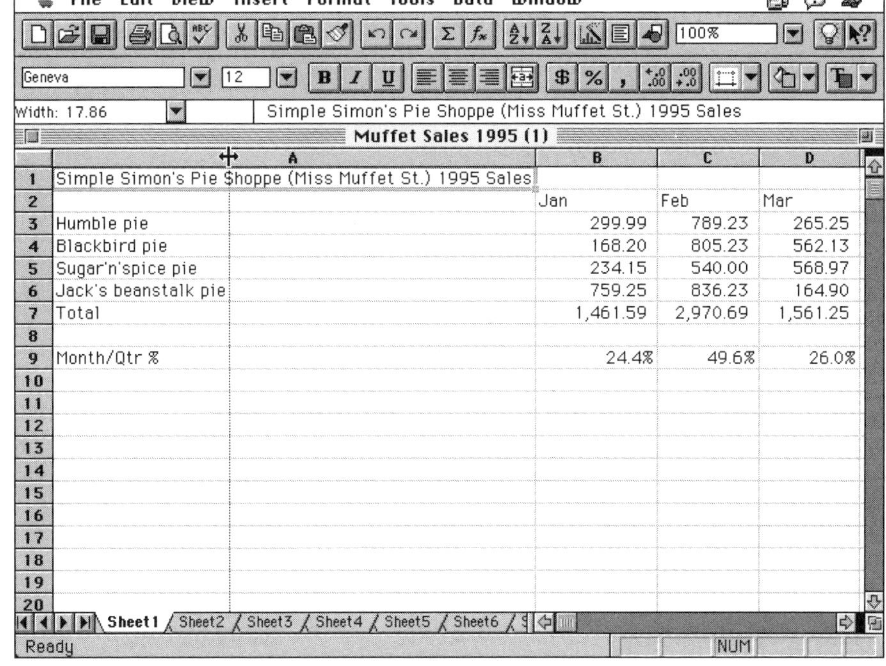

Figure 3-13: Manually narrowing column A after AutoFit widened it enough for the entire title in cell A1.

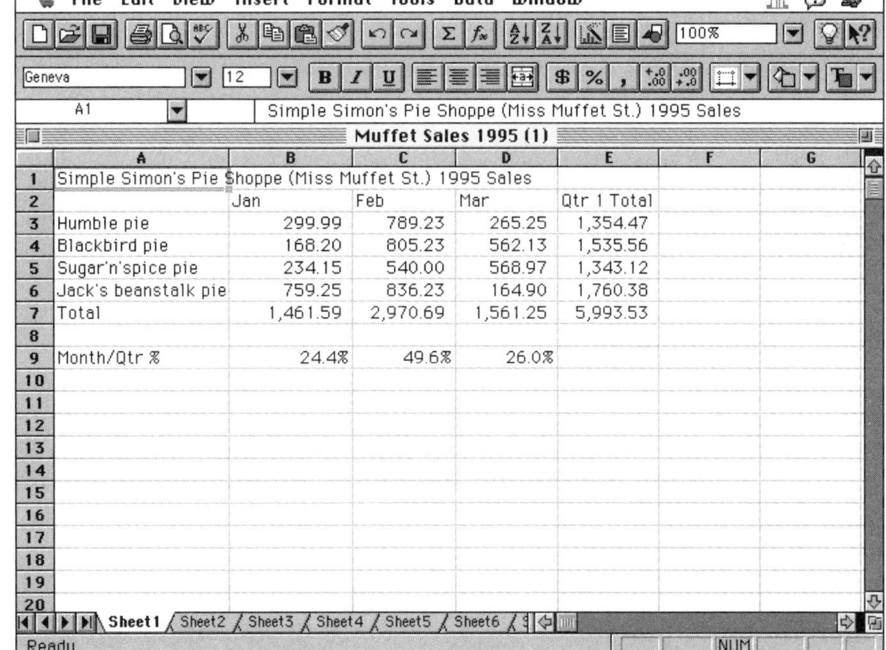

Figure 3-14: Column A after making it just wide enough to display the types of pies.

You also can set the widths of columns from the Column Width dialog box. When you use the dialog box, you enter the number of characters you want for the column width. To open this dialog box, you can choose the Column Width command from the column shortcut menu (which you open by clicking on any selected column or column letter with the mouse button) or choose Format ➪ Column ➪ Width.

The Column Width text box in the Column Width dialog box shows how many characters are in the standard column width in the worksheet. To change the widths of all the columns you've selected in the worksheet (except those already adjusted manually or with AutoFit), enter a new value in the Column Width text box and click on OK.

If you want to have Excel size the column to best fit by using the pull-down menus, choose Format ➪ Column ➪ AutoFit Selection. If you want to return a column selection to the standard (default) column width by using the pull-down menus, you simply choose Format ➪ Column ➪ Standard Width.

Rambling rows

The story for adjusting the height of a row is pretty much the same as that for adjusting the width of a column, except that you do a lot less row adjusting than you do column adjusting because Excel automatically changes the height of the rows to accommodate changes to their entries (such as selecting a larger font size or wrapping text in a cell). Most row-height adjustments come about when you want to increase the amount of space between a table title and the table or between a row of column headings and the table without adding a blank row. (See "Line 'Em Up" later in this chapter for details.)

To increase the height of a row, drag down the bottom border of the row frame until the row is high enough and then release the mouse button. To shorten a row, reverse this process and drag up the bottom row-frame border. To use AutoFit to create a best fit for the entries in a row, double-click on the bottom row-frame border.

As with columns, you also can adjust the height of selected rows with a dialog box. To open the Row Height dialog box, choose the Row Height command from the Row shortcut menu (opened by clicking on any selected row or row number with the mouse button) or choose Format ➪ Row ➪ Height. To set a new row height for the selected row (or rows), enter the number of characters in the Row Height text box and click OK. To return to the best fit for a particular row, choose Format ➪ Row ➪ AutoFit.

Worksheet hide 'n' seek

If you get carried away and make a column too narrow or a row too short, it actually disappears from the worksheet. You may wonder why in the world you would spend all that time entering and formatting information only to go and *hide* it.

Actually, you play hide 'n' seek with worksheet information mostly when setting up printed reports. For example, you may have a worksheet containing a column that lists employee salaries required in calculating the departmental budget figures. You prefer to leave off this column from most printed reports. Rather than spend time moving the salary column outside the area to be printed, you can simply hide the column until after you print the report.

Hiding columns and rows the easy way

Suppose that you need to hide column B in the worksheet because it contains some irrelevant or sensitive information that you don't want printed. To hide this column, follow these steps:

1. **Click on the letter B on the frame to select the column.**
2. **Click and hold down the mouse button on the letter B again, this time while pressing the Control key.**

   The column shortcut menu appears.
3. **Select the Hide command.**

   That's all there is to it — column B goes *poof!* All the information in the column disappears from the worksheet.

   Note: When you hide column B, notice that the row of column letters in the frame now reads A, C, D, E, F, and so forth.

Now, suppose that you've printed the worksheet and you need to make a change to one of the entries in column B. To unhide the column, follow these steps:

1. **Position the mouse pointer on column letter A in the frame, click and hold down the mouse button, and drag the pointer to the right to select both columns A and C.**

   You must drag from A to C to include hidden column B as part of the column selection.
2. **Press the Control key and click and hold down the mouse button somewhere in the selected columns.**

   The column shortcut menu appears.

3. **Select the Unhide command.**

   Excel brings back the hidden B column and selects all three columns: A, B, and C. Click the mouse pointer on any cell in the worksheet to deselect the columns.

You can do the same trick of hiding and unhiding rows in your worksheet with the Hide and Unhide commands on the Row shortcut menu. Remember, too, that both the Column and Row commands on the Format menu have Hide and Unhide commands on their cascading menus that work exactly like the Hide and Unhide commands on the shortcut menus.

Hiding columns and rows the hard way

I won't lie to you — hiding and redisplaying columns with the mouse can be *very* tricky (just ask my assistant Jane!). This process requires a degree of precision that you may not possess (especially if you've only recently started using the rodent). However, if you consider yourself a real mouse master, you can hide and unhide columns solely by dragging the mouse pointer, as follows:

- To hide a column with the mouse, drag the column's right-hand edge to the left until it's on top of the left edge, and then release the mouse button.
- To hide a row with the mouse, drag the row's bottom border upward until it's on top of the upper border.

As you drag a border, Excel replaces the cell address on the formula bar with the current column-width or row-height measurement. When the Width or Height indicator reaches 0.00, you know you can release the mouse button.

Figure 3-15 shows the first-quarter sales worksheet in the process of hiding row 9 by dragging its lower row border (the one it shares with the top of row 10) upward. In this figure, the bottom border of row 9 is pulled up to meet its upper border. As soon as you release the mouse button, this row is history, as illustrated in Figure 3-16.

Unhiding a column or row with the mouse is a reversal of the hiding process. To unhide a row or column, drag the column or row border between the nonsequential columns or rows in the opposite direction — right for columns, down for rows. The only trick to this procedure is that you must position the mouse pointer *just* right on the column or row border so that the pointer changes to a double-headed arrow split in the middle rather than a regular double-headed arrow. (Contrast the shape of the pointer on the frame in Figure 3-15 with the pointer in Figure 3-16.)

Muffet Sales 1995 (1)

Simple Simon's Pie Shoppe (Miss Muffet St.) 1995 Sales

	A	B	C	D	E
1	Simple Simon's Pie Shoppe (Miss Muffet St.) 1995 Sales				
2		Jan	Feb	Mar	Qtr 1 Total
3	Humble pie	299.99	789.23	265.25	1,354.47
4	Blackbird pie	168.20	805.23	562.13	1,535.56
5	Sugar'n'spice pie	234.15	540.00	568.97	1,343.12
6	Jack's beanstalk pie	759.25	836.23	164.90	1,760.38
7	Total	1,461.59	2,970.69	1,561.25	5,993.53
8					
9		24.4%	49.6%	26.0%	

Figure 3-15: To manually hide row 9, drag the border upward between rows 10 and 9.

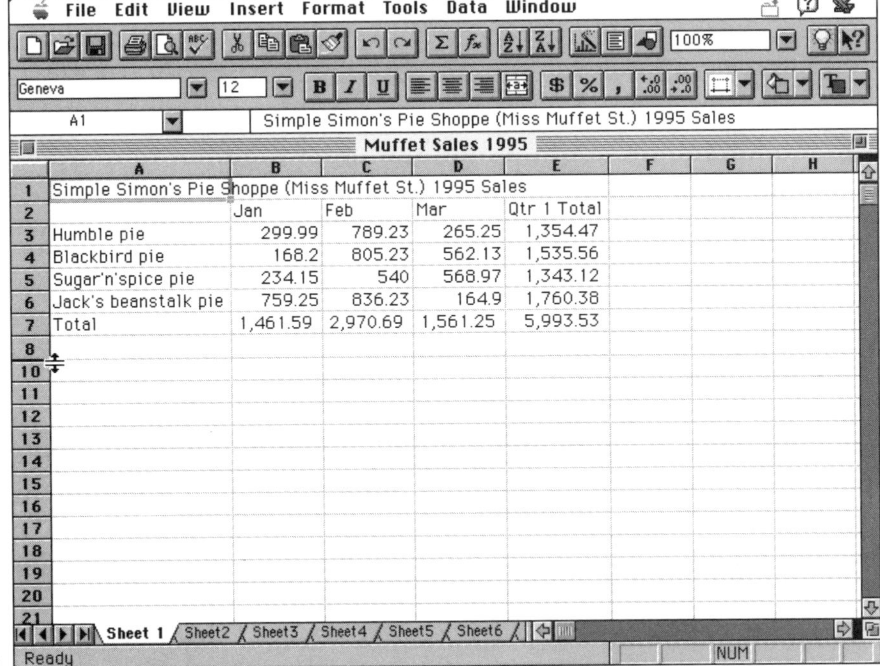

Muffet Sales 1995

	A	B	C	D	E
1	Simple Simon's Pie Shoppe (Miss Muffet St.) 1995 Sales				
2		Jan	Feb	Mar	Qtr 1 Total
3	Humble pie	299.99	789.23	265.25	1,354.47
4	Blackbird pie	168.2	805.23	562.13	1,535.56
5	Sugar'n'spice pie	234.15	540	568.97	1,343.12
6	Jack's beanstalk pie	759.25	836.23	164.9	1,760.38
7	Total	1,461.59	2,970.69	1,561.25	5,993.53
8					
10					

Figure 3-16: After you release the mouse button, no more row 9!

Figure 3-16 shows the first-quarter sales worksheet the moment before row 9 is unhidden with the mouse. In this figure, you see the mouse pointer (with the split in the middle of the double-headed arrow) just as I was about to start dragging downward the lower border of the hidden row 9. Figure 3-17 shows the unhidden row 9, with all its information safe and sound, after I dragged its border down a row and released the mouse button. (I knew to release the mouse button when I saw `Height: 12.75`, the standard row height for this worksheet, on the formula bar, but you don't see this in the figure.) Note that row height is dependent on font size. Choose Format ⇨ Row ⇨ Autofit to make sure that you get the correct row height for your worksheet.

If you ever manually hide a column or row only to find that you can't get that blasted split-bar pointer to appear so that you can drag the column or row back into existence, don't get frantic. Just drag through the columns or rows on either side of the hidden one, hold down the Control key and click the mouse button, and then choose the Unhide command on the shortcut menu.

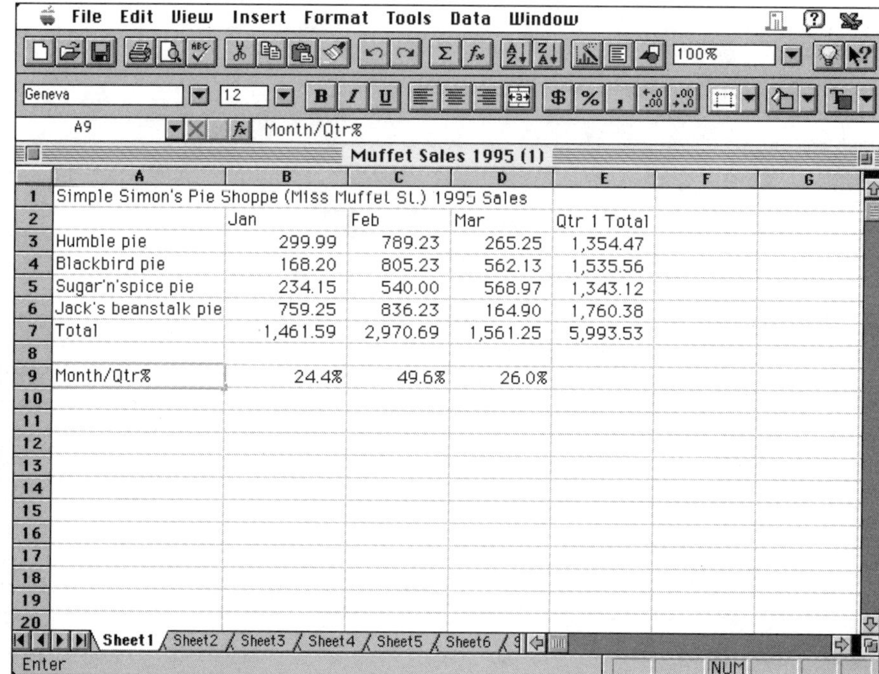

Figure 3-17: To redisplay row 9, drag the split-bar pointer down a row.

Oh, That's Just Fontastic!

When you start a new worksheet, Excel assigns a uniform font and type size to all the cell entries you make. This font varies according to the printer you use — for a laser printer, such as the Apple LaserWriter or HP LaserJet, Excel uses a font called Geneva in a 10-point size. Although this font is fine for normal entries, you may want to use something with a little more zing for titles and headings in the worksheet.

If you don't especially care for the standard font that Excel uses, you can modify it by choosing Tools ➪ Options ➪ General tab. You see an option called Standard Font near the bottom of the Options dialog box. Select the new standard font from its pop-up menu. If you want a different type size, choose the Size option, too, and either enter the new point size for the standard font or select it from this option's pop-up menu.

With the tools on the Formatting toolbar, you can make most font changes (including selecting a new font style or new font size) without having to resort to the Format Cells command on the cell shortcut menu or the Cells command on the Format pull-down menu.

- To select a new font for a cell selection, click on the drop-down button next to the Font list box on the Formatting toolbar and then select the name of the font you want to use from the list box.
- If you want to change the font size, click on the drop-down button next to the Size list box on the Formatting toolbar. Then I select the new font size.

You also can add the attributes of bold, italics, underlining, or strikethrough to the font you're using. The Formatting toolbar contains the Bold, Italic, and Underline tools. Remember that you use these tools not only to add attributes to a cell selection but to remove them as well.

After you click on one of these attribute tools, notice that the tool changes by losing the shading around its right and bottom edge and becoming a lighter shade of gray. These changes occur to make the tool button appear to be pushed in. When you click on a "pushed-in" tool to remove an attribute, Excel changes the tool back to its original form so that it no longer appears pushed in.

Although you'll probably make most font changes with the toolbars, on rare occasions you may find it more convenient to make these changes from the Font tab in the Format Cells dialog box (⌘+1).

As you can see in Figure 3-18, this Font tab in the Format Cells dialog box brings together many choices under one roof: fonts, font styles (such as bold and italic), effects (such as underlining and strikethrough), and color changes. When you want to make many font-related changes to a cell selection, the Font tab may be your best bet. One of the nice things about using this tab is that it contains a Preview box that shows you how your font changes will appear (on-screen, at least).

If you change font colors by using the Color option on the Font tab in the Format Cells dialog box or with the Font Color tool on the Formatting toolbar and then you print the worksheet with a black-and-white printer, Excel renders the colors as shades of gray. The Automatic choice in the Font tab Color pop-up menu box defaults to black unless changed.

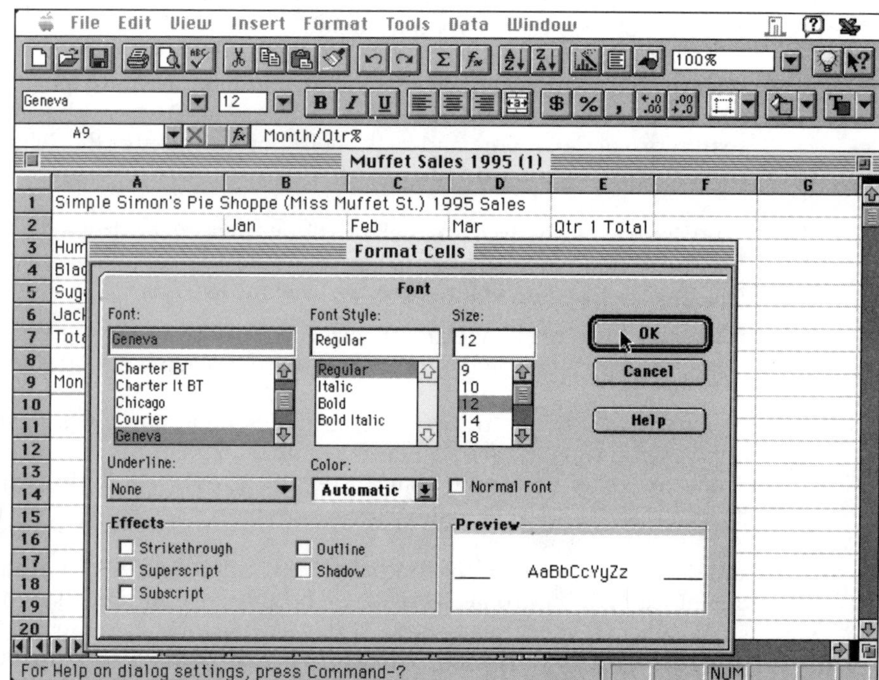

Figure 3-18: The Font tab in the Format Cells dialog box.

Line 'Em Up

You already know that the alignment assigned to a cell entry (when you first make the entry) is simply a function of the type of entry it is: All text entries are left-aligned and all values are right-aligned. You can alter this standard arrangement, though, anytime you choose.

The Formatting toolbar contains three normal alignment tools: Align Left, Center, and Align Right. These tools align the current cell selection exactly as you expect them to. To the right of the Align Right tool, you find a special alignment tool called Center Across Columns.

Despite its rather strange name, you should get to know the Center Across Columns tool. You can use this tool to center a worksheet title across the entire width of a table in seconds (or faster, depending on your computer). In Figure 3-19, notice that the title for the sales table is entered in cell A1 and spills over to the empty cells to the right (B1, C1, and D1) because the title is too long to be in one cell. To center this title over the table (which extends from column A through E), select the cell range A1:E1 (the width of the table), as shown in Figure 3-19, and then click on the Center Across Columns tool on the Formatting toolbar. Figure 3-20 shows the result: a properly centered title over the table.

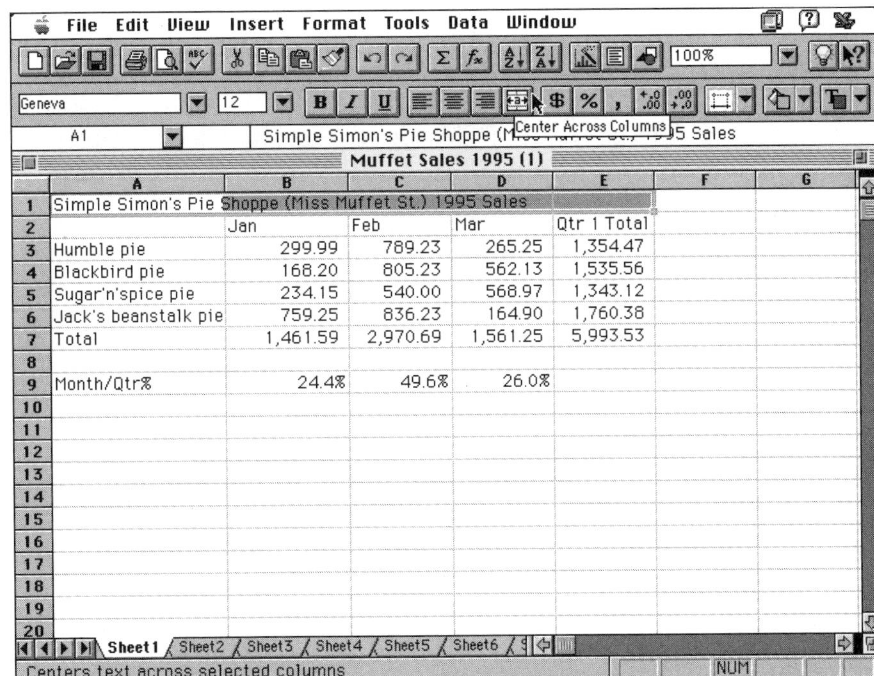

Figure 3-19: Preparing to center a title over an entire table with Center Across Columns.

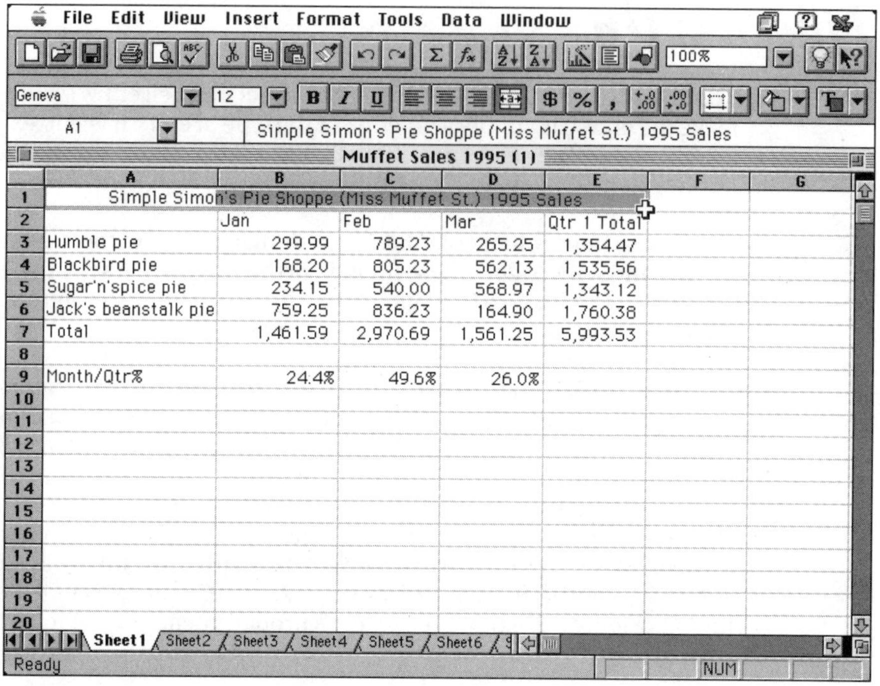

	A	B	C	D	E	F	G
1	Simple Simon's Pie Shoppe (Miss Muffet St.) 1995 Sales						
2		Jan	Feb	Mar	Qtr 1 Total		
3	Humble pie	299.99	789.23	265.25	1,354.47		
4	Blackbird pie	168.20	805.23	562.13	1,535.56		
5	Sugar'n'spice pie	234.15	540.00	568.97	1,343.12		
6	Jack's beanstalk pie	759.25	836.23	164.90	1,760.38		
7	Total	1,461.59	2,970.69	1,561.25	5,993.53		
8							
9	Month/Qtr%	24.4%	49.6%	26.0%			

Figure 3-20: The table title after centering it across columns A through E.

Up, down, and all around

Left, right, and center alignment all refer to the placement of a text entry in relation to the left and right cell borders. You also can align entries in relation to the top and bottom borders of their cells. Normally, all entries are vertically aligned with the bottom of the cells (as though they were resting on the very bottom of the cell). You also can vertically center an entry in its cell or align it with the top of its cell.

To change the vertical alignment of a cell selection, open the Format Cells dialog box (⌘+1). Choose the Alignment tab (shown in Figure 3-21) and click on the Top, Center, or Bottom radio button in the Vertical box.

Figure 3-22 shows the title for the Miss Muffet Street first-quarter sales table after I formatted it to be centered vertically in its cell. (This text entry was previously centered across the cell range A1:E1, illustrated in Figure 3-20. The height of row 1 was increased from the normal 12.75 characters to 22.50 characters. See "Rambling rows" earlier in this chapter.)

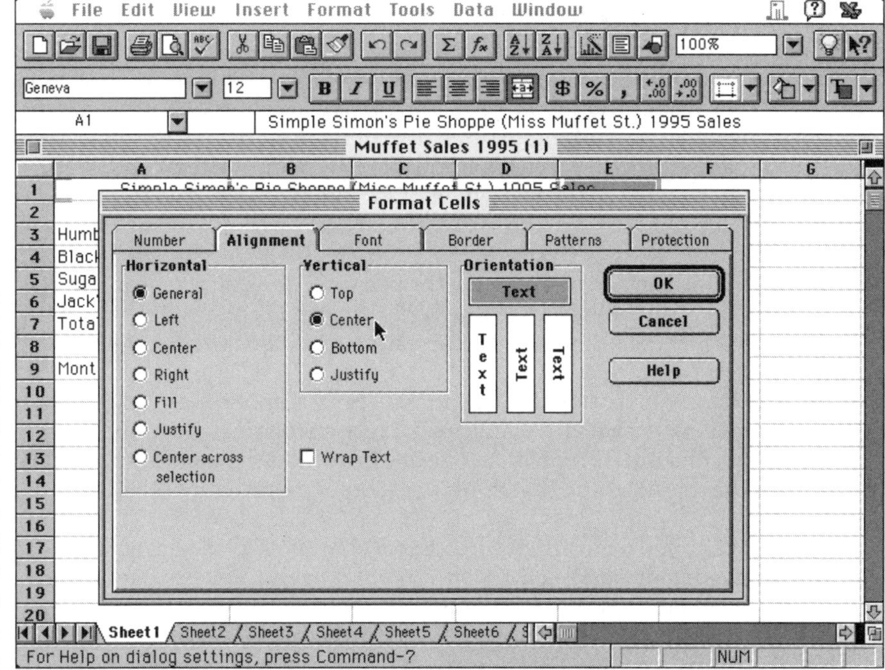

Figure 3-21: Changing the Vertical alignment with the options on the Alignment tab of the Format Cells dialog box.

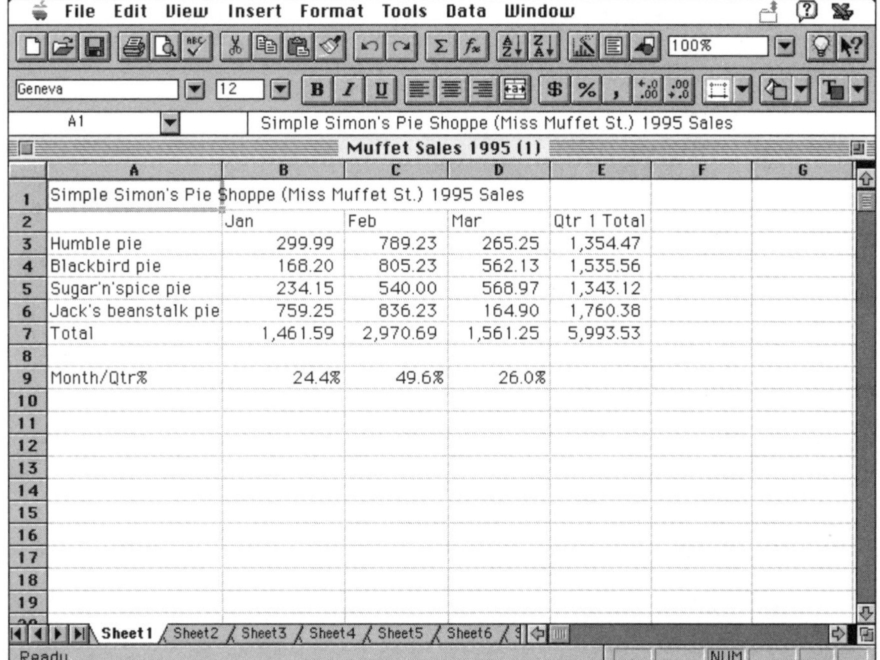

File Edit View Insert Format Tools Data Window
Simple Simon's Pie Shoppe (Miss Muffet St.) 1995 Sales
Muffet Sales 1995 (1)
Jan
Feb
Mar
Qtr 1 Total
Humble pie 299.99 789.23 265.25 1,354.47
Blackbird pie 168.20 805.23 562.13 1,535.56
Sugar'n'spice pie 234.15 540.00 568.97 1,343.12
Jack's beanstalk pie 759.25 836.23 164.90 1,760.38
Total 1,461.59 2,970.69 1,561.25 5,993.53
Month/Qtr% 24.4% 49.6% 26.0%
Ready

Figure 3-22: Centering the table title vertically in row 1.

That's a wrap

Traditionally, column headings in worksheet tables have been a problem because you either had to keep them really short or abbreviate them if you wanted to avoid widening all the columns more than the data warranted. You can get around this problem in Excel by using the text-wrap feature. Figure 3-23 shows an order form in which the column headings use text wrap to avoid widening the columns as much as the types of pie entries would require.

To turn on text wrap, select the cells with the column headings (the cell range B3:F3) and then click on the Wrap Text check box in the Alignment tab in the Format Cells dialog box. (You can see this check box in Figure 3-21.)

When you turn on text wrap, Excel breaks up the long text entries in the selection (that either spill over or are cut off) into separate lines. To accommodate more than one line in a cell, the program automatically expands the row height so that the entire wrapped-text entry is visible.

When you turn on text wrap, Excel continues to use the horizontal and vertical alignment you specified for the cell. Note that you can use any of the Horizontal alignment options, including Left, Center, Right, Justify, or Center Across Selection. You *cannot,* however, use the Fill option. Select the Fill radio button only when you want Excel to repeat the entry across the entire width of the cell.

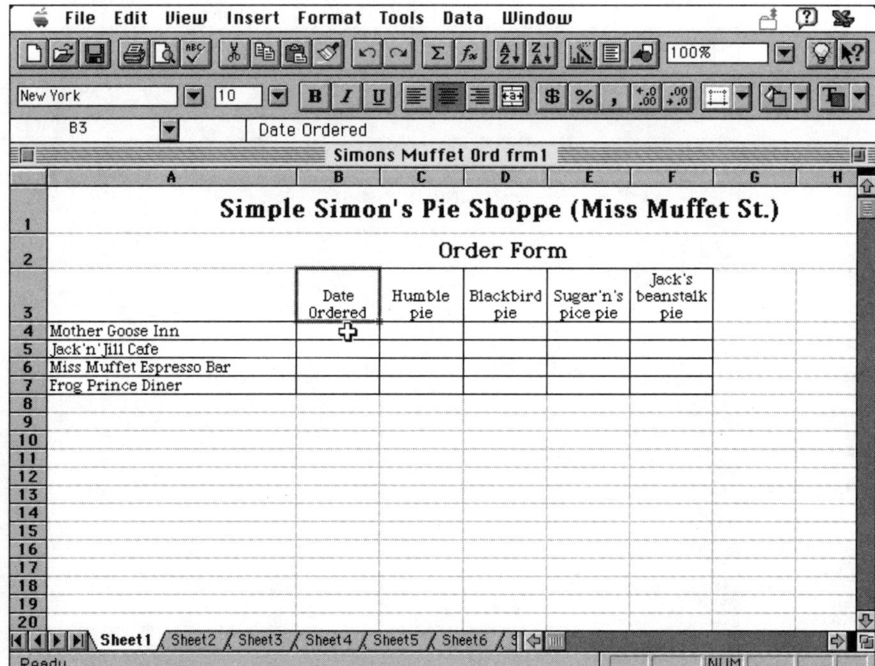

Figure 3-23: An order form with the column headings using text wrap.

If you want to wrap a text entry in its cell and have Excel justify the text with both the left and right border of the cell, select the Justify radio button in the Alignment tab in the Format Cells dialog box.

You can break a long text entry into separate lines by adjusting the cell's column width and row height.

Just point me in the right direction

Instead of wrapping text entries in cells, you may find it more beneficial to change the orientation of the text. Figure 3-24 shows a situation in which changing the orientation of the column headings works much better than wrapping them in their cells.

This example shows the same order form introduced in Figure 3-23 after switching the orientation of the column headings for the various pie types. Notice that switching the text orientation allows you to make the columns very skinny (and rather tall). This change is fine for this order form because it still creates boxes large enough for the pie shop to fill in the number of pies ordered by each of its regular accounts (Mother Goose Inn, Jack'n'Jill Cafe, and so on).

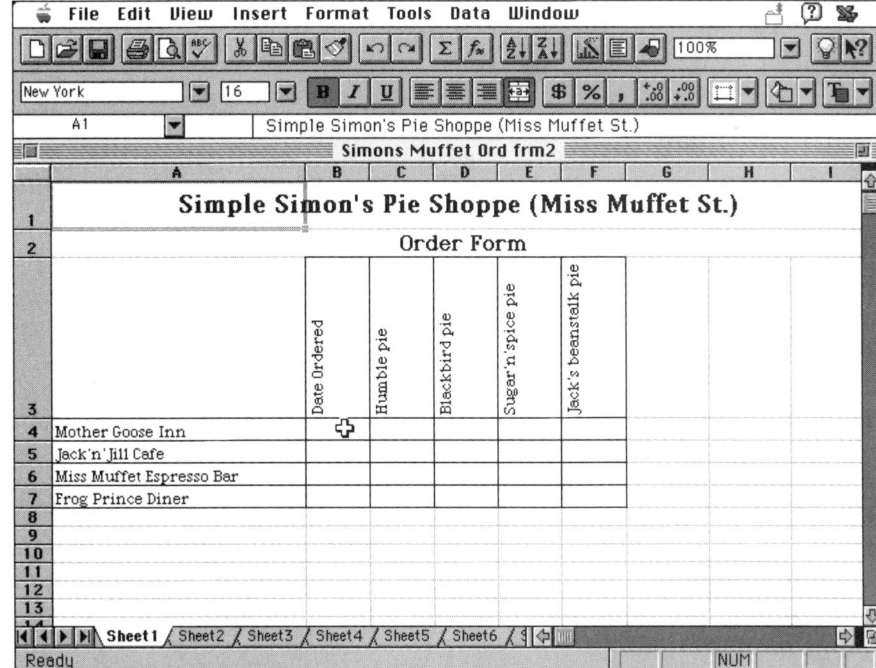

Figure 3-24: The order form after switching the orientation of the various types of pies.

To make this switch in orientation, you select the cell range (B3:F3) and then choose the appropriate Orientation option in the Alignment tab of the Format Cells dialog box (in this case, the one with the text running up). Note that the Orientation options are not available when you select the Fill, Justify, or Center Across Selection radio buttons.

I think I'm borderline

The gridlines displayed in the worksheet are just guidelines to help you keep your place as you work in the document. You can choose either to print them with your data or not. To emphasize sections of the worksheet or parts of a particular table, you can add border lines or shading to certain cells. Don't confuse the border lines you add to accent a particular cell selection with the gridlines used to define cell borders in the worksheet — the border lines you add to a worksheet are printed, whether or not you print the worksheet gridlines.

To better see the border lines you add to the cells in a worksheet, remove the gridlines normally displayed in the worksheet, as follows:

1. **Choose Tools ⇨ Options ⇨ View tab.**
2. **Select the Gridlines option to remove the X from its check box.**
3. **Choose OK or press Return.**

Note that the Gridlines check box in the Options dialog box determines whether or not gridlines are displayed in the worksheet on-screen. To determine whether or not gridlines are printed as part of the worksheet printout, you choose File and then Page Setup; then select the Sheet tab and select or deselect the Gridlines check box under Print.

To add border lines to a cell selection, open the Format Cells dialog box (⌘+1) and then choose the Border tab, as shown in Figure 3-25. Select the type of line you want to use in the Style area of the dialog box and then select from the Border section of the dialog box the edge or edges you want this line applied to.

- To have Excel draw borders around only the outside edges of the entire selection, choose the Outline check box in the Border section.
- If you want border lines to appear around all four edges of each cell in the selection, select the Left, Right, Top, and Bottom check boxes instead.

When you want to add border lines to a single cell or around the outer edge of a cell selection, you don't even have to open the Border dialog box. You simply select the cell or cell range, click on the Border tool's pop-up menu button on the Formatting toolbar, and then select the type of border lines to use in the border palette that appears.

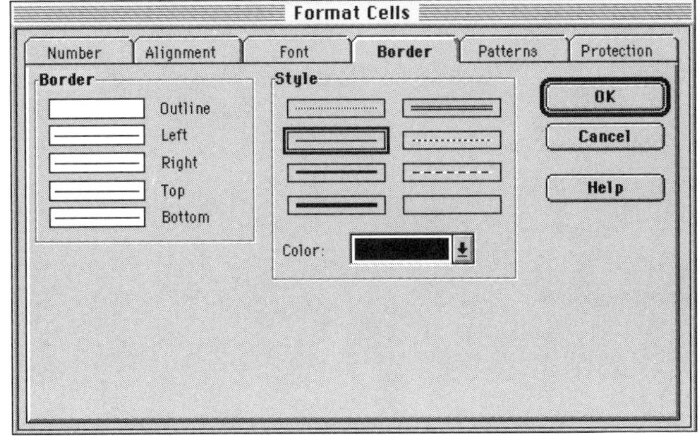

Figure 3-25: Selecting borders with the Border tab in the Format Cells dialog box.

The only problem you may have with border lines occurs when you remove them from the worksheet. To get rid of borders, you must select the cell or cells that currently contain the borders, open the Format Cells dialog box (⌘+1), select the Border tab, and then remove the currently used border style from each and every edge option (Outline, Left, Right, Top, and Bottom).

To remove a border style from an edge, click on the border option, or click on the blank border style (the one in the lower right-hand corner of the Style area)

Of course, the problem you often have is figuring out which cells contain the borders you want to remove. What appears at first glance to be a row of cells with borders on their bottom edges can really be a border on the top edges of the cells in the row below. If you ever try to remove borders from a cell selection only to find that the borders are still there, select the cells in the neighboring ranges and try deleting the borders from them as well.

The patterns of my cells

You also can add emphasis to particular sections of the worksheet or one of its tables by changing the color or pattern, or both, of its cells. If you're using a black-and-white printer (as all but a fortunate few of us are), you may want to restrict your color choices to light gray in the color palette.

When enhancing a cell selection that contains any kind of entry, you may want to restrict your use of patterns to the very open ones with few dots. (Otherwise, the contents of the cells are almost impossible to read when printed.)

To choose a new color or pattern for part of the worksheet, select the cells you want to pretty up, and then open the Format Cells dialog box (⌘+1) and choose the Patterns tab, as shown in Figure 3-26. To change the color of the cells, click on the desired color in the Color palette shown under the Cell Shading heading.

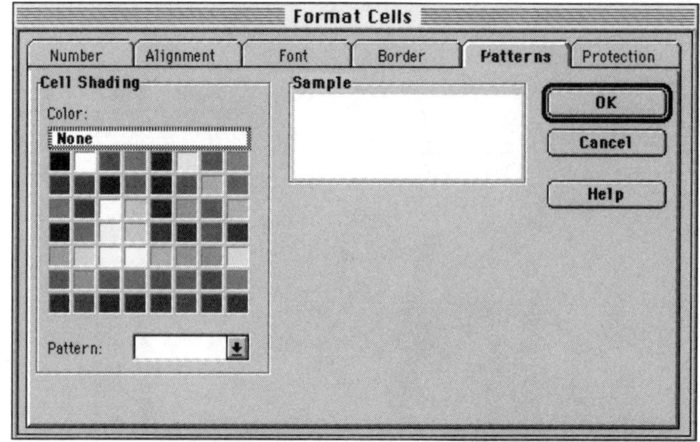

Figure 3-26: Selecting new colors and patterns with the Patterns tab in the Format Cells dialog box.

To change the pattern of the cells, click on the Pattern's pop-up menu box to open an expanded color palette, which contains a number of black-and-white patterns to choose from. Click on the desired pattern in this expanded palette. Excel shows what your creation will look like in the Sample box.

To remove a shading pattern from cells, select the cell range, open the Format Cells dialog box (⌘+1), and select the Patterns tab. Then choose the None option at the top of the Color palette.

You can assign new colors (but not new patterns) to your cell selection with the Color tool (right in front of the Color Font tool) on the Formatting toolbar. Simply select the cells to be colored and then click on the Color tool's pop-up menu button and choose the desired color in the color palette that appears. Although you can't select new patterns (only colors) with the Color tool, you can remove both colors and patterns assigned to a cell selection by selecting the cells and then clicking on the Color tool's pop-up menu button. Then choose None at the top of the color palette that appears.

Going in Style

Cell styles are Excel's way of bringing together under one roof many different kinds of formatting (including the number format, font, alignment, borders, patterns, and protection status). Excel includes six built-in cell styles that you can use in any worksheet: Comma, Comma (0), Currency, Currency (0), Normal, and Percent.

The most common of these styles is the Normal style, which is automatically used in formatting all cells in a new worksheet. The other five styles are used to format cell selections with different number formats. To apply any of these built-in cell styles (or any others you create on your own) to the current cell selection, simply choose Format ➪ Style, and then select a new style in the Style Name pop-up menu box.

Creating new cell styles for a worksheet is as simple as falling off a log. All you do is format one of the cell entries in the worksheet with all the formatting you want in the new style — including the number format, font, alignment, borders, patterns, and protection status. (See Chapter 5 if you don't have a clue as to what protection status is or does.) Then, with the cell pointer located in the sample formatted cell, choose Format ➪ Style to open the Style dialog box, choose the Style Name option, and type in a unique name for your new style in the Style Name text box. Choose OK or press Return.

The next time you save the workbook, Excel saves the new style as part of the document. To apply the new style to other cells in a worksheet, simply select the cells, open the Style dialog box, and select the style name from the Style Name pop-up menu box.

As mentioned, styles are a great way to make custom number formats much easier to use in a workbook. For example, you can create a Hidden style that uses a custom number format to hide all types of entries. You can create a Full Month style that converts dates from an abbreviated date format to a date format that displays the whole shebang. All you do is create these custom number formats, apply them to a sample cell in the worksheet, and create a style named Hidden and one named Full Month. (Refer to "Number Formats Made to Order," earlier in this chapter, for details on how to create custom number formats.) After saving the workbook with these new styles, you can apply them to other cells in the worksheet from the Style dialog box.

In Excel 5.0, you can merge styles created for other workbooks saved on disk into the workbook you're currently creating. To merge the styles, open the workbook that contains the styles you want to copy into the current workbook. Then choose the Window command and select the workbook that is to receive these styles. Choose Style on the Format menu to open the Style dialog box in the workbook that is to receive a copy of the styles from the other workbook. Choose the Merge button to open the Merge Styles dialog box and double-click on the name of the workbook from which you will copy the styles in the Merge Styles From list box.

If the workbook you're currently working on contains styles (other than the standard six that are part of every new workbook) with the same names as some of those in the workbook whose styles you're copying, Excel displays an alert dialog box asking you whether you want to go ahead and merge the styles that have the same name. To overwrite the styles that have the same name in the current workbook, choose Yes. To merge only the styles with different names, choose No. To abandon the whole bloody merger of styles, choose Cancel.

Cell Formatting on the Fly with the Format Painter

Using styles to format worksheet cells is certainly the way to go when you have to apply the formatting over and over again in the workbooks you create. However, there may be times when you simply want to reuse a particular cell format and apply it to select groups of cells in a single workbook without ever bothering to create an actual style for the cell's format.

For those occasions when you feel the urge to format on the fly (so to speak), you can use the Format Painter tool on the Standard toolbar (the one with the paintbrush icon right next to the Paste tool). This wonderful little tool enables you to take the formatting from a particular cell that you've fancied up and apply its formatting to other cells in the worksheet simply by selecting them.

To use the Format Painter tool to copy a cell's formatting to other worksheet cells, just follow these easy steps:

1. **Format an example cell or cell range in your workbook by selecting whatever fonts, alignment, borders, patterns, and color you want it to have.**
2. **With the cell pointer in one of the cells you just fancied up, click on the Format Painter tool in the Standard toolbar.**

   The mouse pointer changes from the standard thick white cross to a thick white cross with a paintbrush by its side.
3. **Drag the white-cross-plus-paintbrush pointer through all the cells you want to format with the formatting you created in the example cell.**

   As soon as you release the mouse button, Excel applies all the formatting used in the example cell to all the cells you just selected!

Chapter 4

How to Make Changes without Messing Up the Entire Workbook

In This Chapter

- How to open a workbook that needs editing
- How to use the Undo feature to recover from a mistake
- How to use the drag-and-drop feature to move or copy entries in the document
- How to use the Cut, Copy, and Paste commands to move and copy information
- How to copy formulas
- How to delete entries from a cell selection
- How to delete rows and columns from a worksheet
- How to insert new rows and columns in a worksheet
- How to use the spell checker to catch and eliminate spelling errors

Picture this: You've just finished creating, formatting, and printing a major project — a workbook with your department's budget for the next fiscal year — with Excel. Because you finally understand a little bit about how Excel works, you get the job done in crack time. You're actually ahead of schedule. You turn over the document to your boss so that he or she can check the numbers. You have plenty of time for making those inevitable last-minute corrections — you're feeling on top of the situation.

Then comes the reality check: Your boss brings the document back and says, plainly agitated, "We forgot to include the estimates for the temps and our overtime hours. They've got to go right here. While you're adding them, can you move these rows of figures up and those columns over?"

As your boss continues to suggest improvements to go along with the one major addition you have to make, your heart begins to sink. These modifications are in a different league from saying, "Let's change these column headings from bold to italics and add shading to that row of totals." Clearly, you're looking at a great deal more work on this baby than you had contemplated. Even worse, you're looking at making structural changes that threaten to unravel the very fabric of your beautiful worksheet.

As this fable points out, editing a worksheet in a workbook can occur on different levels. You can make changes that affect the contents of the cells, such as copying a row of column headings or moving a table to a new area in a particular worksheet. You can make changes that affect the structure of a worksheet itself, such as inserting new columns or rows (so that you can enter new data originally left out) or deleting unnecessary columns or rows from an existing table without leaving any gaps. You can even make changes to the number of worksheets in a workbook by adding or deleting sheets.

In this chapter, you learn how to safely make all these types of changes to a workbook. As you'll see, the mechanics of copying and moving data or inserting and deleting rows are simple to master. The impact that such actions have on the worksheet is what takes a little more effort to understand. But not to worry! You always have the Undo feature to fall back on for those (rare?) times when you make a little change that throws an entire worksheet into complete and utter chaos.

Help, My Workbook's Gone and I Can't Open It Up!

Before you can do any damage (I mean, make any changes) to a workbook document, you have to open it up in Excel. To open a workbook, you can click on the Open tool on the Standard toolbar (the second one from the left with the picture of a file folder opening up). Or you can choose Open from the File menu or press the keystroke shortcut ⌘+O (or ⌘+F12, if you prefer function keys).

When you open a workbook, Excel displays the Open Document dialog box shown in Figure 4-1. Select the document you want to work on from the file-name list box and then open the document by choosing Open or pressing Return. If you're real handy with the mouse, double-click on the document name to open it.

As alternatives to these file-opening methods, you can try the following:

- At the bottom of the File menu, Excel lists the last four documents you opened. If the worksheet you want to work with is one of these four, you can open it by selecting its filename from the menu.
- To select a new folder at a higher level on your hard disk, click on the folder name pop-up menu and then drag to the name of the disk. This procedure causes Excel to display a list of all the folders on the hard disk. You can open a folder either by double-clicking on the folder name or clicking on it and selecting the Open button. When you come across the name of the Excel workbook you want to work with in an open folder, double-click on its name in the list box or click on the name and select the Open button.

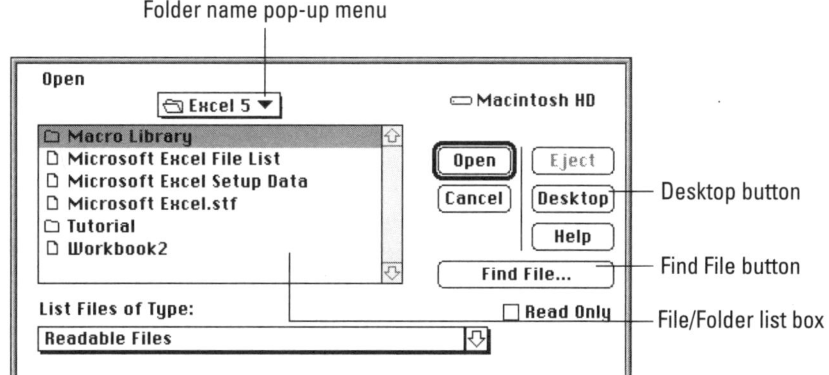

Figure 4-1: The Open dialog box.

Now where did I put that darn workbook?

The only problem you can encounter in opening a document in the Open dialog box is locating the filename. Everything's hunky-dory as long you can find the document in the Folder Name list box.

But what about those times when a file seems to have mysteriously migrated and is now nowhere to be found in the list? (These times seem to happen quite frequently to my students.) I hate to tell you this, but you're going to have to roll up your shirtsleeves and go out on a search for the missing file. Just be thankful you don't have to deal with DOS and its cryptic file names.

The first thing to do before you begin actively searching for the missing document is to find out where in the world you are! What is the current Desktop (hard disk, CD-ROM, or floppy) and folder?

Excel lists this information in the Open dialog box right below the open Folder Name pop-up menu. For example, the first time you display the Open dialog box, you see the contents of the folder in which you placed the Excel program. This is true even if there is an alias of Excel that you double-clicked to launch it. You may select other folders by using the Folder Name pop-up menu as long as you remember that there is a hierarchy (different levels) of folders and their contents.

The Open dialog box tells you that you are looking at the contents of your Microsoft Excel folder. Chances are good that when you first saved and named a worksheet, you didn't save it in this folder, since most users only store their Excel program files here. If you *did* save documents here, you may want to move them to another folder that you've created just for Excel files.

If the file you want is on another hard disk, CD-ROM, or floppy, choose the Desktop button. After you select a new disk from this list box, Excel lists all the folders on this drive.

If you don't find the document in this new list, you may also have to look inside the various folders. You can continue navigating through folders while in the Open dialog box, or you can use the Find command in the Mac Finder. Excel 5 users will have an easier time by clicking the Find File button in the Open dialog box or on the File drop-down menu. You can search by filename and other file info.

If you liken the computer's storage system to a traditional file cabinet, the hard disk, CD-ROM, or floppy compare to the file drawers; the file folders within each drawer compare to the folders on a disk; the paper documents in the folders compare to electronic files. Using this analogy, files on the desktop of a disk are like paper documents stuffed into the very front of a file drawer without being placed in any of the file folders that follow.

Putting out an APB for a document

But what about those times when you haven't the foggiest idea where you saved the worksheet? Now you need to turn to the Finder Find command mentioned earlier. To find a missing Excel file with the Mac Finder, follow these steps:

1. **Click on the Excel icon in the Application menu.**

   This is the farthest right icon at the top of the screen; also known as the menu bar.

2. **Select Finder and release the mouse button.**

   The Finder icon appears along with Finder pull-down menus.

3. **Choose Find from the File menu.**

   The Find dialog box appears.

4. **You have several choices, including the More Choices button. You have three pull-down menus: Name, Contains, and Search on All Disks. You should enter the filename in the top right box.**

5. **You should check out the three pull-down menus to focus the search.**

6. **Choose Find or press Return.**

7. **When the Finder locates the Excel document, the Finder opens the folder that contains the docuwment and selects it. To open the document and reactivate Excel, simply double-click on the selected icon.**

The shortcut to search for the missing Excel document is to press ⌘+F. Enter the name of the file you are searching for, and then choose the Find button or press Return. When the Finder locates the Excel document, the Finder opens the folder that contains the document and selects it. To open the document and reactivate Excel, simply double-click on the selected icon.

A Find File pop-up menu is accessible from both the Open dialog box and the Excel File pull-down menu. You can read up on this feature in IDG's *More Excel for Dummies* by yours truly.

Please Do That Old Undo That You Do So Well

Before you start fooling around with your work of art, you should know how to get to the Undo feature should you somehow manage to do something that messes up the document. The Undo command on the Edit menu is like a chameleon: If you delete the contents of a cell selection with the Clear command on this same menu, Undo changes to Undo Clear. If you move some entries to a new part of the worksheet with the Cut and Paste commands (again, found on the Edit menu), the Undo command changes to Undo Paste.

The Undo command on the Edit menu changes in response to whatever action you have just taken. Because it keeps changing after each action, you must remember to strike while the iron is hot, so to speak, by using the Undo feature to restore the worksheet to its previous state *before* you choose another command. It's imperative that you don't get going so fast that you make several changes in a row without stopping to check how each one affects the worksheet. For example, if you delete a value from a cell and then change the font in another cell and widen its column before you realize that you deleted the wrong value, you can't use the Undo feature to restore the deleted value. All you can use Undo for in this case is to restore the column to its previous width (because changing the width was the last action you completed).

In addition to choosing Undo (in whatever guise it appears) from the Edit menu, you also can choose this command by pressing ⌘+Z (perhaps for *unZap*) or by clicking on the Undo tool on the Standard toolbar (the one with the arrow curving to the left).

Redo that old Undo

After you choose the Undo command (by whatever means you find most convenient), the command changes yet again — this time to a Redo command. If you delete an entry from a cell by using Clear from the Edit menu and then choose Undo Clear from the Edit menu (or press ⌘+Z or click on the Undo tool on the Standard toolbar), the next time you open the Edit menu, you see the following command at the top where Undo normally appears:

```
Redo (u) Clear ⌘+Z
```

The (u) appears after Redo to remind you that the letter *u* remains the command letter, even though *Redo* doesn't have a *u* in it. When you choose the Redo command, Excel redoes the thing you just undid. (Don't worry — this sounds more complicated than it is.) You are simply switching back and forth between the result of an action and the state of the worksheet just before the action. You can continue to Undo and Redo until you decide how you want the worksheet to look (or until they turn off the lights and lock up the building).

Shortcut for extended keyboard users: You have a choice other than ⌘+Z for Undo/Redo. Simply press F1. Try it.

When Undo just won't do

Just when you think it's safe to begin gutting the company's most important workbook, I feel I have to inform you that Undo doesn't work in all situations. Although you can undo your latest erroneous cell deletion, bad move, or unwise copy, you *cannot* undo your latest inaccurate file deletion or imprudent save (such as when you meant to choose Save As from the File menu to save the edited worksheet under a different document name but instead chose Save and ended up saving the changes as part of the current document).

Unfortunately, Excel doesn't let you know when you are about take a step from which there is no return until it's too late. After you've gone and done the "undoable" and you open the Edit menu, right where you expect the Undo *blah blah* command to appear, the screen now says

```
Can't Undo
```

To add insult to injury, this extremely unhelpful command appears dimmed to indicate that you can't choose it — as if being able to choose it would change anything anyway!

For every rule, there is an exception, and Excel does give you advance warning (which you should heed) in one case when you choose a command that is normally undoable. When your computer is low on memory or when the change would affect much of the worksheet (or both), Excel knows when it wouldn't be able to undo the change were it to go through with the command. The program then displays an alert box telling you there isn't enough memory to undo this action and asking whether you want to go ahead anyway. If you click on Yes and complete the edit, just realize that you do so without any possibility of pardon. If you find out — too late — that you deleted a row of essential formulas (that you forgot about because you couldn't see them), you can't bring them back with Undo.

Drag until You Drop

The first editing technique you need to learn is called *drag-and-drop*, a mouse technique that you can use to pick up a cell selection and drop it into a new place on the worksheet. Although drag-and-drop is primarily a technique for moving cell entries around a worksheet, you can adapt it to copy a cell selection as well.

To use drag-and-drop to move a range of cell entries (moving only one cell range at a time), follow these steps:

1. **Select the range as you normally do.**
2. **Position the mouse pointer on one of the edges of the selected range and then press and hold down the mouse button.**

   Your signal that you can start dragging the cell range to its new position in the worksheet is when the pointer changes to the arrowhead.
3. **Drag.**

   As you drag, you actually move only the outline of the cell range. Drag the outline until it's positioned around the new cells in the worksheet where you want the entries to appear.
4. **Release the mouse button.**

   The cell entries within the range reappear in the new location as soon as you release the mouse button.

Figures 4-2 and 4-3 show how you can drag-and-drop to move a cell range. In Figure 4-2, I selected the cell range A7:E7 (containing the quarterly totals) in preparation for moving it to row 9 to make room for the sales figures for two new types of pies: Itsy-bitsy spider pie and Shoo-fly pie (which hadn't been created when this workbook was first made). In Figure 4-3, you see the worksheet after I completed the move, leaving only cell B9 selected.

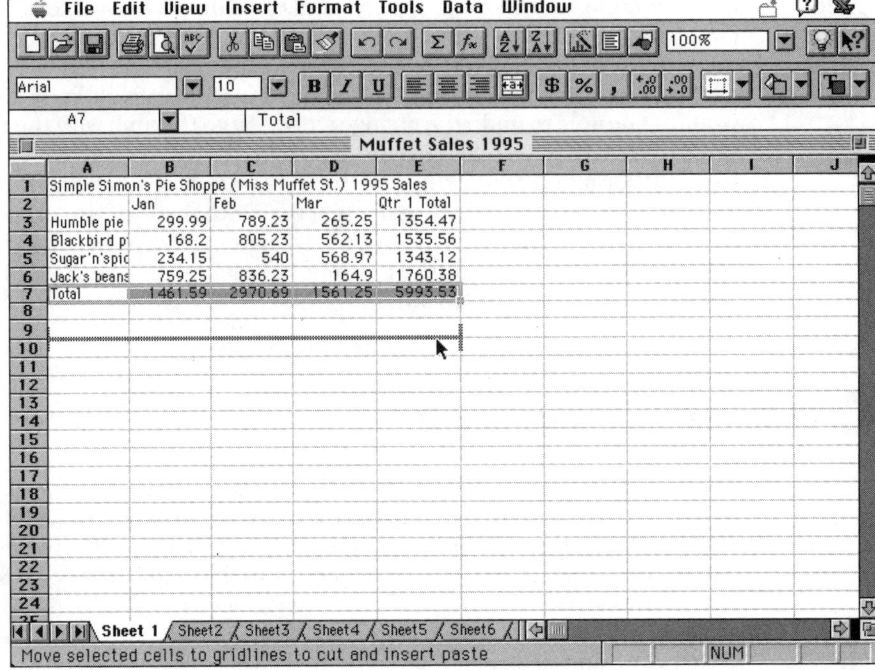

Figure 4-2: Dragging a selection to its new position in the worksheet.

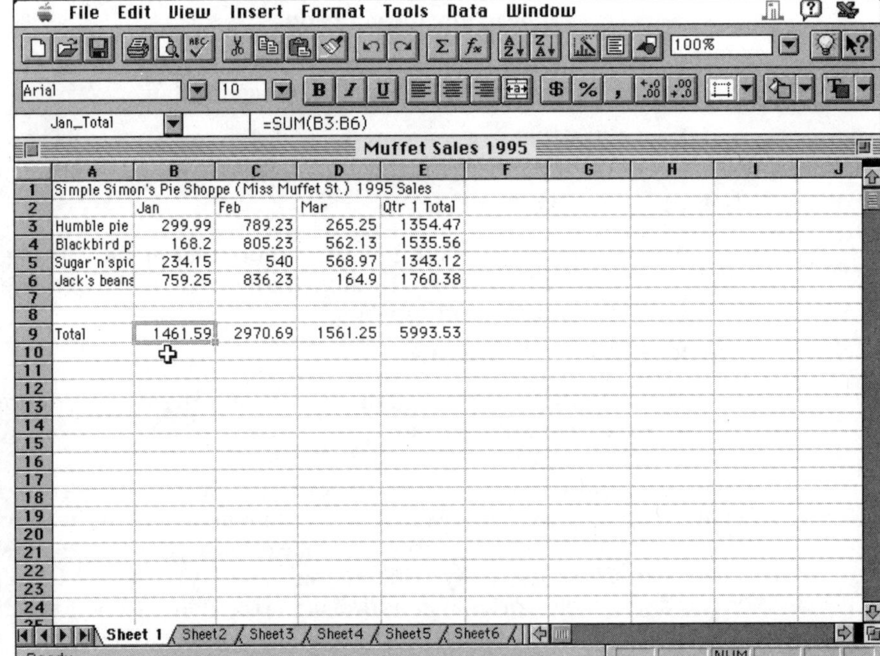

Figure 4-3: The worksheet after the drag-and-drop operation.

In Figure 4-3, notice that the argument for the SUM function in cell B9 has not kept pace with the change — it continues to sum only the range B3:B6. Eventually, this range must be expanded to include cells B7 and B8, the first-quarter sales figures for the new yummy Itsy-bitsy spider pie and the sure-to-please Shoo-fly pie. (You'll see the expansion of the worksheet in the upcoming section "You Really AutoFill Those Formulas.")

Okay, so you know how to move a cell range with drag-and-drop. But what if you want to copy a cell range instead? Suppose that you need to start a new table in rows farther down the worksheet and you want to copy the cell range with the formatted title and column headings for the new table. To copy the formatted title range in the sample worksheet, follow these steps:

1. **Select the cell range.**

   In this example, the relevant cell range is B2:E2.

2. **Press and hold down the Option key as you position the mouse pointer on an edge of the selection.**

   The pointer changes from a thick-shaded cross to an arrowhead with a + (plus sign) to the right of it. This pointer is your signal that drag-and-drop will *copy* the selection rather than *move* it.

3. **Drag the cell-selection outline to the place where you want the copy to appear and release the mouse button.**

The Control key is found only on the extended keyboard. If you have a regular keyboard, you have to use Copy and Paste (see "Pasting the Night Away" later in this chapter for details).

Table 4-1 lists the copy and drag-and-drop commands.

Table 4-1 Copy and Drag-and-Drop Keyboard Commands

Keyboard Combinations	*What's Going On Here?*
Click and drag with arrowhead cursor	Known as drag-and-drop. Moves contents of selected cells to new location in worksheet.
Control+click and drag with arrowhead cursor	Previously known as copying with drag-and-drop. Excel 5 introduces a new drag-and-drop shortcut menu, which enables you to copy contents, formats, and formulas, or you can move the contents of the cells.
Option+click and drag with arrowhead cursor	Known as copying with drag-and-drop. Copies contents of selected cells and cursor (changes by adding a small + [plus sign]) as you copy and drag contents.
Shift+click and drag with arrowhead cursor	Prevents you from copying selected cells into an already-occupied cell range.

Excel 5 Drag-and-Drop shortcut menu

	A	B	C	D	E
1	Simple Simon's Pie Shoppe (Miss Muffet St.) 1995 Sales				
2		Jan	Feb	Mar	Qtr 1 Total
3	Humble pie	299.99	789.23	265.25	1354.47
4	Blackbird p	168.2	805.23	562.13	1535.56
5	Sugar'n'spic	234.15	540	568.97	1343.12
6	Jack's beans	759.25	836.23	164.9	1760.38
7					
8					
9	Total	1461.59	2970.69	1561.25	5993.53

Copy
Move
Copy Formats
Copy Values
Shift Down and Copy
Shift Right and Copy
Shift Down and Move
Shift Right and Move

Place a copy of the dragged cells here

Figure 4-4: The new Drag-and-Drop shortcut menu in Excel 5 that you access with Control+click and drag.

If you try to use drag-and-drop when the cursor is in the lower right-hand corner of a selection and the arrowhead changes to a cross — then instead of drag-and-drop, you wind up copying a series with AutoFill or multiple copies of selected cells (please refer to the section in Chapter 2 called "When You AutoFill It Up").

When using drag-and-drop, if you position the outline of the selection so that it overlaps any part of cells that already contain entries, Excel displays an alert box with the following question:

```
Replace contents of the destination cells?
```

To avoid replacing existing entries and to abort the entire drag-and-drop mission, choose Cancel in this alert box. To go ahead and exterminate the little darlings, choose OK or press Return.

Like the Klingons of Star Trek fame, spreadsheets (including Excel) never take prisoners. When you place or move a new entry into an occupied cell, the new entry completely replaces the old, as though the old entry never existed in that cell.

To insert the cell range that you're moving or copying into a populated region of the worksheet without wiping out existing entries, hold down Shift while you drag the selection (if you're copying, hold down both Shift and Option [or Shift and ⌘]). For this maneuver, rather than dragging a rectangular outline of the cell range, you drag an I-beam shape that shows where the selection will be inserted when you release the mouse button. As you move the I-beam shape, notice that it gloms onto the column and row borders as you move it. When you position the I-beam shape at the column or row border where you want the cell range to be inserted, release the mouse button. Excel inserts the cell range and repatriates the existing entries to neighboring blank cells (out of harm's way).

When using drag-and-drop in insert mode, think of the I-beam shape as a pry bar that pulls apart the columns or rows along the axis of the I-beam. Figures 4-5 and 4-6 show how to use the I-beam to move the quarterly totals in column E to column B. When you drag the cell range E2:E7 to the cell range B2:B7, you can be sure that Excel will insert these totals and move the existing columns of sales entries to the right.

Figure 4-5 shows the worksheet after I selected the cell range of quarterly totals (E2:E7), held down Shift, and dragged the I-beam shape until it rested on the border between columns A and B (between the row headings and the January sales figures). Figure 4-6 shows the results after I released the mouse button.

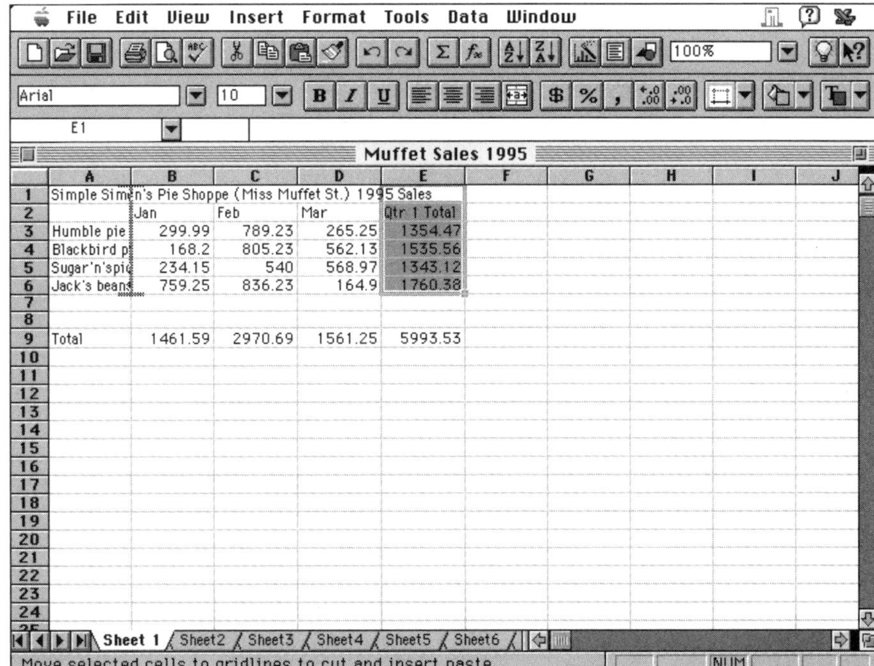

Figure 4-5: Dragging the totals from column E to column B, replacing no existing entries.

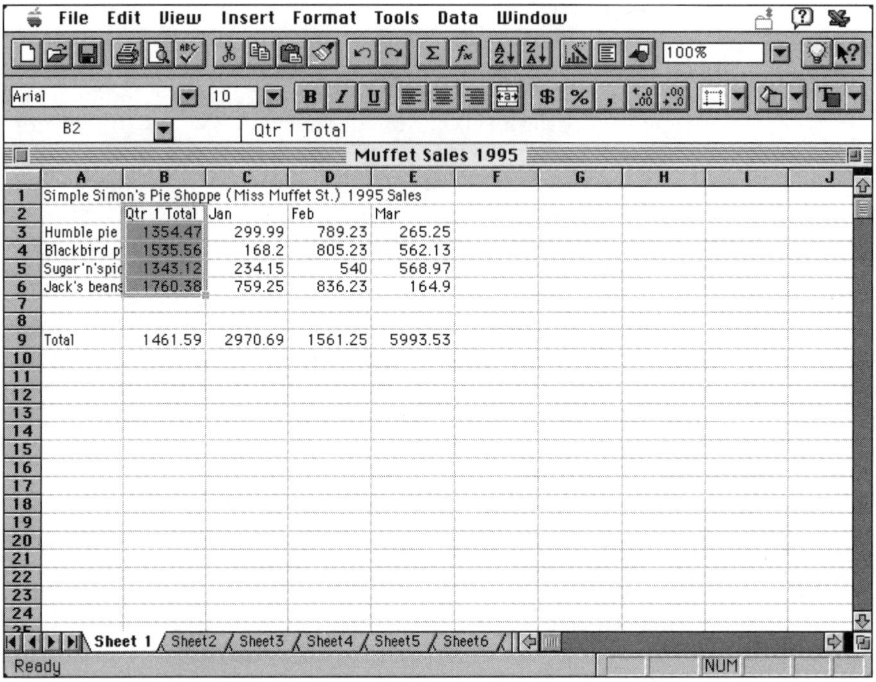

	A	B	C	D	E
1	Simple Simon's Pie Shoppe (Miss Muffet St.) 1995 Sales				
2		Qtr 1 Total	Jan	Feb	Mar
3	Humble pie	1354.47	299.99	789.23	265.25
4	Blackbird p	1535.56	168.2	805.23	562.13
5	Sugar'n'spic	1343.12	234.15	540	568.97
6	Jack's beans	1760.38	759.25	836.23	164.9
9	Total	1461.59	2970.69	1561.25	5993.53

Figure 4-6: After inserting the quarterly total range in column B.

Notice the orientation of the I-beam shape in Figure 4-5: The long part of the "I" runs parallel to the column border. Getting the I-beam selection indicator to assume this orientation can be tricky. To prepare to drag the cell selection, position the mouse pointer on one of the vertical edges (either the left or the right) of the selection. After you drag the selection, position the mouse pointer slightly to the left of the column border and not on it.

You Really AutoFill Those Formulas

Copying with drag-and-drop (by holding down Control) is useful when you need to copy a bunch of neighboring cells to a new part of the worksheet. Frequently, you need to copy the formula you've just created to a bunch of neighboring cells that need to perform the same type of calculation, such as totaling columns of figures. Just copying the cell format doesn't cut it. This type of copying, although quite common, can't be done with drag-and-drop. Instead, you use the AutoFill feature (introduced in Chapter 2) or the Copy and Paste commands (see "Pasting the Night Away," coming right up).

Figures 4-7 and 4-8 show how you can use AutoFill to copy one formula to a range of cells. Figure 4-7 shows the Muffet Street worksheet after I added the Itsy-bitsy spider and Shoo-fly pies to the list (see Figures 4-2 and 4-3 to see how I moved the Total row to row 9 to make room).

Unfortunately, Excel doesn't update the sum formulas to include the new rows (the SUM function still uses B3:B6 when the calculation should extend to include rows 7 and 8). To make the SUM function include all the rows, position the cell pointer in cell B9 and click on the AutoSum tool on the Standard toolbar. Excel suggests the new range B3:B8 for the SUM function.

Figure 4-8 shows the worksheet *after* I recreated the SUM formula in cell B9 with the AutoSum tool to include the expanded range. I dragged the fill handle (the thin black cross — see Table 1-3 in Chapter 1 for a description) to select the cell range C9:E9, where this formula should be copied. Notice that I deleted the original formulas from the cell range C9:E9 in this figure to make it easier to see what's going on; normally, you just copy over the original outdated formulas and replace them with new, correct copies.

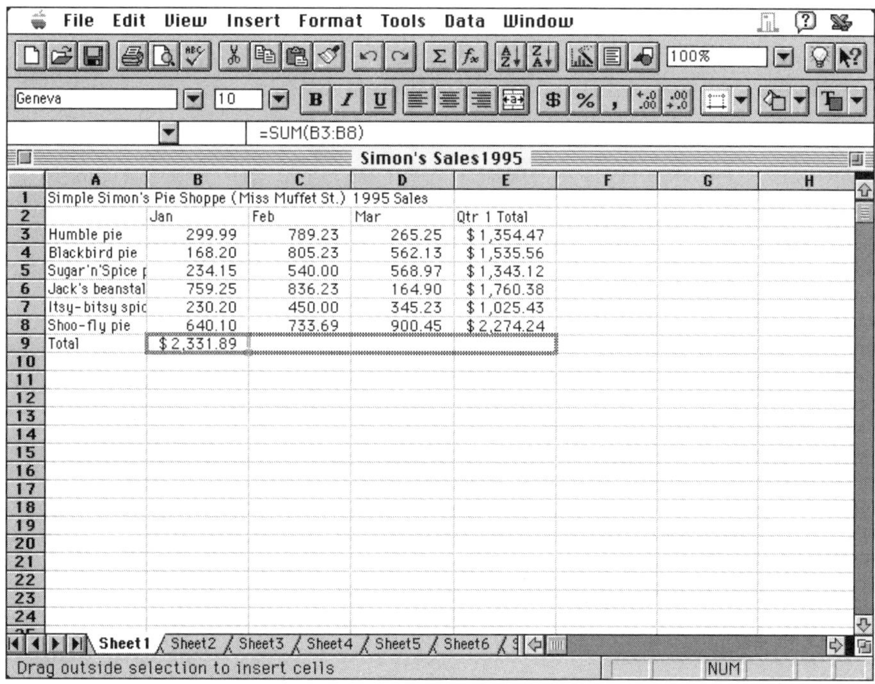

File Edit View Insert Format Tools Data Window
Geneva
10
100%
=SUM(B3:B8)
Simon's Sales1995
Simple Simon's Pie Shoppe (Miss Muffet St.) 1995 Sales
Jan
Feb
Mar
Qtr 1 Total
Humble pie 299.99 789.23 265.25 $1,354.47
Blackbird pie 168.20 805.23 562.13 $1,535.56
Sugar'n'Spice p 234.15 540.00 568.97 $1,343.12
Jack's beanstal 759.25 836.23 164.90 $1,760.38
Itsy-bitsy spic 230.20 450.00 345.23 $1,025.43
Shoo-fly pie 640.10 733.69 900.45 $2,274.24
Total $2,331.89
Sheet1 Sheet2 Sheet3 Sheet4 Sheet5 Sheet6
Drag outside selection to insert cells
NUM

Figure 4-7: Copying a formula to a cell range with AutoFill.

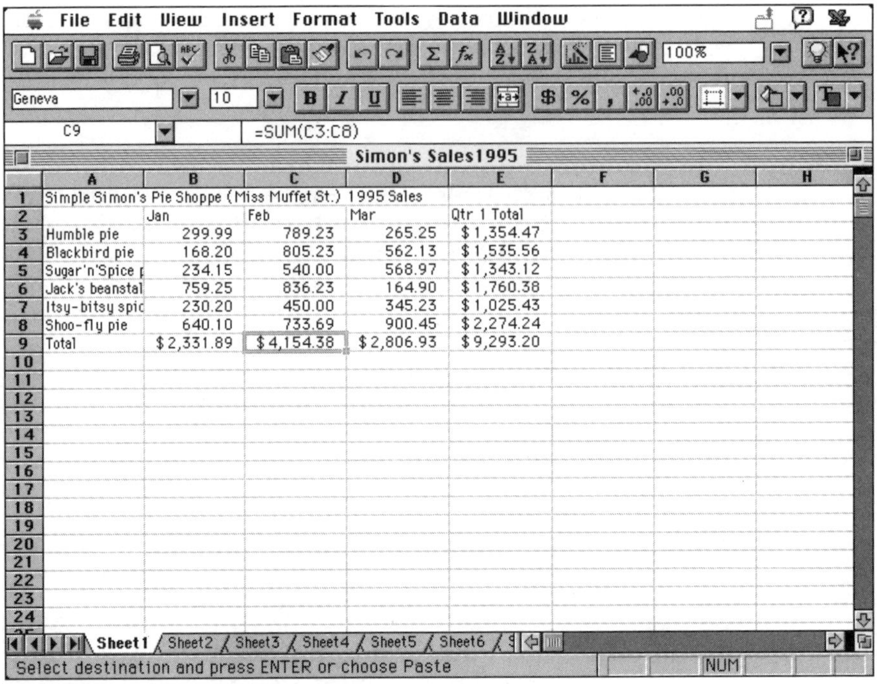

C9 =SUM(C3:C8)

Simon's Sales1995

	A	B	C	D	E
1	Simple Simon's Pie Shoppe (Miss Muffet St.) 1995 Sales				
2		Jan	Feb	Mar	Qtr 1 Total
3	Humble pie	299.99	789.23	265.25	$1,354.47
4	Blackbird pie	168.20	805.23	562.13	$1,535.56
5	Sugar'n'Spice p	234.15	540.00	568.97	$1,343.12
6	Jack's beanstal	759.25	836.23	164.90	$1,760.38
7	Itsy-bitsy spic	230.20	450.00	345.23	$1,025.43
8	Shoo-fly pie	640.10	733.69	900.45	$2,274.24
9	Total	$2,331.89	$4,154.38	$2,806.93	$9,293.20

Select destination and press ENTER or choose Paste

Figure 4-8: The worksheet after I copied the formula for total monthly sales

Everything's relative

Refer to Figure 4-8 to see the worksheet after I copied the formula in cell B9 to the cell range C9:E9 (cell C9 is active). Notice how Excel handles the copying of formulas. The original formula in cell B9 is as follows:

```
=SUM(B3:B8)
```

But I did just what you said...

Drag-and-drop while holding down the Shift key (Insert mode) is one of Excel's most finicky features. Sometimes you do everything just right and you *still* get the alert box indicating that Excel is about to replace existing entries instead of pushing them aside (always choose Cancel).

Fortunately, you can insert values or information with the Cut and Insert Paste commands without worrying about which way the I-beam selection goes. (See "Pasting the Night Away," later in this chapter.)

When Excel copies the original formula next door to cell C9, Excel slightly changes the formula so that it looks like this:

```
=SUM(C3:C8)
```

Notice how Excel adjusts the column reference, changing it from *B* to *C* (because I dragged from left to right across the rows).

When you copy a formula to a cell range that extends across the columns rather than down the rows, Excel adjusts the row numbers in the copies rather than the column letters to suit the position of each copy. For example, cell E3 in the Muffet Street 1995 sales worksheet contains the following formula:

```
=SUM(B3:D3)
```

When you copy this formula down to cell E4, Excel changes the copy of the formula to the following:

```
=SUM(B4:D4)
```

Excel adjusts the row reference to keep current with the new row 4 position. Because Excel adjusts the cell references in copies of a formula relative to the direction of the copying, the cell references are known as *relative cell references.*

Dealing in absolutes

All new formulas you create naturally contain relative cell references unless you say otherwise. Because most copies of formulas that you make require adjustments of their cell references, you rarely have to give this arrangement a second thought. Every once in a while, however, you come across an exception that calls for limiting when and how cell references are adjusted in copies.

One of the most common of these exceptions occurs when you want to compare a range of different values to a single value — in other words, when you want to compute what percentage each part is to the total. For example, in the Muffet Street 1995 sales worksheet, you encounter this situation in creating and copying a formula that calculates what percentage each monthly total (in the cell range B9:D9) is of the quarterly total in cell E9.

Suppose that you want to enter these formulas in row 11 of the Muffet Street 1995 worksheet, starting in cell B11. The formula in cell B11 for calculating the percentage of the January-to-first-quarter-total in cell B11 is very straightforward:

```
=B9/E9
```

This formula divides the January total in cell B9 by the yearly total in E9 (what could be easier?). Look, however, at what happens if you drag the fill handle one cell to the right to copy this formula to cell C11:

```
=C9/F9
```

The adjustment of the first cell reference from B9 to C9 is just what the doctor ordered. However, the adjustment of the second cell reference from E9 to F9 is a disaster. You not only don't calculate what percentage the February sales are of the first quarter sales, you also end up with one of those horrible `#DIV/0!` error things in cell C11.

To stop Excel from adjusting a cell reference in a formula in any copies you make, you have to convert the cell reference from relative to absolute. You can do this by pressing ⌘+T (for *absoluTe?*).

Windows refugees changing to the Mac platform: Please don't try F4 on the extended keyboard to convert from relative to absolute. On the Mac, F4 is the keystroke shortcut for pasting information.

Excel indicates that you've made the cell reference absolute by placing a $ (dollar sign) in front of each column letter and row number in the formula. For example, look at Figure 4-9. Cell B11 in this figure contains the correct formula to copy to the cell range C11:D11:

```
=B9/$E$9
```

Figure 4-10 shows the worksheet after this formula is copied to the range C11:D11 with the fill handle (cell C11 is selected). Notice that the formula bar shows that this cell contains the following formula:

```
=C9/$E$9
```

Because I changed E9 to $E$9 in the original formula, all the copies have this same absolute reference.

If you goof up and copy a formula where one or more of the cell references should have been absolute but you left them all relative, edit the original formula as follows:

1. **Double-click on the cell that contains the formula, or select it and press ⌘+U to edit it.**
2. **Position the insertion point somewhere on the reference you want to convert to absolute.**
3. **Press ⌘+T.**
4. **When you finish editing, press Return and then copy the formula to the messed-up cell range with the fill handle.**

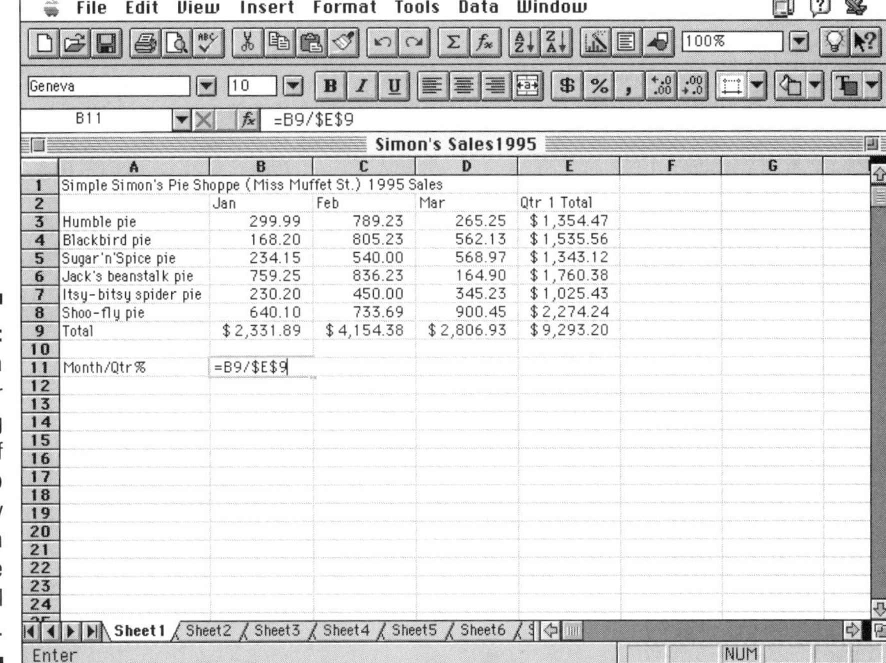

Figure 4-9: The formula for computing the ratio of monthly to quarterly sales with an absolute cell reference.

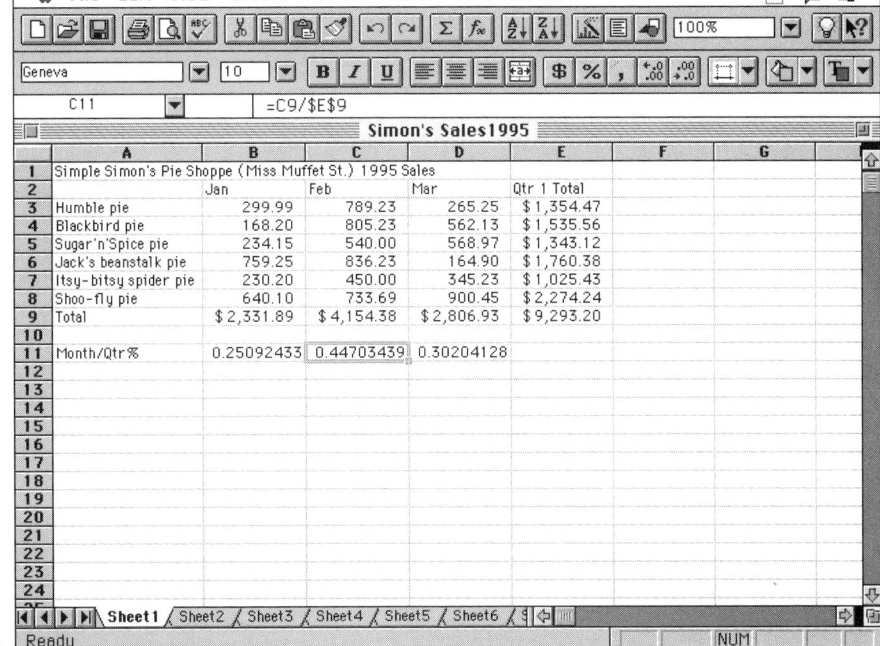

Figure 4-10: The worksheet after copying the formula with the absolute cell reference.

Pasting the Night Away

Instead of drag-and-drop or AutoFill, you can use the standby Cut, Copy, and Paste commands to move or copy information in a worksheet. These commands use the Clipboard as a kind of electronic halfway house, where the information you cut or copy remains until you decide to paste it somewhere. Because of this Clipboard arrangement, you can use these commands to move or copy information to any other worksheet open in Excel, or even to other programs running on the Mac (such as a Word document). This kind of moving or copying across documents is not possible with drag-and-drop or AutoFill.

To move a cell selection with Cut and Paste, follow these steps:

1. **Select the cells you want to move.**
2. **Choose Cut from the cell shortcut menu or Cut from the Edit menu.**

   You can cut through all these menus and just press ⌘+X. Whenever you choose the Cut command in Excel, the program surrounds the cell selection with a *marquee* (a dotted line that "travels" around the cells' outline) and displays the following message on the status bar: `Select destination and press Return or choose Paste.`
3. **Move the cell pointer to, or select, the cell in the upper left-hand corner of the new range to which you want the information moved.**
4. **Press Return to complete the move operation.**

   Alternatively, if you're feeling really ambitious, choose Paste from the cell shortcut menu, choose Paste from the Edit menu, or press ⌘+V.

Notice that when you indicate the destination range, you don't have to select a range of blank cells that matches the shape and size of the cell selection you're moving. Excel only needs to know the location of the cell in the upper left-hand corner of the destination range to figure out where to put the rest of the cells.

In fact, you can mess yourself up if you select more than the first cell of the destination range and the selected range doesn't exactly match the size and shape of the selection you're moving. After you press Return, Excel displays an alert box with the following message:

```
Cut and paste areas are different shapes
```

If you choose OK to get rid of this dialog box, you have to correct the size of the destination range to successfully complete the move operation. As stated earlier, you can select either only the first cell of the destination range or you must select a range that exactly matches the range previously cut.

Copying a cell selection with the Copy and Paste commands follows an identical procedure to the one you use with the Cut and Paste commands. After selecting the range to copy, you have even more choices about how to get the information into the Clipboard. Instead of choosing Copy from the cell shortcut menu or Copy from the Edit menu, you can press ⌘+C or click on the Copy tool on the Standard toolbar (the eighth one from the left, the one with the picture of the duplicate documents).

Copying is much better the second time around

When copying a selection with the Copy and Paste commands and the Clipboard, you can copy the information multiple times. Just make sure that, instead of pressing Return to complete the first copy operation, you choose the Paste command (from the cell shortcut menu or the Edit menu) or press ⌘+V.

When you use the Paste command to complete a copy operation, Excel copies the selection to the range you designated without removing the marquee from the original selection. This marquee is your signal that you can select another destination range (either in the same or a different document).

After selecting the first cell of the next range where you want the selection copied, choose the Paste command again. You can continue in this manner, pasting the same selection to your heart's content. When you make the last copy, press Return instead of choosing the Paste command. If you forget and choose Paste, you can get rid of the marquee around the original cell range by pressing Esc.

Special pasting

Normally, Excel copies all the information in the range of cells you selected — formatting, formulas, text, and other values you have entered. If you want, you can specify that only the entries be copied (without the formatting) or that just the formatting be copied (without the entries). You can even have Excel copy only values in a cell selection, which means that Excel copies all text entries and values entered in a cell selection but does *not* include formulas or formatting. When you paste values, all formulas in the cell selection are discarded and only the calculated values are retained — these values appear in the new cell range just as though you entered them manually.

To paste particular parts of a cell selection while discarding others, you choose the Paste Special command on the cell shortcut menu or on the Edit pull-down menu, rather than the standard Paste command (which means you don't get the benefit of using the nifty ⌘+V keyboard shortcut). When you choose Paste Special instead of Paste, Excel displays the Paste Special dialog box shown in Figure 4-11. Here, you can specify which parts of the current cell selection to use by choosing the appropriate Paste radio button.

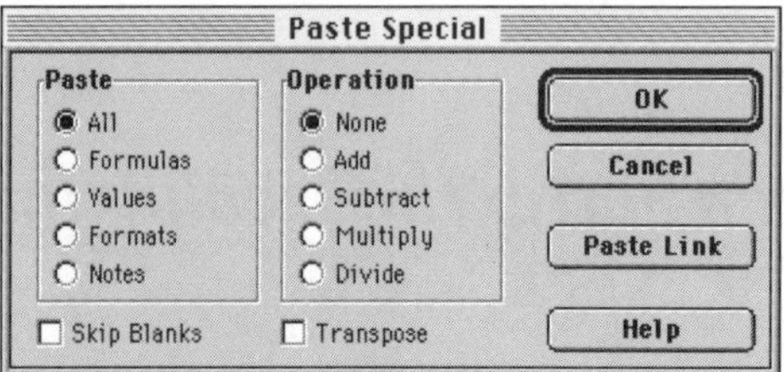

Figure 4-11: The Paste Special dialog box.

- By default, Excel chooses All to paste all the stuff in the cell selection (formulas, formatting — you name it).
- Choose the Formulas radio button to paste all the text, numbers, and formulas in the current cell selection while, at the same time, omitting all the current formatting applied to the cells.
- Choose the Values radio button to convert formulas in the current cell selection to their calculated values.
- Choose the Formats radio button to paste only the formatting from the current cell selection and leave the cell entries in the dust.
- Choose the Notes radio button to paste all text, numbers, and formulas in the current selection along with any notes that you've attached to the cells (kinda like electronic sticky notes — see Chapter 5 for details).

- By default, Excel chooses the operation None. None replaces all existing cell entries with the values being pasted.
- Choose Add, Subtract, Multiply, or Divide if you want to modify the previous cell entries with the new entries being pasted. If you choose Add, for example, they are added to existing values. The other options operate in a similar manner. It is not often that you elect to choose operations other than the default None.

To Clear or to Delete: That Is the Question

You can perform the following two kinds of deletions in a worksheet:

- The first type of deletion is rightfully referred to as *clearing* a cell: It deletes or empties the cell's contents without removing the cell from the worksheet (which would alter the layout of the surrounding cells).
- The second type of deletion, correctly referred to as *deleting* a cell, gets rid of the whole-kit-and-caboodle — deleting the cell structure along with all the contents and formatting. When you delete a cell, Excel has to shuffle the position of entries in the surrounding cells to plug up any gaps made by its demise.

Clearing the air

To clear the contents of a selection rather than delete it, select the range of cells to be cleared and press ⌘+B or choose Clear Contents from the cell shortcut menu (or Edit ⇨ Clear ⇨ Contents).

If you select a cell range on the Mac and use either the Delete key or the Clear key, only the contents of the first cell are cleared, and the cell format doesn't change. Pressing ⌘+B is the fastest means of clearing the contents from a range of cells without altering formats.

If you want to get rid of more than just the contents of a cell selection, choose Clear on the Edit menu and then choose from among the following cascading menu commands:

- Choose All to get rid of all formatting, notes, and entries in the cell selection.
- Choose Formats to delete only the formatting from the current cell selection without touching anything else.
- Choose Notes if you want to remove only the notes in the cell selection but leave everything else behind.

This cell range is condemned

To delete a cell selection rather than clear out its contents, select the cell range and press ⌘+K or choose Delete from the cell shortcut menu or Delete from the Edit menu. Excel displays a Delete dialog box that you use to indicate how Excel should shift the cells left behind to fill in the gaps made by the deletion. Use the Delete dialog box for these options:

- By default, Excel selects the Shift Cells Left radio button, which means that Excel moves entries from neighboring columns on the right to the left to fill in gaps created when you delete the cell selection by choosing OK or pressing Return.
- If you want Excel to move up entries from neighboring rows below, click on the Shift Cells Up radio button.
- If you decide to remove all the rows selected in the cell range (instead of restricting the deletion to just those few columns selected), click on the Entire Row radio button in the Delete dialog box.
- If you decide to delete all the columns highlighted in the cell range (instead of restricting the deletion to just those few rows selected), click on the Entire Column radio button.
- If you know ahead of time that you want to delete an entire column or row from the worksheet, you can select the column or row on the window frame and then press ⌘+K or choose Delete from the shortcut menu or Delete from the Edit menu. You can remove more than one column or row at a time, provided that they all neighbor one another and that you select them by dragging through their column letters or row numbers. (Excel cannot delete nonadjacent selections.)

Deleting entire columns and rows from a worksheet is risky business unless you are sure that the columns and rows in question contain nothing of value. Remember, when you delete an entire row from the worksheet, you delete *all information from column A through IV* in that row (and you can see only a very few columns in this row). Likewise, when you delete an entire column from the worksheet, you delete *all information from row 1 through row 16384* in that column.

Under New Construction

For those inevitable times when you need to squeeze new entries into an already-populated region of the worksheet, you can insert new cells in the area instead of going through all the trouble of moving and rearranging several individual cell ranges. To insert a new cell range, select the cells (many of which are already occupied) where you want the new cells to appear, and then press ⌘+I or choose Insert on the cell shortcut menu or the Cells command on the Insert pull-down menu to display the Insert dialog box. When you insert new cells, you can decide how Excel should shift existing entries to make room for the new cells by using the following options:

- Choose the Shift Cells Right radio button to shift existing cells to the right to make room for the ones you want to add before choosing OK or pressing Return.
- To instruct the program to shift existing entries down, choose the default Shift Cells Down radio button before choosing OK or pressing Return.
- As when you delete cells, when you insert cells with the Insert dialog box, you can insert complete rows or columns in the cell range by clicking on either the Entire Row or the Entire Column radio button. You also can select the row number or column letter on the frame before you choose the Insert command.

Note that you also can insert entire columns and rows in a worksheet by choosing the Columns or Rows command on the Insert menu without having to open the Insert dialog box.

Keep in mind that just as when you delete whole columns and rows, inserting entire columns and rows affects the entire worksheet, not just the part you see. If you don't know what's out in the hinterlands of the worksheet, you cannot be sure how the insertion will impact (perhaps even sabotage) entries in the other unseen areas.

Dispelling Your Misspellings

You'll be happy to know that Excel has a spelling checker that can catch and eliminate most of those embarrassing little spelling errors. However, this means you no longer have any excuse for putting out worksheets with typos in the titles or headings.

To check the spelling in a worksheet, either choose the Spelling command from the Tools menu, click on the Check Spelling tool (the one with a check mark under ABC) on the Standard toolbar, or press F7.

Any way you access the spelling checker, Excel begins checking the spelling of all text entries in the worksheet. When the program comes across an unknown word, Excel displays the Spelling dialog box, similar to the one shown in Figure 4-12.

Figure 4-12: Checking spelling in the Spelling dialog box.

Excel suggests replacements for the unknown word, with the most likely replacement appearing in the Change To list box. Use the Spelling dialog box options as follows:

- To replace the word listed after the Not in Dictionary prompt with the word listed in the Change To list box, click on the Change button.
- To change all occurrences of this misspelled word in the worksheet, click on the Change All button.
- If you want to add the unknown word to a custom dictionary so that it isn't flagged when you check the spelling in the worksheet later on, click on the Add button.

Notice that the Excel spelling checker not only flags words not found in its built-in or custom dictionary but also flags occurrences of double words in a cell entry (such as *total total*) or words with unusual capitalization (such as *NEw York* instead of *New York*).

Keep in mind that you can check the spelling of just a particular group of entries by selecting the cells before you either choose Spelling from the Tools menu, click on the Check Spelling tool in the Standard toolbar, or press F7.

Part III

Ferreting Out the Information

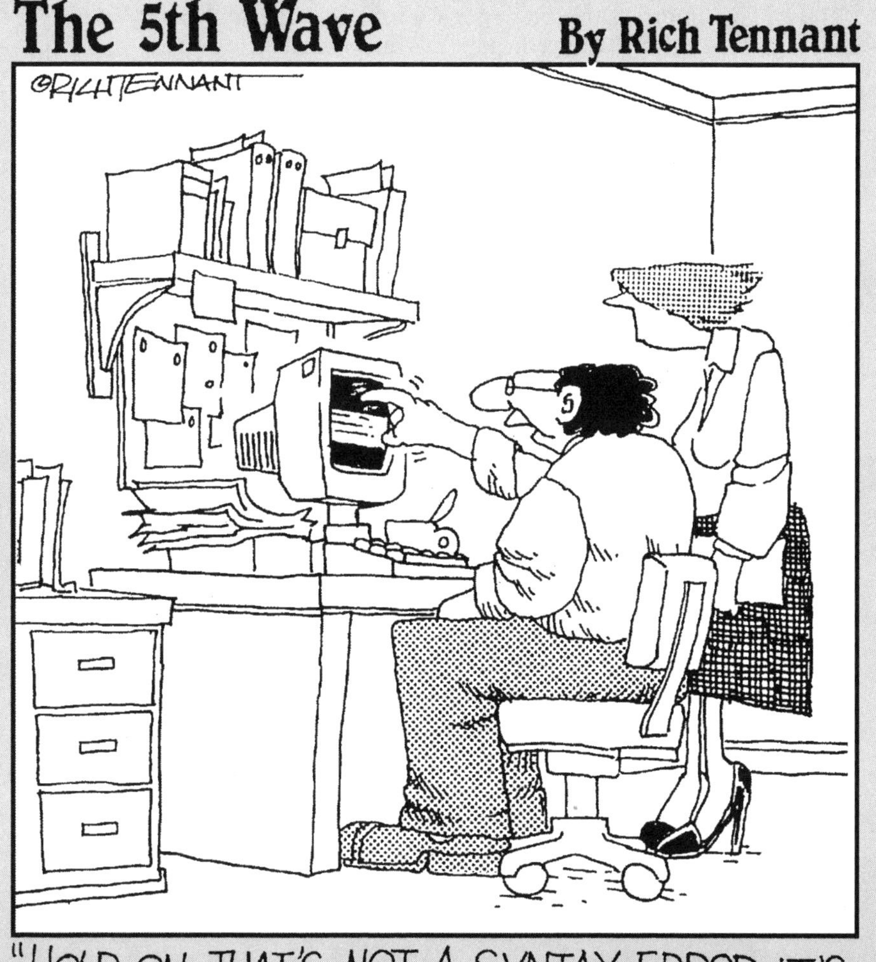

"HOLD ON, THAT'S NOT A SYNTAX ERROR, IT'S JUST A DONUT CRUMB ON THE SCREEN."

The part in which . . .

You learn all kinds of neat tricks for overseeing the information you've got in your worksheet and for getting it down on paper. First, you learn how to unearth stuff you thought was lost forever by using a series of strategems, such as zooming in and out of the worksheet, splitting the document window into panes, marking your place with electronic sticky notes, assigning English-like names to worksheet cells, and last but not least, using the Find command to hunt down specific text or values.

After learning how to stay on top of the info, you're ready to print it. You learn how to print all or just part of your worksheet, how to get the whole thing to fit on a single page, and how to print reports with headers and footers. You can print certain rows and columns with worksheet headings on each page, insert your own page breaks, and print a copy of your worksheet that shows the formulas in each cell along with the worksheet row and column frame. Whew!

Chapter 5

Keeping on Top of the Information (or How to Avoid Losing Stuff)

In This Chapter

- How to use the Zoom feature to enlarge or reduce the worksheet display
- How to split a document window into two or four panes
- How to freeze information on-screen as worksheet titles
- How to attach notes to cells
- How to assign descriptive names to cell ranges
- How to use the Find feature for locating information in the worksheet
- How to use the Replace feature to replace existing entries with new ones
- How to switch to manual recalculation to control when a worksheet is recalculated
- How to protect a worksheet from further changes

You already know that each Excel worksheet offers an awfully big place in which to store information and that each workbook you open offers you 16 of these babies. Because your computer monitor only lets you see a tiny bit of any of the worksheets in a workbook at any one time, the issue of keeping on top of information is not a small one.

Although the Excel worksheet employs a coherent cell-coordinate system you can use to get anywhere in the great big worksheet, you've got to admit that this A1, B2 stuff, although highly logical, remains fairly alien to human thinking. I mean, saying, "Go to cell IV88" just doesn't have anywhere near the same impact that saying, "Go to the corner of Hollywood and Vine" does. Consider for a moment how hard it would be to come up with a meaningful association between the 1992 depreciation schedule and its location in the cell range AC50:AN75 — do you think you could remember where to find it?

In this chapter, you learn some of the more effective techniques for keeping on top of information. First, you learn how to change the perspective on a worksheet by zooming in and out on the information, how to split the document window into separate panes, and how to keep particular rows and columns on-screen at all times.

And as if *that* weren't enough, you also learn how to add reminders to cells with notes; how to assign descriptive, Englishy names to cell ranges (like *Hollywood and Vine*); and how to use the Find and Replace commands to locate and, if necessary, replace entries anywhere in the worksheet. Finally, you learn how to control the timing of when Excel recalculates the worksheet and how to limit where changes can be made.

Zoom, Zoom, Zoom Went the Window

So what are you going to do now that the boss won't spring for that 19-inch monitor for your computer? All day long you're either straining your eyes to read all the information in those tiny cells or you're scrolling like mad trying to locate a table you can't seem to find. Never fear, the Zoom feature is here! You can use Zoom like a magnifying glass to blow up part of the worksheet or to shrink it down to size.

Figure 5-1 shows a blowup of a worksheet after increasing it to 200 percent magnification (twice normal size). To blow up a worksheet to this size, choose the pull-down menu button for the Zoom Control tool on the Standard toolbar and then drag up or click on the 200% setting. (You also can blow up a worksheet by choosing Zoom on the View menu and then selecting the 200% radio button in the Zoom dialog box — if you really want to go to all that trouble.) One thing is for sure: You don't have to scramble for your glasses to read the names in Figure 5-1's cells! The only problem with 200 percent magnification is that you can see so few cells at one time.

Figure 5-2 shows the same worksheet, this time at 25 percent magnification (roughly one-quarter normal size). To reduce the display to this magnification, choose the 25% setting in the pull-down menu box attached to the Zoom Control tool on the Standard toolbar (unless you're just dying to open the Zoom dialog box so that you can accomplish the task via its 25% radio button).

Whew! At 25 percent of normal screen size, the only thing you can be sure of is that you can't read a thing! However, notice that with this bird's-eye view, you can see at a glance how far over and down the data in this worksheet extends.

The Zoom command has five built-in, precise magnification settings (200%, 100%, 75%, 50%, and 25%). To use other percentages besides these, you can use the following options:

- If you want to use other precise percentages in between the five preset percentages (such as 150% or 85%) or use settings greater or less than the highest or lowest (such as 400% or 15%), open the Zoom dialog box by choosing View ⇨ Zoom. Then choose the Custom radio button and enter the magnification percentage in its text box before choosing OK or pressing Return.

File Edit View Insert Format Tools Data Window

200%

Geneva 12

A1 Simple Simon's Pie Shoppe (Miss Muffet St.) 1995 Sales

Muffet Sales 1995 (1)

	A	B	C	D
1	Simple Simon's Pie Shoppe (Miss Muffet St.) 1			
2		Jan	Feb	Mar
3	Humble pie	299.99	789.23	265.2
4	Blackbird pi	168.2	805.23	562.1
5	Sugar'n'spic	234.15	540	568.9
6	Jack's beans	759.25	836.23	164
7	Total	1461.59	2970.69	1561.2
8				
9				

Sheet1 Sheet2 Sheet3 Sheet4 Sheet5 Sheet6

Ready NUM

Figure 5-1: Zooming in at 200 percent magnification.

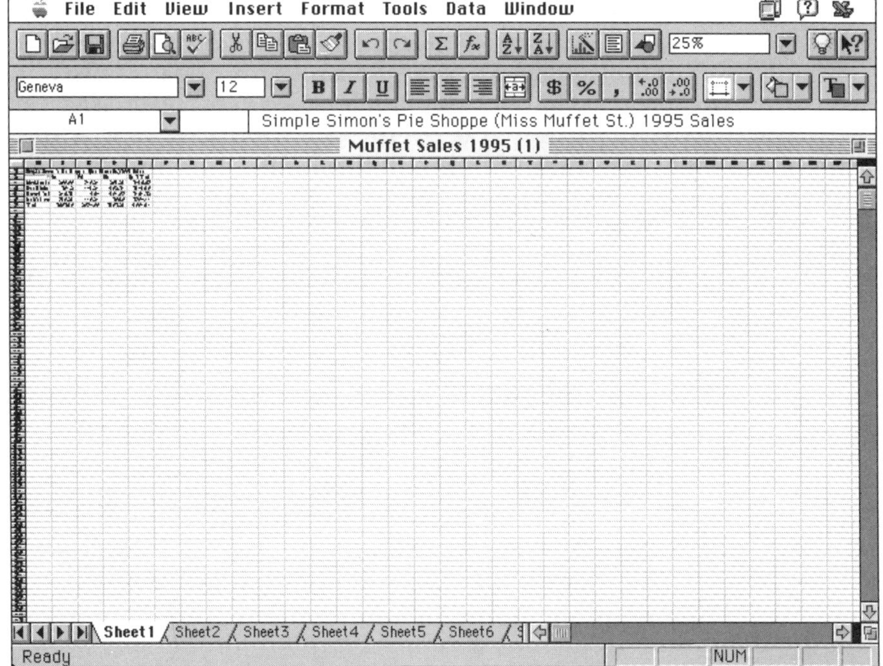

Figure 5-2: Zooming out to 25 percent magnification.

- If you don't know what percentage to enter to display a particular cell range on-screen, select the range and then choose the Selection option in the Zoom Control pull-down menu box. Or you can open the Zoom dialog box and then choose the Fit Selection radio button and choose OK or press Return. Excel figures out the percentage necessary to fill up your screen with just the selected cell range.

You can use the Zoom feature to locate and move to a new cell range in the worksheet. First, select a small magnification, such as 25%. Then locate the cell range you want to move to and select one of its cells. Finally, use the Zoom feature to return the screen magnification to 100% again. When Excel returns the display to normal size, the cell you selected and its surrounding range appear on-screen.

Tapping on My Window Panes

Although zooming in and out on the worksheet can help you get your bearings, zooming can't bring together two separate sections so that you can compare their data on-screen (at least not at a normal size where you can actually read the information). To manage this kind of trick, split the document window into separate panes and then scroll through the worksheet in each pane so that the worksheets display the parts you want to compare.

Splitting the window is easy. Figure 5-3 shows a sample income statement after splitting its worksheet window horizontally into two panes and scrolling to rows 24 through 30 in the second pane. Each pane has its own vertical scroll bar, which enables you to scroll different parts of the worksheet into view.

To split a worksheet into two horizontal panes, you can drag down the *split bar* — located right above the scroll arrow at the very top of the vertical scroll bar — until the window is divided as you want it. Use the following steps:

1. **Click on the split bar located at the top edge of the vertical scroll bar.**

   The mouse pointer changes to a double-headed arrow with a split in its middle (such as the one used to display hidden rows).

2. **Hold down the mouse button and drag downward until you reach the row at which you want the document window divided.**

   A gray dividing line appears in the workbook document window as you drag down, indicating where the document window will be split.

3. **Release the mouse button.**

   Excel divides the window into horizontal panes at the pointer's location and adds a vertical scroll bar to the new pane.

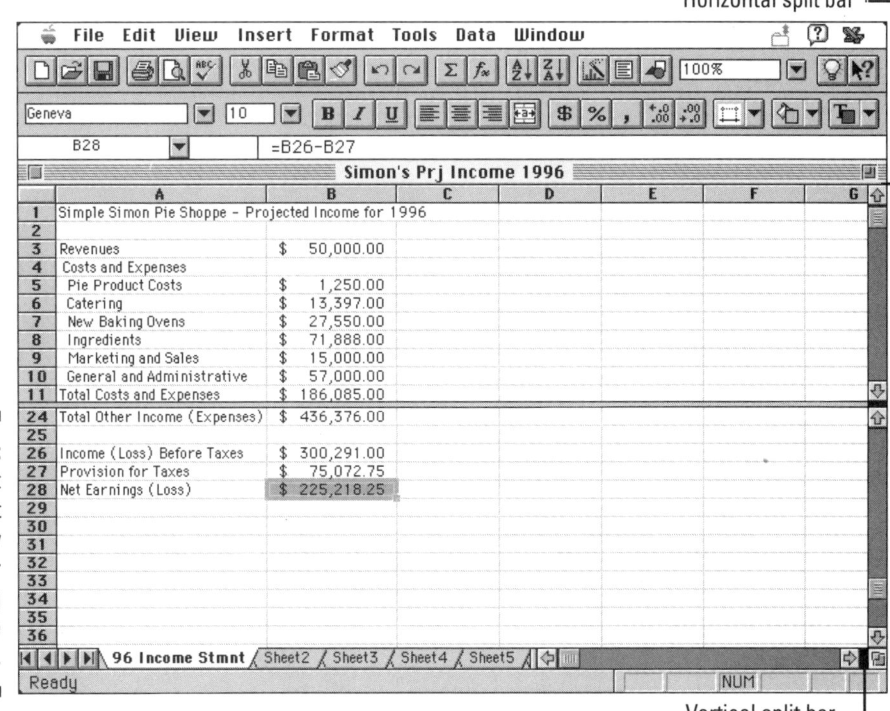

Figure 5-3: A split document window after scrolling down in the lower pane.

You can also split the document window into vertical panes. Follow these steps:

1. **Click on the split bar located at the right edge of the horizontal scroll bar.**
2. **Hold down the mouse button and drag to the left until you reach the column at which you want the document window divided.**
3. **Release the mouse button.**

   Excel splits the window at that column and adds a second horizontal scroll bar to the new pane.

You can make the panes in a document window disappear by double-clicking anywhere on the split bar that divides the window.

Instead of dragging split bars, you can divide a document window with the Split command on the Window menu. When you choose the Split command, Excel uses the position of the cell pointer to determine where to split the window into panes. The program splits the window vertically at the left edge of the pointer and horizontally along the top edge. If you want the window split into only two panes (instead of four), position the cell pointer either in the first column of the desired row (for two horizontal panes at that row) or in the first row of the desired column (for two vertical panes at that column).

When the left edge of the cell pointer is right up against the left edge of the document window (as it is when the pointer is in any cell in column A), the program doesn't split the window vertically. When the top edge of the pointer is right up against the top edge of the document window (as it is when the pointer is in row 1), the program doesn't split the window horizontally — Excel splits the window vertically along the left edge of column C when the pointer is in cell C1.

If you position the cell pointer in cell D6 and choose Split from the Window menu, the window splits into four panes: A horizontal split occurs between rows 5 and 6, and a vertical split occurs between columns C and D.

After the window is split into panes, you can move the cell pointer into a particular pane by clicking on one of its cells. To remove the panes from a window, choose Remove Split from the Window menu or double-click on the split bar that divides the windows.

Immovable Titles on My Frozen Window Panes

Window panes are great for viewing different parts of the same worksheet that normally can't be seen together. Window panes also can be used to *freeze* headings in the top rows and first columns so that the headings stay in view at all times — no matter how you scroll through the worksheet. Frozen headings are especially helpful when you work with a table that contains information extending beyond the rows and columns shown on-screen.

Figure 5-4 shows just such a table. The client list worksheet contains many more rows than you can see at one time (unless you decrease the magnification to 25% with Zoom, which makes the data too small to read). As a matter of fact, this worksheet continues down to row 34.

By splitting the document window into two horizontal panes between rows 2 and 3 and then freezing the top pane, you can keep in row 2 the column headings that identify each column of information on-screen as you scroll up and down the worksheet to review information on different employees. If you further split the window into vertical panes between columns B and C, you can keep the identification numbers and last names on-screen as you scroll left and right through the worksheet.

Figure 5-4 shows the client list after splitting the window into four panes and freezing two of them. To create and freeze these panes, follow these steps:

1. **Position the cell pointer in cell C3.**
2. **Choose Window ➪ Split.**

   Alternatively, you can create the panes by dragging to the left the vertical split bar until it is on the border between columns B and C, and dragging down the horizontal split bar until it is on the border between rows 2 and 3.

3. **Choose Window ➪ Freeze Panes.**

   Excel freezes the top and left window panes above row 3 and left of column C.

Because the upper and left panes are frozen, the program does not add a second horizontal and vertical scroll bar to the new panes. Notice that the borders of frozen panes are represented by a single line rather than a thin bar as is the case with unfrozen panes. (To help you see the frozen panes in Figures 5-4 through 5-6, I removed the worksheet gridlines. See Chapter 10 for information about how *you* can remove the gridlines from a particular worksheet in a workbook.)

File Edit View Insert Format Tools Data Window

Helvetica 10 100%

C3 Christian

Simons Client Database

	A	B	C	D	E	F	G	H	I	J	
1			Simple Simon Pie Shoppe -- Client List								
2	ID No	Last Name	First Name	Street	City	State	ZIP	Anniversary	In Years	Grs Rcpts	Cr
3	101-920	Andersen	Christian	340 The Shadow	Scholar	MN	58764	12/29/86	7.4	$12,000	Y
4	101-014	Andersen	Hans	341 The Shadow	Scholar	MN	58764	12/30/90	3.4	$21,000	N
5	103-023	Appleseed	Johnny	6789 Fruitree Tr	Along The Way	SD	66017	02/25/92	2.2	$4	Y
6	102-013	Baggins	Bingo	99 Hobbithole	Shire	ME	04047	12/21/90	3.4	$45,678	N
7	103-007	Baum	L. Frank	447 Toto Too Rd	Oz	KS	65432	06/29/88	5.9	$24,962	N
8	104-026	Brown	Charles	59 Flat Plains	Saltewater	UT	84001	07/10/92	1.9	$956	N
9	101-001	Bryant	Michael	326 Chef's Lane	Paris	TX	78705	02/02/85	9.3	$42,500	Y
10	101-028	Cassidy	Butch	Sundance Kidde	Hole In Wall	CO	80477	11/12/92	1.5	$12	N
11	102-006	Cinderella	Poore	8 Lucky Maiden Way	Oxford	TN	07557	03/20/88	6.2	$13	N
12	103-004	Cupid	Eros	97 Mount Olympus	Greece	CT	03331	11/14/90	3.5	$78,655	N
13	104-011	Dragon	Kai	2 Pleistocene Era	Ann's World	ID	00001	08/24/90	3.7	$2	N
14	104-031	Eaters	Big	444 Big Pigs Court	Dogtown	AZ	85257	09/03/96	-2.3	$66,666	Y
15	106-022	Foliage	Red	49 Maple Syrup	Waffle	VT	05452	12/19/91	2.4	$4,200	Y
16	102-020	Franklin	Ben	1789 Constitution	Jefferson	WY	20178	10/22/91	2.6	$34,400	Y
17	104-019	Fudde	Elmer	8 Warner Way	Hollywood	CA	33461	08/14/91	2.8	$2	Y
18	102-002	Gearing	Shane	1 Gunfighter's End	LaLa Land	CA	90069	03/05/85	9.2	$12,180	Y
19	102-012	Gondor	Aragorn	2956 Gandalf	Midearth	WY	80342	10/12/90	3.6	$145,000	Y
20	104-005	Gookin	Polly	4 Feathertop Hill	Hawthorne	MA	01824	07/14/87	6.8	$25	Y
21	105-008	Harvey	Chauncey	60 Lucky Starr Pl	Shetland	IL	60080	08/16/89	4.8	$1,555	N
22	106-021	Horse	Seabisquit	First Place Finish	Raceway	KY	23986	11/03/91	2.5	$195	N
23	101-015	Humperdinck	Engelbert	6 Hansel+Gretel Tr	Gingerbread	MD	20815	02/15/91	3.3	$1	Y
24	103-017	Jacken	Jill	Up the Hill	Pail of Water	OK	45678	03/02/91	3.2	$55	N
25	105-027	Laurel	Stan	2 Oliver Hardy	Celluloyde	NM	82128	09/14/92	1.7	$5	N
26	101-030	Liberty	Statuesque	31 Gotham Centre	Big Apple	NY	10011	01/04/93	1.4	$459	N

Sheet1 / Sheet2 / Sheet3 / Sheet4 / Sheet5 / Sheet6

Ready NUM

Figure 5-4: Frozen panes keep the column headings and last names on screen even while scrolling.

Figure 5-5 shows what happens when you scroll the worksheet after freezing the window panes. In this figure, I scrolled the worksheet so that rows 22 through 34 appear under rows 1 and 2. Because the vertical pane with the worksheet title and column headings is frozen, this pane remains on-screen. (Normally, of course, rows 1 and 2 would have been the first to disappear as you scrolled through the worksheet.)

Figure 5-6 shows what happens if you scroll the worksheet to the left. In this figure, I scrolled the worksheet so that columns E through K appear after columns A and B. Because the first two columns are frozen, they remain on-screen, helping you identify who belongs to what information.

To unfreeze the window panes in a worksheet, choose Window ⇨ Unfreeze Panes. If you want to remove the panes from the document window at the same time, choose Window ⇨ Remove Split instead.

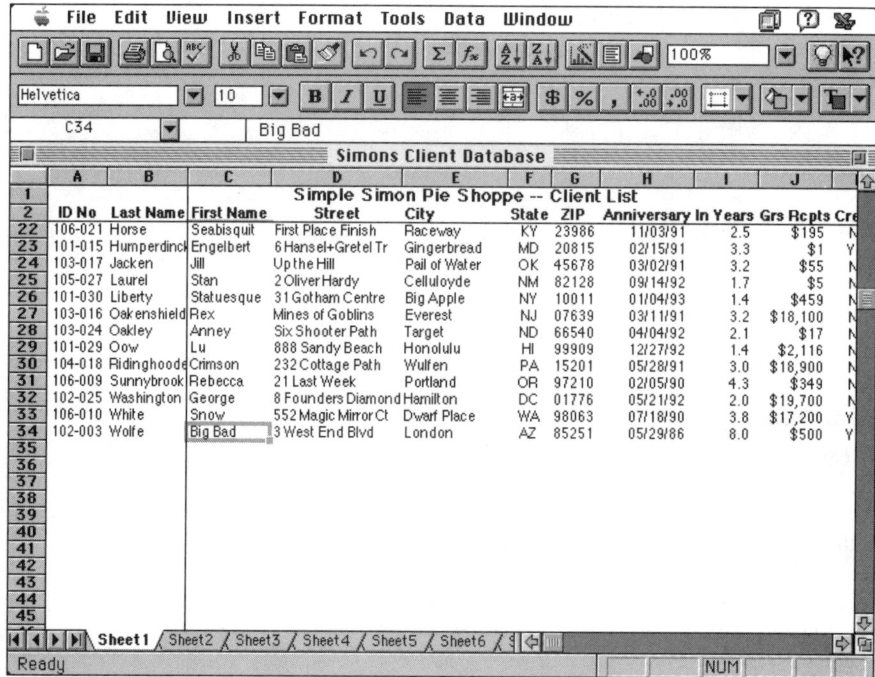

	A	B	C	D	E	F	G	H	I	J	K
1			Simple Simon Pie Shoppe -- Client List								
2	ID No	Last Name	First Name	Street	City	State	ZIP	Anniversary	In Years	Grs Rcpts	Cre
22	106-021	Horse	Seabisquit	First Place Finish	Raceway	KY	23986	11/03/91	2.5	$195	N
23	101-015	Humperdinck	Engelbert	6 Hansel+Gretel Tr	Gingerbread	MD	20815	02/15/91	3.3	$1	Y
24	103-017	Jacken	Jill	Up the Hill	Pail of Water	OK	45678	03/02/91	3.2	$55	N
25	105-027	Laurel	Stan	2 Oliver Hardy	Celluloyde	NM	82128	09/14/92	1.7	$5	N
26	101-030	Liberty	Statuesque	31 Gotham Centre	Big Apple	NY	10011	01/04/93	1.4	$459	N
27	103-016	Oakenshield	Rex	Mines of Goblins	Everest	NJ	07639	03/11/91	3.2	$18,100	N
28	103-024	Oakley	Anney	Six Shooter Path	Target	ND	66540	04/04/92	2.1	$17	N
29	101-029	Oow	Lu	888 Sandy Beach	Honolulu	HI	99909	12/27/92	1.4	$2,116	N
30	104-018	Ridinghoode	Crimson	232 Cottage Path	Wulfen	PA	15201	05/28/91	3.0	$18,900	N
31	106-009	Sunnybrook	Rebecca	21 Last Week	Portland	OR	97210	02/05/90	4.3	$349	N
32	102-025	Washington	George	8 Founders Diamond	Hamilton	DC	01776	05/21/92	2.0	$19,700	N
33	106-010	White	Snow	552 Magic Mirror Ct	Dwarf Place	WA	98063	07/18/90	3.8	$17,200	Y
34	102-003	Wolfe	Big Bad	3 West End Blvd	London	AZ	85251	05/29/86	8.0	$500	Y
35											
36											
37											
38											
39											
40											
41											
42											
43											
44											
45											

Figure 5-5: Scroll down to display the last rows of the worksheet.

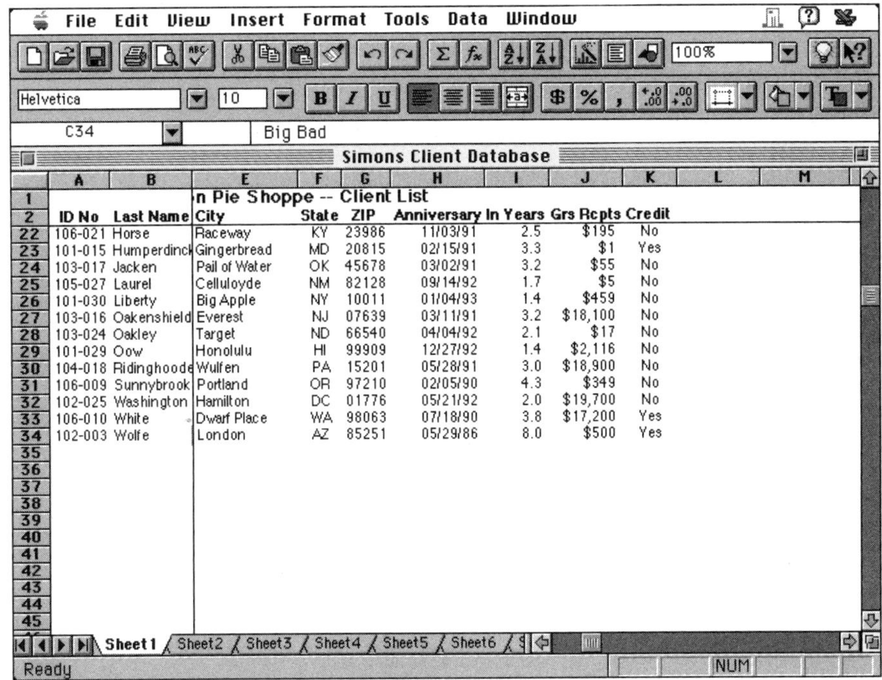

Figure 5-6: Scroll left to display the worksheet columns E through K.

Electronic Sticky Notes

Excel lets you add text notes — which kind of work like electronic sticky notes — to particular cells in a worksheet. For example, you can add a note to yourself to verify a particular figure before printing the worksheet or to remind yourself that a particular value is only an estimate (or even to remind yourself that it's your anniversary and you'd better pick up a little something special on the way home). In addition to using text notes to remind yourself of something you've done or that still remains to be done, you can use a note to mark your current place in a large worksheet. You then can use the note's location to quickly find your starting place the next time you work with that worksheet.

To add a text note to a cell, follow these steps:

1. **Select the cell to which you want to add the note.**
2. **Choose Insert ⇨ Note.**

   The Cell Note dialog box appears with the insertion point located in the Text Note list box.

3. **Type the text of your note in the Text Note list box.**

   If you want to add notes to more than one cell, click on the Add button, select the cell to which you want to add the next note, and type its text.

4. **Choose OK or press Return after you finish adding notes.**

   Excel marks the location of notes in a cell by adding a tiny square in the upper right-hand corner of the cell (this square appears in red on a color monitor).

5. **To display the note in a cell, position the cell pointer on the cell with the note indicator (the tiny dot) and press Shift+F2.**

   Alternatively, you can position the pointer in the cell with the note you want to see and then select Note on the Insert menu.

   Excel opens a Cell Note dialog box, similar to the one in Figure 5-7, where you can read the text of your note. This dialog box also shows the location of all other notes in the worksheet.

6. **To read other notes, select the note location from the Notes in Sheet list box.**

7. **After you finish looking over your notes, click on Close.**

   The Cell Note dialog box closes.

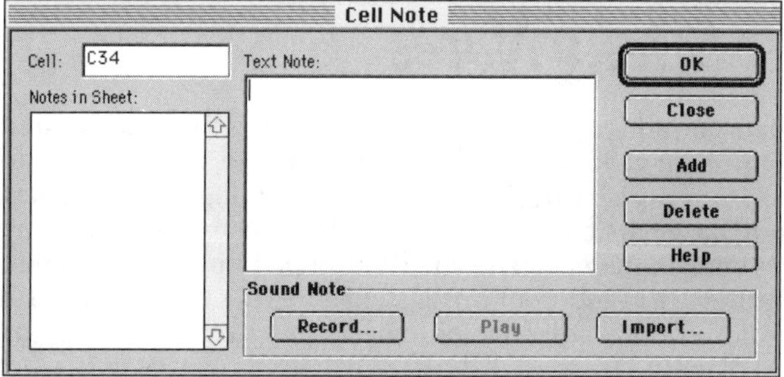

Figure 5-7: The Cell Note dialog box.

My cells are alive with the sound of music

If you have a Mac with built-in sound capabilities, you can use the microphone (if you can find it) that came with the Mac to record sound notes in cells. Just follow these steps:

1. **Open the Cell Note dialog box (Shift+F2).**
2. **Click on the Record button to open up a dialog box where you can record the note.**

3. **Click on the Record button (the large dot) in this dialog box.**
4. **Speak the text of your note into the microphone.**
5. **Click on the Stop button (the square) after you've finished recording.**
6. **Click on the Save button to close the dialog box.**
7. **Click on the Add button in the Cell Note dialog box.**

In the Notes in Sheet list box in the Cell Note dialog box, Excel indicates that you have a sound note by placing an asterisk after the cell reference. To play a sound note, double-click on the cell in the worksheet or select the sound note from the Notes in Sheet list box and then click on the Play button.

Selecting and removing cell notes

If you use a note as a placeholder and you want to go to that cell, first select all the cells in the worksheet that contain notes by choosing Go To on the Edit menu (F5) to open the Go To dialog box, selecting the Special button, and pressing Return. Press Tab to move from selected cell to selected cell.

To remove all notes from the worksheet, after selecting all the cells in the worksheet, choose Edit ⇨ Clear ⇨ Notes. To remove just the notes from a particular cell selection (as opposed to all the notes in the worksheet), select the range as you would any other range and choose Edit ⇨ Clear ⇨ Notes.

When printing a worksheet, you can print the notes alone or the notes plus selected worksheet data. See Chapter 6 for details on choosing what information to print.

Name That Cell

By assigning descriptive names to cells and cell ranges, you can go a long way toward keeping on top of the location of important information in a worksheet. Rather than trying to associate random cell coordinates with specific information, you just have to remember the name of the cell range. And best of all, after you name a cell or cell range, you can use the name with the Go To feature.

When assigning range names to a cell or cell range, you need to follow a few guidelines:

- Range names must begin with a letter of the alphabet — not a number. For example: instead of *93Profit,* use *Profit93.*

- Range names cannot contain spaces. Instead of a space, use the underscore (Shift+hyphen) to tie the parts of the name together. For example: instead of *Profit 93*, use *Profit_93*.
- Range names cannot correspond to cell coordinates in the worksheet. For example, you can't name a cell *Q1* because this is a valid cell coordinate. Instead, use something like *Q1_sales*.

To name a cell or cell range in a worksheet, follow these steps:

1. **Select the cell or cell range.**
2. **Choose Insert ➪ Name ➪ Define (or press ⌘+L).**

   Excel opens the Define Name dialog box, as shown in Figure 5-8. The references for the selected cell or cell range appear in the Refers To text box (including the worksheet name, followed by the absolute cell references of the range).
3. **Type the name for the selected cell or cell range in the Names in Workbook text box.**
4. **Click on OK or press Return.**

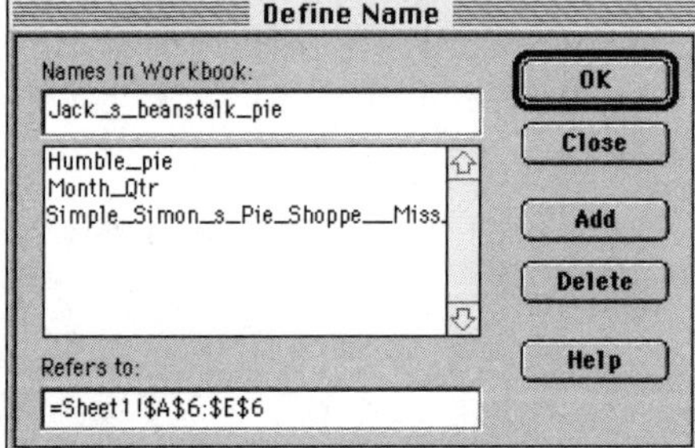

Figure 5-8: The Define Name dialog box.

If you want to define more than one range name at a time, do the following:

1. **Type the name for the first range that's already selected in the worksheet.**
2. **Click on the Add button.**

   Excel adds that name to the Names in Workbook list box.
3. **Replace the current range name in the Name text box with the name of the next range.**
4. **Press Tab until the Refers To text box is selected and you see a marquee around the currently selected range.**

You may have to drag the Define Name dialog box out of the way to see the marquee and to select the cell range to which the new name refers, as indicated in the next step.

5. **Select the cell or cell range in the worksheet to which this new range name applies.**

6. **Click on the Add button.**

7. **After you finish naming cells and cell ranges in this manner, click on the Close button.**

To select a named cell or range in a worksheet, press F5 or choose Go To on the Edit menu. The Go To dialog box appears, as you see in Figure 5-9. Double-click on the desired range name in the Go To list box. (Alternatively, select the name and click OK or press Return.) Excel moves the cell pointer directly to the named cell. If you selected a cell range, the program selects all the cells in that range.

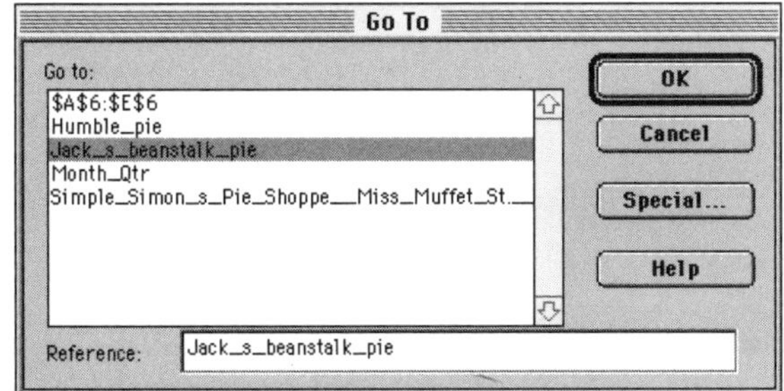

Figure 5-9: The Go To dialog box.

Finders Keepers

When all else fails, you can use Excel's Find feature to locate specific information in the worksheet. After you choose Find on the Edit pull-down menu or press ⌘+F or Shift+F5, Excel opens the Find dialog box, as shown in Figure 5-10. In the Find What text box, enter the text or values you want to locate and then choose Find Next or press Return to start the search.

When you search for a text entry with the Find feature, be mindful of whether the text or number you enter in the Find What text box is separate in its cell or occurs as part of another word or value. For example, Figure 5-10 shows the characters `id` in the Find What text box. Because the Find Entire Cells Only check box is not selected, Excel finds the field name `ID No` in cell A2, the state code `ID` (for Idaho) in cell F13, as well as the `id` that occurs in `Midearth` in cell E19. If you checked the Find Entire Cells Only check box in the Find dialog box before starting the search, Excel would consider neither the ID in ID No nor the id in Midearth to be a match.

When you search for text, you also can specify whether you want Excel to match the case you use when entering the search text in the Find What text box. By default, Excel ignores case differences between text in cells of your worksheet and the search text you enter in the Find What text box. To conduct a case-sensitive search, you need to select the Match Case check box to put an X in it.

When you search for values in the worksheet, be mindful of the difference between formulas and values. For example, Figure 5-10 shows the value 10.2 in cell I11 of the employee roster. However, if you enter **10.2** in the Find What dialog box and press Return to start the search, Excel displays an alert box with the following message:

```
Cannot find matching data
```

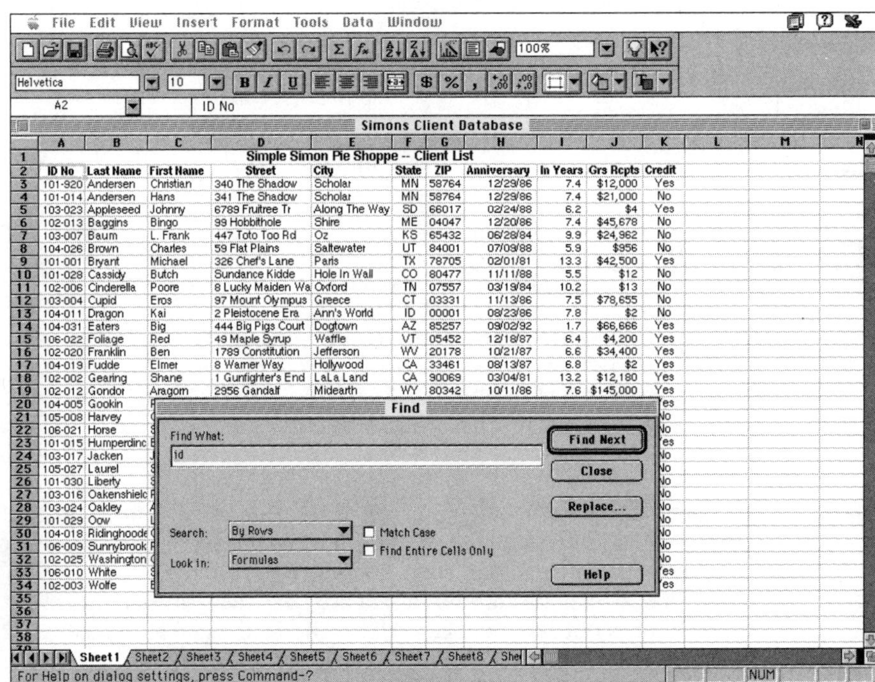

Figure 5-10: The Find dialog box.

Excel does not find the value 10.2 in cell I11 because this value is calculated by the following formula and Excel normally searches the formulas (not the values returned by the formulas):

=(NOW()-H3)/365

To search for the 10.2 value calculated by the formula in I11, you need to select Values in the Look In pull-down menu box (in the Find dialog box) rather than the normally used Formulas option. If you are looking for text or values entered in notes added to the worksheet cells, you need to select the Notes option in the Look In pop-up menu box to have Excel search there.

If you don't know the exact spelling of the word or name or the precise value or formula you're searching for, you can use *wildcards*. Use the question mark (?) to stand for a single unknown character or the asterisk (*) for any number of missing characters.

Suppose that you enter the following in the Find What text box and choose the Values option in the Look In pull-down menu box:

```
7*4
```

Excel stops at cells that contain the values 74,704 and 75,234, and even finds the text entry *782 4th Street*.

If you actually want to search for an asterisk in the worksheet, precede it with a ~ (tilde), as follows:

```
~*4
```

This arrangement enables you to search the formulas in the worksheet for one that multiplies by the number 4 (remember, Excel uses the asterisk as the times sign).

```
J?n*
```

This entry in the Find What text box finds cells that contain *Jan, January, June, Janet*, and so on.

Normally, Excel searches only the current worksheet for the search text you enter. If you want the program to search all the worksheets in the workbook, you must select all the worksheets prior to entering the search text in the Find dialog box and starting the search. To select all the worksheets in a workbook, click on one of the tabs at the bottom of the document window while holding down ⌘+Option or the Control key, and choose the Select All Sheets command on the shortcut menu that appears. See Chapter 9 for more information on working with more than one worksheet in a workbook.

When Excel locates a cell in the worksheet that contains the text or values you're searching for, it selects that cell while leaving the Find dialog box open at the same time (remember, you can move the Find dialog box if it obscures your view of the cell). To search for the next occurrence of the text or value, choose Find Next or simply press Return.

Excel normally searches down the worksheet by rows. To search across the columns first, choose the By Columns option in the Search pop-up menu box. To reverse the search direction and revisit previous occurrences of matching cell entries, press Shift as you click on the Find Next button in the Find dialog box.

Replacement Costs

If your purpose for finding a cell with a particular entry is to change its content, you can automate this process by choosing Replace instead of Find from the Edit menu or by pressing ⌘+H. After entering the text or value you want to find in the Find What text box, enter the text or value you want as the replacement in the Replace With text box.

When you enter replacement text, enter it *exactly* as you want it to appear in the cell. In other words, if you replace all occurrences of *Jan* in the worksheet with *January*, enter the following in the Replace With text box:

```
January
```

Make sure that you use the capital *J* in the Replace With text box, even though you can enter the following in the Find What text box (provided you don't check the Match Case check box):

```
jan
```

After specifying what to find and what to replace it with, you can have Excel replace occurrences in the worksheet on a case-by-case basis or globally. To replace all occurrences in a single operation, click on the Replace All button.

Be careful with global search-and-replace operations; they can really mess up a worksheet in a hurry if you inadvertently replace values, parts of formulas, or characters in titles and headings that you hadn't intended to change. As a precaution:

1. **Never undertake a global search-and-replace operation on an unsaved worksheet.**
2. **Verify that the Find Entire Cells Only check box is selected before you begin.**

You can end up with a mess of unwanted replacements if you leave this check box unselected when you *really* only want to replace entire cell entries rather than matching parts in cell entries. If you do make a mess, choose the Undo Replace command on the Edit menu (⌘+Z) to restore the worksheet. If you don't discover the problem in time to use Undo, close the messed-up worksheet without saving the changes and open the unreplaced version you saved.

To see each occurrence before you replace it, choose the Find Next button or press Return. Excel selects the next cell with the text or value you entered in the Find What text box. To have the program replace it, click on Replace. To skip this occurrence, click on the Find Next button to continue the search. When you finish replacing occurrences, click on Close to close the Replace dialog box.

To Calc or Not to Calc

Locating information in a worksheet, although extremely important, is only part of the story of keeping on top of the information in a worksheet. In large workbooks that contain many completed worksheets, you may want to switch to manual recalculation so that you can control when the formulas in the worksheet are calculated. You need this kind of control when you find that Excel's recalculation of formulas each time you enter or change information in cells has slowed down the program's response to a *crawl*. By holding off recalculations until you are ready to save or print the workbook, you can work with its worksheets without interminable delays. However, if you recently laid your hands on some additional system memory (RAM), you may want to boost Excel's memory. (Refer to Figure 2-1 in Chapter 2, "Concocting Your First Workbook.")

To put the workbook on manual recalculation, choose Tools ⇨ Options ⇨ Calculation tab. Then select the Manual radio button in the Calculation area. Don't remove the `X` from the Recalculate before Save check box so that Excel still automatically recalculates all formulas before saving the workbook. By keeping this setting active, you are assured of saving only the most up-to-date values.

After switching to manual recalculation, Excel displays the message `Calculate` on the status bar whenever you make a change to the worksheet that somehow affects the current values of its formulas. Whenever you see `Calculate` on the status bar, it means that you need to bring the formulas up-to-date before saving the workbook (as you would do before printing its worksheets).

To recalculate the formulas in a workbook when calculation is on manual, press ⌘+= or click on the Calc Now (⌘+=) button in the Calculation tab of the Options dialog box. You also can press F9.

Excel then recalculates the formulas in all the worksheets in your workbook. If you've only made changes to the current worksheet and don't want to wait around for Excel to recalculate every other worksheet in the workbook, you can restrict the recalculation to the current worksheet by clicking on the Calc Sheet button on the Calculation tab of the Options dialog box or by pressing Shift+F9.

Protect Yourself!

After you've more or less finalized a worksheet by checking out its formulas and proofing its text, you may want to guard against any unplanned changes by protecting the document.

Each cell in the worksheet can be locked or unlocked. By default, Excel locks all the cells in a worksheet after you choose Tools ⇨ Protection ⇨ Protect Sheet and then choose OK or press Return in the Protect Sheet dialog box. If you want to lock all the cells in the workbook, choose Protect Workbook on the Protection cascading menu and then choose OK or press Return in the Protect Workbook dialog box.

Selecting the Protect Sheet command makes it impossible to make further changes to the contents of any of the locked cells in that worksheet. Selecting the Protect Workbook command makes it impossible to make further changes to the contents of any locked cells in any worksheet in that workbook. However, because Excel automatically assigns a locked status to every single cell in every worksheet (or workbook), selecting Protect Sheet (or Protect Workbook) is tantamount to protecting every single solitary cell in the whole darned worksheet (or workbook).

If you try to edit or replace an entry in a locked cell, Excel displays an alert dialog box with the following message:

```
Locked cells cannot be changed
```

Usually, your intention in protecting a worksheet or an entire workbook is not to prevent *all* changes but to prevent changes in certain areas of the worksheet. For example, in a budget worksheet, you may want to protect all the cells that contain headings and formulas but allow changes in all the cells where you enter the budgeted amounts. By setting up the worksheet in this way, you cannot inadvertently wipe out a title or formula in the worksheet simply by entering a value in the wrong column or row (not an uncommon occurrence).

To leave certain cells unlocked so that you can still change them after protecting the worksheet or workbook, follow these steps before you choose the Protect Sheet or the Protect Workbook command:

1. **Select the cells you want to be able to change after turning on the worksheet or workbook protection.**
2. **Open the Format Cells dialog box by choosing Format ⇨ Cells (or by pressing ⌘+1) and then choose the Protection tab.**
3. **Remove the X from the Locked check box in the Protection tab and then choose OK or press Return.**
4. **Turn on protection in the worksheet or workbook by choosing Tools ⇨ Protection and then selecting either Protect Sheet or Protect Workbook on the cascading menu.**
5. **Choose OK or press Return.**

To remove protection from the current worksheet or workbook document so that you can once again make changes to its cells, be they locked or unlocked, choose Tools ⇨ Protection and then select either Unprotect Sheet or Unprotect Workbook on the cascading menu.

To make it impossible to remove protection from a document unless you know the password, you can enter a password in the Password (optional) text box of the Protect Sheet or Protect Workbook dialog box. Excel masks each character in the password with a tiny asterisk as you enter it. After you choose OK, Excel makes you reenter the password before protecting the worksheet or workbook. From then on, you can remove protection from a worksheet or workbook *only* if you can reproduce the password *exactly* as you assigned it — including any case differences! ***Be very careful with passwords.*** If you forget the password, you cannot ever again change any locked cells, and you cannot unlock any more cells in the worksheet.

Chapter 6

Getting the Information Down on Paper (or Spreadsheet Printing 101)

In This Chapter

- How to use the Print Preview feature to see how a report will appear when printed
- How to use the Print tool to print the current worksheet
- How to print all the worksheets in a workbook
- How to print only a particular section of the worksheet
- How to fit an entire report on a single page
- How to change the orientation of the printing of a report
- How to change the margins for a report
- How to add a header and footer to a report
- How to print column and row headings on every page of a report
- How to insert page breaks in a report
- How to print the formulas in a worksheet

Getting it all down on paper — when all is said and done, this is really what it's about. All the data entry, all the formatting, all the formula checking, all the things you do to get a worksheet ready you do in preparation for printing its information. In this chapter, you learn how easy it is to print reports with Excel. And you find that by just following a few simple guidelines, you can produce top-notch reports the first time you send the document to the printer (instead of the second, or even the third, time around).

The only trick to printing a worksheet is becoming accustomed to the *paging* scheme and learning how to control it. Many of the worksheets you create with Excel are not only longer than one printed page but are also wider. Unlike word processors — like Word 6.0 — which only page the document vertically (because you can't create a document wider than the page size you're using), spreadsheet programs like Excel often have to break up pages both vertically and horizontally to print a worksheet document.

When paging a worksheet, Excel first pages the document vertically down the rows in the first columns of the print area (just like a word processor). After paging the first columns, the program pages down the rows of the second set of columns in the print area. Excel pages down and then over until all the document in the print area (which can include the entire worksheet or just sections of the worksheet) is paged.

Keep in mind that, when paging the worksheet, Excel does not break up the information within a row or column. If all the information in a row won't fit at the bottom of the page, the program moves the entire row to the following page. Similarly, if all the information in a column won't fit at the right edge of the page, Excel moves the entire column to a new page. (Because Excel pages down and then over, chances are that the column will not appear on the next page of the report.)

There are several ways to deal with such paging problems — and you're going to learn them all! After you have these page problems under control, printing is the proverbial piece of cake.

Look before You Print!

Do the world a favor and save a forest or two by using the Print Preview feature before you print any worksheet, section of worksheet, or entire workbook. Because of the peculiarities in paging worksheet data, check the page breaks for any report that requires more than one page. Print Preview mode not only shows you exactly how the worksheet data will be paged when printed, but also enables you to modify the margins, change the page settings, and even go ahead and print the report when everything looks okay.

To switch to Print Preview mode, click on the Print Preview tool on the Standard toolbar (the Print Preview tool is the one with the magnifying glass on the page right next to the Print button) or choose the Print Preview command from the File menu. Excel displays in a separate window all the information on the first page of the report. Figure 6-1 shows the Print Preview window with the first page of a three-page sample report.

When Excel displays a full page in the Print Preview window, you can barely read its contents. Increase the view to actual size if you need to verify some of the information. You can zoom up to 100 percent by clicking on the Zoom button at the top of the window. Alternatively, click on the part of the page you want to see in full size (note that the mouse pointer assumes the shape of a magnifying glass). Figure 6-2 shows the first page of the three-page report after you click on the upper left-hand portion of the page.

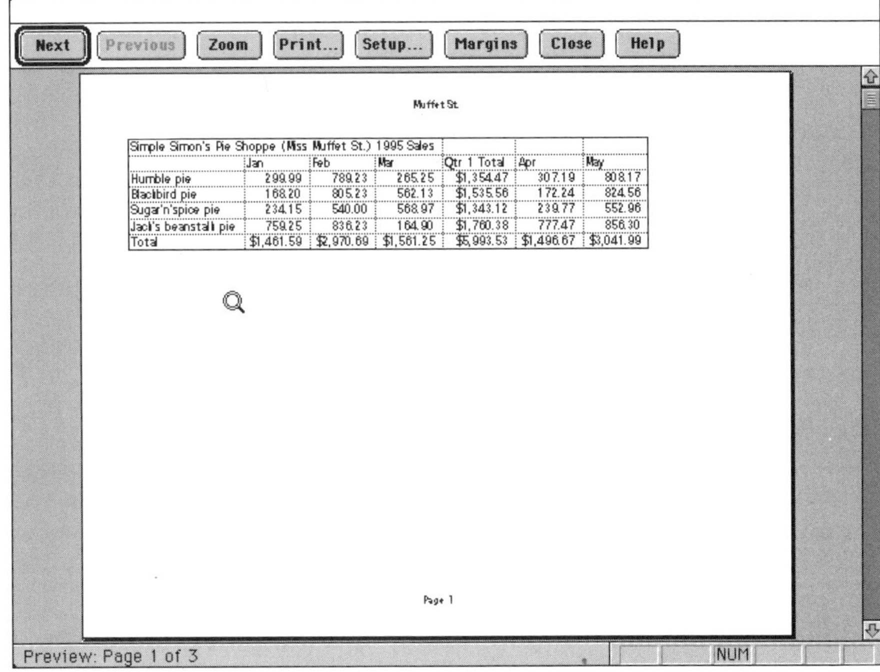

Figure 6-1: The first page of a three-page report in Print Preview mode.

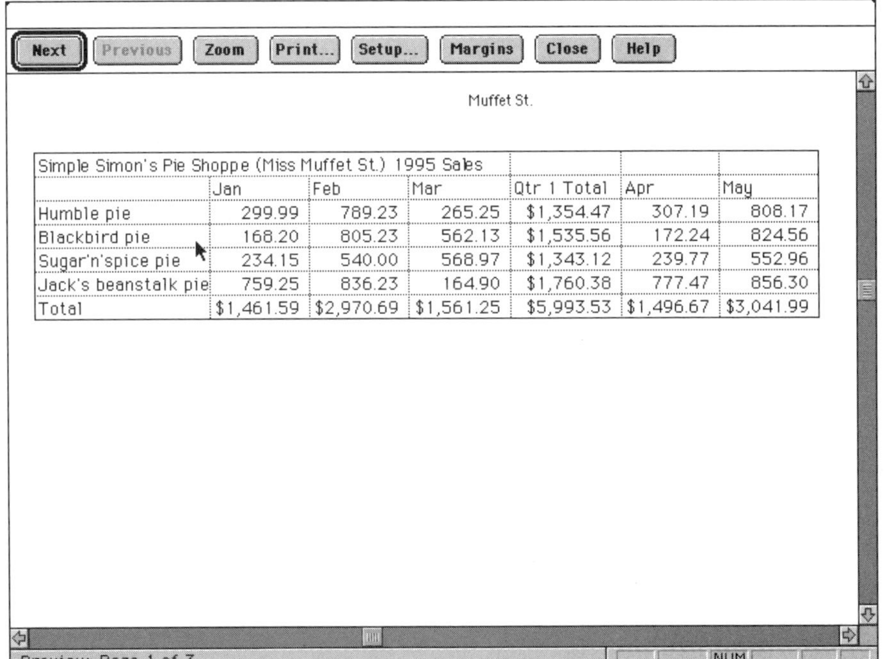

Simple Simon's Pie Shoppe (Miss Muffet St.) 1995 Sales						
	Jan	Feb	Mar	Qtr 1 Total	Apr	May
Humble pie	299.99	789.23	265.25	$1,354.47	307.19	808.17
Blackbird pie	168.20	805.23	562.13	$1,535.56	172.24	824.56
Sugar'n'spice pie	234.15	540.00	568.97	$1,343.12	239.77	552.96
Jack's beanstalk pie	759.25	836.23	164.90	$1,760.38	777.47	856.30
Total	$1,461.59	$2,970.69	$1,561.25	$5,993.53	$1,496.67	$3,041.99

Figure 6-2: The report after zooming in on the upper left-hand part of the page.

After a page is enlarged to actual size, use the scroll bars to bring new parts of the page into view in the Print Preview window. If you prefer to use the keyboard, press the ↑ and ↓ keys or Page Up and Page Down to scroll up or down the page. Press ← and → or Home and End to scroll left and right. ⌘+Page Up and ⌘+Page Down will also scroll left and right; however, using the arrow keys is much less confusing. ⌘+Home and ⌘+End will jump to the top left-hand corner of the page and the lower right-hand corner of the page. Please remember that these navigation keys work in the Zoom mode of Print Preview. Some of these same keys work to send you to different pages of the worksheet in full-page view.

To return to the full-page view, click the mouse pointer (in its arrowhead form) anywhere on the page or click on the Zoom button at the top of the window. On the status bar of the Print Preview window, Excel indicates the number of pages in a report. If your report has more than one page, you can view pages that follow the one you are currently previewing by clicking on the Next command button at the top of the window. To review a page you've already seen, back up a page by clicking on the Previous button. You also can advance to the next page by pressing the Page Down or ↓ key. Move to the previous page by pressing the Page Up or ↑ key when the page view is full-page rather than actual size.

When you finish previewing the report, you have the following options:

- If the pages look okay, you can click on the Print button to display the Print dialog box and start printing the report from there.
- If you notice some paging problems you can solve by choosing a new paper size, page order, orientation, or margins, or if you notice a problem with the header or footer in the top or bottom margin of the pages, you can click on the Setup button and take care of these problems in the Page Setup dialog box.
- If you notice some problems with the margins or the column widths and you want to adjust them in Print Preview mode, you can click on the Margins button and drag the margin markers into place (see "Marginal thinking," later in this chapter, for details).
- If you notice any other kind of problem, such as a typo in a heading or a wrong value in a cell, click on the Close button and return to the normal worksheet document window — you cannot make any kind of editing changes in the Print Preview window.

After you make corrections to the worksheet, you can print the report from the normal document window by choosing Print from the File menu. Alternatively, you can switch back to Print Preview mode to make a last-minute check and click on the Print button, or use the Print button (fourth from left, with the picture of the printer) on the Standard toolbar.

The page breaks automatically

Excel automatically displays the page breaks in the normal document window after you preview the document. Page breaks appear on-screen as dotted lines between columns and rows that will appear on different pages.

To get rid of page breaks in the document window, choose Options on the Tools menu and then choose the View tab and clear the `X` from the Automatic Page Breaks check box. Finally, choose OK or press Return.

Printing in a nutshell

As long as you want to use Excel's default print settings to print all the cells in the current worksheet, printing in Excel is uncomplicated: Click on the Print tool on the Standard toolbar (the fourth tool from the left), and the program prints one copy of all the information in the current worksheet, including any charts and graphics — but excluding notes you added to cells. (See Chapter 7 for details about charts and graphics.)

After you click on the Print tool, Excel routes the print job to the Mac Print Monitor, the middleman responsible for sending the job to the printer. While Excel is sending the print job to the Print Monitor, the Print Monitor displays a Printing dialog box to keep you informed of its progress. This dialog box displays a message like `Printing Page 2 of 3`. If your printer driver supports background printing and you have selected it, then the Print Monitor dialog box hides on the Application menu at the top right-hand of the screen. After this dialog box disappears, you are free to go back to work in Excel — be aware, however, that Excel may move like a slug until the job is actually printed. To abort the print job while it's being sent to the Print Monitor, click on the Cancel button in the Printing dialog box.

In Figure 6-3 you see the Chooser, which allows you to choose between different printer drivers if you have more than one, or you can select or deselect background printing. The Chooser is located on the rainbow-colored Apple menu.

If you want to cancel the print job but you don't get it done before Excel ships the entire job to the Print Monitor (that is, the Printing dialog box disappears before you've had a chance to cancel the print job), you must leave Excel, activate the Print Monitor window, and cancel printing from there. To cancel a print job from the Print Monitor, follow these steps:

1. **Click on the Excel Icon in the Application menu and select the Print Monitor.**

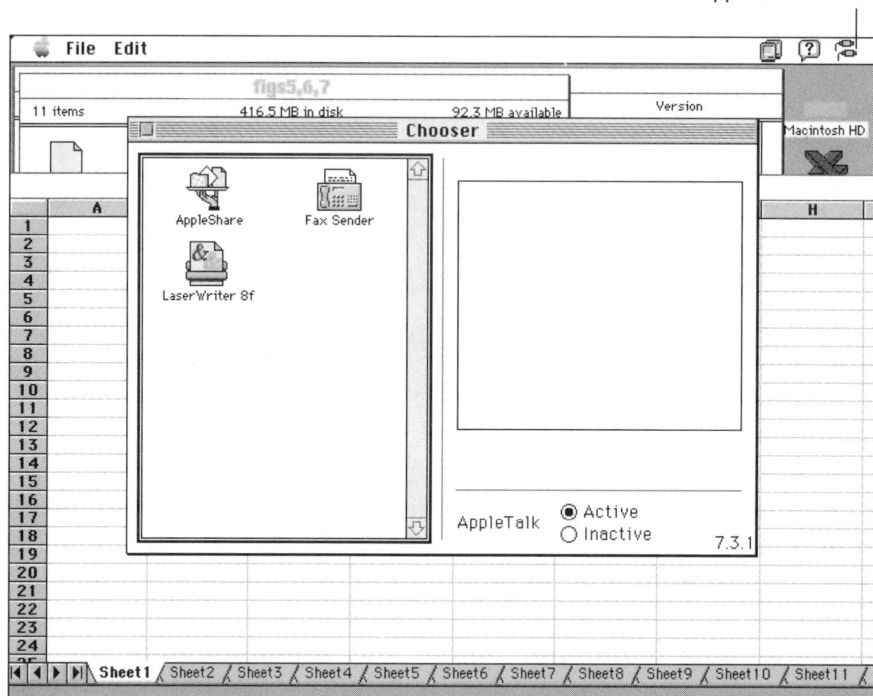

Figure 6-3: The Chooser dialog box.

2. **In the Print Monitor dialog box, select the print job you want to delete (see Figure 6-4).**
3. **Click on the Cancel Printing button.**

   After you confirm that you want to delete the job, you can return to Excel by clicking somewhere on the Excel window (it should still be visible in the background).

Variations on a print theme

Printing with the Print tool on the Standard toolbar is fine, provided that all you want is a single copy of all the information in the current worksheet. If you want more copies or more or less data (such as all the worksheets in the workbook or just a cell selection within a particular worksheet), or if you need to change some of the page settings (like the size of the page or the orientation of the printing on the page), you need to print from the Print dialog box, shown in Figure 6-5.

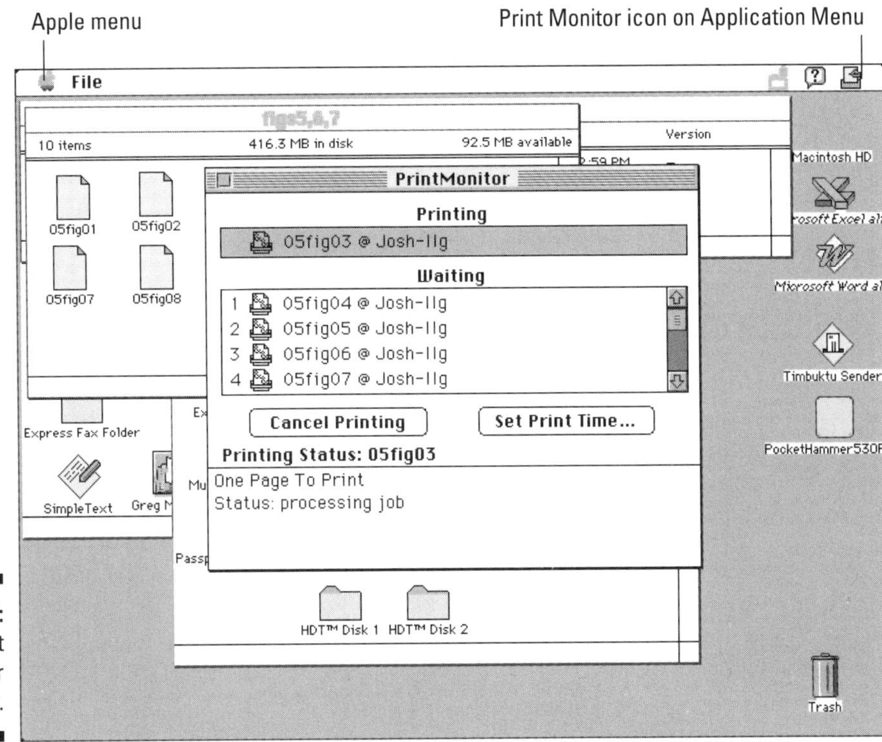

Figure 6-4: The Print Monitor dialog box.

Printer: "Josh-IIg" 8.1.2
Print
Copies: 1 Pages: ◉ All ○ From: To:
Cancel
Paper Source
◉ All ○ First from: Cassette
Remaining from: Cassette
Destination
◉ Printer
○ File
Options
Help
Print
○ Selection
◉ Selected Sheets
○ Entire Workbook
Print Preview...
Help

Figure 6-5: The Print dialog box.

Excel provides a number of ways to open the Print dialog box:

- Press ⌘+P.
- Choose the Print command from the File menu.
- Press ⌘+Shift+F12.

The keystroke you use to cancel a print job being sent to the Print Monitor is ⌘+. (yes, that's a period).

Printing just the good parts

After you open the Print dialog box, you can select how much of the information is to be printed. You can also change the number of copies printed, using one of the following:

- *Selection.* Choose this radio button if you want Excel to print just the cells that are currently selected in your workbook — you must remember, though, to select them before opening the Print dialog box and choosing this radio button!
- *Selected Sheet(s).* Excel automatically chooses this radio button and prints all of the information in whatever worksheets are selected in your workbook. Normally, this option prints only the data in the current worksheet. To print other worksheets in the workbook when this radio button is chosen, cancel from the Print dialog box and hold down the ⌘ key as you click on the sheet's tab. To include all the sheets between two sheet tabs, click on the first tab, and then hold down Shift as you click on the second tab. Excel selects all the tabs in between. Then you must bring back the print dialog box by pressing ⌘+P.
- *Entire Workbook.* Choose this radio button if you want Excel to print all the data in each of the worksheets in your workbook.
- *Copies.* To print more than one copy, enter the number of copies you want to print in the Copies text box, or use ↑ and ↓ to select the required number (Excel collates each copy of the report for you).
- *All.* Normally, Excel prints all the pages required to produce the information in the areas of the workbook that you want printed. Sometimes, however, you may only need to reprint a page or a range of pages that you modified within a particular section. To reprint a single page, enter its page number in both the From and To text boxes. To reprint a range of pages, put the first page number in the From text box and the last page number in the To text box.

After you finish choosing new print options, you can send the job to the printer by choosing Print or pressing Return. To preview the document with your setting changes before you print, choose the Print Preview button. To change some of the page settings (as explained in the following section "In Pursuit of the Perfect Page"), select the Setup tab after selecting the Print Preview button.

In Pursuit of the Perfect Page

As I said at the beginning of this chapter, about the only thing that is the slightest bit complex in printing a worksheet is figuring out how to get the pages right. Fortunately, the options in the Page Setup dialog box give you a great deal of control over what goes on which page. You can open the Page Setup dialog box in one of the following ways: You can choose Page Setup from the File menu, you can click on the Page Setup button if the Print dialog box is open, or you can click on the Setup button if the Print Preview window is open. The Page Setup dialog box contains four tabs: Page, Margins, Header/Footer, and Sheet.

The particular options offered in the Page tab of the Page Setup dialog box may vary slightly with the type of printer you use. Figure 6-6 shows the Page Setup dialog box when the Apple LaserWriter is the current printer (all the options you see here are also present when using other laser printers, such as the Hewlett-Packard LaserJet printer).

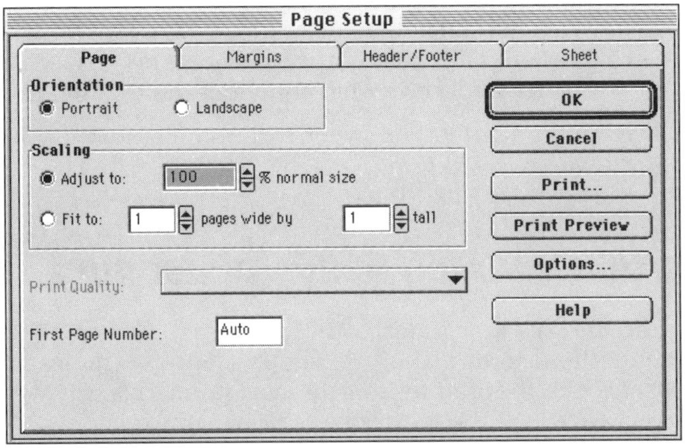

Figure 6-6: The Page Setup dialog box.

The Print dialog box in Excel for the Macintosh doesn't contain a Page Setup button. To open the Page Setup dialog box, choose Page Setup from the File pull-down menu or click on the Setup button in the Print Preview window.

For most types of printers, the Page tab of the Page Setup dialog box includes options for changing the orientation, scaling the printing, and choosing a new paper size:

- *Orientation.* Portrait positions the printing with the short side of the paper horizontal. Landscape positions the printing with the long side of the paper horizontal (see the following section, "Orienting yourself to the landscape").
- *Adjust to.* This option lets you increase or decrease the size of the printing by a set percentage (much like using the Zoom feature to zoom in and out on worksheet data on-screen). When entering values in the Adjust to text box, keep in mind that 100% represents normal size and that any percentage below that reduces the size of the printing, resulting in more on each page. Any percentage above 100% increases the size of the printing, resulting in less on each page.
- *Fit to.* This option lets you fit all the printing on a single page (by default) or on a set number of pages wide by a set number of pages tall (see "Squeezing it all on one page" later in this chapter).
- *Print Quality.* On some printers (like dot-matrix printers), you can change the quality of the printing, depending on whether you're producing a first rough draft or a final printout.
- *First Page Number.* This option lets you change the starting page number when you want the first number to be higher than 1. Use this numbering option only when you're printing page numbers in the header or footer (see " My header don't know what my footer's doing" later in this chapter).
- *Options.* This option lets you switch to the options for the Macintosh printer driver.

Orienting yourself to the landscape

For many printers (including most of the dot-matrix, laser, or inkjet persuasions), the Page tab of the Page Setup dialog box includes an Orientation option for changing the printing from the more normal *portrait* (where the printing runs parallel to the short edge of the paper) to *landscape* (where the printing runs parallel to the long edge of the paper). With these types of printers, you can usually use the Adjust To or Fit To options to scale the size of the printing (see the following section, "Squeezing it all on one page"). By scaling the size of the printing, you can enlarge or reduce the printing by a particular percentage or force all the information onto a single page or a set number of pages.

Many worksheets are far wider than they are tall — consider budgets or sales tables that track expenditures over 12 months. If your printer enables you to change the orientation of the page, you may find that such worksheets page better if you switch the orientation from portrait mode to landscape mode.

Figure 6-7 shows the Print Preview window with the first page of a report in landscape mode. By using landscape mode rather than portrait mode for this report, Excel fits two more columns of information on this page. In addition, in landscape mode, the total page count for a report can be reduced.

Squeezing it all on one page

If your printer supports the scaling options, you're in luck. You can always get a worksheet to fit on a single page simply by clicking on the Fit To radio button. When you click on this radio button, Excel figures out how much to reduce the size of the information you're printing to get it all on one page.

If you preview this one page and find that the printing is just too small to read comfortably, reopen the Page tab of the Page Setup dialog box and try changing the number of pages in the Page(s) Wide By and Page(s) Tall text boxes, located to the immediate right of the Fit To radio button (again see Figure 6-6). Instead of trying to stuff everything on one page, for example, check out how your information looks when you fit the worksheet on two pages across: Enter **2** in the Page(s) Wide By text box and leave 1 the in the Page(s) Tall text box. Alternatively, see how the worksheet looks when you fit it on two pages down: Leave the 1 in the Page(s) Wide By text box and enter **2** in the Page(s) Tall text box.

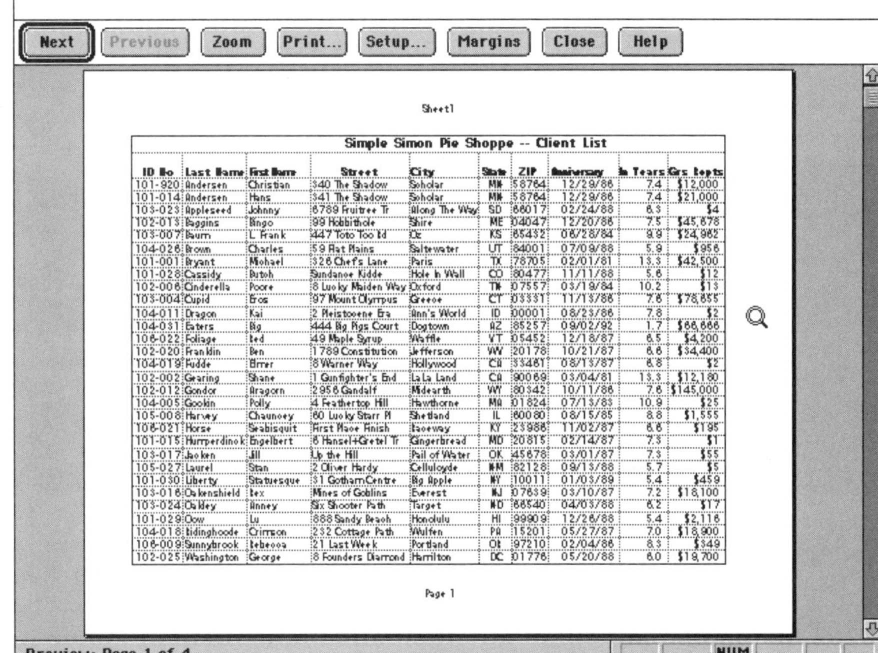

Simple Simon Pie Shoppe -- Client List

ID No	Last Name	First Name	Street	City	State	ZIP	Anniversary	In Years	Grs Rcpts
101-920	Andersen	Christian	340 The Shadow	Scholar	MN	58764	12/29/88	7.4	$12,000
101-014	Andersen	Hans	341 The Shadow	Scholar	MN	58764	12/29/88	7.4	$21,000
103-023	Appleseed	Johnny	6789 Fruitree Tr	Along The Way	SD	66017	02/24/88	6.3	$4
102-013	Baggins	Bingo	99 Hobbithole	Shire	ME	04047	12/20/88	7.5	$45,678
103-007	Baum	L. Frank	447 Toto Too Rd	Oz	KS	65432	06/28/84	9.9	$24,962
104-026	Brown	Charles	59 Flat Plains	Saltewater	UT	84001	07/09/88	5.9	$956
101-001	Bryant	Michael	326 Chef's Lane	Paris	TX	78705	02/01/81	13.3	$42,500
101-028	Cassidy	Butch	Sundance Kidde	Hole In Wall	CO	80477	11/11/88	5.6	$12
102-006	Cinderella	Poore	8 Lucky Maiden Way	Oxford	TN	07557	03/19/84	10.2	$13
103-004	Cupid	Eros	97 Mount Olympus	Greece	CT	03331	11/13/88	7.6	$78,655
104-011	Dragon	Kai	2 Pleistocene Era	Ann's World	ID	00001	08/23/88	7.8	$2
104-031	Eaters	Big	444 Big Pigs Court	Dogtown	AZ	85257	09/02/92	1.7	$66,666
106-022	Foliage	Red	49 Maple Syrup	Waffle	VT	05452	12/18/87	6.5	$4,200
102-020	Franklin	Ben	1789 Constitution	Jefferson	WV	20178	10/21/87	6.6	$34,400
104-019	Fudde	Elmer	8 Warner Way	Hollywood	CA	33461	08/13/87	6.8	$2
102-002	Gearing	Shane	1 Gunfighter's End	LaLa Land	CA	90069	03/04/81	13.3	$12,180
102-012	Gondor	Aragorn	2956 Gandalf	Midearth	WY	80342	10/11/88	7.6	$145,000
104-005	Gookin	Polly	4 Feathertop Hill	Hawthorne	MA	01824	07/13/83	10.9	$25
105-008	Harvey	Chauncey	60 Lucky Starr Pl	Shetland	IL	60080	08/15/85	8.8	$1,555
106-021	Horse	Seabisquit	First Place Finish	Raceway	KY	23986	11/02/87	6.6	$195
101-015	Humperdinck	Engelbert	6 Hansel+Gretel Tr	Gingerbread	MD	20815	02/14/87	7.3	$1
103-017	Jacken	Jill	Up the Hill	Pail of Water	OK	45678	03/01/87	7.3	$55
105-027	Laurel	Stan	2 Oliver Hardy	Celluloyde	NM	82128	09/13/88	5.7	$5
101-030	Liberty	Statuesque	31 GothamCentre	Big Apple	NY	10011	01/03/89	5.4	$459
103-016	Oakenshield	Rex	Mines of Goblins	Everest	NJ	07639	03/10/87	7.2	$18,100
103-024	Oakley	Anney	Six Shooter Path	Target	ND	66540	04/03/88	6.2	$17
101-029	Oow	Lu	888 Sandy Beach	Honolulu	HI	99909	12/26/88	5.4	$2,116
104-018	Ridinghoode	Crimson	232 Cottage Path	Wulfen	PA	15201	05/27/87	7.0	$18,900
106-009	Sunnybrook	Rebecca	21 Last Week	Portland	OR	97210	02/04/86	8.3	$349
102-025	Washington	George	8 Founders Diamond	Hamilton	DC	01776	05/20/88	6.0	$19,700

Figure 6-7: A report shown in landscape mode in the Print Preview window.

After using the Fit To option, you may find that you don't want to scale the printing. Cancel scaling by clicking on the Adjust To radio button right above the Fit To button and enter **100** in the text box.

Marginal thinking

Excel uses a standard top and bottom margin of one inch on each page of the report and a standard left and right margin of three-quarters of an inch.

Frequently, you find that you can squeeze the last column or the last few rows of the worksheet data you're printing on a page by simply adjusting the margins for the report. To get more columns on a page, try reducing the left and right margins. To get more rows on a page, try reducing the top and bottom margins.

You can change the margins in two ways:

- Open the Page Setup dialog box, select the Margins tab, shown in Figure 6-8, and enter the new settings in the Top, Bottom, Left, and Right text boxes.
- Open the Print Preview window, click on the Margins button, and drag the margin markers to their new positions (see Figure 6-9).

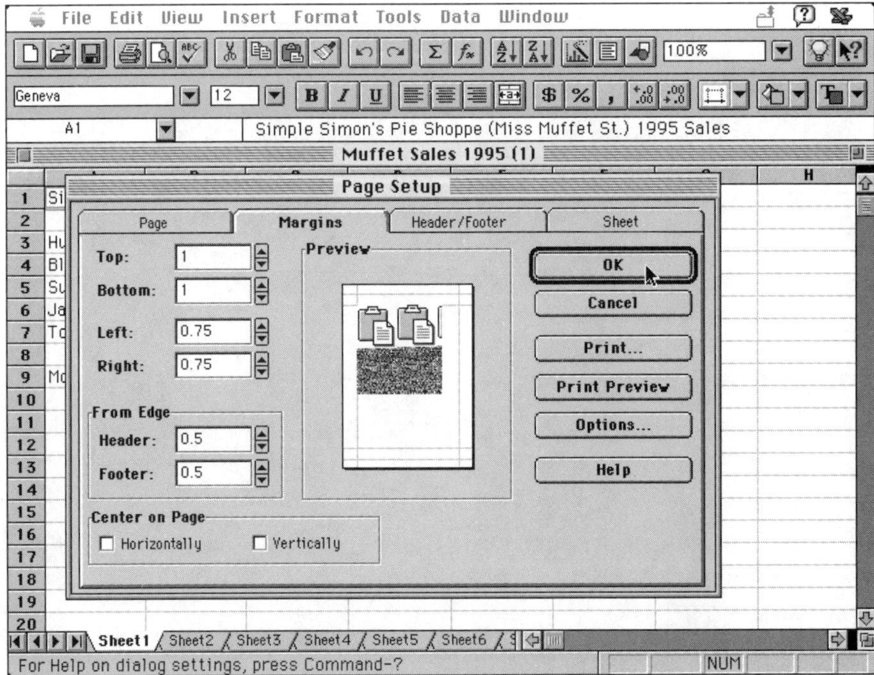

Figure 6-8: The Margins tab of the Page Setup dialog box.

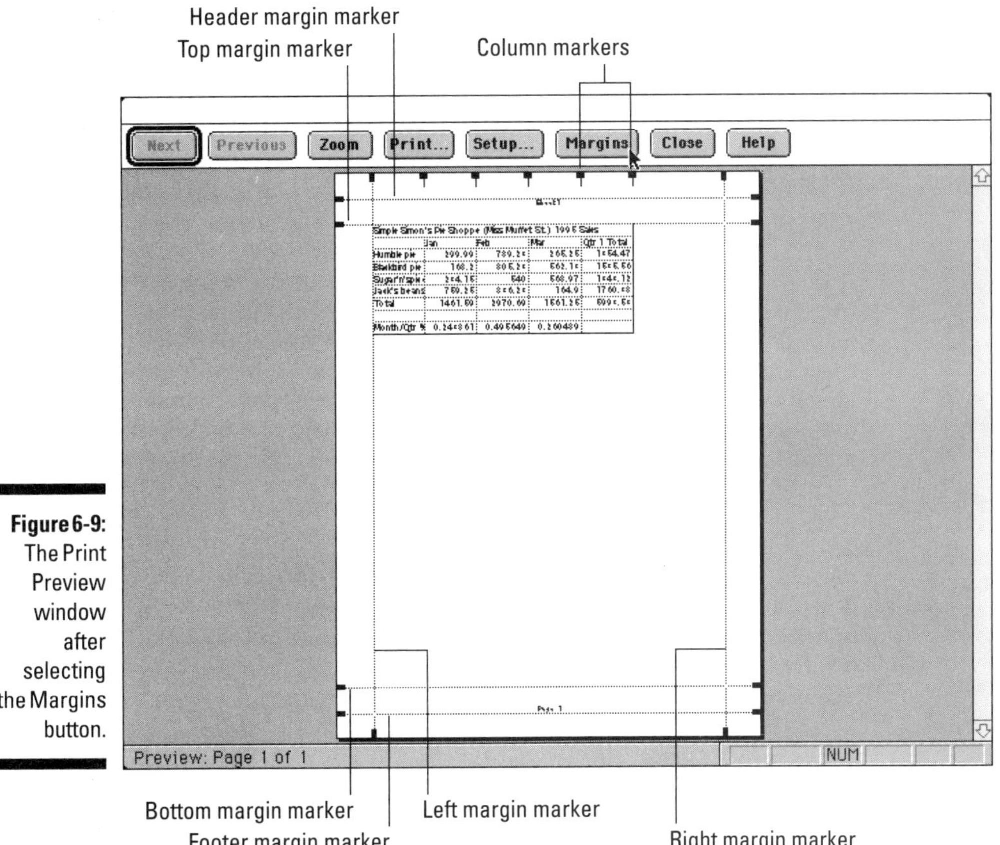

Figure 6-9: The Print Preview window after selecting the Margins button.

You can use the Center on Page options in the Margins tab of the Page Setup dialog box to center a selection of data — that is, a selection that takes up less than a full page, of course — between the current margin settings (refer to Figure 6-8). Choose the Horizontally check box to center the data between the left and right margins. Choose the Vertically check box to center the data between the top and bottom margins. Choose both check boxes to center the selection in the middle of your page.

If you use the Margins button in the Print Preview window to change the margin settings, you can modify the column widths as well as the margins. Figure 6-9 shows the margin and column markers that appear when you click on the Margins button in the Print Preview window. To change one of the margins, position the mouse pointer on the desired margin marker (the pointer's shape changes to a double-headed arrow) and drag the marker in the appropriate direction. When you release the mouse button, Excel redraws the page using the new margin setting. You may gain or lose columns or rows, depending on what kind of adjustment you make. Changing the column widths is the same story: Drag the column marker to the left or right to decrease or increase the width of a particular column.

My header don't know what my footer's doing

Headers and footers are simply text that appears on every page. The header is printed in the top margin of the page, and, not surprisingly, the footer is printed in the bottom margin. Both the header and footer are centered horizontally in the margins. You can use a header and footer in a report to identify the document used to produce the report and to display the page numbers and the date and time of printing. Unless you specify otherwise, Excel automatically adds a header that shows the name of the worksheet being printed and a footer that shows the current page number.

To modify the header or footer in some way, open the Header/Footer tab in the Page Setup dialog box and make your changes in the Header and Footer pull-down menu box (see Figure 6-10). The Header and Footer pull-down menu boxes both contain a wide number of stock pieces of information for your header and footer, including the following information (or various combinations of this information):

- *The name of the worksheet.* Excel gets this information from the sheet tab. (See Chapter 9 to learn how to rename a sheet tab.)
- *The name of the person who prepared the worksheet.* Excel gets this information from the User Name option in the General tab of the Options dialog box. (See Chapter 10 for details.)
- *The page number.*
- *The current date.*
- *The name of the workbook document.*

Figure 6-10 shows the Header/Footer tab of the Page Setup dialog box after choosing

```
Greg Harvey, Simons Client Database
```

in the Header pull-down menu box and

```
Page 1 of ?
```

in the Footer pull-down menu box.

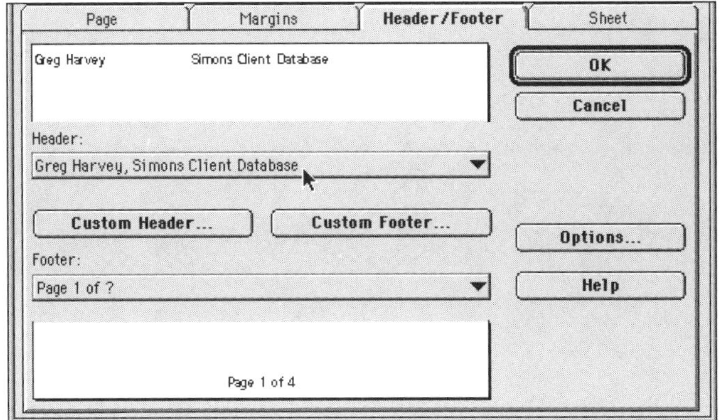

Figure 6-10: The Header/ Footer tab of the Page Setup dialog box with a header and footer.

In the header information, Greg Harvey, Simons Client Database is the company to which Excel is registered (this name is the same as the one listed as the registered user on the About Microsoft Excel dialog box). `Page 1` is, of course, the current page number. For the footer information, `Page 1 of ?`, Excel puts in the current page number and the total number of pages in the report. You can choose this paging option in either the Header or Footer pull-down menu box.

Figure 6-11 shows the first page of a report in the Print Preview screen. Here, you can see the header and footer as they will print. Fortunately, in the Print Preview window, you can verify that the header information won't all print on top of each other as it appears in the header preview area of the Page Setup dialog box. You can also see how the `Page 1 of ?` works in the footer. On the first page, you see the centered footer `Page 1 of 4`. On the second page, you would see the centered footer `Page 2 of 4`.

If you don't want *any* header or footer printed in your report, you simply open the Header/Footer tab in the Page Setup dialog box and then choose the `(none)` option at the very top of the Header and Footer pull-down menu boxes.

When only a custom header or footer will do

Most of the time, the stock headers and footers available in the Header and Footer pull-down menu boxes are sufficient for your report needs. Every once in a while, though, you may want to insert information that is not available in these list boxes or in an arrangement that is not offered in the stock headers and footers. For those times, you need to turn to the Custom Header and

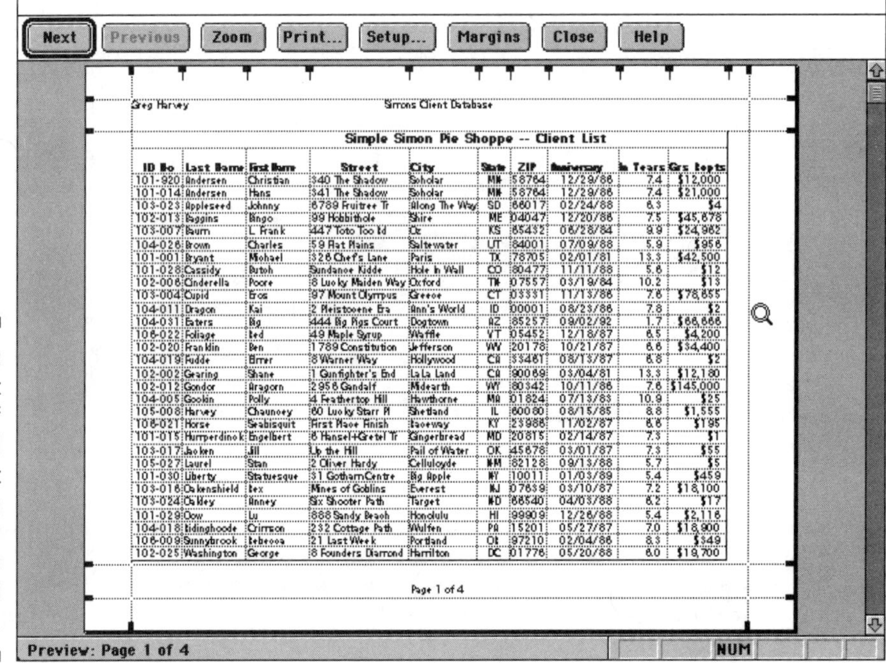

Simple Simon Pie Shoppe -- Client List

ID No	Last Name	First Name	Street	City	State	ZIP	Anniversary	In Years	Grs Rcpts
101-920	Andersen	Christian	340 The Shadow	Scholar	MN	58764	12/29/88	7.4	$12,000
101-014	Andersen	Hans	341 The Shadow	Scholar	MN	58764	12/29/88	7.4	$21,000
103-023	Appleseed	Johnny	6789 Fruitree Tr	Along The Way	SD	66017	02/24/88	6.3	$4
102-013	Baggins	Bingo	99 Hobbithole	Shire	ME	04047	12/20/88	7.5	$45,678
103-007	Baum	L. Frank	447 Toto Too Rd	Oz	KS	65432	08/28/84	9.9	$24,962
104-026	Brown	Charles	59 Flat Plains	Saltewater	UT	84001	07/09/88	5.9	$958
101-001	Bryant	Michael	326 Chef's Lane	Paris	TX	78705	02/01/81	13.3	$42,500
101-028	Cassidy	Butch	Sundance Kidde	Hole In Wall	CO	80477	11/11/88	5.6	$12
102-006	Cinderella	Poore	8 Lucky Maiden Way	Oxford	TN	07557	03/19/84	10.2	$13
103-004	Cupid	Eros	97 Mount Olympus	Greece	CT	03331	11/13/88	7.6	$78,655
104-011	Dragon	Kai	2 Pleistocene Era	Ann's World	ID	00001	08/23/86	7.8	$2
104-031	Eaters	Big	444 Big Pigs Court	Dogtown	AZ	85257	09/02/92	1.7	$66,666
106-022	Foliage	Red	49 Maple Syrup	Waffle	VT	05452	12/18/87	6.5	$4,200
102-020	Franklin	Ben	1789 Constitution	Jefferson	WV	20178	10/21/87	6.6	$34,400
104-019	Fudde	Elmer	8 Warner Way	Hollywood	CA	33461	08/13/87	6.8	$2
102-002	Gearing	Shane	1 Gunfighter's End	LaLa Land	CA	90069	03/04/81	13.3	$12,180
102-012	Gondor	Aragorn	2956 Gandalf	Midearth	WY	80342	10/11/86	7.6	$145,000
104-005	Gookin	Polly	4 Feathertop Hill	Hawthorne	MA	01824	07/13/83	10.9	$25
105-008	Harvey	Chauncey	60 Lucky Starr Pl	Shetland	IL	60080	08/15/85	8.8	$1,555
106-021	Horse	Seabisquit	First Place Finish	Raceway	KY	23986	11/02/87	6.6	$195
101-015	Humperdinck	Engelbert	6 Hansel+Gretel Tr	Gingerbread	MD	20815	02/14/87	7.3	$1
103-017	Jacken	Jill	Up the Hill	Pail of Water	OK	45678	03/01/87	7.3	$55
105-027	Laurel	Stan	2 Oliver Hardy	Celluloyde	NM	82128	09/13/88	5.7	$5
101-030	Liberty	Statuesque	31 GothamCentre	Big Apple	NY	10011	01/03/89	5.4	$459
103-016	Oakenshield	Rex	Mines of Goblins	Everest	NJ	07639	03/10/87	7.2	$18,100
103-024	Oakley	Anney	Six Shooter Path	Target	ND	66540	04/03/88	6.2	$17
101-029	Oow	Lu	888 Sandy Beach	Honolulu	HI	99909	12/26/88	5.4	$2,116
104-018	Ridinghoode	Crimson	232 Cottage Path	Wulfen	PA	15201	05/27/87	7.0	$18,900
106-009	Sunnybrook	Rebecca	21 Last Week	Portland	OR	97210	02/04/86	6.3	$349
102-025	Washington	George	8 Founders Diamond	Hamilton	DC	01776	05/20/88	6.0	$19,700

Figure 6-11: The first page of printed report showing header and footer as they will print.

Custom Footer buttons in the Header/Footer tab of the Page Setup dialog box. With the Custom Header and Custom Footer buttons, you can create your header or footer by inserting your own information.

Figure 6-12 shows the Header dialog box that appeared when I clicked on the Custom Header button after selecting the stock header shown in Figure 6-10.

Notice that in the custom Header dialog box, the header is divided into three sections: Left section, Center section, and Right section. All header text entered in the Left section of this dialog box is justified with the left margin of the report. All header text entered in the Center Section box is centered between the left and right margins, and — you guessed it — all text entered in the Right section box is justified with the right margin of the report.

You can use Tab to advance from section to section in the header and to select the contents of that section. If you want to break the header text in one of the sections, press Return to start a new line. If you want to clear the contents of a section, press Delete.

Figure 6-12: The Header dialog box.

As you can see in Figure 6-12, Excel puts some weird codes with &s (ampersands) in the center of this stock header (&[File]. When creating a custom header or footer, you too can mix weird ampersand codes with the standard text (like "For Eyes Only" and such). To insert the weird ampersand codes in a section of the header (or footer), click on the appropriate button, as described in the following:

- Click on the Page button to insert the &[Page] code, which puts in the current page number.
- Click on the Total Page button to insert the &[Pages] code, which puts in the total number of pages. If you want Excel to display the Page 1 of 3 kind of information, type the word **Page** and press the spacebar, click on the Page button and press the spacebar again, type **of** and press the spacebar a third time, and finally press the Total Page button. Excel inserts Page &[Page] of &[Pages] in the custom header or footer.
- Click on the Date button to insert the &[Date] code, which puts in the current date.

- Click on the Time button to insert the `&[Time]` code, which puts in the current time.

Previous versions of Excel allowed some shortcut codes — such as `&T` (insert Time), which is now `&[Time]` — therefore, it should be faster to select the buttons instead. In addition to inserting ampersand codes in the custom header or footer, you can choose a new font, font size, or font attribute for information in any of its sections by clicking on the Font button. When you click on the Font button, Excel opens the Font dialog box, where you can select a new font, size, style, or special attributes like strikethrough.

When you've finished creating your custom header or footer, choose OK to close the Header or Footer dialog box and return to the Header/Footer tab of the Page Setup dialog box. The effect of your work now appears in the sample boxes.

Setting up the sheet

The Sheet tab of the Page Setup dialog box, shown in Figure 6-13, contains a variety of printing options that may come in handy from time to time:

- *Print Area.* Use this text box to designate the range of cells that you want printed. (You only use this option when your workbook contains a section that you routinely need to print and you don't want to waste your time selecting the range and choosing the Selection radio button in the Print dialog box every blasted time you print this information.)

  To specify a print area, select this text box and then type in the cell references or range names or click and drag the mouse pointer through the cell range in the worksheet. To designate nonadjacent areas, separate individual cell ranges with a comma (for example, **A1:G72, K50:M75**).
- *Rows to Repeat at Top.* Use this option to designate rows of a worksheet as print titles to be printed across the top of each page of the report (see the following section, "Entitlements"). Select this text box and then enter the row references (such as **2:3**) or drag down the rows.
- *Columns to Repeat at Left.* Use this option to designate columns of a worksheet as print titles to be printed at the left edge of each page of the report (see the following section, "Entitlements"). Select this text box and then enter the column row references (such as **A:B**) or drag across the columns.
- *Gridlines.* Use this option to hide or show the cell gridlines in the printed report. (Figure 6-14 shows a page of a report in Print Preview after removing the `X` from the Gridlines check box.)

- *Notes.* When this check box is selected, Excel prints the text of any text notes attached to cells that are included in the report. Leave this check box deselected when you don't want the notes included at the end of the printout.
- *Draft Quality.* When you select this check box, Excel doesn't print cell gridlines (regardless of the status of the Gridlines check box) and omits some graphics from the printout. Select this option when you want to get a fast and dirty copy of the report and are only concerned with checking the text and numbers.
- *Black and White.* When you select this check box, Excel prints the different colors assigned to cell ranges in black and white. You would select this option, for example, when you used colors for text and graphics in a workbook you created on a color monitor but you want to print these elements in monochrome on a black-and-white printer. If you don't select this option, the colors become shades of gray on a black-and-white printer.
- *Row and Column Headings.* When you select this check box, Excel includes the worksheet frame with the column letters and row numbers on each page of the report. Select this option when you want to be able to identify the location of the printed information — see "Printing by Formula," later in this chapter, for an example.
- *Down, then Across.* Normally, Excel selects this radio button, which tells the program to number and page a multipage report by proceeding down the rows and then across the columns to be printed.
- *Across, then Down.* Choose this radio button to alter the way a multipage report is numbered and paged. When you select this option, Excel proceeds to number and page across the columns and then down the rows to be printed.

Entitlements

Just as you can freeze rows and columns of information on-screen so that you can always identify the data you're seeing, you can print particular rows and columns on each page of the report. Excel refers to such rows and columns in a printed report as *print titles.* Don't confuse print titles with the header of a report. Even though both are printed on each page, header information is printed in the top margin of the report; print titles always appear in the body of the report. If you use rows as print titles, the titles appear at the top; if you use columns as print titles, the titles appear on the left.

To designate print titles for a report, follow these steps:

1. **Open the Page Setup dialog box and then choose the Sheet tab.**

   The Sheet tab of the Page Setup dialog box appears (refer to Figure 6-13).

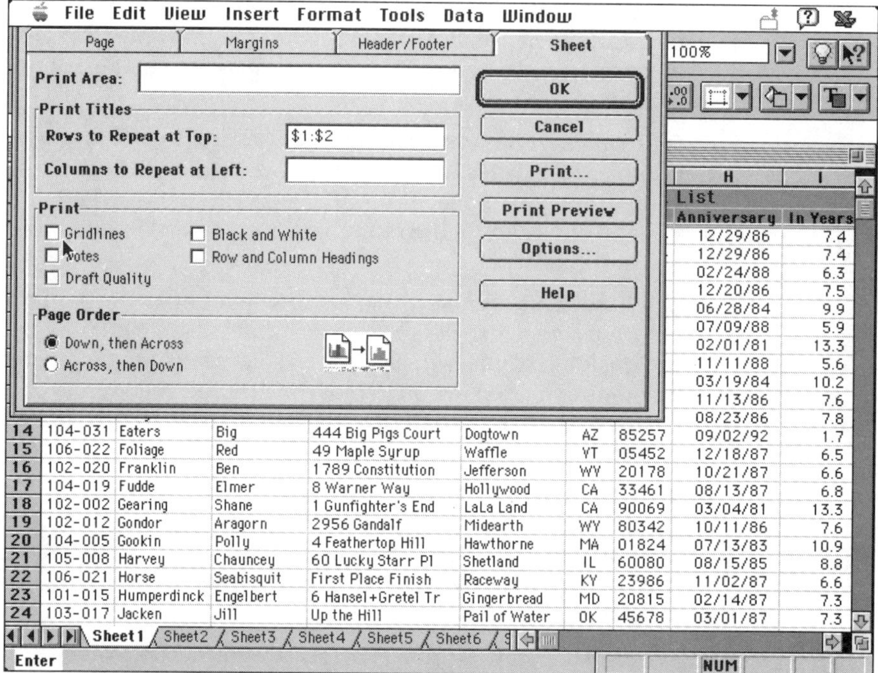

Figure 6-13: Setting the print titles for the sample report.

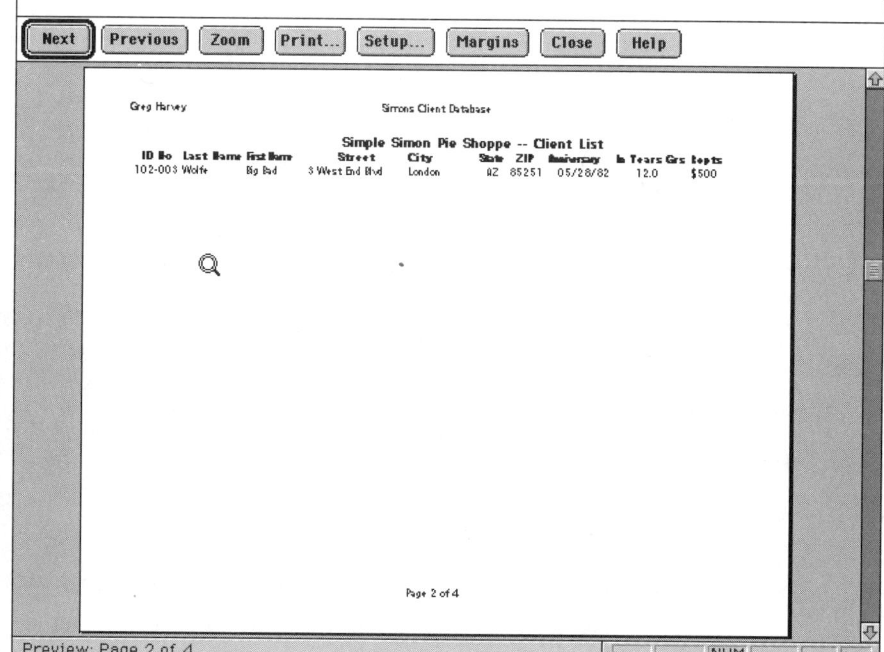

Figure 6-14: The second page of the sample report showing print titles set in Figure 6-13.

2. **To designate worksheet rows as print titles, choose the Rows to Repeat at Top text box and then drag through the rows whose information is to appear at the top of each page in the worksheet.**

   To designate worksheet columns as print titles, choose the Columns to Repeat at Left and then drag through the range of columns whose information is to appear at the left edge of each page of the printed report in the worksheet. In the example shown in Figure 6-13, I dragged through rows 1 and 2 in column A of the Simons Client Database worksheet, and Excel entered the row range `$1:$2` in the Rows to Repeat at Top text box.

   Excel indicates the print-title rows in the worksheet by placing a dotted line (that moves like a marquee — in fact, it's *called* a marquee) on the border between the titles and the information in the body of the report.

3. **Click on OK or press Return.**

   After you close the Page Setup dialog box, the marquee showing the border of the row or column titles disappears from the worksheet.

In Figure 6-13, rows 1 and 2, containing the worksheet title and column headings for the clients database worksheet, are designated as the print titles for the report. Figure 6-14 shows the Print Preview window with the second page of the report. In this figure, you can see how these print titles appear in the report. Note that I deselected the Gridlines check box in the Sheet tab of the Page Setup dialog box so that the worksheet gridlines would not appear in this figure.

If you no longer need print titles, you can clear them from a report by opening the Sheet tab of the Page Setup dialog box and clearing the row and column ranges from the Rows to Repeat at Top and the Columns to Repeat at Left text boxes before choosing OK or pressing Return.

Give Your Page a Break!

Sometimes as you preview a report, you see that Excel has split across different pages information that you know should always appear together on the same page. If, after trying other approaches (such as changing the page size, orientation, or margins), you still can't remedy the bad page break, you can insert a manual page break to force Excel to print the information on the same page.

Inserting a manual page break is much like dividing the document window into panes. You use the top and left-hand edges of the cell pointer to determine where the manual page break is placed. (This is very similar to how you use the top and left-hand edges of the cell pointer to determine how Excel divides the document window into panes.) The top edge of the cell pointer determines where the page break occurs horizontally, and the left edge of the cell pointer determines where the page break occurs vertically.

Figure 6-15 shows an example of a bad vertical page break. Given the page size, orientation, and margin settings for this report, Excel breaks the page between columns L and M. This break separates the sales figures for July, August, and September in columns J, K, and L from the Quarter 3 Totals in column M. You can remedy a problem like this with a manual page break.

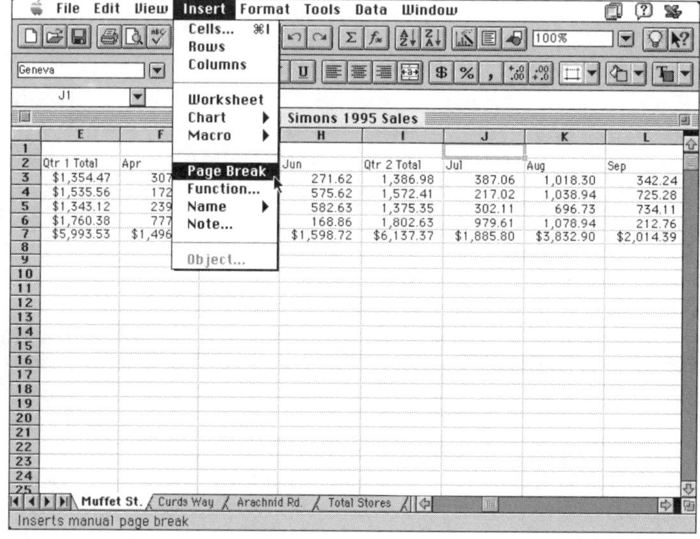

Figure 6-15: You can use the Insert menu to insert a manual page break.

To keep all the third-quarter figures on the same page, you need to insert a manual page break so that the sales information in columns J, K, and L is forced onto the page containing the quarterly totals in column M, as illustrated in Figure 6-16. You should note that you can use this method when none of the other treatments — short of using the Fit To radio button in the Page tab — squeezes the quarterly total information in column M onto the page containing the sales information in columns J, K, and L.

You can create the vertical page break by following these steps (refer to Figure 6-15):

1. **Position the cell pointer in cell J1.**

   Make sure that the pointer is in row 1 of column J. Otherwise, Excel inserts a horizontal page break at the row and a vertical page break at column J.

2. **Choose Page Break from the Insert menu.**

   Excel inserts a manual vertical page break between columns I and J (see Figure 6-16). The manual page break removes the automatic page break that previously appeared between columns L and M and forces all the third-quarter sales figures with their totals together on another page.

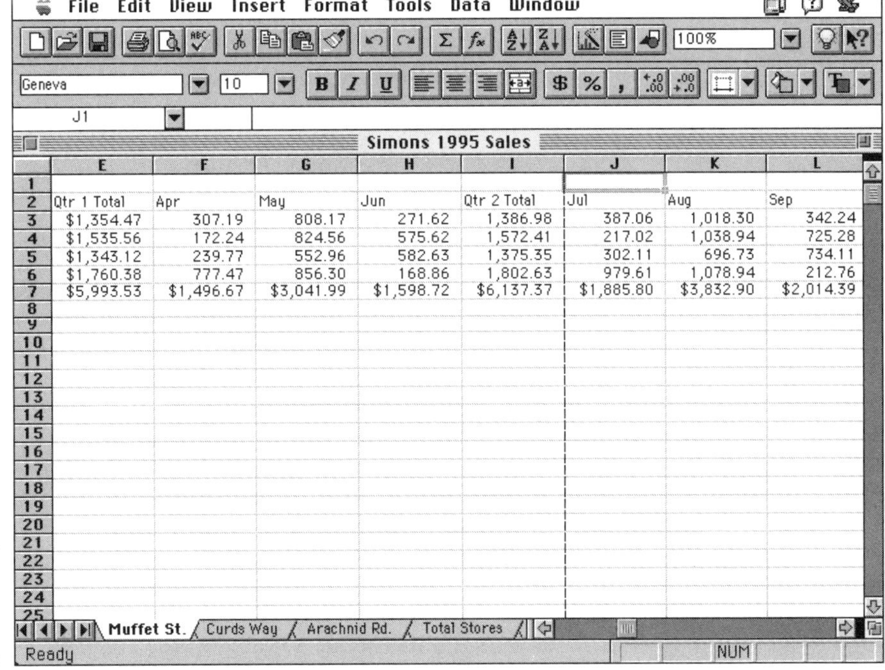

Figure 6-16: The page after inserting a manual page break between columns I and J.

To remove a manual page break from a worksheet, position the cell pointer somewhere in the row below a horizontal page break or somewhere in the column to the right of a vertical page break. (Manual page breaks are indicated in the worksheet by dotted lines that are indistinguishable from automatic page breaks.) Then choose Remove Page Break from the Insert menu. The Page Break command changes to the Remove Page Break command on the Insert menu, depending on where you place the cell pointer. If you inserted both a vertical and a horizontal page break at the same time, you must position the cell pointer in the same cell you used to create the two page breaks in order to get rid of them both in a single operation.

Printing by Formula

You may need to know one more basic printing technique every once in a while: how to print the formulas in a worksheet rather than printing the calculated *results* of the formulas. You may want to print the formulas in the worksheet to make sure that you haven't done anything stupid like replace a formula with a number or use the wrong cell references in a formula — before you distribute the worksheet company-wide (which can be really embarrassing).

Before you can print a worksheet with its formulas, you have to display the formulas instead of their results in the cells, as follows:

1. **Choose Tools ⇨ Options ⇨ View Tab.**
2. **Choose the Formulas check box to put an X in it, and then choose OK or press Return.**

Excel displays the contents of each cell in the worksheet as they generally appear only in the formula bar or when you're editing them in the cell. Notice that value entries lose their number formatting, formulas appear in their cells (Excel widens the columns with best-fit so that the formulas appear in their entirety), and long text entries no longer spill over into neighboring blank cells.

Excel allows you to toggle between the normal cell display and the formula cell display by pressing ⌘+`. That is, press ⌘ plus that weird backward accent key (`**)**, which appears on the same key housing the ~ (tilde). Don't mistake this symbol (`) for the apostrophe ('), which appears on the same key as the quotation mark ("). You can toggle between the normal and the formula cell display by pressing ⌘+` or Control+` — either way, you have to locate that ~ key.

After Excel displays the formulas in the worksheet, you are ready to print it as you do any other report. You can include the worksheet column letters and row numbers as headings in the printout so that if you *do* spot an error, you can pinpoint the cell reference right away. To include the row and column headings in the printout, click on the Row & Column Headings check box in the Sheet tab of the Page Setup dialog box before you send the report to the printer. Figure 6-17 shows the Print Preview window containing part of the first page of a report that prints the formulas and includes the worksheet column letters and row numbers as headings.

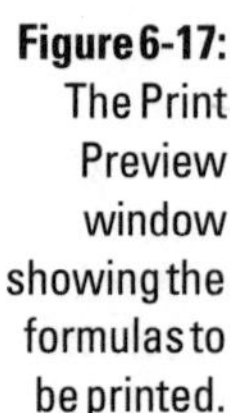

	A	B	C
1	Simple Simon's Pie Shoppe (Miss Muffet St.) 1995 S		
2		Jan	Feb
3	Humble pie	299.99	789.23
4	Blackbird pie	168.2	805.23
5	Sugar'n'Spice pie	234.15	540
6	Jack's beanstalk pie	759.25	836.23
7	Itsy-bitsy spider pie	230.2	450
8	Shoo-fly pie	640.1	733.69
9	Total	=SUM(B3:B8)	=SUM(C3:C8)
10			

Figure 6-17: The Print Preview window showing the formulas to be printed.

When you display formulas in the cells, all entries — text, values, and formulas — are left-aligned in their cells, and all formatting for the values is missing.

After you print the worksheet with the formulas, you can return the worksheet to normal by opening the Page Setup dialog box, choosing the View tab, and deselecting the Formulas check box. Then choose OK or press Return.

Part IV

Amazing Things You Can Do with Excel (for Fun and Profit)

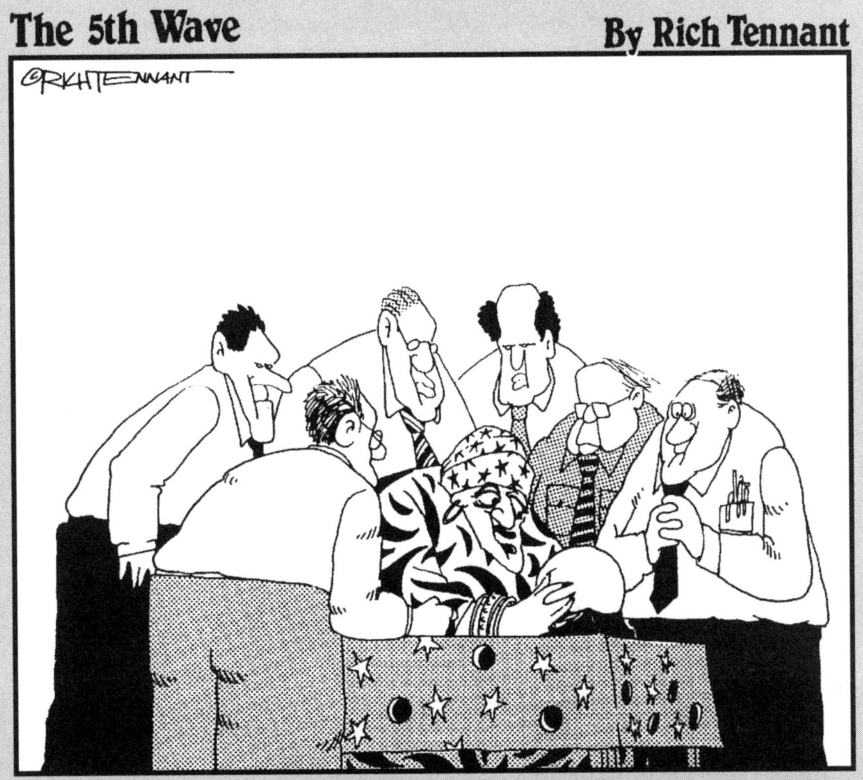

"THE IMAGE IS GETTING CLEARER NOW... I CAN ALMOST SEE IT... YES! THERE IT IS–THE GLITCH IS IN A FAULTY CELL REFERENCE IN THE FOOTBALL POOL SPREADSHEET."

The part in which . . .

You get exposed to something more exciting than the standard, anybody-can-do-it worksheet. First, you learn how easy it is to win friends and influence people by creating super-looking charts that make the folks who read them sit up and take notice of your otherwise mundane numbers. Then you discover how to use Excel to maintain and organize the huge quantities of facts and figures you need to track. You find out how to sort the data into any order that you can dream up, as well as how to search for and retrieve only the information you *really* want.

Finally, you learn how to work with more than one Excel worksheet at a time: how to arrange the worksheets in your workbooks so that you can compare, transfer, and summarize their information.

Chapter 7

A Picture Worth a Thousand Numbers

In This Chapter

- How to create a chart in a worksheet with the ChartWizard
- How to change the chart type with the Chart toolbar
- How to select a new chart type
- How to add and format chart titles
- How to add a text box and arrow to a chart
- How to format the chart's axes
- How to change the orientation of a 3-D chart
- How to use the drawing tools to add graphics to charts and worksheets
- How to print a chart without printing the rest of the worksheet data

As Rod Stewart once observed, "Every picture tells a story, don't it?" By adding charts to worksheets, you not only heighten interest in the worksheet but you also illustrate trends and anomalies that may not otherwise be apparent from just looking at the numbers. Because Excel makes it so easy to chart the information in a worksheet, you can experiment with different types of charts until you find the one that best represents the data — in other words, the picture that best tells the particular story.

Just a word about charts before you start learning how to make them in Excel. Do you remember your high school algebra teacher valiantly trying to teach you how to graph equations by plotting different values on an x-axis and a y-axis on graph paper? Of course, you were probably too busy with more important things, like sex, drugs, and rock 'n' roll, to pay too much attention to an old algebra teacher. Besides, you probably told yourself, "I'll never need this junk when I'm out on my own and get a job!"

Well, see? You just never know. Even though Excel automates almost the entire process of charting worksheet data, you may need to be able to tell the x-axis from the y-axis, just in case Excel doesn't draw the chart the way you had in mind. To refresh your memory, the x-axis is the horizontal axis; the y-axis is the vertical one.

In most charts that use these two axes, Excel plots the categories along the x-axis and their relative values along the y-axis. The x-axis is sometimes referred to as the *time axis* because the chart often depicts values along this axis at different time periods, such as months, quarters, years, and so on.

Charts as if by Magic

Well, that's enough background on charts. Now let's get on with the charting itself. Excel makes the process of creating a new chart in a worksheet as painless as possible with the ChartWizard. The ChartWizard walks you through a five-step procedure, at the end of which you have a complete and beautiful new chart.

Before you start the ChartWizard, first select the cell range that contains the information you want charted. Keep in mind that to end up with the chart you want, the information should be entered in standard table format. With the information in this format, you can select it all as a single range, as in Figure 7-1.

If you create a chart that uses an x-axis and y-axis (as most do), the ChartWizard naturally uses the row of column headings in the selected table for the category labels along the x-axis. If the table has row headings, the ChartWizard uses these as the headings in the *legend* of the chart (if you choose to include one). The legend identifies each point, column, or bar in the chart that represents the values in the table.

After you select the information to chart, follow these steps to create the chart:

1. **Click on the ChartWizard tool on the Standard toolbar.**

   The ChartWizard tool is the sixth tool from the right, with the picture of a magic wand over a Column chart. When you click on this tool, the mouse pointer changes to a crosshair with a small Column chart below and to the right.

2. **Drag the crosshair pointer through the cells in the worksheet to indicate the location and size of the finished chart.**

   To remind you that you're creating a chart, Excel displays the following message in the status bar: `Drag in document to create a chart.`

   Position the crosshair at the upper left-hand corner of the place in the worksheet where you want the chart. Drag diagonally down until you've drawn the outline of the chart, as shown in Figure 7-2. Don't worry if you don't get the outline exactly the right size or in the just the right place — you easily can move or resize the chart after it's created.

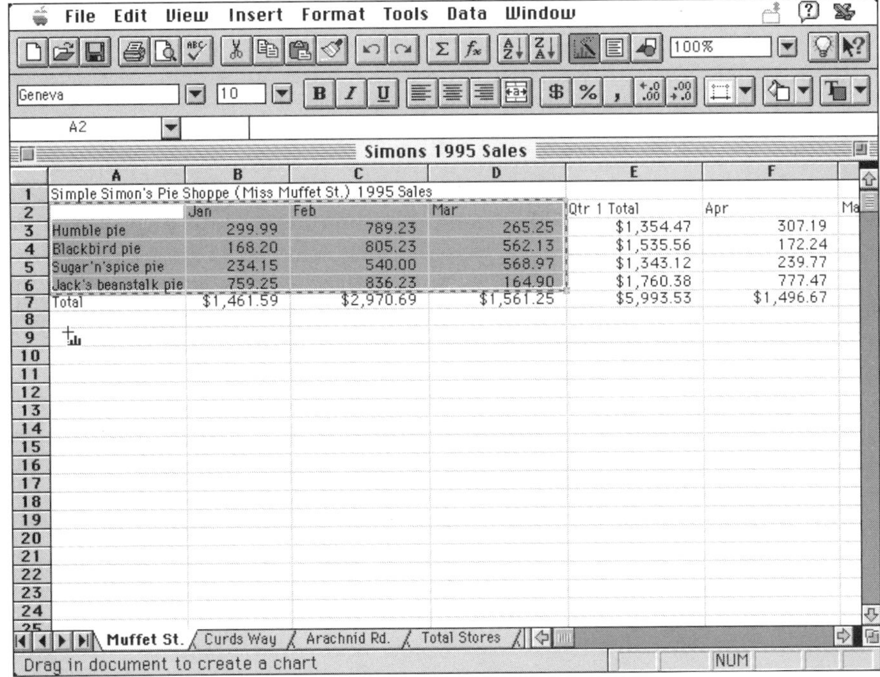

Figure 7-1: Selecting the information to be charted.

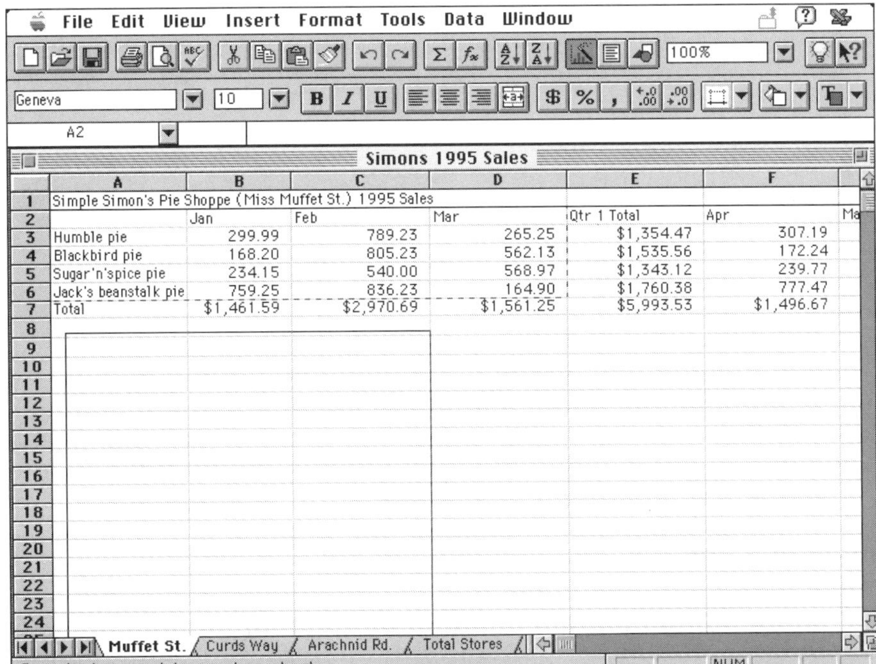

Figure 7-2: Indicating the location and size of the chart in the worksheet.

If you want to put the chart on a worksheet different from the one containing the selected data that you're charting, position the crosshair pointer on the appropriate sheet tab at the bottom of the document window, click on the tab, and then drag it through the cells of that worksheet.

3. **Release the mouse button.**

   Excel displays the ChartWizard — Step 1 of 5 dialog box , as you can see in Figure 7-3. Notice that the outline of the shape of the finished chart no longer appears in the worksheet. (Notice, too, that the step numbers in this procedure don't correspond with the step numbers in the dialog boxes on-screen. Oh, well.)

4. **Verify the cell range.**

   While the first ChartWizard dialog box is displayed, verify that the cell range surrounded by the marquee in your worksheet and specified in formula form (with absolute cell references) in the Range text box is correct. To modify this range (perhaps to include the row of column headings or the column of row headings), either reselect the range with the mouse or edit the cell references in the Range text box.

5. **Click on the Next button in the dialog box or press Return after the selected range is correct.**

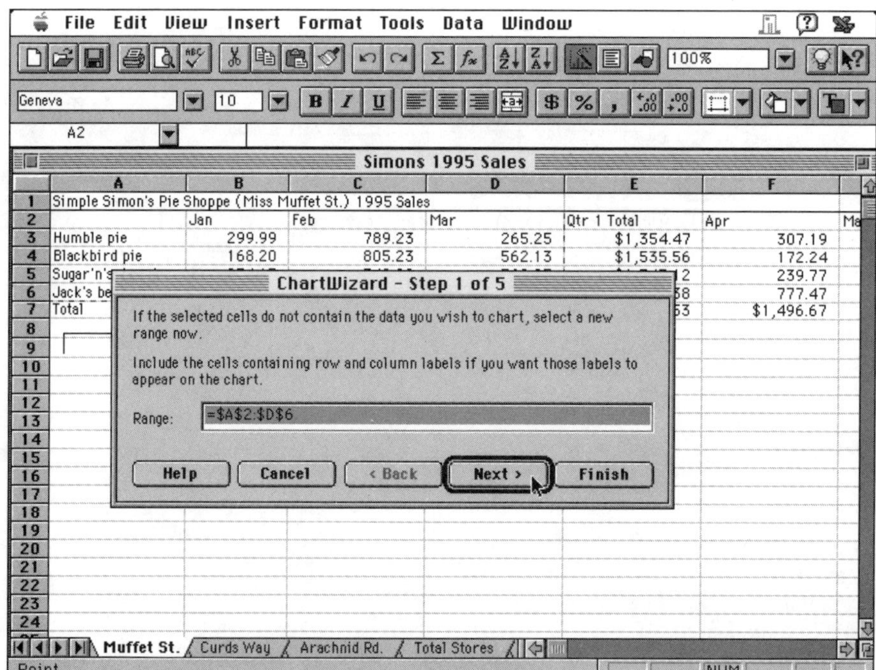

Figure 7-3: Step 1: Verifying the range to be charted.

Excel displays the ChartWizard — Step 2 of 5 dialog box, shown in Figure 7-4. Left to itself, the ChartWizard represents your data in a Column chart; however, the Step 2 of 5 dialog box offers a wide range of chart types.

6. **Select a chart type other than the default Column type, if you want.**

   To select another chart type, click on its sample chart.

7. **Click on the Next button or press Return.**

   The ChartWizard — Step 3 of 5 dialog box appears (see Figure 7-5). Each chart type is available in one of many different formats and has a default format (referred to as the *preferred format*).

8. **Choose a preferred format for your chart.**

   To choose a new format, click on its sample in the dialog box or type its number. (Press 0 [zero] if you want to choose format 10.) Figure 7-5 shows the dialog box with format 6 selected as the preferred format for the Column chart.

9. **Click on the Next button or press Return.**

   The ChartWizard shows you a preview of the chart in the ChartWizard — Step 4 of 5 dialog box, as shown in Figure 7-6.

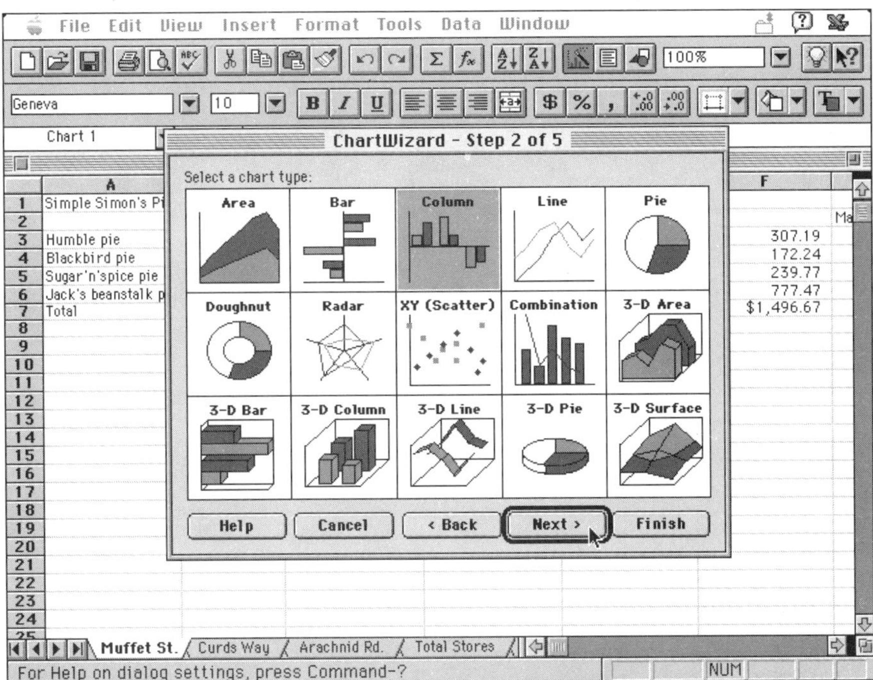

Figure 7-4: Step 2: Selecting the type of chart you want.

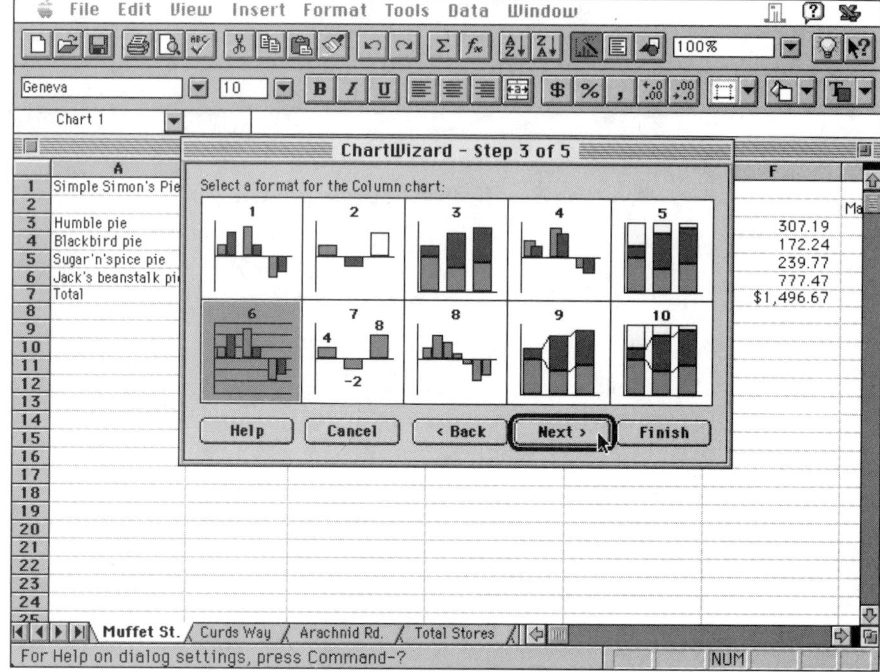

Figure 7-5: Step 3: Selecting a format for the type of chart you've selected.

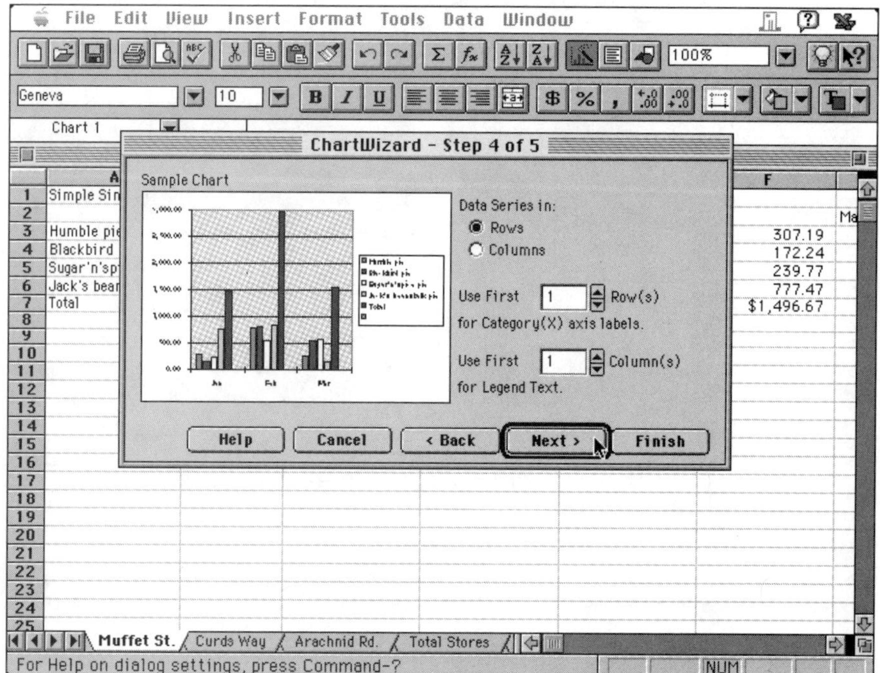

Figure 7-6: Step 4: Verifying that the data is charted correctly.

10. **Verify that Excel has charted the data correctly.**

    Normally, the ChartWizard makes each column of values in the selected table into a separate *data series* on the chart. The *legend* (the boxed area with samples of the colors or patterns used in the chart) identifies each data series in the chart.

    In terms of the worksheet data selected in the Muffet Street first-quarter sales worksheet (shown in Figure 7-1), each bar in the Column chart represents a different month's sales, and these sales are clustered together by the four different types of pies sold. If you want, you can switch the data series from columns to rows by clicking on the Rows radio button, as I did in Figure 7-6.

    Choosing the Rows radio button in this example makes each bar represent the sales of one of the four different types of pies and causes them to be clustered together by month. Figure 7-6 shows the sample chart for the Miss Muffet Street first-quarter sales after changing the Data Series In option from Columns to Rows. (Note that the default settings of 1 as the row for the category labels and 1 as the column for the legend text are still in effect.)

    Because the chart forms the data series by rows, the ChartWizard uses the entries in the first row (the column headings in cell range B2:D2) to label the x-axis (the so-called *category labels*). The ChartWizard uses the entries in the first column (the row labels in cell range A3:A6) as the headings in the legend.

11. **Click on the Next button or press Return.**

    The ChartWizard — Step 5 of 5 dialog box appears, as you can see in Figure 7-7.

12. **Enter the titles for the chart.**

    You can enter a title for the entire chart as well as individual titles for the category axis (the x-axis) and the value axis (the y-axis). You also can remove the legend from the chart (not recommended for any chart that contains more than one data series) by clicking on the No radio button.

    Figure 7-7 shows the dialog box after I entered a title for the chart in the Chart Title text box. The Sample Chart area shows the title as it is entered. Because of space limitations in the dialog box, the text may not wrap in the worksheet the same way it does in the Sample Chart area. If you add a title for the x-axis in the Category (X) text box, the title appears right under the category labels in the chart. If you add a title for the y-axis in the Value (Y) text box, the title appears to the left of the values, running up the side of the chart.

13. **Click on the Finish button or press Return to close the last ChartWizard dialog box.**

    The chart you have created appears in the worksheet in the area you selected earlier, and the Chart toolbar magically appears, floating in the workbook document window. Figure 7-8 shows the Column chart created for the Miss Muffet Street first-quarter sales.

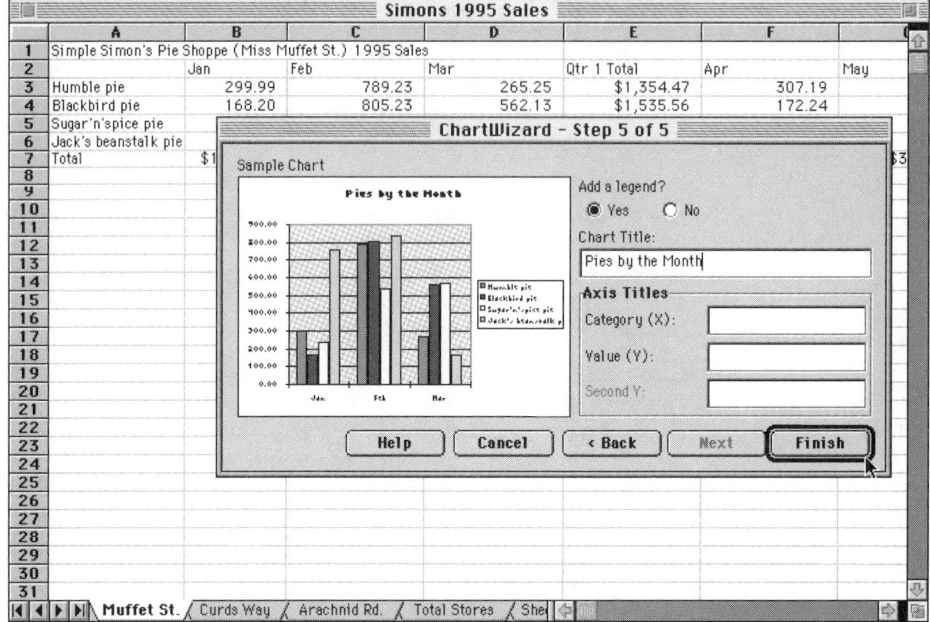

Figure 7-7: Step 5: Adding the titles to the chart.

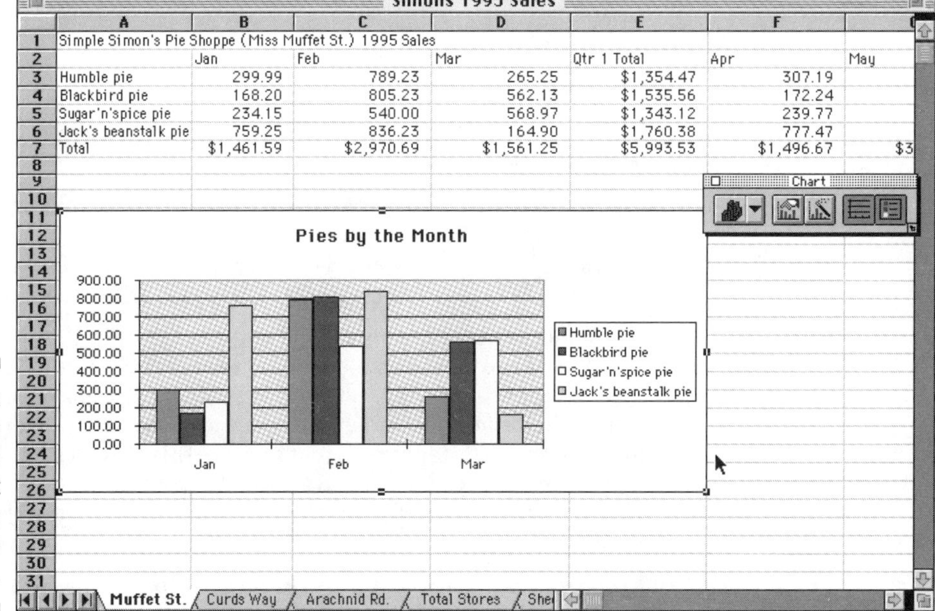

Figure 7-8: The completed chart as it appears in the worksheet.

You easily can move or resize the chart right after creating it because the chart is still selected. (You always can tell when a graphics object, such as a chart, is selected: You see *selection handles* — the tiny squares — around the edges of the object.) Immediately after creating the chart, the Chart toolbar appears, floating above in the workbook document window. To move the chart, position the mouse pointer somewhere inside the chart and drag it to a new location. To resize the chart (to make it bigger or smaller if it seems distorted in any way), position the mouse pointer on one of the selection handles. When the pointer changes from the arrowhead to a double-headed arrow, drag the side or corner (depending on which handle you select) to enlarge or reduce the chart.

After the chart is properly sized and positioned in the worksheet, set the chart in place by deselecting it (clicking the mouse pointer on any cell outside of the chart). As soon as you deselect the chart, the selection handles disappear, as does the Chart toolbar, from the document window. To reselect the chart (to edit, size, or move it), click anywhere on the chart with the mouse pointer.

To create a chart in a separate chart sheet, select the cell range that contains the information you want graphed, and press F11 (see Figure 7-9). Excel represents your data as a column bar chart in the new chart sheet, which you then can edit by using techniques you learn in this chapter.

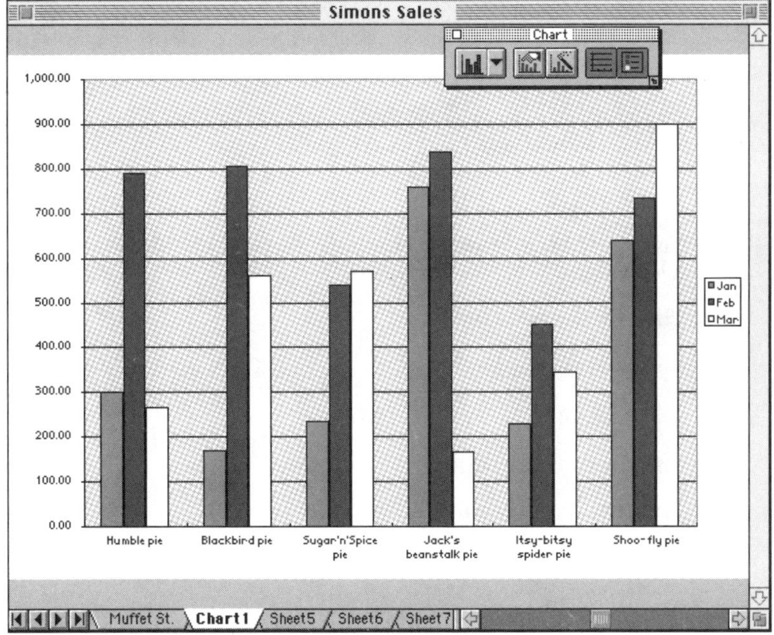

Figure 7-9: A new Chart1 created from the Simons Sales worksheet by using the F11 shortcut key.

A Little Change of Chart

After you create a chart, you can use the tools on the Chart toolbar to make some changes to the chart. Remember that this toolbar appears whenever you select the chart in the worksheet. To change the chart type, simply click on the Chart Type tool's pull-down menu button and then select the new type of chart in the pull-down palette that appears (see Figure 7-10).

To add or get rid of gridlines for the major values (on the y-axis), click on the Horizontal Gridlines tool. To hide or display the chart's legend, click on the Legend tool.

Figure 7-10 shows the chart created in the preceding section after I changed the chart type from a simple Column to a 3-D Column chart. Figure 7-11 shows the same chart after I changed the chart type from 3-D Column to 3-D Bar (where the columns are arranged horizontally rather than vertically) and added gridlines.

In addition to being able to change the type of chart and add or remove gridlines and the legend, you also can use the Chart toolbar to change the data included in the chart. To change the data represented in the chart, follow these steps:

1. **Click on the chart in the worksheet to select the chart and then click on the ChartWizard tool.**

   The ChartWizard tool is located both on the Standard toolbar or on the Chart toolbar that appears as soon as you select the chart. The Chart-Wizard displays a ChartWizard — Step 1 of 2 dialog box that contains the Range text box with the current cell range being charted.

2. **Change this cell range to include more or less data or labels in the worksheet.**

3. **Click on the Next button.**

   The ChartWizard — Step 2 of 2 dialog box appears. It contains the same options for changing the way you chart the data as the Step 4 of 5 dialog box does when you create the chart.

4. **Change the chart options if you want.**

5. **Click on the Finish button or press Return.**

   Your changes show up immediately in the selected chart.

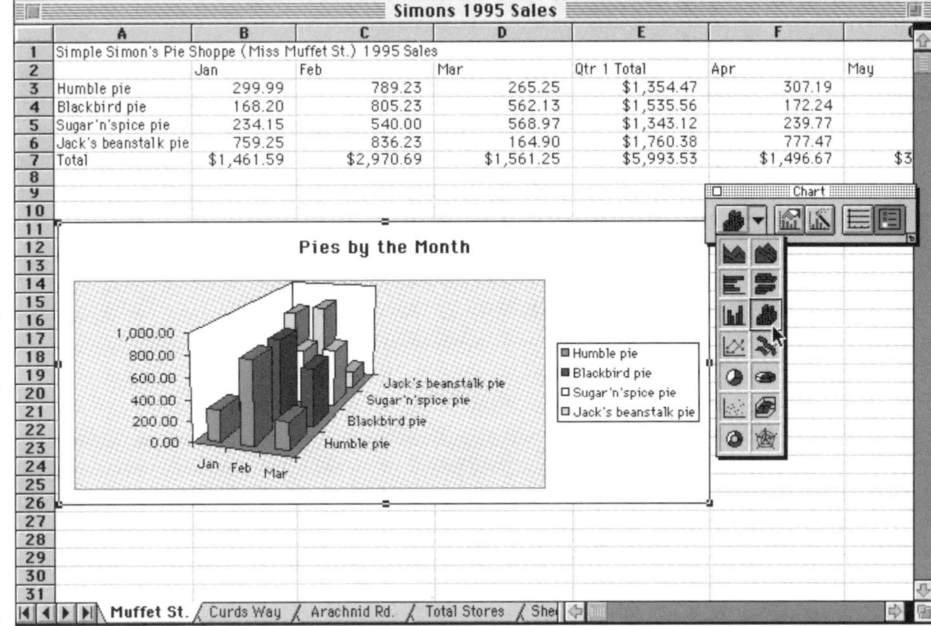

Figure 7-10: The chart type changed to a 3-D Column chart and the gridlines removed.

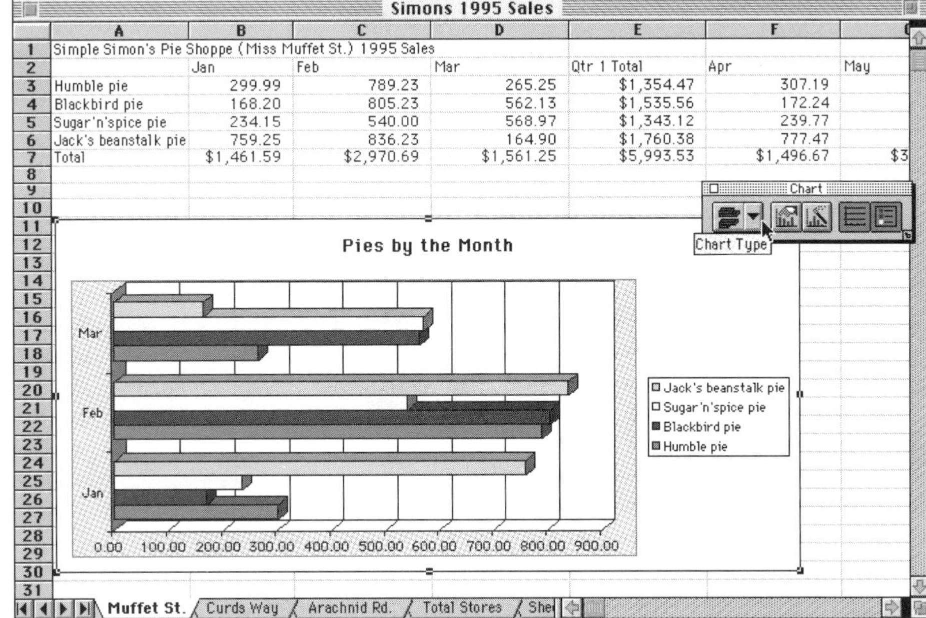

Figure 7-11: The chart type changed to a 3-D Bar chart and gridlines added.

Accentuate the positive

Besides changing the type of chart or adding or removing gridlines with the tools on the Chart toolbar, you may want to make changes to specific parts of the chart (such as selecting a new font for titles or repositioning the legend). To make these kinds of changes, you must double-click on the chart and then select the particular object (title, legend, plot area, and so on). When you double-click on a chart, Excel displays a heavy border (made up of diagonal lines) around the chart, as shown in Figure 7-12.

After you double-click on the chart, you can select the individual parts of the chart where you want to change the formatting.

- To select one of these chart objects, simply click on the object.
- You can tell when an object is selected because selection handles appear around it. Figure 7-12 shows the selection handles around the chart title, for example. With some objects, you can use the selection handles to resize or reorient the object.

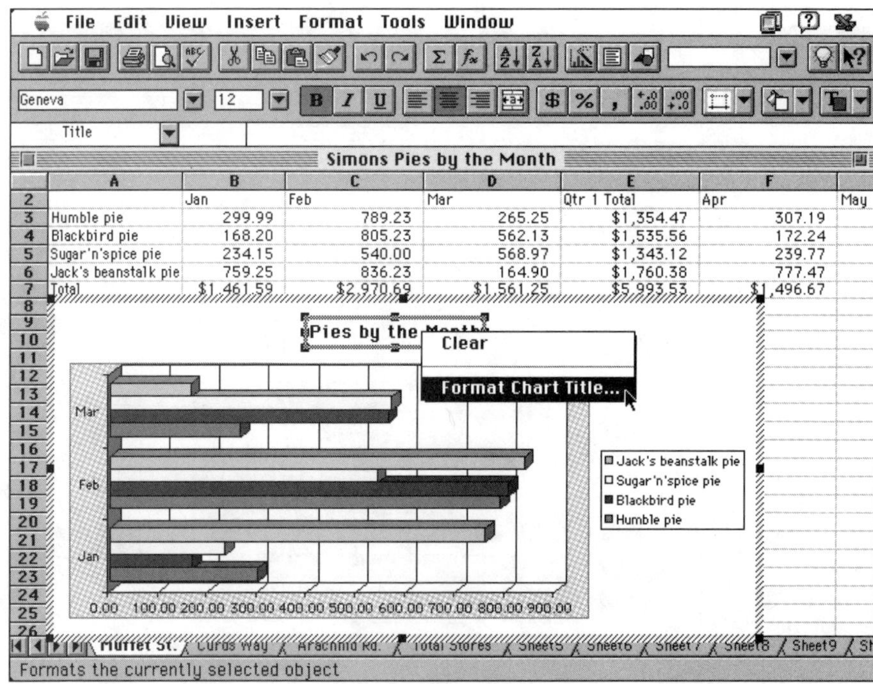

Figure 7-12: Selecting the Format Chart Title command in the title's shortcut menu.

- After selecting some chart objects, you can move them within the chart by positioning the arrowhead pointer in their midst and then dragging their boundaries.
- To display a chart object's shortcut menu, click on the object with the either the Control key or the ⌘+Option keys and then drag to the desired command on the menu or click on the command to select it.

All the parts of the chart you can select in a chart window have shortcut menus attached to them. If you want to select a command from the shortcut menu as soon as you select a part of the chart, you can click on the object with the either the Control key or the ⌘+Option keys and then drag to the desired command on the menu or click on the command to select it.

Figure 7-12 shows the 3-D Bar version of the chart for the first-quarter sales after double-clicking on the chart, selecting the chart's title, and then pressing Control and clicking on the chart's title to display its shortcut menu. To change the formatting of this title, you simply choose the Format Chart Title command in the shortcut menu. When you select this command, the Format Chart Title dialog box appears, similar to the one shown in Figure 7-12. This dialog box has three tabs — Patterns, Fonts, and Alignment — each with its own options for formatting the title.

- Select the Patterns tab and use its options to place a border or to change the pattern or color within the title area.
- Select the Font tab, shown in Figure 7-13, and use its options to choose a new font, size, or style for the title.
- Select the Alignment tab and use its options to change the alignment or orientation of the title.

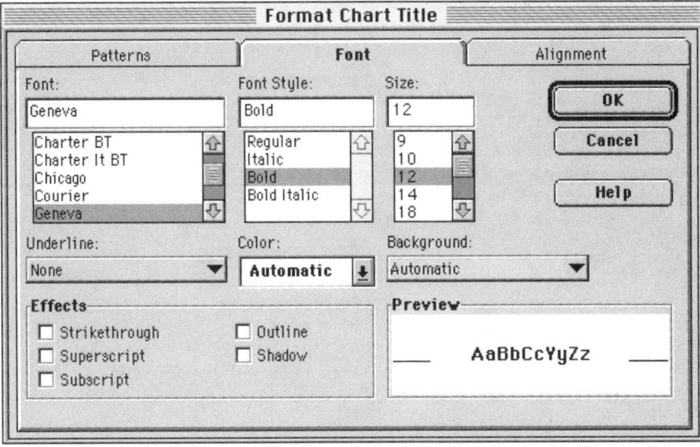

Figure 7-13: The Font tab of the Format Chart Title dialog box.

Note that you can move the chart title by dragging it to a new position within the chart. In addition to moving the title, you can break up the title on several different lines. Then, if you want, you can use options in the Alignment tab of the Format Chart Title dialog box to change the alignment of the broken-up text.

To force part of the title onto a new line, click the insertion point at the place in the text where the line break is to occur on the formula bar (the text of the title appears there whenever you select the title). After the insertion point is positioned in the title, press ⌘+Return to start a new line.

In addition to changing the way the titles appear in the chart, you can modify the way the data series, legend, and x- and y-axes appear in the chart by opening their shortcut menus and selecting the appropriate commands from them.

Singularly unattached

Figure 7-14 shows a couple of other changes you easily can make to a chart. In this figure, you see the first-quarter sales chart (as a 3-D Bar chart) after I added a text box with an arrow that points out how good the pie sales were in February. I also formatted the values on the x-axis (which is normally the y-axis when the chart isn't turned on its side) with the Currency number format.

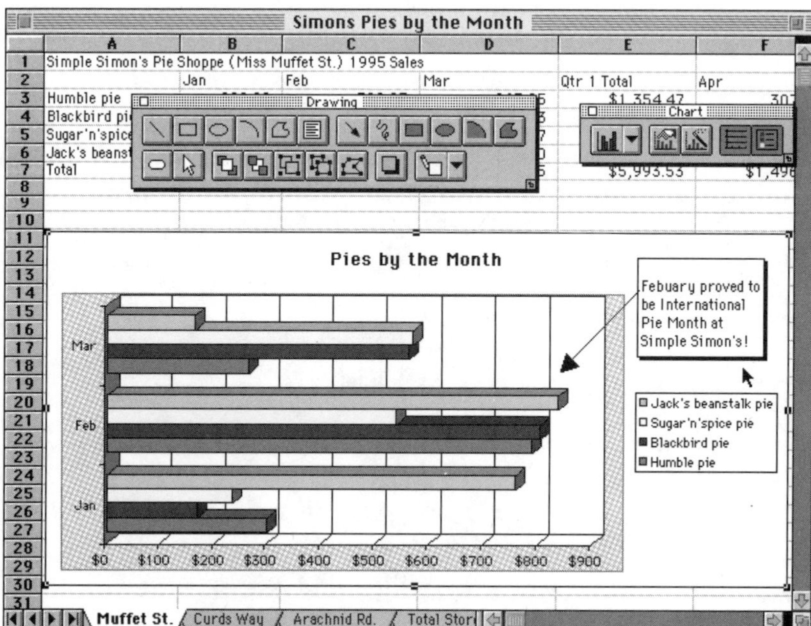

Figure 7-14: After adding a text box with an arrow and formatting the values on the x-axis with the Currency style.

To add a text box to the chart, click on the Text Box tool on either the Standard toolbar (right next to the ChartWizard tool) or on the Drawing toolbar, which is shown in Figure 7-14 and is displayed by choosing Drawing on the toolbar shortcut menu.

When you choose the Text Box tool, Excel changes the pointer to a crosshair, which you use to draw the text box in either the chart or the worksheet by dragging the text box's outline. When you release the mouse button, the program positions the insertion point at the top of the text box and you can then type the text you want to appear within it. The text you type appears in the text box and wraps to a new line when you reach the right edge of the text box. (Remember that you can press ⌘+Return when you want to force text to appear on a new line.) After you've finished entering the message for your text box, click anywhere outside of the box to deselect it.

After adding a text box to a chart (or worksheet), you can edit the text box as follows:

- You can move the text box to a new location in the chart by dragging the text box.
- You can resize the text box by dragging the appropriate selection handle after it's selected.
- To make a change to a border of the text box or to remove a border entirely, choose the Format Object command on the text box's shortcut menu and then choose the Patterns tab in the Format Object dialog box. To remove all borders from the text box, click on the None radio button.
- To add the drop-shadow effect (such as the one shown in the text box in Figure 7-14), click on the Shadow check box in the Patterns tab of the Format Object dialog box or click on the Drop Shadow tool in the Drawing toolbar (the one with the picture of a drop shadow on a rectangle).

When annotating a particular part of the chart with a text box, you may want to add an arrow to point directly to the object or part of the chart you are describing. To add an arrow, click on the Arrow tool (immediately to the right of the Text Box tool) on the Drawing toolbar. Then drag the crosshair from the place where the end of the arrow (without the arrowhead) is to appear to the place where the arrow starts (and the arrowhead appears) and release the mouse button.

Excel then draws a new arrow that remains selected (with selection handles at the beginning and the end of the arrow). You then can modify the arrow as follows:

- To move the arrow, drag it into position.
- To change the length of the arrow, drag one of the selection handles.

- As you change the length, you also can change the direction of the arrow by pivoting the mouse pointer around the stationary selection handle.
- If you want to change the shape of the arrowhead or the thickness of the arrow's shaft, choose the Format Object command from the arrow's shortcut menu and make changes to the options in the Patterns tab of the Format Object dialog box.

Formatting the values on the x- or y-axis

When charting a bunch of values, Excel isn't too careful about how it formats the values that appear on the y-axis (or the x-axis, when you choose a chart, such as the 3-D Bar chart shown in Figure 7-14). If you're not happy with the way the values appear on either the x- or y-axis, you can change the appearance of the values as follows:

1. **Double-click on the chart.**
2. **With the mouse button, ⌘+Option+click (or Control+click) on the x- or y-axis that contains the values to be formatted.**
3. **Choose the Format Axis command on the axis shortcut menu.**
4. **Choose the Number tab in the Format Axis dialog box and then choose the appropriate options in the Category and Format Codes list box.**

   For example, to select the Currency format with no decimal places, choose Currency in the Category list box and then select $#,##0_);($#,##0) in the Format Codes list box.
5. **Choose OK or press Return.**

After you choose a new number format for a chart, Excel immediately formats all the numbers that appear along the selected axis.

Modifying a chart by changing charted values in the worksheet

As soon as you finish modifying the objects in a chart, you can deselect the chart and return to the normal worksheet and its cells by clicking the pointer anywhere outside the chart. After a chart is deselected, you once again can move the cell pointer all over the worksheet. Just keep in mind that if you use the arrow keys to move the cell pointer, the cell pointer disappears when you move to a cell in the worksheet that's hidden behind the chart. (Of course, if you try to select a cell covered by a chart by clicking on the cell with the mouse pointer, you only succeed in selecting the chart itself anyway.)

The worksheet values represented graphically in the chart remain dynamically linked to the chart so that if you make a change to one or more of the charted values in the worksheet, Excel automatically updates the chart to suit the changes in the values.

Figure 7-15 illustrates this dynamic relationship. This figure shows the same chart as shown in Figure 7-14, except that I increased the value in cell D6 (the March sales of Jack's beanstalk pie) from 164.90 to 1,640.90. After I made this change, Excel immediately redrew the bar representing this value — the very top bar in the charts shown in both Figure 7-14 and 7-15. Note how the bar has grown like Pinocchio's nose in Figure 7-15 and how Excel automatically increased the x-axis scale from a maximum of $900 to $1,200 so that the chart adequately can represent this new high value.

Getting a new perspective on things

Figure 7-16 shows the chart in a chart window in yet another guise — this time as a 3-D Area chart. After you select this kind of chart (or the 3-D Column, 3-D Line, and 3-D Surface charts), Excel draws the chart in perspective view by adding a third axis to the chart. Now you have the Category (x) axis with the months running along the bottom of the closest side, the Data Series (y) axis with the types of pies running along the bottom of the other side, and the Value (z) axis with the dollar amounts running up the left wall.

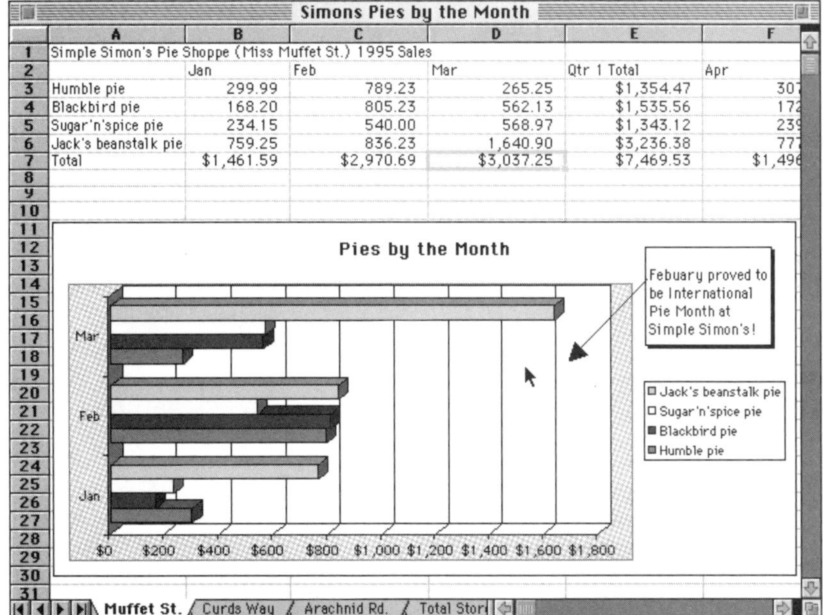

Figure 7-15: The chart shows an increase in cell D6 from 164.90 to 1640.90.

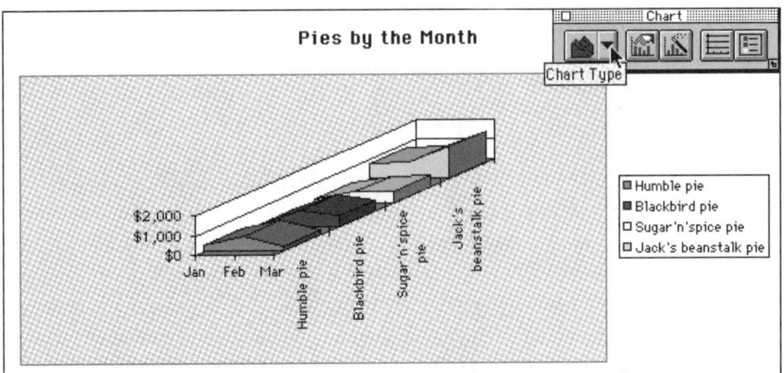

Figure 7-16: Changing the chart type to a 3-D Area chart.

These three axes form a kind of open box with the Category and Series axes on the two sides of the floor and the Value axis on the left side of the wall of the box. You can modify the view of this type of 3-D perspective chart by rotating the box, thereby changing the viewing angles of its walls and floor.

To modify the view of the chart, double-click on the chart and then select the frame of the 3-D chart by clicking on one its corners and holding down the mouse button. In a second (assuming that you really clicked on a corner of the frame and not on one of data series inside the frame), everything disappears from the chart except for the wire frame representing the orientation of the 3-D chart (see Figure 7-17).

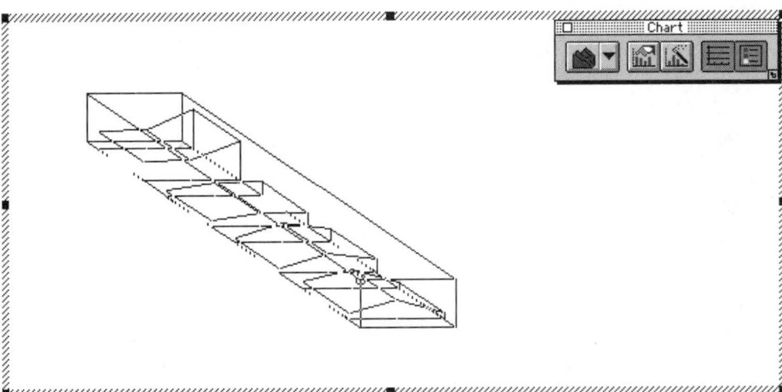

Figure 7-17: Modifying the view of the 3-D Area chart by rotating the wire-frame box.

You then can drag around a corner of the wire-frame box to reorient the entire 3-D chart. After the wire-frame box is positioned the way you want the 3-D chart to be, release the mouse button. Excel draws the 3-D chart by using the new viewing angles. Figure 7-17 shows the wire frame of the 3-D Area chart after rotating the frame down and to the right. Figure 7-18 shows you how the rotated 3-D Area chart appears after releasing the mouse button.

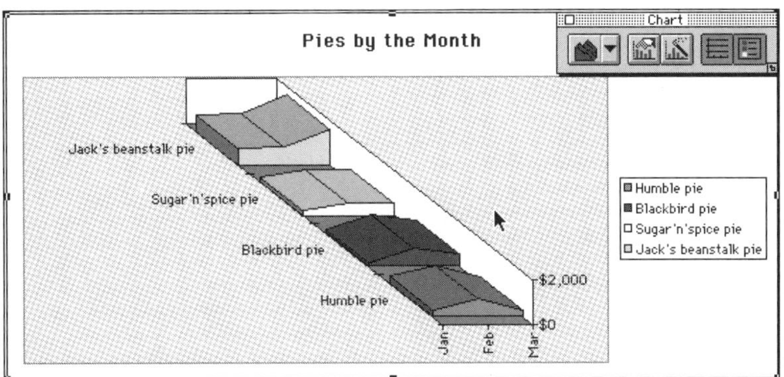

Figure 7-18: The 3-D Area chart after rotating it.

Notice how this change to the orientation of the 3-D Area chart causes Excel to flip the category labels with the names of the types of pies all the way from the right side of the chart over to the left side.

A Worksheet without Graphics Is Like . . .

Charts are not the only kind of graphics you can add to a worksheet. Indeed, Excel lets you spruce up a worksheet with drawings, text boxes, and even graphics images imported from other sources, such as scanned images or drawings created in other graphics programs.

Figure 7-19 shows some of the other types of graphics you can include in the worksheet. In the upper left-hand corner of the table is a drawing of a pie (OK, it's a windowsill pie, but what the heck). I borrowed this graphics image from Adobe's Photoshop program and brought the image directly into the worksheet with the Clipboard by copying it with ⌘+C and pasting it with ⌘+V.

In addition to the imported windowsill pie graphic, the worksheet shown in Figure 7-19 contains other graphics: a text box with a drop shadow, an arrow, and an oval drawn around the quarterly sales total in cell E7. I added these three graphics objects by using the tools on the Drawing toolbar, which is shown as a floating toolbar in the middle left-hand corner of the workbook document window.

The Drawing toolbar contains all sorts of drawing tools you can use to draw outlined or filled shapes. The following suggestions may spur you on to further creativity:

- To draw the oval around the yearly total in cell E7, click on the Oval tool on the Drawing toolbar and drag the crosshair pointer until the oval is the size and shape you want. (To draw a circle rather than an oval with this tool, hold down the Shift key as you drag the pointer.)

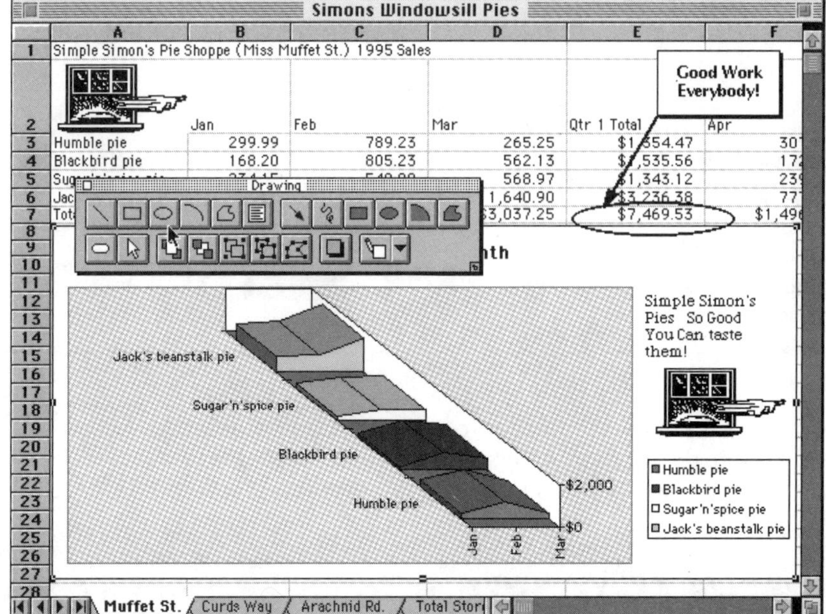

Figure 7-19: The worksheet is enhanced with a variety of graphics.

- To create the text box with the drop shadow, click on the Text Box tool on the Drawing toolbar (the Text Box tool uses the same picture as its counterpart on the Standard toolbar). Drag the crosshair pointer to create the size and shape of the box. After you release the mouse button, Excel draws the text box in the worksheet and positions the insertion point inside the text box, where you can enter text. After you've finished entering text, click the mouse pointer somewhere outside of the new text box to deselect the box. If you want, you can change the font and alignment of the text in the box by selecting the Format Object command on the box's shortcut menu and selecting the options on the Font and Alignment tabs.
- To draw the arrow from the text box to the yearly total, click on the Arrow tool on the Drawing toolbar, drag the crosshair from the box to the oval, and then release the mouse button. When drawing an arrow in the worksheet with the Arrow pointer, the direction you drag the pointer determines which end of the shaft gets the arrowhead. If you drag the crosshair pointer from the oval to the text box, the arrowhead points up to the box instead of down to the cell with the yearly total.

Putting one graphic in front of the other

In case you haven't noticed, graphics objects float on top of the cells of the worksheet. Most graphics objects, including charts, are opaque — meaning that they hide (not replace) information in the cells underneath. If you move one opaque graphic on top of another, the one on top hides the one below, just as putting one sheet of paper over another hides the information on the one below. For the most part, then, be sure that graphics objects don't overlap one another or overlap cells that have worksheet information you want to display.

Sometimes, however, you can create some interesting special effects by placing a transparent graphics object (such as a circle) in front of an opaque graphics object. The one problem you may encounter is if the opaque object gets on top of the transparent one. If this happens, switch their positions by selecting the opaque object and then choosing the Send to Back command on its shortcut menu.

Now you see them, now you don't

One more thing you'll want to know about the graphics that you add to a worksheet is how to *hide* the graphics. You see, adding graphics to a worksheet can appreciably slow down the screen response, because Excel has to take time to redraw each and every little picture in the document window whenever you scroll the view even slightly. To keep this sluggishness from driving you crazy, either hide the display of all the graphics (including charts) while you edit other things in the worksheet, or replace the graphics with gray rectangles (called *placeholders*) that continue to mark their places in the worksheet but don't take nearly as long to redraw.

To hide all the graphics or replace them with gray placeholders, choose the Options command on the Tool menu and then choose the View tab. Click on the Hide All radio button under Objects to get rid of the display of all graphics. Click on the Show Placeholders radio button to replace the graphics with shaded rectangles. This option is the safest bet because the placeholders give you a general idea of how changes to the cells of the worksheet impact the graphics.

Before you print the worksheet, be sure that you redisplay the graphics objects by opening the Options dialog box, choosing the View tab, and then clicking on the Show All radio button.

Putting Out the Chart

Sometimes, you may want to print only a particular chart in the worksheet, independent of the worksheet data the chart represents or any of the other stuff you've added. To print only a chart, first make sure that the graphics objects are displayed in the worksheet. Then double-click on the chart to display the heavy border drawn with diagonal lines. Next, choose the Print command from the File pull-down menu (⌘+P) or click on the Print tool on the Standard toolbar.

If you select the Print command on the File menu rather than click on the Print tool, you see that the Selected Sheets radio button under Print is selected. By default, Excel prints the selected sheet full size on the page, which may mean that not all the chart can be printed on a single page. Choose the Print Preview button to make sure.

If you find in Print Preview that you need to change the selected sheet's size or the orientation of the printing (or both), choose the Setup button in the Print Preview window. To change the orientation of the printing or the paper size, choose the Page tab in the Page Setup dialog box and change these options. When everything looks all right in the Print Preview window, start printing the chart by selecting the Print button.

Chapter 8

Facts and Figures at Your Fingertips

In This Chapter

- How to set up a database in Excel
- How to create a data form for a database
- How to add records with the data form
- How to find, edit, and delete records with the data form
- How to sort records in the database
- How to filter records in the database
- How to set up custom criteria when filtering records

The purpose of all the worksheet tables you've been exposed to up until now has been to perform essential calculations (such as to sum monthly or quarterly sales figures) and then present the information in an understandable form. But you can create another kind of worksheet table in Excel: a *database*. The purpose of a database is not so much to calculate new values as to store lots and lots of information in a consistent manner. For example, you can create a database that contains the names and addresses of all your clients, or you can create a database that contains all the essential facts about your employees.

Believe it or not, you already know everything you need to know about setting up and creating a database from your experience with creating other types of worksheet tables. When setting up a database, you start by entering a row of column headings, technically known as *field names* in database parlance, to identify the different kinds of items you need to keep track of, such as First Name, Last Name, Street, City, State, and so on. After you enter the row of field names, you start entering the information for the database in the appropriate columns of the rows immediately below the field names.

As you proceed, notice that each column of the database contains information for a particular item you want to track in the database, such as the client's company name or an employee's telephone extension. Each column is also known as a *field* in the database. In looking back over your work, you see that each row of the database contains complete information about a particular person or thing you're keeping track of in the database, whether it's a corporation, such as PBC Broadcasting, Inc., or a particular employee, such as Butch Cassidy or Lu Oow. The individuals or entities described in the rows of the database are also known as the *records* of the database. Each record (row) contains many fields (columns).

Maintaining vast quantities of data in a tabular format is but one small part of the database story in Excel. You will find that Excel provides you with very powerful features for organizing the data as well as for displaying just the information you need.

For example, you may have entered the clients in a database alphabetically by company name but now want to see them listed alphabetically by company name *and* grouped by states and cities. No problem: Sort the records of the database by their State, City, and then Company fields.

Suppose that you only want to work with clients who live in New York City and who have already established credit accounts with you. It's simple: You choose Data ➪ Filter ➪ AutoFilter to add pull-down menus (complete with pull-down buttons) to each field name in the database. Then, to display only the records you want to see, you click on the pull-down button for the appropriate field(s) and select the entry in the pull-down menu by which you want the database filtered. For this example, you would select New York in the City pull-down menu and Yes in the Credit pull-down menu. And just like that, Excel hides all the records in your database except those containing the entries you selected, referred to as filter criteria. In our example, Excel would display only the records in the database where the City field contains New York and the Credit field contains Yes.

Data in What Form?

Setting up and maintaining a database is easy with Excel's handy, built-in *data form.* You use the data form to add, delete, or edit records in the database. To create a data form for a new database, you first enter the row of column headings used as field names and one sample record in the following row (check out the client database in Figure 8-1).

Format each field entry just as you want all subsequent entries in that column of the database to appear. Then select the two rows of cells and choose the Form command on the Data menu.

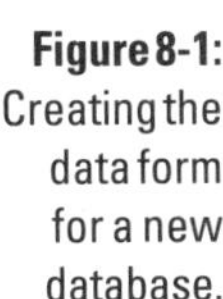

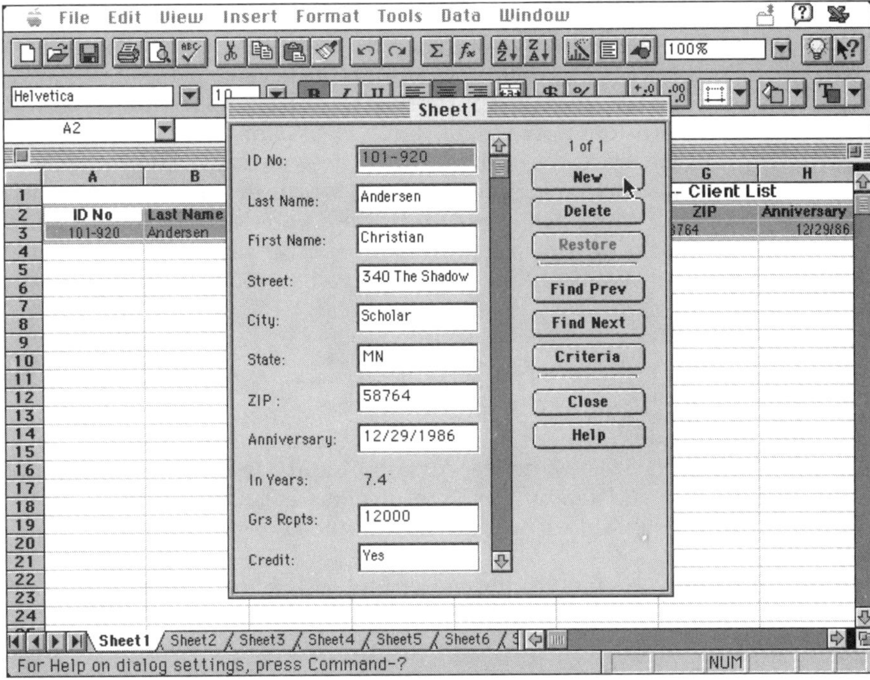

Figure 8-1: Creating the data form for a new database.

Creating a data form from field names alone

In Excel 5.0, it is possible to create a data form for a new database simply by entering a row of field names and selecting them before you choose Form on the Data menu. When you create a data form in this way, Excel displays an alert dialog box indicating that no headers (that is, the row with the field names for the new database) have been detected. This alert box also asks you to confirm the top row of the selection (which happens to be the only row of the selection) as the header row. Go ahead and choose OK or press Return to create a blank data form listing all the fields down the form in the same order as they appear across the selected row.

Creating a blank data form from only the field names is just fine, provided that your database doesn't contain any calculated fields (that is, fields whose entries result from a formula's computation rather than from manual entry). If your new database is to contain calculated fields, you need to build their formulas in the appropriate fields of the first record. Then select both the row of field names and the first database record with the formulas indicating how they are calculated before you choose Form on the Data menu. Excel knows which fields are calculated and which are not. (You can tell that a field is a calculated field in the data form because Excel lists its field name but does not provide a text box for you to enter any information for it.)

As soon as you choose the Form command on the Data menu, Excel analyzes the row of field names and entries for the first recording and creates a data form that lists the field names down the left side of the form with the entries for the first record in the appropriate text boxes next to them. Figure 8-1 shows the data form for this new database: It looks like a customized dialog box. The data form Excel creates includes the entries you made in the first record. The data form also contains a series of buttons on the right side that you use to add, delete, or find specific records in the database. Right above the first button (New), the data form lists the number of the record you're viewing followed by the total number of records (`1 of 1` when you first create the data form).

The more the merrier — adding new records

After you create the data form with the first record, you then can use the form to add the rest of the records to the database. The process is simple. When you click on the New button, Excel displays a blank data form (marked `New Record` at the right side of the data form), which you get to fill in.

After you enter the information for the first field, press Tab to advance to the next field in the record.

Whoa! *Don't* press Return. If you do, you'll insert the new, incomplete record into the database.

Continue entering information for each field, pressing Tab to go to the next field in the database.

- If you notice that you've made an error and want to edit an entry in a field you already passed, press Shift+Tab to return to that field.
- To replace the entry, just start typing.
- To edit some of the characters in the field, press ← or click the I-beam pointer in the entry to locate the insertion point and then edit the entry from there.

When entering information in a particular field, you can copy the entry made in the same field of the preceding record by pressing Control+" (quotation marks). Press Control+", for example, to carry forward the same entry in the State field for each new record of people who live in the same state.

When entering dates in a date field, use a consistent date format that Excel knows — for example, enter something like **2/19/94**. When entering numbers that use leading zeros that you don't want to disappear from the entry (such as ZIP codes like 00102), put an apostrophe (') before the first 0. The apostrophe tells Excel to treat the number like a text label.

Press ↓, press Return, or click on the New button after you've entered all the information for the new record (see Figure 8-2). Excel inserts the new record as the last record in the database and displays a new blank data form where you can enter the next record (see Figure 8-3).

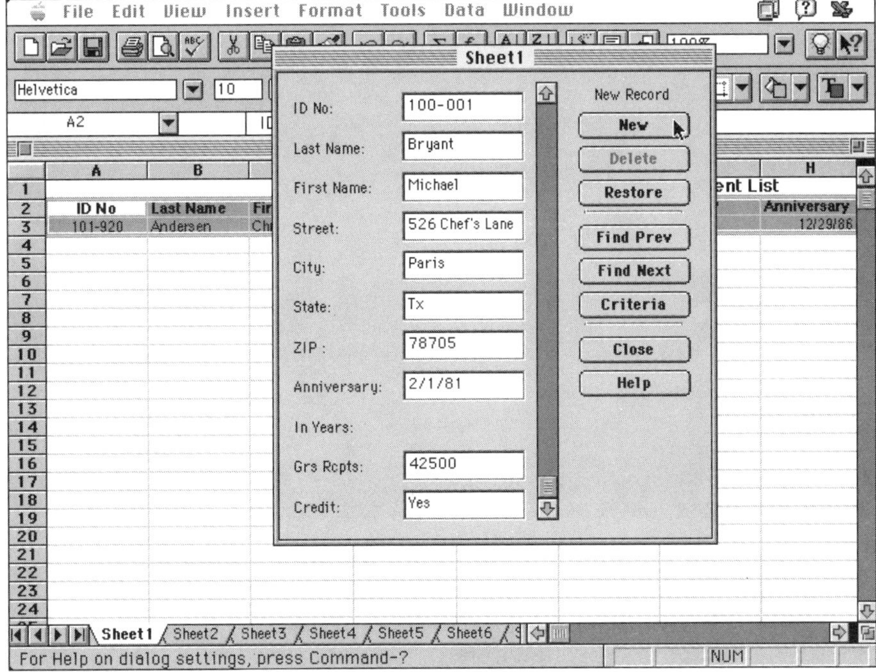

Figure 8-2: Entering information in the data form for the second record.

Getting Excel to calculate a field entry

Remember that if you want the entry for a particular field to be calculated by the program, you need to enter the formula for that field in the first record of the database and then select both the row field names and first record when creating the data form. Excel copies the formula for this calculated field to each new record you add with the data form.

In the client database, for example, the Years field in cell I3 of the first record is calculated by the formula =(NOW()-H3)/365 (computing the number of years someone has been a client by subtracting the anniversary date from the current date returned by the NOW function and dividing the resulting number of days by 365). As you can see, Excel adds the calculated field, Years, to the data form but doesn't provide a text box for this field (calculated fields cannot be edited). When you enter additional records into the database, Excel calculates the formula for the Years field. If you then redisplay the data for these records, you see the calculated value following Years (although you cannot change the value).

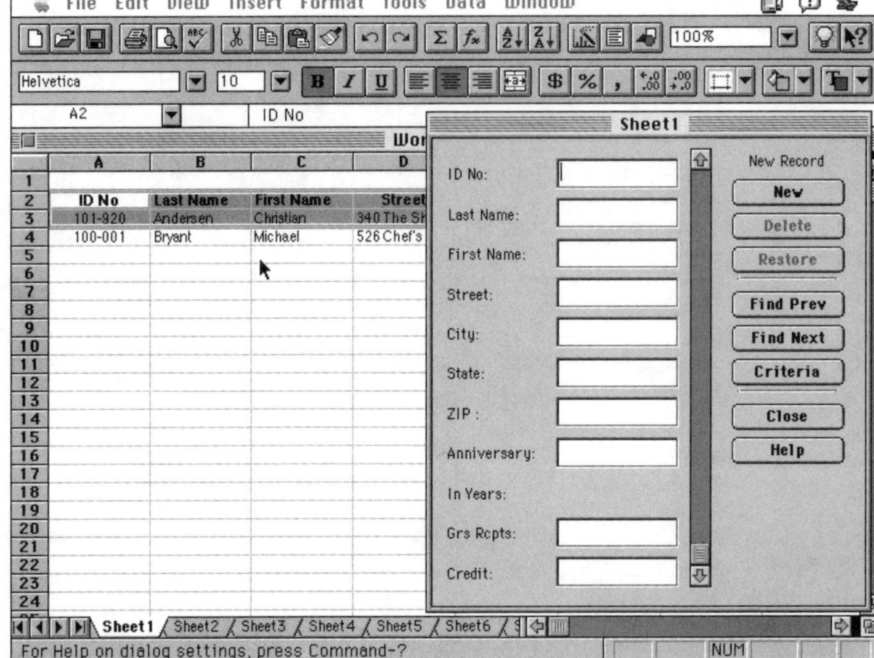

Figure 8-3: The database after the second record was entered in the data form.

When you finish adding records to the database, press Esc or click on the Close button to close the data form. Then save the worksheet with the Save command on the File pull-down menu or click on the Save tool on the Standard toolbar.

Finders keepers: locating, changing, and deleting records

After the database is underway and you're caught up with entering new records, you can start using the data form to perform routine maintenance on the database. For example, you can use the data form to locate a record you want to change and then make the edits to the particular fields. You also can use the data form to find a specific record you want to remove and then delete it from the database.

- Begin editing by selecting the row of field names along with all the records in the database. To make this selection, simply position the cell pointer in the first field name, hold down the Shift key, and press ⌘+→ followed by ⌘+↓. Then choose Form on the Data menu.

- Locate the record you want to edit in the database by bringing up its data form. See Table 8-1 and the following two sections, "Scroll me up, Scotty" and "Eureka! (or, 'Look me up when you're in town')," for hints on locating records.
- To edit the fields of the current record, move to that field by pressing Tab or Shift+Tab and replace the entry by typing a new one.
- Alternatively, press ← or → or click the I-beam cursor to reposition the insertion point and then make your edits.
- To clear a field entirely, select it and then press Delete.

To delete the entire record from the database, click on the Delete command button. Excel displays an alert box with the following dire warning:

```
Displayed record will be deleted permanently
```

To go ahead and get rid of the record displayed in the data form, choose OK. To play it safe and keep the record intact, choose Cancel.

Please keep in mind that you *cannot* use the Undo feature to bring back a record you removed with the Delete button! Excel definitely is *not* kidding when it uses words like `deleted permanently`. As a precaution, always save a backup version of the worksheet with the database before you start removing old records.

Table 8-1 Ways to Get to a Particular Record

Keystrokes or Scroll Bar Technique	*Result*
Press ↓ or Return, or click on the ↓ scroll arrow or the Find Next button	Moves to the next record in the database and leaves the same field selected
Press ↑ or Shift+Return, or click on the ↑ scroll arrow or the Find Prev button	Moves to the preceding record in the database and leaves the same field selected
Press Page Down	Moves 10 records forward in the database
Press Page Up	Moves 10 records backward in the database
Press Control+↑ or Control+Page Up, or drag the scroll box to the top of the scroll bar	Moves to the first record in the database
Press Control+↓ or Control+Page Down, or drag the scroll box to the bottom of the scroll bar	Moves to the last record in the database

⌘ does not work interchangeably with the Control key in many Excel 5 shortcut keyboard commands such as the Data ⇨ Form procedure. Microsoft is trying to force us Mac heads to use Microsoft Windows commands.

Scroll me up, Scotty

After you display the data form in the worksheet by selecting the entire database (field names and all), choose the Form command from the Data pull-down menu. You now can use the scroll bar to the right of the list of field names or various keystrokes (both summarized in Table 8-1) to move through the records in the database until you find the one you want to edit or delete.

- To move to the data form for the next record in the database, press ↓, press Return, or click on the scroll arrow at the bottom of the scroll bar.
- To move to the data form for the preceding record in the database, press ↑, press Shift+Return, or click on the scroll arrow at the top of the scroll bar.
- To move to the data form for the first record in the database, press Control+↑, press Control+Page Up, or drag the scroll box to the very top of the scroll bar.
- To move to the data form for the last record, press Control+↓, press Control+Page Down, or drag the scroll box to the very bottom of the scroll bar.

Eureka! (or, "Look me up when you're in town")

In a really large database, trying to find a particular record by moving from record to record — or even moving ten records at a time with the scroll bar — can take all day. Rather than waste time trying to manually search for a record, you can use the Criteria button in the data form to look up the record.

When you click on the Criteria button, Excel clears all the field entries in the data form (and replaces the record number with the word `Criteria`) so that you can enter the criteria to search for in the blank text boxes.

Suppose that you need to edit Cinderella's credit rating (she finally makes enough money sweeping chimneys to earn her a line of credit at any of the three Simple Simon Pie Shoppe locations). Unfortunately, her paperwork doesn't include her ID number. All you know is that she currently doesn't have credit, and you're pretty sure she spells her last name with a *C* instead of a *S*.

To find her record, you can use this information to narrow down the search to the records where the last name begins with the letter *C* and the Credit field contains *No*. To narrow the search, open the data form for the client database, click on the Criteria button, and then enter the following in the text box for the Last Name field:

```
C*
```

Also enter the following in the text box for the Credit field (see Figure 8-4):

```
No
```

When you enter search criteria for records in the blank text boxes of the data form, you can use the **?** (question mark) and ***** (asterisk) wildcard characters. Remember that you use these wildcard characters with the Find command on the Edit menu to locate cells with particular entries (see Chapter 5 for more on using these wildcard characters with the Find feature).

Now choose the Find Next button. Excel displays in the data form the first record in the database where the last name begins with the letter *C* and the Credit field contains *No*. As shown in Figure 8-5, the first record in this database that meets these criteria is for Butch Cassidy. To press on and find our dear Cinderella's record, choose the Find Next button again. Figure 8-6 shows Poore Cinderella's record. Having located Cinderella's record, you then can edit her credit status in the text box for the Credit field. After you click on the Close button, Excel records her well-deserved credit rating in the database itself.

Figure 8-4: Entering the search criteria in the text boxes.

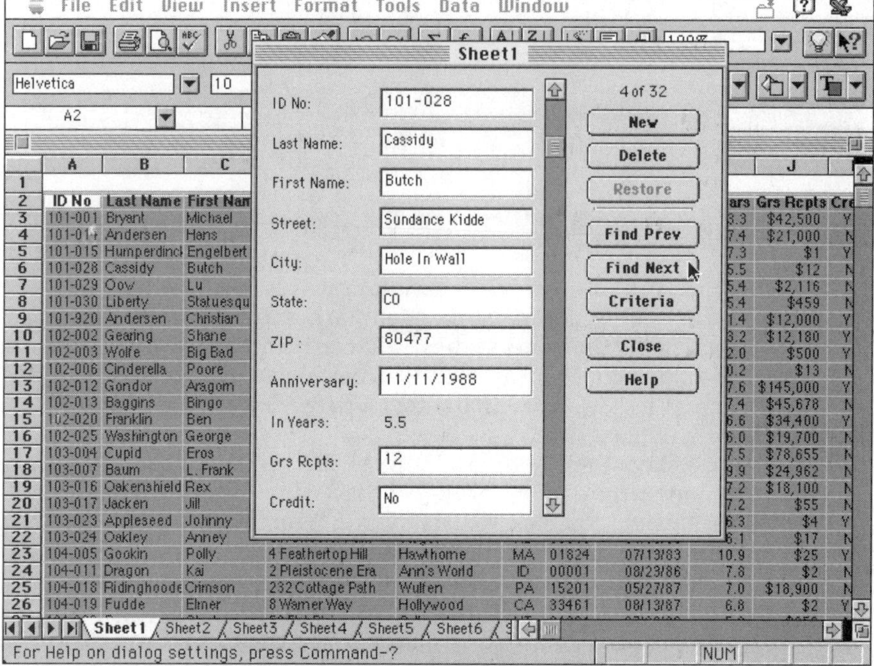

Figure 8-5: The first record in the database that meets the search criteria.

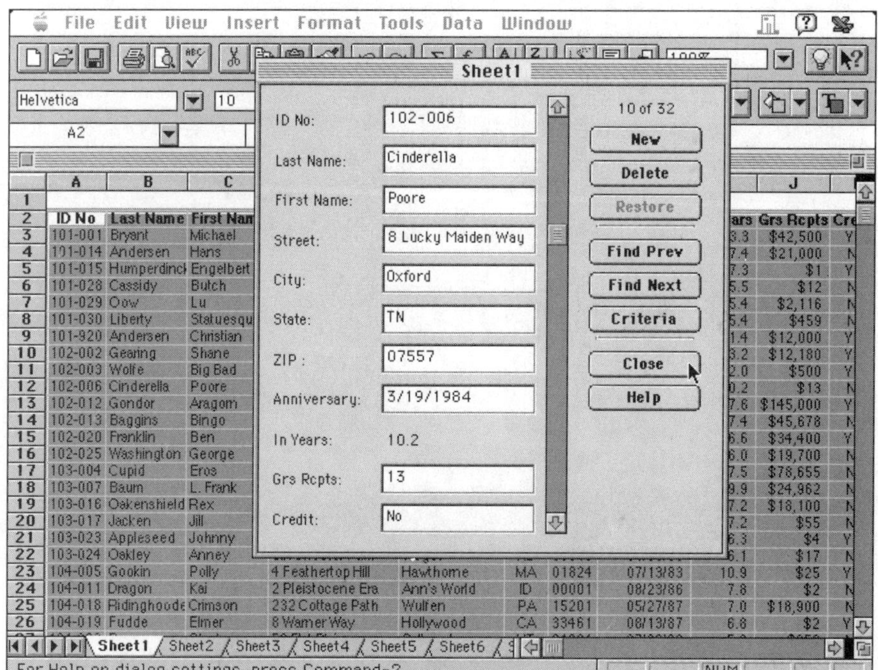

Figure 8-6: Eureka! The long-lost record appears.

When you use the Criteria button in the data form to find records, you can include the following operators in the search criteria you enter to locate a specific record in the database:

Operator	*Meaning*
=	Equal to
>	Greater than
>=	Greater than or equal to
<	Less than
<=	Less than or equal to
<>	Not equal to

For example, to display only those records where a client's gross receipts are greater than or equal to $30,000 a year, enter **>=30000** in the text box for the Grs Rcpts field before choosing the Find Next button.

When specifying search criteria that fit a number of records, you may have to click on the Find Next or Find Prev button several times to locate the record you want. If no record fits the search criteria you enter, the computer beeps at you when you click on one of these buttons.

To change the search criteria, if necessary, first clear the data form by choosing the Criteria button again. Then select the appropriate text boxes and clear out the old criteria before you enter the new. (You can just replace the criteria if you're using the same fields.)

To switch back to the current record without using the search criteria you enter, click on the Form button (this button replaces the Criteria button as soon you click on the Criteria button).

Data from A to Z (or, "So, Sort Me!")

Every database you put together in Excel has some kind of preferred order for maintaining and viewing the records. Depending on the database, you may want to see the records in alphabetical order by last name. In the case of a database of clients, you may want to see the records arranged alphabetically by company name. In the sample client database used in this chapter, the preferred order is a numerical order by the number assigned to each client when he or she first put in an order.

When you initially enter records for a new database, you no doubt enter them in whatever order is the preferred one. However, as you will soon discover, you don't have the option of adding subsequent records in that preferred order. Whenever you add a new record with the New button in the data form, Excel tacks that record onto the bottom of the database by adding a new row.

Therefore, if you originally entered all the records in alphabetical order by company name (from ABC Supplies to Zastrow and Sons) and then you add the record for a new client named Digital Products of America, Excel puts the new record at the bottom of the barrel, in the last row right after Zastrow and Sons instead of inserting the new record in its proper position — somewhere after ABC Supplies but definitely before Zastrow and his wonderful boys!

Putting a new record at the bottom of the database is not the only problem you can have with the order used when originally entering records. Even if the records in the database remain fairly stable, the preferred order merely represents the order you use *most* of the time. But what about those times when you need to see the records in another, special order?

Suppose that you usually like to work with the client database in alphabetical order by company name but when you use the records to generate mailing labels for a mass mailing, you want the records in ZIP code order. Or if you want to generate for your account representatives a list that shows which clients are in whose territory, you need the records in alphabetical order by state and maybe even by city.

Flexibility in the record order is exactly what's required to keep up with the different needs you have for the data. Flexibility is precisely what the Sort command offers you — after you understand how to use it, of course.

To have Excel correctly sort the records in a database, you must specify which fields determine the new order of the records (such fields are technically known as the *sorting keys*). Further, you must specify what type of order should be created with the information in these fields. There are two possible orders: *ascending order,* in which text entries are placed in alphabetical order (A to Z) and values are placed in numerical order (from smallest to largest), and *descending order,* which is the exact reverse of alphabetical order (Z to A) and numerical order (largest to smallest).

When you sort records in a database, you can specify up to three fields on which to sort, and you also can choose between ascending and descending order for each key that you use. You need to specify more than one field only when the first field you use in sorting contains duplicate values and you want a say in how the records with duplicate values are arranged. (If you don't specify another field to sort on, Excel just puts the records in the order in which you entered them.)

Ascending and descending

When you use the ascending sort order with a key field that contains many different kinds of entries, Excel places numbers (from smallest to largest) before text entries (in alphabetical order), followed by any logical values (TRUE first and then FALSE), error values, and finally, blank cells.

When you use the descending sort order, Excel arranges the different entries in reverse: Numbers are still first, arranged from largest to smallest, text entries go from Z to A, and the FALSE logical value precedes the TRUE logical value.

The best and most common example of when you need more than one key occurs when you sort a large database alphabetically in last-name order. Consider, for example, a database that contains several people with the last name of Smith, Jones, or Zastrow (as is the case when you work at Zastrow and Sons). If you specify the Last Name field as the only field to sort on (using the default ascending order), all the duplicate Smiths, Joneses, and Zastrows are placed in the order in which their records were originally entered. To better sort these duplicates, you can specify the First Name field as the second field to sort on, again using the default ascending order (making the second field the tie-breaker), so that Ian Smith's record precedes that of Sandra Smith, and Vladimir Zastrow's record comes after that of Mikhail Zastrow.

To sort records in an Excel database, follow these steps:

1. **Position the cell pointer in the first field name of the database.**
2. **Choose the Sort command from the Data menu.**

   Excel selects all the records of the database (without including the first row of field names) and opens the Sort dialog box shown in Figure 8-7. By default, the first field name appears in the Sort By pull-down menu and the Ascending radio button, at the top of the Sort dialog box, is selected.
3. **In the Sort By pull-down menu, select the name of the first field on which you want the database records to be sorted.**

   If you want the records arranged in descending order, remember also to choose the Descending radio button to the right.
4. **If the first field contains duplicates, and you want to specify how these records are sorted, select a second field on which to sort in the Then By pull-down menu and select between the Ascending and Descending radio buttons to its right.**
5. **If necessary, specify a third field on which to sort the records in the second Then By pull-down menu and decide on the sort order to use.**
6. **Choose OK or press Return.**

Figure 8-7: The Sort dialog box set up to sort alphabetically by last name and then first name.

Excel sorts the selected records. If you see that you sorted the database on the wrong fields or in the wrong order, choose the Undo Sort command from the Edit menu or press Ô+Z to immediately restore the database records to their previous order.

Figure 8-7 shows the Sort dialog box after I selected the Last Name field as the first field to sort on and the First Name field as the secondary field on which to sort the records. The settings in this dialog box specify that records in the client database be sorted in alphabetical (Ascending) order by last name and then first name. Figure 8-8 shows the client database right after sorting.

You can use the Sort Ascending tool (with the *A* above the *Z*) or the Sort Descending tool (with the *Z* above the *A*) on the Standard toolbar to sort records in the database. These tools use either the very first field or the very last field in the database as the sorting key.

- To sort the database by the values in the very *first* field of the database, position the cell pointer in the cell with the first field name (the first cell in the row of field names at the top of the database) and then click on the Sort Ascending tool or Sort Descending tool.

File Edit View Insert Format Tools Data Window

A3 101-920

Simons Client Database

	A	B	C	D	E	F	G	H	I	J	
1	Simple Simon Pie Shoppe -- Client List										
2	ID No	Last Name	First Name	Street	City	State	ZIP	Anniversary	In Years	Grs Rcpts	Cre
3	101-920	Andersen	Christian	340 The Shadow	Scholar	MN	58764	12/28/82	11.4	$12,000	Y
4	101-014	Andersen	Hans	341 The Shadow	Scholar	MN	58764	12/29/86	7.4	$21,000	N
5	103-023	Appleseed	Johnny	6789 Fruitree Tr	Along The Way	SD	66017	02/24/88	6.3	$4	Y
6	102-013	Baggins	Bingo	99 Hobbithole	Shire	ME	04047	12/20/86	7.4	$45,678	N
7	103-007	Baum	L. Frank	447 Toto Too Rd	Oz	KS	65432	06/28/84	9.9	$24,962	N
8	104-026	Brown	Charles	59 Flat Plains	Saltewater	UT	84001	07/09/88	5.9	$956	N
9	101-001	Bryant	Michael	326 Chef's Lane	Paris	TX	78705	02/01/81	13.3	$42,500	Y
10	101-028	Cassidy	Butch	Sundance Kidde	Hole In Wall	CO	80477	11/11/88	5.5	$12	N
11	102-006	Cinderella	Poore	8 Lucky Maiden Way	Oxford	TN	07557	03/19/84	10.2	$13	N
12	103-004	Cupid	Eros	97 Mount Olympus	Greece	CT	03331	11/13/86	7.5	$78,655	N
13	104-011	Dragon	Kai	2 Pleistocene Era	Ann's World	ID	00001	08/23/86	7.8	$2	N
14	104-031	Eaters	Big	444 Big Pigs Court	Dogtown	AZ	85257	09/02/92	1.7	$66,666	Y
15	106-022	Foliage	Red	49 Maple Syrup	Waffle	VT	05452	12/18/87	6.4	$4,200	Y
16	102-020	Franklin	Ben	1789 Constitution	Jefferson	WY	20178	10/21/87	6.6	$34,400	Y
17	104-019	Fudde	Elmer	8 Warner Way	Hollywood	CA	33461	08/13/87	6.8	$2	Y
18	102-002	Gearing	Shane	1 Gunfighter's End	LaLa Land	CA	90069	03/04/81	13.2	$12,180	Y
19	102-012	Gondor	Aragorn	2956 Gandalf	Midearth	WY	80342	10/11/86	7.6	$145,000	Y
20	104-005	Gookin	Polly	4 Feathertop Hill	Hawthorne	MA	01824	07/13/83	10.9	$25	Y
21	105-008	Harvey	Chauncey	60 Lucky Starr Pl	Shetland	IL	60080	08/15/85	8.8	$1,555	N
22	106-021	Horse	Seabisquit	First Place Finish	Raceway	KY	23986	11/02/87	6.6	$195	N
23	101-015	Humperdinck	Engelbert	6 Hansel+Gretel Tr	Gingerbread	MD	20815	02/14/87	7.3	$1	Y
24	103-017	Jacken	Jill	Up the Hill	Pail of Water	OK	45678	03/01/87	7.2	$55	N
25	105-027	Laurel	Stan	2 Oliver Hardy	Celluloyde	NM	82128	09/13/88	5.7	$5	N
26	101-030	Liberty	Statuesque	31 Gotham Centre	Big Apple	NY	10011	01/03/89	5.4	$459	N

Sheet1 Sheet2 Sheet3 Sheet4 Sheet5 Sheet6

Ready NUM

Figure 8-8: The database sorted in alphabetical order by last name and then first name.

- To sort the database by the values in the very *last* field, position the cell pointer in the cell with the last field name (the last cell in the row of field names at the top of the database) and then click on the Sort Ascending tool or Sort Descending tool.

You AutoFilter the Database to Find the Records You Want

Excel's new AutoFilter feature makes it a breeze to hide everything in a database except the records you want to see. To filter a database with this incredibly nifty feature, position the cell pointer in any one of the cells containing the database field names and choose Data ⇨ Filter ⇨ AutoFilter. When you choose the AutoFilter command, Excel adds pull-down buttons to every cell with a field name in that row (like those shown in Figure 8-9).

To filter the database to just those records that contain a particular value, click on the appropriate field's pull-down button to open a pull-down menu containing all the entries made in that field. Select the value you want to use as a filter. Excel then displays only those records that contain the value you selected in that field (all other records are temporarily hidden).

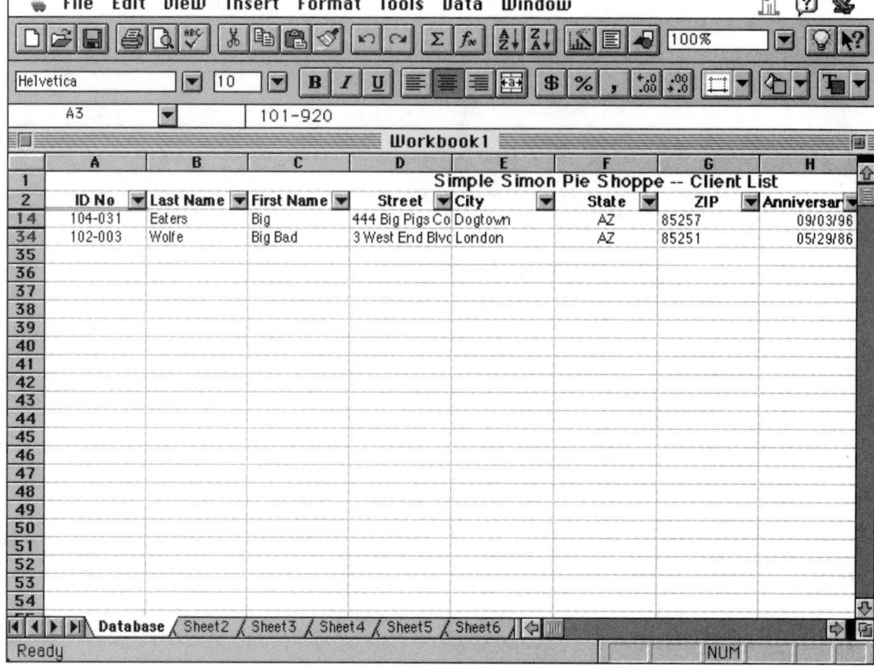

Figure 8-9: The database after filtering for State (AZ) and Credit (Yes).

For example, in Figure 8-9, I filtered the client database to show only those records where the State field contains AZ (for Arizona). To filter the database, I clicked on the State's pull-down menu and then clicked on AZ in the pull-down menu — it was as simple as that.

After you've filtered a database so that only the records you want to work with are displayed, you then can copy the records to another part of the worksheet to the right of the database (or better yet, to another worksheet in the workbook). Simply select the cells and then choose Copy on the Edit menu (⌘+C). Move the cell pointer to the first cell where the copied records are to appear and press Return. After copying the filtered records, you then can redisplay all the records in the database or apply a slightly different filter.

If you find that filtering the database by selecting a single value in a field pull-down menu gives you more records than you really want to contend with, you can further filter the database by selecting another value in a second field's pull-down menu. Suppose that you select CA as the filter value in the State pull-down menu and end up with hundreds of California records still displayed in the worksheet. To reduce the number of California records to a more manageable number, you can select a value, such as San Francisco, in the City field's pull-down menu to further filter the database and reduce the records you have to work with on-screen. Then, when you've finished working with the San Francisco records, you can display another set by choosing the City's pull-down menu again and changing the filter value from San Francisco to some other city (such as Los Angeles).

When you're ready to once again display all the records in the database, choose Data ➪ Filter ➪ Show All. You also can remove a filter from a particular field by selecting its pull-down button and then selecting the (All) option at the top of the pull-down menu.

Note that if you've only applied a single field filter to the database, choosing the (All) option is tantamount to selecting the Show All command.

Creating Custom AutoFilters

In addition to filtering a database to records that contain a particular field entry (such as Newark as the City or CA as the State), you can create custom AutoFilters that enable you to filter the database to records that meet less-exacting criteria, such as last names starting with the letter *M,* or ranges of values, like salaries between $25,000 and $35,000 a year.

To create a custom filter for a field, click on the field's pull-down button and then choose the (Custom) option at the top of the pull-down menu. After you choose the (Custom) option, Excel displays the Custom AutoFilter dialog box, similar to the one shown in Figure 8-10.

In this dialog box, you first select the operator that you want to want to use in the first pull-down menu (=, >, <, >=, <=, or <> — see Table 8-2 for details). In the text box to the right, enter the value (be it text or numbers) that should meet, exceed, fall below, or not be found in the records of the database. Note that you can select any of the entries made in that field of the database by choosing the pull-down button and selecting the entry in the pull-down menu (much like you do when selecting an AutoFilter value in a database itself).

If you only want to filter records where a particular field entry matches, exceeds, falls below, or simply is not the same as the one you enter in the text box, you then choose OK or press Return to apply this filter to the database. However, you can use the Custom AutoFilter dialog box to filter the database to records with field entries that fall within a range of values or meet either one of two criteria.

To set up a range of values, you choose the > or >= operator for the top operator and then enter or select the lowest (or first) value in the range. Then make sure that you select the And radio button and choose the < or <= operator as the bottom operator and enter the highest (or last) value in the range.

Table 8-2 Operators Used in Creating Custom AutoFilters

Operator	*Meaning*	*Example*	*What It Locates in the Database*
=	Equal to	LastName=D*	Records in which the last name starts with the letter *D*
>	Greater than	ZIP>42500	Records in which the number in the ZIP field comes after 42500
<	Less than	Salary<25000	Records in which the value in the Salary field is less than $25,000 a year
>=	Greater than or equal to	Hired>=1/11/92	Records in which the date in the Hired field is on or after January 11, 1992
<=	Less than or equal to	Joined<=2/15/91	Records in which the date in the Joined field is on or before February 15, 1991
<>	Not equal to	State<>NY	Records where the entry in the State field is not *NY* (New York)

Figures 8-10 and 8-11 illustrate how to filter the records in the client database so that only those records where gross receipts are between $10,000 and $75,000 are displayed. As shown in Figure 8-10, you set up this range of values as the filter by first selecting >= as the operator and **10000** as the lower value of the range. Then, with the And radio button selected, you choose <= as the operator and **75000** as the upper value of the range. Figure 8-11 shows the result of applying this filter to the client database.

To set up an either/or condition in the Custom AutoFilter dialog box, you normally choose between the = (equal) and <> (unequal) operators (whichever is appropriate) and then enter or select the first value that must be met or not be equaled. Then you select the Or radio button and choose whichever operator is appropriate and enter or select the second value that must be met or not equaled.

For example, if you wanted to filter the database so that only records where the state is WA (Washington) or OR (Oregon), you would choose = as the first operator and then select or enter **WA** as the first entry. Next, you select the Or radio button and then choose = as the second operator and select or enter **OR** as the second entry. After you filter the database by choosing OK or pressing Return, Excel displays only those records in which either WA or OR is entered as the code in the State field.

Custom AutoFilter

Show Rows Where:
Grs Rcpts
>= 10000
(•) And ( ) Or
<= 75000
Use ? to represent any single character
Use * to represent any series of characters

OK
Cancel
Help

Figure 8-10: The Custom AutoFilter dialog box.

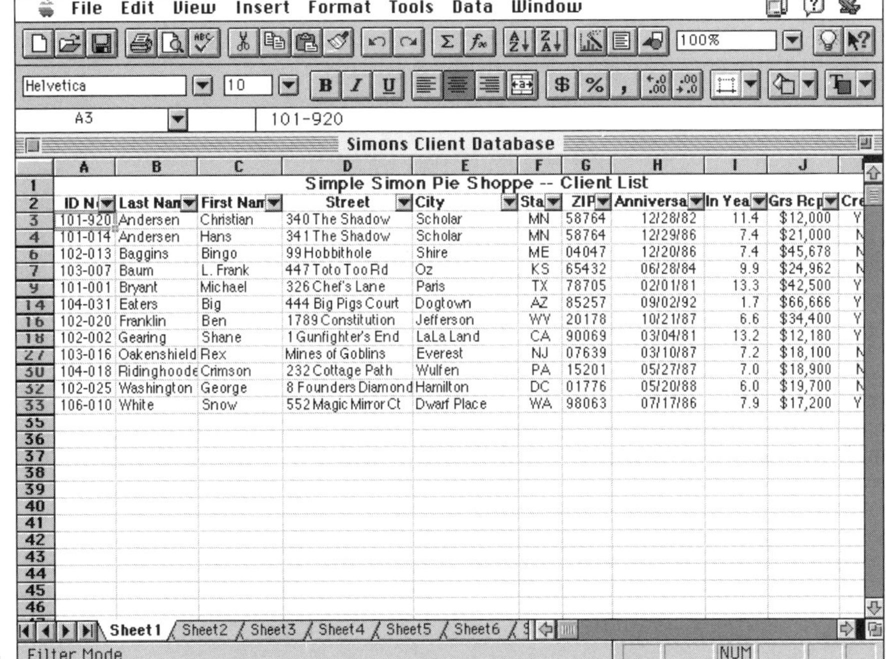

Simple Simon Pie Shoppe -- Client List

	ID N	Last Nan	First Nan	Street	City	Sta	ZIP	Anniversa	In Yea	Grs Rcp	Cr
3	101-920	Andersen	Christian	340 The Shadow	Scholar	MN	58764	12/28/82	11.4	$12,000	Y
4	101-014	Andersen	Hans	341 The Shadow	Scholar	MN	58764	12/29/86	7.4	$21,000	N
6	102-013	Baggins	Bingo	99 Hobbithole	Shire	ME	04047	12/20/86	7.4	$45,678	N
7	103-007	Baum	L. Frank	447 Toto Too Rd	Oz	KS	65432	06/28/84	9.9	$24,962	N
9	101-001	Bryant	Michael	326 Chef's Lane	Paris	TX	78705	02/01/81	13.3	$42,500	Y
14	104-031	Eaters	Big	444 Big Pigs Court	Dogtown	AZ	85257	09/02/92	1.7	$66,666	Y
16	102-020	Franklin	Ben	1789 Constitution	Jefferson	WY	20178	10/21/87	6.6	$34,400	Y
18	102-002	Gearing	Shane	1 Gunfighter's End	LaLa Land	CA	90069	03/04/81	13.2	$12,180	Y
27	103-016	Oakenshield	Rex	Mines of Goblins	Everest	NJ	07639	03/10/87	7.2	$18,100	N
30	104-018	Ridinghoode	Crimson	232 Cottage Path	Wulfen	PA	15201	05/27/87	7.0	$18,900	N
32	102-025	Washington	George	8 Founders Diamond	Hamilton	DC	01776	05/20/88	6.0	$19,700	N
33	106-010	White	Snow	552 Magic Mirror Ct	Dwarf Place	WA	98063	07/17/86	7.9	$17,200	Y

Figure 8-11: The database after applying the custom AutoFilter.

Chapter 9

Coping with More Than One Worksheet at a Time

In This Chapter

- How to move between the worksheets in your workbook
- How to add worksheets to a workbook
- How to delete worksheets from a workbook
- How to select more than one worksheet for group editing
- How to name sheet tabs in a workbook
- How to reorder the worksheets in a workbook
- How to put different worksheets in different windows and display them together on-screen
- How to move or copy a worksheet from one workbook to another
- How to create a worksheet that summarizes the values in other worksheets in your workbook

When you are brand new to spreadsheets, you probably have enough trouble keeping track of one worksheet — let alone 16 worksheets — and the very thought of working with more than one worksheet may be a little more than you can take. As soon as you get a little experience under your belt, however, you will find that working with more than one worksheet in a workbook is no more taxing than working with just a single worksheet.

Don't confuse workbook with worksheet. The *workbook* forms the document (file) that you open and save, copy, or delete, as the case may be. Each workbook (file) normally contains 16 blank *worksheets*. These worksheets are like the loose-leaf pages, which you can delete and add as you need, in a notebook binder. To help you keep track of the worksheets in your workbook and navigate among them, Excel provides sheet tabs (Sheet1 through Sheet16), which are analogous to tab dividers in a loose-leaf notebook.

Before you see *how* to work with more than one worksheet in a workbook, I'll discuss *why* you'd want to do such a crazy thing in the first place. The most common situation is, of course, when you have a bunch of worksheets that are somehow related to each other and that, therefore, naturally belong together in the same workbook. For example, take the Simple Simon Pie Shoppe with its three store locations: Miss Muffet Street, Curds Way, and Arachnid Road. Each location is given its own worksheet in the Simons 1995 Sales workbook that tracks the monthly sales for each type of pie sold. By keeping the sales figures for each location in the same workbook, you gain all the following benefits:

- You can speed up the creation of new worksheets by entering the standard information that all the worksheets require in just one of the worksheets in the workbook (see the "Group Editing (or, 'One Cut, All Is Cut')" section later in this chapter).
- You can attach the macros that you create to help you build the worksheet for the first store sales to the current workbook so that they are readily available when you create the worksheets for the other stores (see Chapter 10 for details on recording macros in the current workbook).
- You quickly can compare the sales of one store to that of another (see "Windows on Your Worksheets" later in this chapter).
- You can print all the sales information for each store as a single report in one printing operation (see Chapter 6 for specifics on printing an entire workbook or particular worksheets in a workbook).
- You can easily create a summary worksheet that totals the quarterly and annual sales of all three store locations (see "Summary Time..." later in this chapter).

Dancing Sheet to Sheet

Each workbook that you create contains 16 worksheets, named Sheet1 through Sheet16. These sheet names appear on tabs at the bottom of the workbook window. To move to another worksheet, you simply click on its sheet tab. Excel then brings that worksheet to the top of the stack by displaying its information in the current workbook window. You always can tell which worksheet is current because its tab is displayed in bold type and appears in white as part of the current worksheet.

To move with the keyboard to the next worksheet in a workbook, press ⌘+Page Down (or Option+→). To move to the preceding worksheet in a workbook, press ⌘+Page Up (or Option+←).

Of course, not all 16 sheet tabs are visible at any one time. Therefore, Excel provides tab scrolling buttons, shown in Figure 9-1, that you can use to bring into view the new sheet tabs. Click on the scroll button with the right-pointing triangle to bring into view the next unseen tab to the right. Click on the scroll button with the left-pointing triangle to bring into view the next unseen tab to the left. Click on the scroll button with the right-pointing triangle and the vertical bar to bring into view the last group of sheet tabs, including the very last tab. Click on the scroll button with the left-pointing triangle and the vertical bar to bring into view the first group of sheet tabs, including the very first tab. Remember that scrolling tabs into view is not the same as selecting a sheet tab: You still need to click on the tab to make the appropriate sheet active after you scroll it into view.

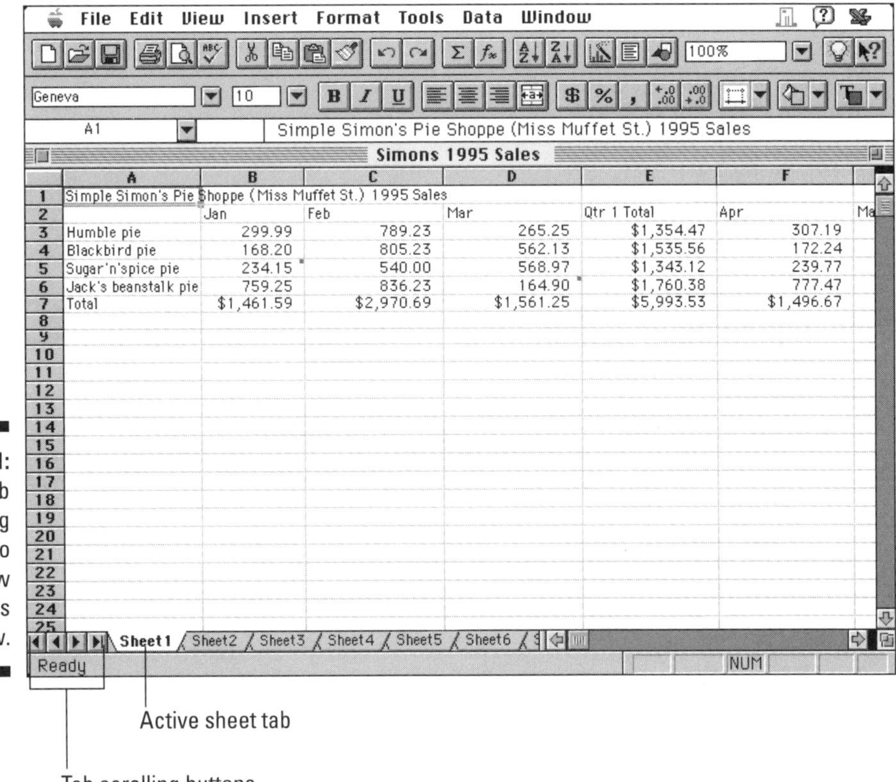

Figure 9-1: Use the tab scrolling buttons to bring new sheet tabs into view.

To make it easier to find the sheet tab you want to select without having to do an inordinate amount of tab scrolling, you can drag the tab split box, shown in Figure 9-2, to the right to reveal more sheet tabs (and thereby make the horizontal scroll bar shorter). If you later decide that you then want to restore the horizontal scroll bar to its normal length, you simply double-click on the tab split box.

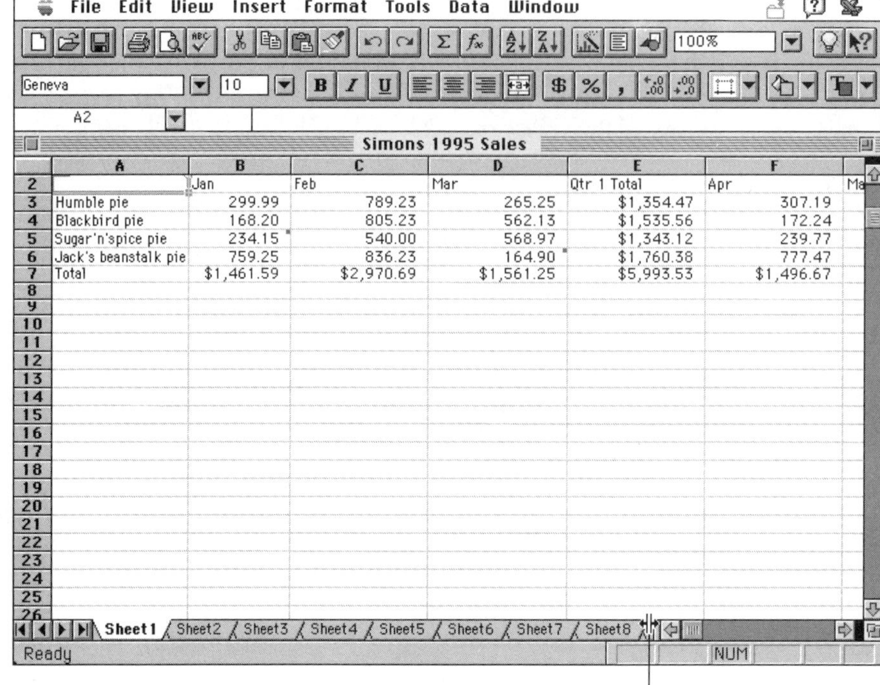

Figure 9-2: Using the tab split box to display more sheet tabs by making the horizontal scroll bar shorter.

Group Editing (or "One Cut, All Is Cut")

Each time you click on a sheet tab, you select that worksheet and make it active, enabling you to make whatever changes are necessary to its cells. You may come across times, however, when you want to select more than one worksheet before you make some editing changes. When you select multiple worksheets, the editing changes you make (such as entering information in a cell range or deleting worksheets) affect all the selected sheets.

Suppose that you need to create three worksheets in a new workbook, all of which contain the names of the 12 months in row 3, starting in column B. Prior to entering **January** in cell B3 and then using the AutoFill handle to fill in the rest of the 11 months across row 3, you select all three worksheets (Sheet1, Sheet2, and Sheet3, for argument's sake). After you select all three worksheets, Excel inserts the names of the 12 months in row 3 in all three worksheets because you entered them once in the third row of the first sheet. Pretty slick, huh?

Likewise, suppose that you have another workbook where you need to get rid of Sheet2, Sheet5, and Sheet9. Instead of clicking on Sheet2, selecting the Delete Sheet command on the Edit menu, clicking on Sheet5 and repeating the Delete

Sheet command, and finally clicking on Sheet9 and repeating the command yet again, you can select all three worksheets and then zap them out of existence in one fell swoop with a single selection of the Delete Sheet command.

To select a bunch of worksheets in a workbook, you have the following choices:

- To select a group of neighboring worksheets, click on the first sheet tab and then scroll the sheet tabs until you see the tab of the last worksheet to be selected. Hold down the Shift key as you click on the last sheet tab to select all the tabs in between (the old Shift-click method applied to worksheet tabs).
- To select a group of non-neighboring worksheets, click on the first sheet tab and then hold down the ⌘ key as you click on the tabs of the other sheets to be selected.

Excel shows you which worksheets are selected by turning their sheet tabs white (although only the active sheet's tab name appears in bold).

To deselect the group of worksheets after you've finished your "group editing," you simply click on a nonselected (that is, gray) worksheet tab. You also can deselect all the selected worksheets by choosing the Ungroup command on one of the tab's shortcut menus.

One Sheet More or Less

For some of you, the 16 worksheets automatically put into each new workbook are far more than you will ever need (or want) to use. For others of you, the measly 16 worksheets may seldom, if ever, be sufficient for the workbooks you create (if, for example, your company operates in 20 locations or routinely creates budgets for 30 different departments or tracks expenses for 40 account representatives).

Excel makes it easy to insert additional worksheets in a workbook or to remove those that you don't need.

- To insert a new worksheet in the workbook, select the tab of the sheet where the new worksheet is to be inserted. Then choose Worksheet on the Insert menu or choose Insert on the tab's shortcut menu. Choose OK in the Insert dialog box or press Return (because Worksheet is already selected in the New list box as the type of sheet to insert).
- To insert a bunch of new worksheets in a row in the workbook, select a group with the same number of tabs as the number of new worksheets to be inserted, starting with the tab where the new worksheets are to be inserted. Then choose Worksheet on the Insert menu or choose Insert on the tab's shortcut menu and choose OK in the Insert dialog box or press Return.

- To delete a worksheet from the workbook, click on its tab and then choose Delete Sheet on the Edit menu or choose Delete on the tab's shortcut menu. Excel then displays a scary message in an alert box about how you're about to permanently delete the selected sheet. Go ahead and select the Yes button if you're really sure that you want to zap the entire sheet (just keep in mind that this is one of those situations where Undo is powerless to put things right by restoring the deleted sheet to the workbook).
- To delete a bunch of worksheets from the workbook, select them all and choose Delete Sheet on the Edit menu or choose Delete on the tab's shortcut menu. Then, if you're sure that none of them will be missed, choose the Yes button in the alert dialog box that appears.

If you find that you're constantly having to monkey around with the number of worksheets in a workbook, either by adding new worksheets or deleting a bunch, you may want to think about changing the default number of worksheets in a workbook. To change the magic number 16 sheets to a more realistic number for your needs, select Tools ⇨ Options ⇨ General tab and enter a new number in the Sheets in New Workbook text box.

A Sheet by Any Other Name

You can attach the macros you created to help you build the first worksheet to the current workbook so that they are readily available when you create the other worksheets (see Chapter 10 for details on recording macros in the current workbook).

Let's face it: The sheet names that Excel comes up with for the tabs in a workbook (Sheet1 through Sheet16) are, to put it mildly, not very descriptive! Luckily, you easily can rename a worksheet tab so that you can remember what you put on the worksheet (provided that this descriptive name is no longer than 32 characters).

To rename a worksheet tab, follow these steps:

1. **Double-click on the sheet tab or choose the Rename command on the sheet's tab shortcut menu to open the Rename Sheet dialog box (similar to the one shown in Figure 9-3).**
2. **Replace the current name in the Name text box with a name of your creation and then choose OK or press Return.**

Excel displays the new sheet name on its tab at the bottom of the workbook window. Figure 9-4 shows you the result of renaming Sheet1 to Muffet St. (the location of the first Simple Simon Pie Shoppe) with the Rename Sheet dialog box.

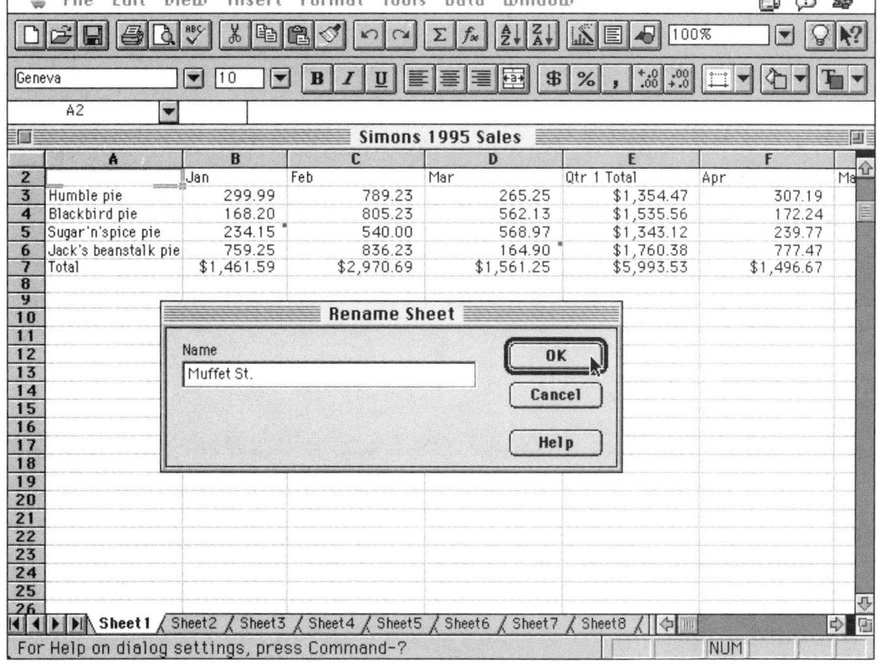

Figure 9-3: Giving a sheet tab a civilized name in the Rename Sheet dialog box.

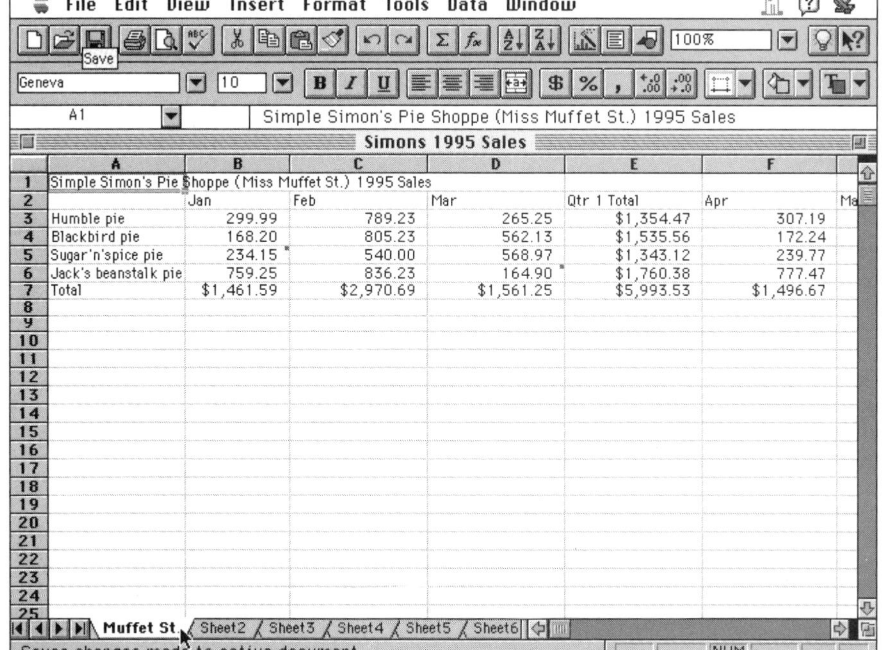

Figure 9-4: The workbook with the new Muffet St. sheet name displayed.

Several good reasons for shorting your sheet's (name)

Although Excel allows up to 32 characters (including spaces) for a sheet name, you should keep your sheet names much briefer, for two reasons. First, the longer the name, the longer the sheet tab; the longer the sheet tab, the fewer tabs that can be displayed; the fewer the tabs that can be displayed, the more tab scrolling you have to do to select the sheets you want to work with. Second, if you start creating formulas that use cells in different worksheets (see "Summary Time..." later in this chapter for an example), Excel uses the sheet name as part of the cell reference in the formula (how else can Excel keep straight the value in cell C1 on Sheet1 from the value in cell C1 on Sheet2?). Therefore, if your sheet names are long, you end up with unnaturally long formulas in the cells and on the formula bar, even when you're dealing with simple formulas that only refer to cells in a few different worksheets.

Arranging Worksheets for Fun and Profit

Sometimes, you may find that you need to change the order in which the sheets appear in the workbook. Excel makes changing the order possible by letting you drag the tab of the sheet you want to arrange in the workbook to the place where it should be inserted. As you drag the tab, the pointer changes to a sheet icon with the arrowhead on it, and the program marks your progress among the sheet tabs (see Figures 9-5 and 9-6 for an example). After you release the mouse button, Excel reorders the worksheets in the workbook by inserting the sheet at the place where you dropped off the tab.

If you hold down the ⌘ key as you drag the tab, Excel inserts a copy of the worksheet at the place where you release the mouse button. You can tell that Excel is copying the sheet rather than just moving it in the workbook because the pointer shows a plus on the sheet icon containing the arrowhead. After you release the mouse button, Excel inserts the copy in the workbook, which is designated by the addition of *(2)* after the tab name. For example, if you copy Sheet5 to another place in the workbook, the sheet tab of the copy is named Sheet5 (2). You then can rename the tab to something civilized (see "A Sheet by Any Other Name," earlier in this chapter, for details).

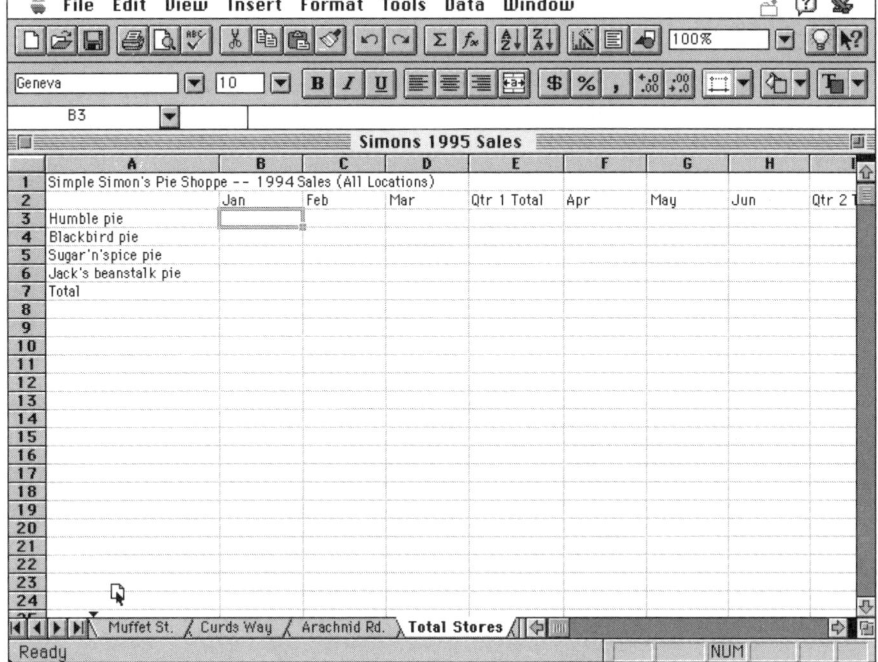

Figure 9-5: Reordering the sheets in the Simons 1995 Sales workbook by dragging the Total Stores tab to the front.

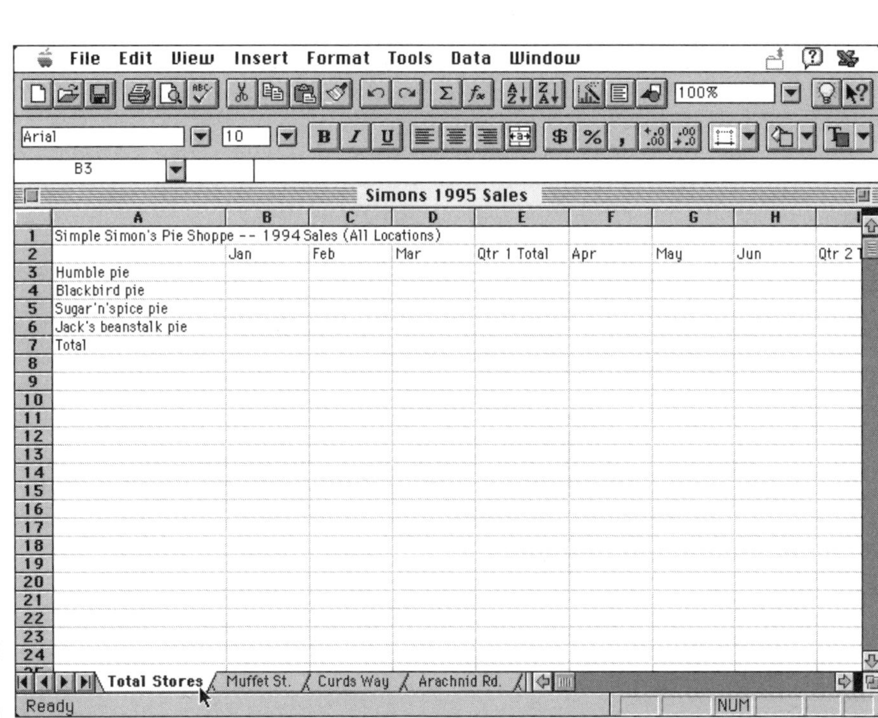

Figure 9-6: The workbook after moving the Total Stores sheet to the front.

Windows on Your Worksheets

Just as you can split up a single worksheet into window panes so that you can view different parts of the sheet on-screen at the same time (Chapter 5), you can split up a single workbook into worksheet windows and then arrange them so that you can view different parts of each worksheet on-screen.

To open the worksheets that you want to view in different windows, you simply insert new document windows (in addition to the one that is automatically opened when you open the workbook file itself) and then select the worksheet that you want displayed in each new window. To accomplish this task, follow these steps:

1. **Choose the New Window command on the Window menu to create a second worksheet window.**
2. **Click on the tab of the worksheet that you want displayed in this second window (indicated by the** :2 **added on to the end of the filename in the title bar).**
3. **Choose the New Window command on the Window menu to create a third worksheet window and then click on the tab of the worksheet that you want displayed in this third window (indicated by the** :3 **added on to the end of the filename in the title bar).**
4. **Continue in this manner, using the New Window command to create a new window and then selecting the tab of the worksheet to be displayed in that window for each worksheet that you want to compare.**

After creating windows for the worksheets you want to compare, you can use the Arrange command on the Window pull-down menu to determine how the windows are to be displayed on-screen. After you select this command, Excel displays the Arrange Windows dialog box with the following options (see Figure 9-7):

- Select the Tiled radio button to have Excel arrange and size the windows so that they all fit side by side on-screen in the order in which they were opened. Figure 9-8 shows the screen after clicking on this button when three document windows were open.
- Select the Horizontal radio button to have Excel size the windows equally and then place them one above the other. Figure 9-9 shows the screen after clicking on this button when three worksheet windows were open.
- Select the Vertical radio button to have Excel size the windows equally and then place them next to each other. Figure 9-10 shows the screen after I clicked on the Vertical radio button when three worksheet windows were open.

- Select the Cascade radio button to have Excel arrange and size the windows so that they overlap one another with only their title bars showing. Figure 9-11 shows the screen after clicking on this button when three document windows were open).

- Select the Windows of Active Workbook check box to have Excel show only the windows that you've opened in the current workbook. (Otherwise, the program also displays all the windows in any other workbooks you have open — yes, Virginia, it is possible to open more than one workbook as well as more than one window within each open workbook, provided your computer has enough memory and you have enough stamina to keep track of all that information.)

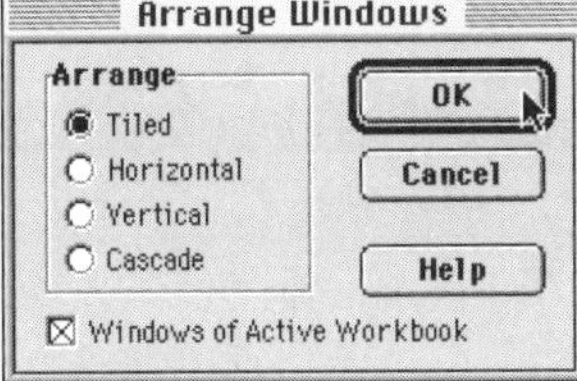

Figure 9-7: The Arrange Windows dialog box.

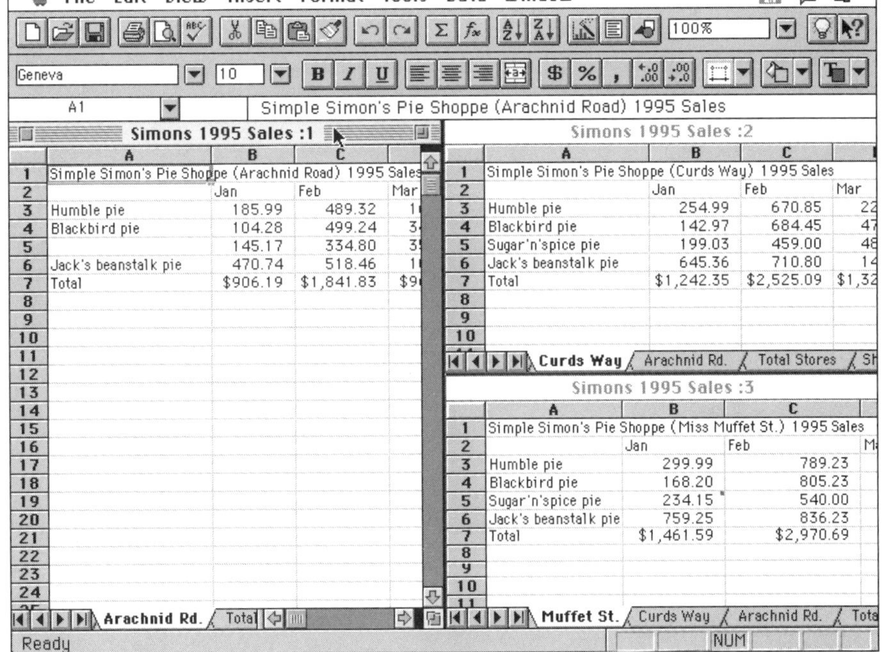

Figure 9-8: Worksheet windows after arranging them with the Tiled radio button.

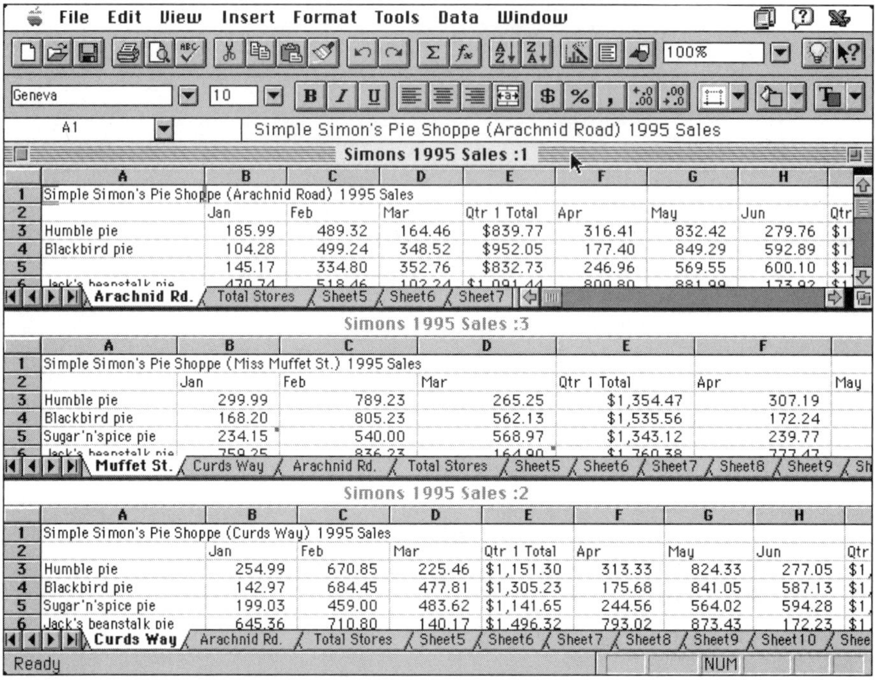

File Edit View Insert Format Tools Data Window

A1 Simple Simon's Pie Shoppe (Arachnid Road) 1995 Sales

Simons 1995 Sales :1

	A	B	C	D	E	F	G	H	
1	Simple Simon's Pie Shoppe (Arachnid Road) 1995 Sales								
2		Jan	Feb	Mar	Qtr 1 Total	Apr	May	Jun	Qtr
3	Humble pie	185.99	489.32	164.46	$839.77	316.41	832.42	279.76	$1
4	Blackbird pie	104.28	499.24	348.52	$952.05	177.40	849.29	592.89	$1
5		145.17	334.80	352.76	$832.73	246.96	569.55	600.10	$1

Arachnid Rd. / Total Stores / Sheet5 / Sheet6 / Sheet7

Simons 1995 Sales :3

	A	B	C	D	E	F	
1	Simple Simon's Pie Shoppe (Miss Muffet St.) 1995 Sales						
2		Jan	Feb	Mar	Qtr 1 Total	Apr	May
3	Humble pie	299.99	789.23	265.25	$1,354.47	307.19	
4	Blackbird pie	168.20	805.23	562.13	$1,535.56	172.24	
5	Sugar'n'spice pie	234.15	540.00	568.97	$1,343.12	239.77	

Muffet St. / Curds Way / Arachnid Rd. / Total Stores / Sheet5 / Sheet6 / Sheet7 / Sheet8 / Sheet9 / Sh

Simons 1995 Sales :2

	A	B	C	D	E	F	G	H	
1	Simple Simon's Pie Shoppe (Curds Way) 1995 Sales								
2		Jan	Feb	Mar	Qtr 1 Total	Apr	May	Jun	Qtr
3	Humble pie	254.99	670.85	225.46	$1,151.30	313.33	824.33	277.05	$1
4	Blackbird pie	142.97	684.45	477.81	$1,305.23	175.68	841.05	587.13	$1
5	Sugar'n'spice pie	199.03	459.00	483.62	$1,141.65	244.56	564.02	594.28	$1
6	Jack's beanstalk pie	645.36	710.80	140.17	$1,496.32	793.02	873.43	172.23	$1

Curds Way / Arachnid Rd. / Total Stores / Sheet5 / Sheet6 / Sheet7 / Sheet8 / Sheet9 / Sheet10 / Shee

Ready NUM

Figure 9-9: Worksheet windows after arranging them with the Horizontal radio button.

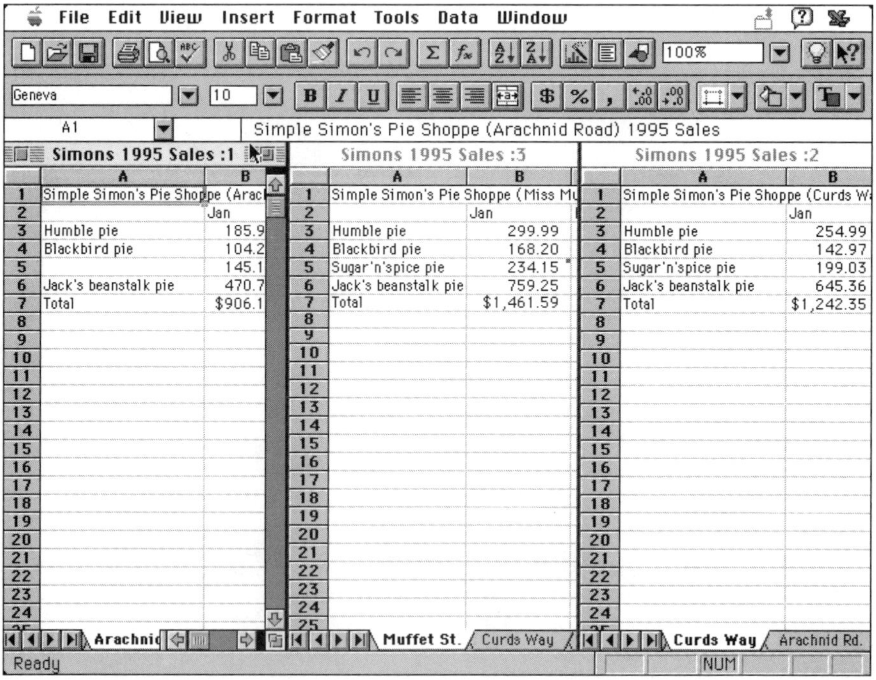

File Edit View Insert Format Tools Data Window

A1 Simple Simon's Pie Shoppe (Arachnid Road) 1995 Sales

Simons 1995 Sales :1

	A	B
1	Simple Simon's Pie Shoppe (Arac	
2		Jan
3	Humble pie	185.9
4	Blackbird pie	104.2
5		145.1
6	Jack's beanstalk pie	470.7
7	Total	$906.1

Arachnid

Simons 1995 Sales :3

	A	B
1	Simple Simon's Pie Shoppe (Miss Mu	
2		Jan
3	Humble pie	299.99
4	Blackbird pie	168.20
5	Sugar'n'spice pie	234.15
6	Jack's beanstalk pie	759.25
7	Total	$1,461.59

Muffet St. / Curds Way

Simons 1995 Sales :2

	A	B
1	Simple Simon's Pie Shoppe (Curds W	
2		Jan
3	Humble pie	254.99
4	Blackbird pie	142.97
5	Sugar'n'spice pie	199.03
6	Jack's beanstalk pie	645.36
7	Total	$1,242.35

Curds Way / Arachnid Rd.

Ready NUM

Figure 9-10: Worksheet windows after arranging them with the Vertical radio button.

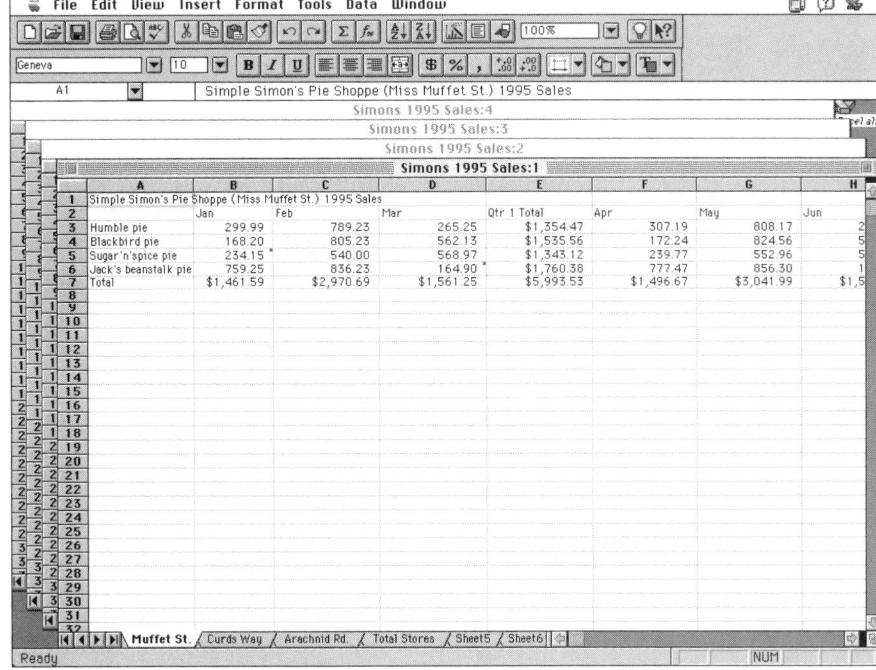

Figure 9-11: Worksheet windows after arranging them with the Cascade radio button.

After the windows are placed in one arrangement or another, you can activate the one you want to use (if it's not already selected) by clicking on it. (In the case of the cascade arrangement, you need to click on the window's title bar.)

After you click on a worksheet window that's been tiled or placed in the horizontal or vertical arrangement, Excel indicates that the window is selected by highlighting its title bar and adding scroll bars to the window. After you click on the title bar of a worksheet window that's been placed in the cascade arrangement, the program displays the window on the top of the stack as well as highlights its title bar and adds scroll bars.

You can temporarily zoom up the window to full size by clicking on the Zoom box in the window's upper right-hand corner. After you finish the work you need to do in the full-size worksheet window, return it to its preceding arrangement by clicking on the window's Zoom box.

To select the next tiled, horizontal, or vertical window on-screen or to display the next window in a cascade arrangement when using the keyboard, press ⌘+F6 (or Control+F6). To select the preceding tiled, horizontal, or vertical window or to display the preceding window in a cascade arrangement, press ⌘+F6. Note that these keystrokes work to select the next and preceding worksheet window even when the windows are maximized in the Excel program window.

If you close one of the windows you've arranged by clicking on its Close box, Excel does not automatically resize the other open windows to fill in the gap. Likewise, if you create another window with the New Window command, Excel does not automatically arrange it in with the others (in fact, the new window sits on top of the other open windows).

To fill in the gap created by closing a window or to integrate a newly opened window into the current arrangement, open the Arrange Windows dialog box and click on the OK button or press Return. (The same radio button you clicked on the last time is still selected; if you want to choose a new arrangement, click on the new radio button before you click on OK.)

Don't try to close a particular worksheet window with the Close command on the File menu, because you'll succeed only in closing the entire workbook file while at the same time getting rid of all the worksheet windows you've created.

When you save your workbook, Excel saves the current window arrangement as part of the file along with all the rest of the changes. If you don't want the current window arrangement saved, close all but one of the windows (by clicking on their Close boxes). Then, before saving the file, click on the last window's Zoom box and select the tab of the worksheet that you want displayed the next time you open the workbook.

From One Workbook to Another

In some situations, you may want to move a particular worksheet or copy it from one workbook to another. To move or copy worksheets between workbooks, follow these steps:

1. **Open both the workbook with the worksheet(s) you want to move or copy and the workbook that is to contain the worksheet(s).**

   Use the Open tool on the Standard toolbar or select the Open command from the File menu (⌘+O) to open the workbooks.

2. **Select the workbook that contains the worksheet(s) to be moved or copied.**

   To activate the workbook with the sheet(s) to be moved or copied, choose its name on the Window pull-down menu.

3. **Select the worksheet(s) to be moved or copied.**

   To select a single worksheet, click on its sheet tab. To select a group of neighboring sheets, click on the first tab and hold down Shift as you click on the last tab. To select various nonadjacent sheets, click on the first tab and then hold down ⌘ as you click on each of the other sheet tabs.

4. **Choose Move or Copy Sheet on the Edit menu or choose the Move or Copy command on one of the tab's shortcut menus.**

   Excel opens up the Move or Copy dialog box (similar to the one shown in Figure 9-12), where you indicate whether you want to move or copy the selected sheet(s) and where to move or copy them.

Figure 9-12: The Move or Copy dialog box, where you select the workbook to move the selected sheets to.

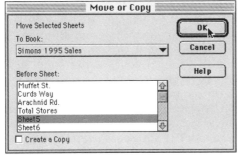

5. **In the To Book pull-down menu, select the name of the workbook to copy or move the worksheet(s) to.**

   If you want to move or copy the selected worksheet(s) to a new workbook rather than an existing one that you have open, choose the (new book) option that appears at the very top of the To Book pull-down menu.

6. **In the Before Sheet list box, select the name of the worksheet in the designated workbook that the worksheet(s) you're about to move or copy should precede.**

7. **To copy the selected worksheet(s) to the designated workbook (rather than move them), select the Create a Copy check box.**

8. **Click on OK or press Return to complete the move or copy operation.**

If you prefer the direct approach, you can move or copy a single worksheet between open workbooks by dragging its sheet tab from one workbook window to another. Note that this method only works with one worksheet: You can't select a bunch of worksheets and then drag their tabs to a new workbook.

To drag a worksheet from one workbook to another, you must open both workbooks and then use the Arrange command on the Window menu and select an arrangement (such as Horizontal or Vertical to put the workbook windows either on top of each other or side by side). Before you close the Arrange Windows dialog box, be sure that the Windows of Active Workbook check box does *not* contain an X.

After arranging the workbook windows, drag the worksheet tab from one workbook to another. If you want to copy rather than move the worksheet, hold down the ⌘ key while you drag the sheet icon. To locate the worksheet in the new workbook, position the downward-pointing triangle that moves with the sheet icon in front of the worksheet tab where the worksheet is to be inserted and then release the mouse button.

Figures 9-13 and 9-14 illustrate how easily you can move or copy a worksheet from one workbook to another by using this drag-and-drop method. In Figure 9-13 you see two workbook windows, the Simons 1995 Sales workbook placed above a new workbook (Workbook1) with the Horizontal option in the Arrange Windows dialog box. To move the Muffet St. worksheet from the Simons 1995 Sales workbook to Workbook1, you simply click on the Muffet St. tab and drag it down to its new position among the sheet tabs of the Workbook1 workbook. Figure 9-14 shows the workbooks after releasing the mouse button. As you can see, Excel moves the Muffet St. worksheet into the Workbook1 workbook at the place indicated by the triangle that accompanies the sheet icon (in between Sheet1 and Sheet2 in this example). (If you had wanted to copy the worksheet to the workbook instead of move it, you would have held down ⌘ as you dragged it to the new workbook.)

Summary Time . . .

To wrap up this fascinating subject of working with more than one worksheet in a workbook, I want to introduce you to the equally fascinating subject of creating a summary worksheet that recaps or totals the values stored in a bunch of other worksheets in the workbook. I'll walk you through the procedure of creating a summary worksheet (called Total Stores) for the Simons 1995 Sales workbook that totals the monthly, quarterly, and annual sales for all three Simple Simon Pie Shoppes (the ones on Miss Muffet Street, Curds Way, and Arachnid Road).

Because the Simons 1995 Sales workbook already contains the worksheets with the sales figures for all these store locations and these worksheets are all laid out in the same arrangement, creating this summary worksheet is a piece of cake (or should I say *easy as pie?*):

1. **I started by adopting Sheet4 in the Simons 1995 Sales workbook as the summary worksheet (the first three sheets already contain the sales for each of the three store locations) by double-clicking on its sheet tab and then renaming the sheet Total Stores.**

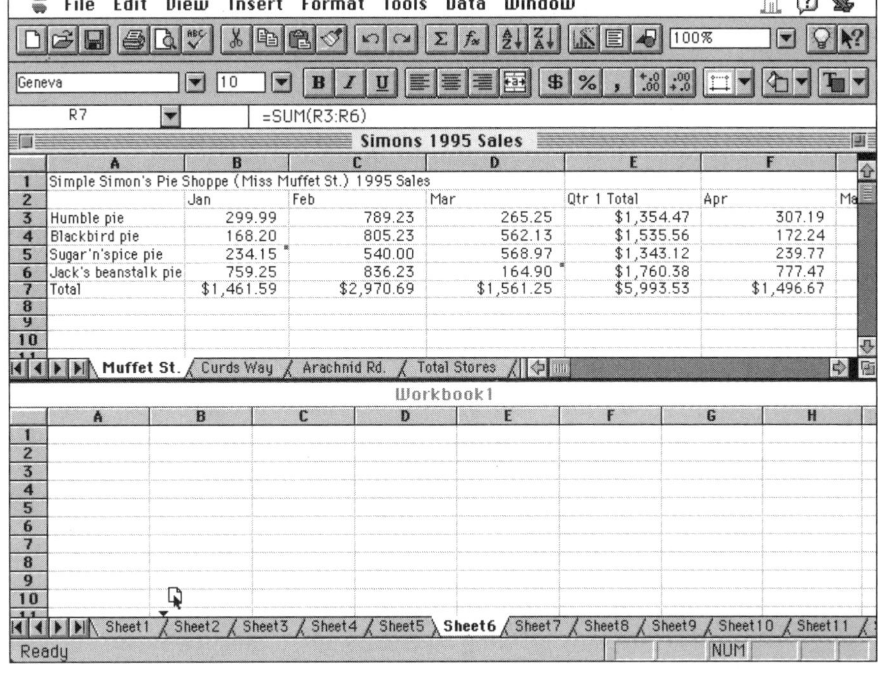

Figure 9-13: Moving the Muffet St. worksheet to a new workbook via drag-and-drop.

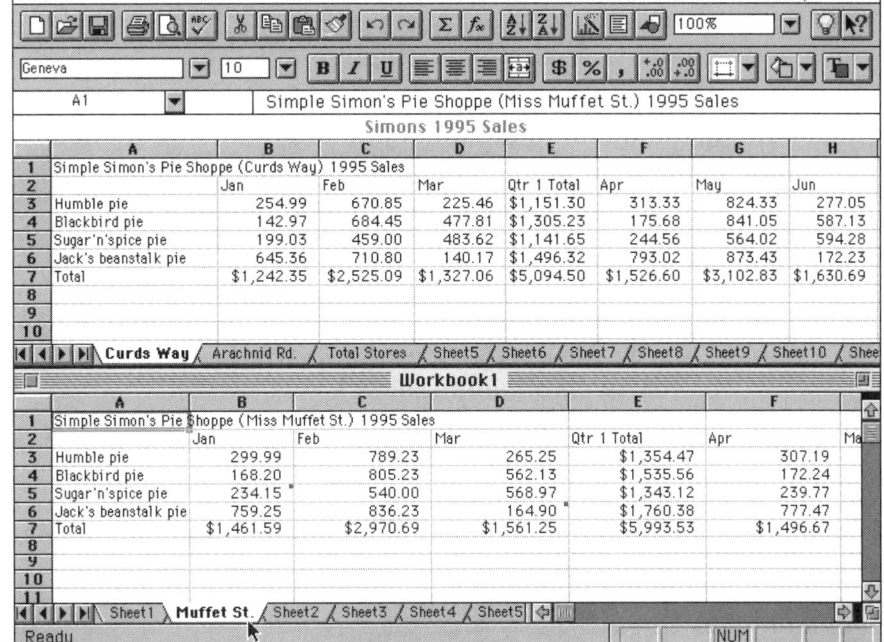

Figure 9-14: After moving the Muffet St. worksheet between Sheet1 and Sheet2 of the new workbook.

2. **Next, I copied the column and row headings (containing the pie names and the names of the months and quarters) from the Arachnid Road worksheet to the Total Stores worksheet.**

   Simply select the cell range A1:A7 in Arachnid Road sheet, press ⌘+C, click on the Total Stores tab, select cell A1 in this worksheet, and press Return. Then go back to Arachnid Road by clicking on its sheet tab. Next, you select the cell range B2:R2, once again press ⌘+C, click on the Total Stores tab, select cell B2, and press Return. Finally, I edited the worksheet title in cell A1 so that it says `All Locations` instead of `Arachnid Road`.

3. **Then I moved the Total Stores sheet with the copied headings to the top of the Simons 1995 Sales workbook by dragging its sheet tab to the location before the Muffet St. tab (as shown earlier in Figures 9-5 and 9-6).**

   I moved the Total Stores sheet simply because I prefer to see the summary sheet at the beginning of the workbook and the supporting worksheets bringing up the rear.

Now, I was ready to create the "master" SUM formula that totals the January sales of Humble pie for Muffet St., Curds Way, and Arachnid Road in cell B3 by doing the following:

1. **I started by clicking on cell B3 and then clicking on the Sum tool on the Standard toolbar.**

   Excel then puts `=SUM()` in the cell, with the insertion point placed between the two parentheses.

2. **I clicked on the Muffet St. sheet tab and then on its cell B3 to select the January sales of Humble pie in the Muffet St. worksheet.**

   The formula bar reads `=SUM('Muffet St.'!B3)` after selecting this cell.

3. **Next, I typed , (the comma starts a new argument) and then clicked on the Curds Way sheet tab followed by its cell B3 to select the January sales of Humble pie in the Curds Way worksheet.**

   The formula bar reads `=SUM('Muffet St.'!B3,'Curds Way'!B3)` after selecting this cell.

4. **Not quite finished yet, I then typed , (comma) and clicked on the Arachnid Rd. sheet tab followed by its cell B3 to select the January sales of Humble pie in the Arachnid Rd. worksheet.**

   The formula bar reads `=SUM('Muffet St.'!B3,'Curds Way'!B3, 'Arachnid Rd.'!B3)` after selecting this cell.

5. **To complete the SUM formula in cell B3 of the Total Sales worksheet, I then clicked on the Return box in the formula bar (I could have pressed the Return key as well).**

Figure 9-15 shows you the result. As you can see in the formula bar, the master SUM formula that returns 740.98 to cell B3 of the Total Sales worksheet gets its result by summing the values in B3 in all three of the supporting worksheets.

All that's left to do now is to format cell B3 with the Currency style, use AutoFill to copy the master formula in cell B3 down to row 7 and over to column R, and then use AutoFit to widen the columns, as follows:

1. **With cell B3 still selected, I clicked on the Currency Style tool on the Formatting toolbar.**
2. **Next, I dragged the AutoFill handle in the lower right-hand corner of cell B3 down to cell B7 to copy the formula for summing the values for the three stores down this column.**
3. **With the cell range B3:B7 still selected, I dragged the AutoFill handle in the lower right-hand corner of cell B7 to the right to column R and then released the mouse button.**
4. **Finally, I widened columns B through R with the AutoFit feature to display the formatted values by dragging through the column letters to select them and then double-clicking on the right border of column R.**

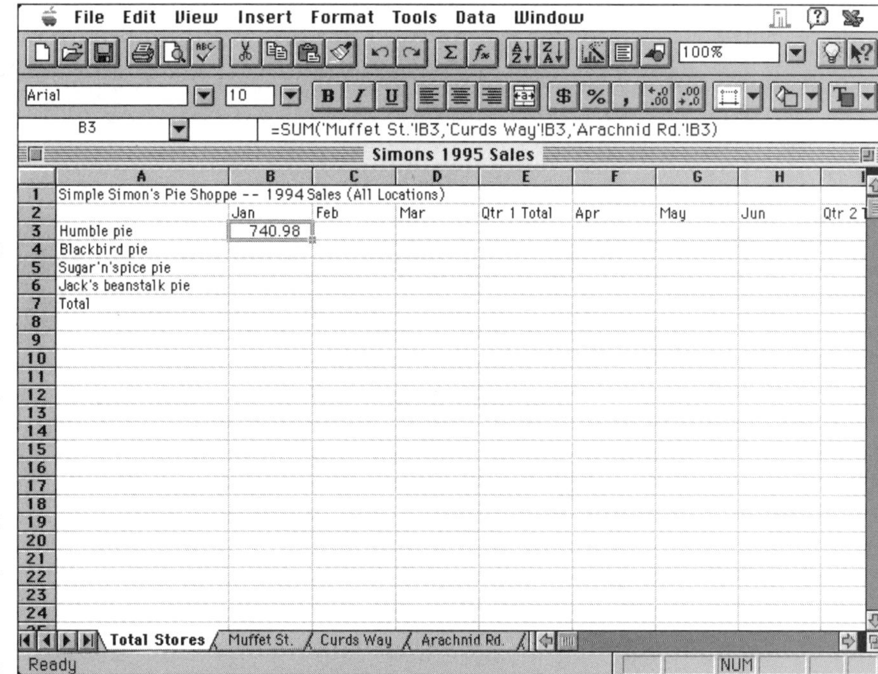

Figure 9-15: The Total Sales worksheet, after creating the SUM formula in cell B3 that totals all January Humble pie sales.

In Figure 9-16, you see the first section of the final summary worksheet after copying the formula created in cell B3 and widening the columns with AutoFit. Although at first glance this Total Stores summary worksheet looks like it was a great deal of work to create, it really was quite simple to put together. And the best part is that because the values in the summary worksheet are tied by formula to the values entered in the supporting sheet for each store, any update or correction made to these figures will be automatically reflected in the summary values in the Total Stores, giving 100-percent accuracy in the totals without requiring any extra work!

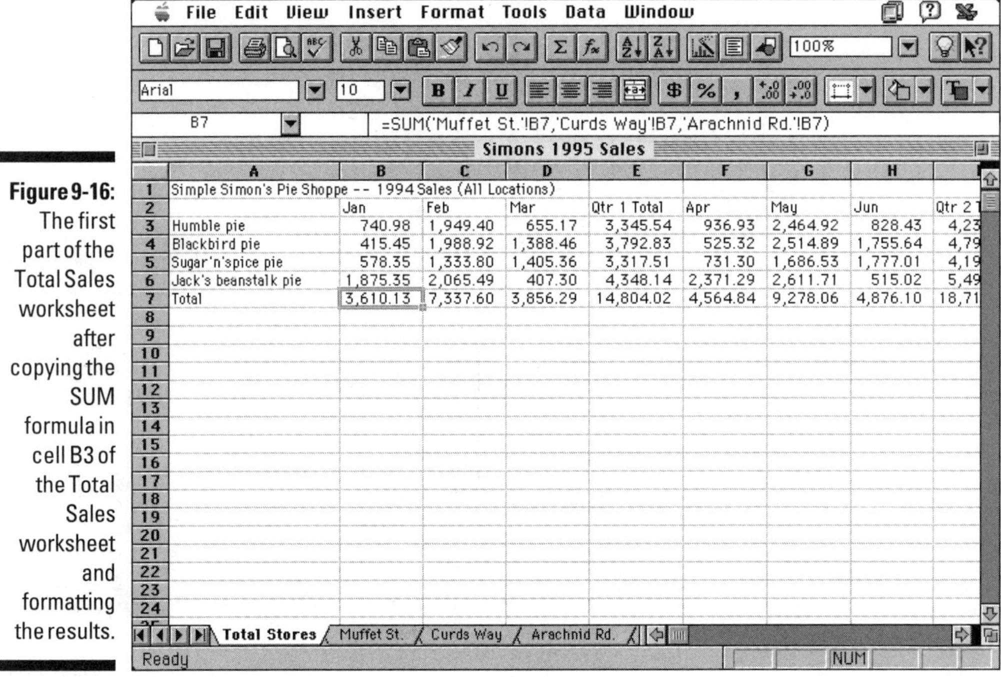

	A	B	C	D	E	F	G	H	
1	Simple Simon's Pie Shoppe -- 1994 Sales (All Locations)								
2		Jan	Feb	Mar	Qtr 1 Total	Apr	May	Jun	Qtr 2 T
3	Humble pie	740.98	1,949.40	655.17	3,345.54	936.93	2,464.92	828.43	4,23
4	Blackbird pie	415.45	1,988.92	1,388.46	3,792.83	525.32	2,514.89	1,755.64	4,79
5	Sugar'n'spice pie	578.35	1,333.80	1,405.36	3,317.51	731.30	1,686.53	1,777.01	4,19
6	Jack's beanstalk pie	1,875.35	2,065.49	407.30	4,348.14	2,371.29	2,611.71	515.02	5,49
7	Total	3,610.13	7,337.60	3,856.29	14,804.02	4,564.84	9,278.06	4,876.10	18,71

Figure 9-16: The first part of the Total Sales worksheet after copying the SUM formula in cell B3 of the Total Sales worksheet and formatting the results.

Part V

Excel — Have It Your Way

"IT WAS CLASHING WITH THE SOUTHWESTERN MOTIF."

The part in which . . .

You learn how to put your own personality into the way Excel works for you and how it looks on-screen. You find out that you can streamline tedious, repetitive tasks by composing and recording macros that you can play back anytime you need them — at the touch of a couple of keys.

You discover how to customize the toolbars by modifying Excel's toolbars and by creating ones of your own design. And you learn how to jazz up the look of the Excel window as well as the look of your documents.

Chapter 10

Excel Made to Order

In This Chapter

- How to record and play back simple macros that perform common tasks
- How to change the way stuff is displayed on-screen
- How to customize the general default settings, such as number of worksheets in a workbook, fonts used in cells, and the folder to save workbooks in
- How to customize the colors displayed on a color monitor

Now that you're familiar with the basics of Excel and how it normally appears and operates, it's high time you learned how to add your own touches to the program. In this chapter, you first learn how to automate some of those everyday tasks that take up so much of your valuable time. Then you take a look at how to control what's displayed on-screen in each workbook document window and in the Excel program window itself. You also learn how to customize all kinds of settings that you don't find quite up to snuff.

As you will soon see, doing your own thing with Excel is quite easy. Not only can customizing help you be more productive with the program, but it also makes you feel like you're in control of Excel instead of the other way around.

Holy Macros!

Macros! Just hearing the word is enough to make you want to head for the hills. Rather than think of this term as *technobabble*, keep in mind that *macro* is short for *macro instruction* and that the word *macro* refers to the Big Picture. A macro (at least at the level of this book) is nothing more than a way to record the actions you take to get a particular task done and have Excel play them back for you. You can create macros to enter a company name in a worksheet, save and print a worksheet, format row headings, and much more.

Using a macro to perform a routine task rather than performing the task by hand has some definite advantages. First, Excel can execute the commands involved *much* faster than you can — no matter how good you are with a keyboard or how familiar you are with Excel. Also, Excel performs the task flawlessly each and every time because the macro plays back your actions exactly as you recorded them. Your only concern, then, is to record the actions correctly. You can even streamline the playback process by assigning keystroke shortcuts to your favorite macros — reducing common tasks that require quite a few steps to just two keystrokes.

The process of creating a macro is surprisingly straightforward:

1. **Open the Record New Macro dialog box to turn on the macro recorder by choosing Tools ➪ Record Macro ➪ Record New Macro.**
2. **Name the macro and (optionally) assign it a keystroke shortcut or assign it to the Tools pull-down menu.**
3. **Perform the sequence of actions you want recorded in the macro just as you would normally perform these actions in Excel.**

   You can choose commands from the pull-down or shortcut menus, click on tools in the toolbars, or use shortcut keystrokes in your macro.
4. **Turn off the macro recorder by clicking on the Stop Macro tool that appears in its own toolbar as soon as you start recording.**

   Alternatively, you can choose Tools ➪ Record Macro ➪ Stop Recording.
5. **Perform the task anytime by typing your keyboard shortcut or choose Tools ➪ Macro to open the Macro dialog box and then double-click on the macro name (or select the name and choose Run).**

   If you assigned the macro to the Tools menu when you recorded it, you can run the macro by selecting the macro on the Tools menu.

You'll be happy to know that when you record your actions, Excel doesn't record your mistakes (don't you wish everyone were so forgiving?). In other words, if you mean to enter the heading **January** in the macro but you type **Janaury** by mistake and then correct your error, Excel does not record your backspacing, deleting *aury,* and typing **uary**. The only thing the macro records is the final, corrected result of January!

To record your actions, Excel 5.0 uses a language called *Visual Basic* (a language, by the way, that you *don't* need to know diddley about in order to create and use *simple* macros, which are the only kind you're going to learn in this book). For those who can't get enough, you'll learn more macros stuff in *More Excel for Dummies* by yours truly and IDG Books (shameless plug). *More Excel for Dummies* is designed for Windows users, but most Mac Excel users would have no trouble ignoring the Windows-only stuff, and it's easier to read than the documentation for sure. Visual Basic commands are recorded in a separate *module sheet,* a fancy name for a worksheet that doesn't use cells and that therefore looks more like a page in a typical word processor.

Put that macro in my personal workbook

Excel automatically assumes that you want to record your macro as part of the current workbook. Recording the macro as part of the workbook means that you can only run the macro when this workbook is open. But you may want to have access to some of your macros any old time you're using Excel, regardless of whether the workbook that happened to be current when you originally recorded the macro is now open, and regardless of whether you're creating a new workbook or editing an existing one.

To record a macro so that it's available to use anytime and anywhere in Excel, you must record the macro in your *personal macro workbook* rather than in the current workbook. Because your personal macro workbook is automatically opened whenever you start up Excel (though it remains hidden at all times), you can run any of its macros no matter which workbook or workbooks are open.

To record a macro in the personal macro workbook, follow these steps:

1. **Choose Tools ⇨ Record Macro ⇨ Record New Macro to open the Record New Macro dialog box.**
2. **Choose Options.**
3. **Choose the Personal Macro Workbook radio button under Store In before you start recording the new macro.**
4. **Record your macro as you normally would.**

Recording macros in good old Excel 4.0 style!

Although Excel 5.0 prefers recording macros in the newfangled Visual Basic (instead of in the good old standby macro language that we all knew and loved in Excel 4.0 and earlier versions), the program hasn't adopted a Visual-Basic-only spoken here attitude. Indeed, Excel 5.0 not only enables you to run existing macros in this earlier macro language, but it also enables you to record new macros in this "obsolete" language. To record a macro in the Excel 4.0 language, choose the Options button in the Record New Macro dialog box, choose the MS Excel 4.0 Macro radio button under Language, and then start recording the new macro. Excel records all your actions in the old macro language, which you'll find in a Macro1 worksheet appended to the end of the current workbook.

A macro a day

To get a feel for how easy recording and playing back a simple macro is, perform the following steps for creating a couple of simple macros. The first sample macro enters and formats a company name in a cell. In the example, you'll turn on the macro to record your actions as you change the font to 18-point Brush Script and enter the company name — that's right, it's the Simple Simon Pie Shoppe. If you're actually following along at your computer as you read these steps, be sure to adapt the basic macro so that it enters the name of your company in the font and type size you want to use.

The very first thing you need is to be in a place where you can perform the actions you're going to have Excel record in the macro. For this example, open a new worksheet (or use a blank cell in an existing worksheet) and then follow these steps:

1. **Position the cell pointer in the cell where you want to enter the company name.**

   For this example, position the pointer in cell A1 in a blank worksheet in the current workbook. If necessary, choose a new blank worksheet by clicking on the next sheet tab or by pressing ⌘+Page Down.

2. **Choose Tools ⇨ Record Macro ⇨ Record New Macro.**

   The Record New Macro dialog box appears, similar to the one shown in Figure 10-1.

   If you display the Visual Basic toolbar, shown in Figure 10-1, you can open the Record New Macro dialog box by clicking on the Record Macro tool (the one with the red dot).

Taking a look at your personal macro workbook

Excel doesn't actually create a personal macro workbook until you record your first macro in that location (no sense creating something until you have occasion to use it). After you create your first macro in the personal macro workbook, you also have to save your changes in this file (called PERSONAL MACRO WORKBOOK in the Macintosh version) when Excel prompts you to do so upon exiting the program. Excel saves this file in the Startup folder.

After you create and save your first macro in the personal macro workbook, you can make the workbook visible and take a gander at its contents. Choose Unhide on the Window menu and then select the workbook's name in the Unhide dialog box. After you finish scratching your head over all those strange Visual Basic commands in the macros of the Module1 sheet of this workbook (the only sheet that this workbook happens to contain), be sure to hide this workbook again by choosing Hide on the Window menu. If you don't hide the workbook, you'll have to look at those Visual Basic macro commands every time you fire up Excel. Not a pleasant thought.

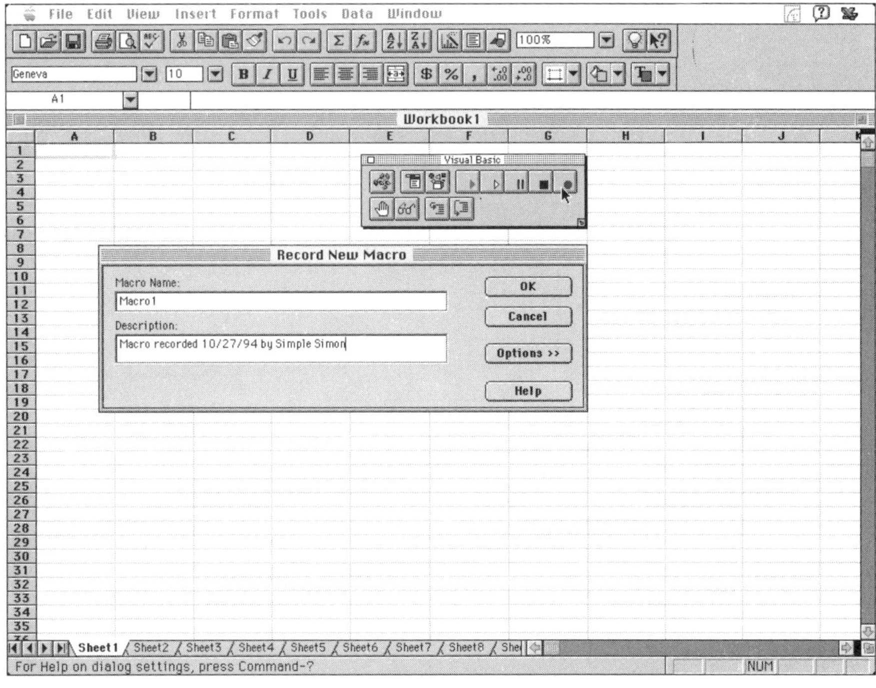

Figure 10-1: The Record New Macro dialog box and Visual Basic toolbar.

3. **In the Macro Name text box, replace the temporary macro name** `Macro1` **with a more descriptive macro name of your own choosing.**

   When naming a macro, follow the same guidelines you use when naming ranges — that is, start the name with a letter, not a number, and don't use spaces. Instead, use an underscore — Shift+- (hyphen). And don't use weird punctuation characters in the name. See Chapter 5 for more information about these guidelines.

   For this example, replace `Macro1` with **Company_Name.**

4. **If you want, edit or annotate the macro description in the Description text box, which appears beneath the Macro Name text.**

   This text box is a good place to briefly describe the purpose of the macro you're creating (entering the name of your company).

5. **If you want to assign the macro to the Tools pull-down menu, assign a shortcut key to run the macro and store the macro in your personal macro workbook (so that you can use it anywhere, anytime). Or you can record the macro actions in an old-fashioned macro sheet in the Excel 4.0 macro language (rather in a module sheet in Visual Basic) and choose the Options button to expand the Record New Macro dialog box, as shown in Figure 10-2.**

   If none of these macro options holds any appeal, skip to Step 10.

6. **To be able to play your macro by selecting it from the Tools pull-down menu, in the expanded Record New Macro dialog box, choose Menu Item from the Tools menu in the Assign to area so that an X appears in that check box. Then, in the text box below, type the name of the command that will play this macro. Be sure to type the name exactly as you want it to appear on the Tools menu.**

   For example, if you want to be able to play your macro by choosing the command Company Name from the Tools menu, you select this text box and then type **Company Name** in its text box (see Figure 10-2).

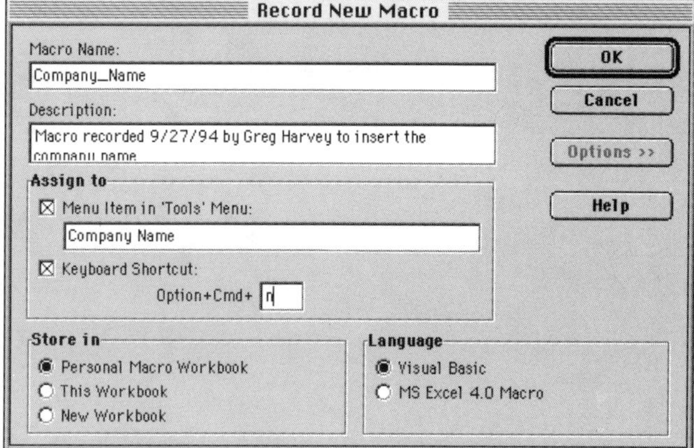

Figure 10-2: The expanded Record New Macro dialog box after pressing the Option button.

7. **To assign a shortcut key to play your macro, choose Shortcut Key in the Assign to area to put an X in its check box and then enter a letter from A to Z (in upper- or lowercase).**

   The number or letter you enter is the key you'll use (in combination with the Option+⌘ key) to run the macro. Try to avoid using letters that are already assigned to standard Excel shortcuts. For example, don't use Option+⌘+P, which very close to Excel's shortcut for displaying the Print dialog box (⌘+P), or Option+⌘+S, which is likely to get confused with Excel's shortcut for saving a workbook (⌘+S). See the table on the front of the *Excel 5 For Macs For Dummies* Cheat Sheet at the very beginning of this book for a complete list of these Excel keyboard shortcuts.

   For this example, you may want to enter the letter **n** as the shortcut key so that you can insert the company name by pressing Option+⌘+n.

8. **To store your macro in your personal macro workbook, choose the Personal Macro Workbook radio button under Store In.**

   If you want to save the macro in a module in a brand new workbook (which you can save later after recording the macro) rather than in either the current workbook (in which you will perform the actions recorded in the new macro) or in your personal macro workbook, choose the New Workbook radio button instead.

9. **To save the macro in the old Excel 4.0 macro language rather than in the new and cool Visual Basic language, choose the MS Excel 4.0 Macro radio button in the Language area.**

   Figure 10-2 shows the expanded Record New Macro dialog box after the various settings have been made. As you can see, the Tools menu item will be called Company_Name and the shortcut keystroke will be Option+⌘+n (for name). Also, because the company name is so often added to new workbooks, the Personal Macro Workbook radio button is selected so that this macro is available anytime Excel is being used.

10. **Choose OK or press Return to start recording your macro.**

   The Record Macro dialog box closes, and Excel shows you that the macro recorder is turned on by displaying the message `Recording` on the status bar.

11. **Perform the task you want to record.**

   For the Company_Name sample macro, you first select the new font (Brush Script in this case) from the Font tool pull-down menu and the font size (18 points) from the Size tool pull-down menu, or you can select a custom font size from the ⌘+1 ⇨ Font dialog box. Second, enter the company name in cell A1.

12. **When you finish recording all the actions you want your macro to perform, turn off the macro recorder by clicking on the Stop Macro button in its own toolbar, shown in Figure 10-3, or in the Visual Basic toolbar if that's displayed. You also can turn off the macro recorder by choosing Tools ⇨ Record Macro ⇨ Stop Recording.**

   As soon as you stop recording a macro, the Recording message disappears from the status bar.

Play you back with interest

After you turn off the macro recorder, you are ready to test the macro. If your macro enters or deletes text as part of its actions, be very careful where you test it out. Be sure that the cell pointer is in a part of the worksheet where existing cell entries won't be trashed when you play back the macro. When you are ready to test the macro, you can do any of the following:

- The easiest way to play back a macro is to press the shortcut keystrokes (Option+⌘+n for the sample Company_Name macro, for example), assuming, of course, that you assigned a shortcut to your macro.
- You can select the macro name from the bottom of the Tools pull-down menu (Tools ⇨ Company_Name for the sample macro), assuming that you assigned the macro to the Tools menu. Notice that Excel does not assign a command letter (the underlined letter you can press to select a given command) to a macro that you add to the Tools menu.

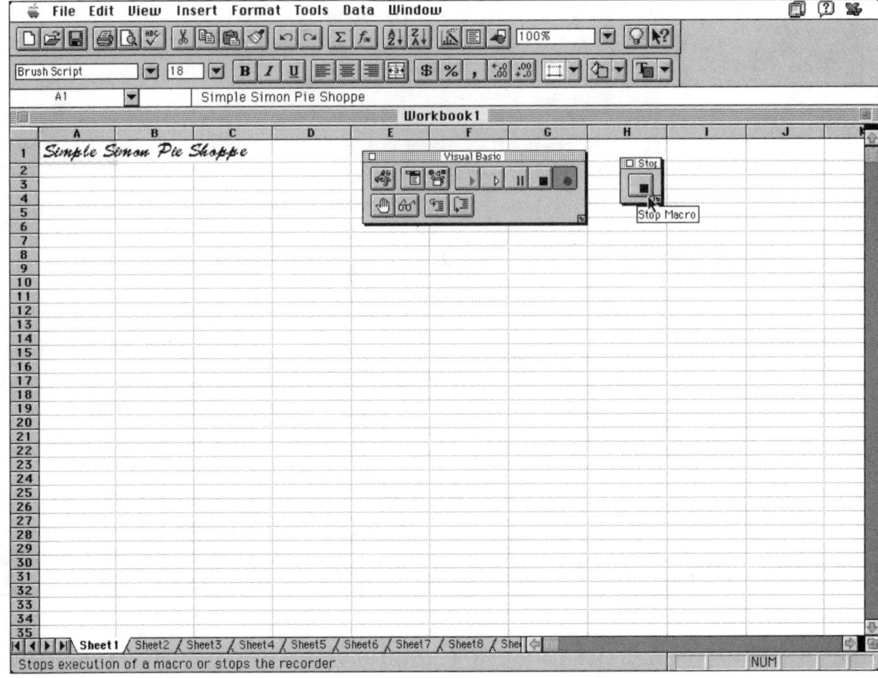

Figure 10-3: Turning off the macro recorder by clicking on the Stop tool.

- You can choose Macro on the Tools menu to open the Macro dialog box and then double-click on the macro's name (or select the name and choose the Run button). This method works for any macro, regardless of whether it has shortcut keys or is assigned to the Tools pull-down menu.

If, when you play back the macro, you find the little devil running amok in your worksheet, press ⌘+. (period) to stop the macro prematurely. Excel displays a macro error dialog box that indicates the point at which the macro was interrupted. Click on the Halt button in this dialog box to shut the macro down.

If you created the macro as part of the current workbook, Excel places the macro in a module sheet (called Module1) that is appended to the end of the workbook.

If you created the macro as part of the personal macro workbook, Excel places the macro in a hidden workbook called PERSONAL MACRO WORKBOOK.

If you saved the macro as part of a new workbook, Excel puts the macro in a module sheet (Module1) appended to a new workbook and given a temporary filename like Workbook1, Workbook2, or whatever the next available number is.

When you save the current workbook or the new workbook, Excel saves the macros in its module sheets as part of the files. In the case of the hidden personal macro workbook, when you exit Excel, the program asks whether you want to save changes to this macro workbook. Be sure to select the Yes button so that you can still use the macros you've placed there the next time you work in Excel.

January, February, June, and July

The second sample macro enters the 12 months of the year (from January to December) across a single row of a worksheet. After entering the names, the macro makes the names of the months bold and italic and then widens the columns with the best-fit feature.

As with the first macro, first you must find a place in a worksheet where you can enter and format the names. For this macro, select a new worksheet in your workbook. Or you might use a region of an existing worksheet that has 12 unused columns (so that existing cell entries don't skew how wide the best-fit feature makes the columns). Remember, you want the length of the name of the month to determine the width of its column.

Figure 10-4 shows the Record New Macro dialog box for this macro. Its name, appropriately enough, is Months_of_the_Year, its shortcut keystroke is Option+⌘+m, and its menu item name is just plain Months.

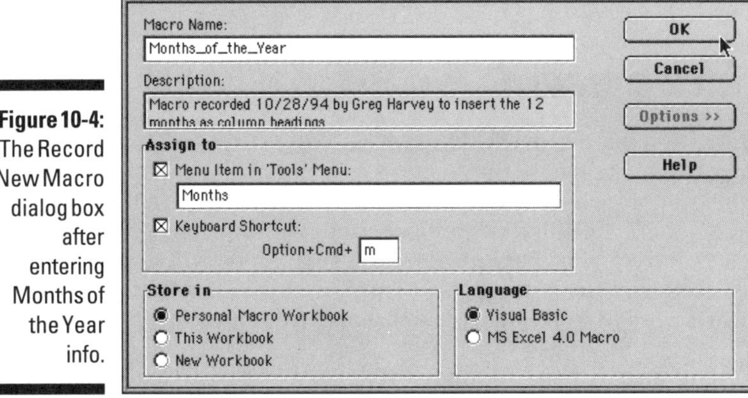

Figure 10-4: The Record New Macro dialog box after entering Months of the Year info.

Follow these steps:

1. **Put the cell pointer in cell A1 and turn on the macro recorder by choosing Tools ⇨ Record Macro ⇨ Record New Macro.**
2. **Enter** January **in cell A1 and then use the AutoFill handle to select the range through cell L1.**

   You didn't think you were going to have to type out all those names of the months, did you?
3. **Click on the Bold and Italic tools on the Formatting toolbar**.

   This step adds these enhancements to the entries (the cell range A1:L1 with the month names is still selected).
4. **Select the range of columns containing the months (columns A through L) and double-click on the right border of one of them to widen the columns with best fit.**

   Click in the first cell of the range to deselect the range of columns.

Now turn off the macro recorder and test the macro. To adequately test the macro, use new columns to the right. For example, I tested this macro on the virginal columns N through Y in Sheet2 by placing the cell pointer in cell N1 and then pressing Option+⌘+m. As expected, the macro entered in cell range N1:Y1 the names of the 12 months, *January* through *December,* and then dutifully made them bold and italic. Unfortunately, however, the macro did not select columns N through Y and use best fit to match the column widths to their entries as I had intended. Instead, the macro selected and applied best fit to columns A through L a second time and then selected cell A1. Bad macro!

The relative record

What, you may well ask, causes the Months_of_the_Year macro to screw up so that it always applies best fit to the columns A through L instead of applying best fit to the columns where the 12 months were actually entered? Well, Chapter 4 talks about the differences between copying a formula with *relative* cell references and copying one with *absolute* cell references. It turns out that Excel adjusts cell references in copies of a formula unless you take steps to convert them to *absolute* references, which makes them unchanging.

When recording macros, just the opposite is true: When you select a cell range, a range of columns in this case, Excel records the cell references as absolute references rather than as relative ones. And this is the reason that the Months_of_the_Year macro keeps selecting columns A through L instead of the columns where you worked so hard to enter the months (by pressing Option+⌘+m).

To change this macro so that it works correctly, you have to (sorry) re-record the macro, this time using relative cell references. Open up a new worksheet where you can perform the actions to be recorded, choose Tools ➪ Record Macro ➪ Record New Macro, and set up the Record New Macro dialog box the same way you did when you first created the macro. Excel asks whether you want to overwrite the existing keystroke assignments and later prompts you to overwrite the macro itself. In both cases, click on the Yes button.

Before you start recording the macro steps, choose Tools ➪ Record Macro ➪ Use Relative Reference. Then perform all actions (typing **January,** using AutoFill to generate the rest of the months, applying bold and italics to the cell range, and selecting the columns and adjusting their widths with best fit). This time, Excel records the command for selecting the columns with relative column references so that the selection of the columns in the macro is always relative to the cell range containing the names of the months.

After stopping the macro, test it in columns in the worksheet. Now, no matter where you enter the names of the months, the Months_of_the_Year macro always adjusts the widths of the columns that contain the months. Good macro!

The Vision Thing

Excel gives you a lot of control over what appears on-screen and how it looks. The options for controlling the appearance of Excel program and workbook windows mostly appear on the View tab of the Options dialog box. You also can use the General tab of the Options dialog box to customize the cell reference style, the menus used, how many worksheets to a new workbook, and what font each new workbook uses.

The view from my window

Figure 10-5 shows the options on the View tab of the Options dialog box. To open this dialog box, choose Options on the Tools menu and then choose the View tab. The View tab contains a mess of check boxes that turn on and off the display of various elements in both the Excel program window and a particular workbook document window. As you would expect, all the options with Xs in their check boxes are turned on, and all the options with empty check boxes are turned off.

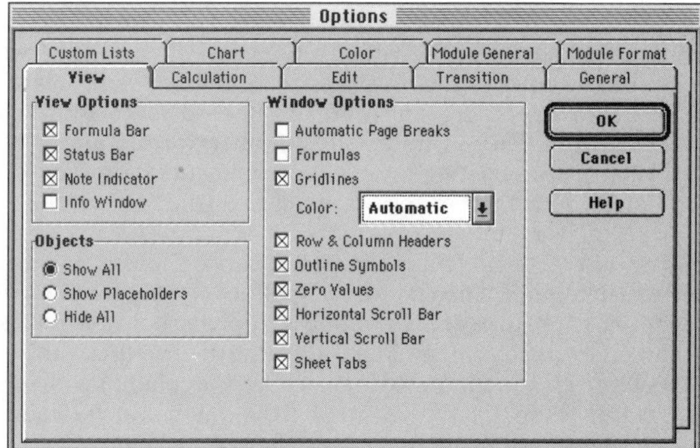

Figure 10-5: The View tab in the Options dialog box.

The check box options in the Show area of this dialog box control which elements are displayed in the Excel program window:

- *Formula Bar.* Hides or shows the formula bar right below the Formatting toolbar at the top of the program window.
- *Status Bar.* Hides or shows the status bar at the bottom of the program window.
- *Note Indicator.* Hides or shows a little red dot in the upper right-hand corner of a cell that contains a note. (See Chapter 5 for details.)
- *Info Window.* Hides or shows a separate window, displaying information about the contents of whatever cell is current in your worksheet.

The check box options in the Window Options area of the View tab determine whether or not a number of elements in the current worksheet are displayed. Keep in mind that turning off a particular element in the current worksheet does not turn off that element in any other worksheet in that workbook. All the following option settings, except for the Automatic Page Breaks option, are saved as part of your worksheet when you save the workbook (the Automatic Page Breaks option always reverts back to the default of being hidden):

- *Automatic Page Breaks.* When you print or look at a worksheet in Print Preview, hides or shows the page breaks that Excel puts in the worksheet.
- *Formulas.* Switches between showing the formulas in the cells of your worksheet rather than the calculated values, which are shown as the normal state of affairs. When you put an X in this check box, Excel also automatically removes the cell gridlines, widens all the columns, and left-aligns all the information in the cells.

- *Gridlines.* Hides or shows the column and row separators that define the cells in your worksheet. Note that you also can change the color of the gridlines (when they're displayed, of course) by choosing a new color in the Color palette, which appears when you click on its pull-down menu button. (I find that navy blue is rather fetching.)
- *Row & Column Headers.* Hides or shows the row of column letters at the top of the worksheet and the column of row numbers at the left.
- *Outline Symbols.* Hides or shows the various symbols that appear when you outline a worksheet table. (Generally, you outline only really large tables so that you can collapse the table to its essentials by hiding all but particular levels.)
- *Zero Values.* Hides or displays zero entries in the worksheet. Deselect this check box if you want to suppress the display of all zeros in a worksheet. (You may want to suppress the display of zeros, for example, in a worksheet template if you don't want to see those zeros in a new worksheet that you generate from the template.)
- *Horizontal Scroll Bar.* Hides or displays the horizontal scroll bar to the right of the worksheet tabs at the bottom of the workbook document window. When you hide the horizontal scroll bar and leave the sheet tabs displayed (see the following Sheet Tabs item), Excel fills the area normally reserved for the horizontal scroll bar with sheet tabs. Note that this option affects the display of every worksheet in your workbook.
- *Vertical Scroll Bar.* Hides or displays the vertical scroll bar on the right side of the workbook document window. This option also affects the display of every worksheet in your workbook.
- *Sheet Tabs.* Hides or displays the tabs that enable you to activate the various worksheets in your workbook. Note that when you remove the display of the sheet tabs, you can still use ⌘+Page Down and ⌘+Page Up to move between worksheets. However, without the tabs, you won't know which worksheet you're looking at unless you can recognize the sheet from its data alone.

Chapter 7 introduces you to the Objects radio buttons in the View tab of the Options dialog box. Remember that these settings determine how graphics objects, including charts and other types of graphics, are displayed in the worksheet. To speed up the screen-response time when making editing changes, you can replace the detailed display of graphics objects with placeholders (shaded rectangles) by clicking on the Show Placeholders radio button. To hide the graphics objects altogether, select the Hide All radio button. When you finish editing and are again ready to display the charts and graphics in a worksheet, click on the Show All radio button.

The General tab in the Options dialog box, shown in Figure 10-6, contains a number of program setting options that you may want to change (if not right away, then after working with Excel a little more).

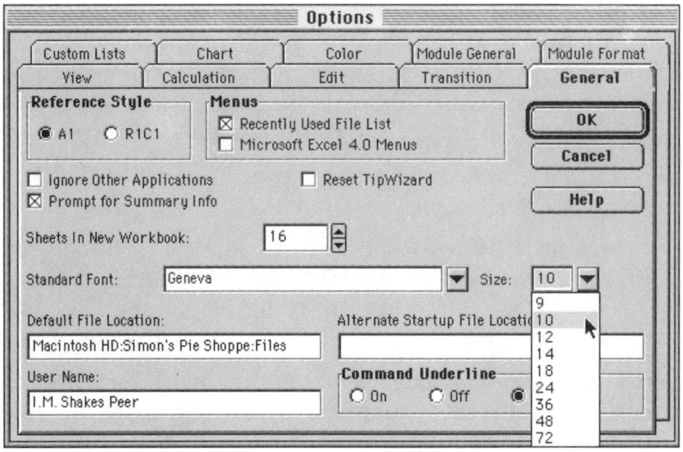

Figure 10-6: The General tab in the Options dialog box.

Of special interest in the General tab is the Sheets in New Workbook option, which sets the number of blank worksheets in each new workbook. After all, you may never need 16 worksheets and may want to choose a more realistic number instead, like 3 or (if you're feeling wild) 4. Standard Font sets the font used in every cell of a new workbook. Default File Location determines which folder Excel automatically chooses when you try to open or save a workbook document. These and the other options in this tab are explained in more detail in the following:

- *Reference Style.* Contains the A1 and R1C1 radio buttons. The A1 style (sounds like a steak sauce, I know) is the reference style you know from this book and the one that Excel normally uses. The R1C1 style is the creepy alternative that you don't know, in which each column is numbered like the rows, and the row (that's the *R* part) reference number precedes the column (the *C* part) reference number. In this system, the cell you know and love as B2 would be cell R2C2, a name very similar to that of the lovable vacuum-cleaneresque droid in *Star Wars*.
- *Recently Used File List.* With this check box selected, Excel lists the last four documents you opened (in order from most recently used) at the bottom of the File menu. You can open any of these four files simply by selecting its name or number after you open the File menu.
- *Microsoft Excel 4.0 Menus.* When you select this check box, the program resets the pull-down menus to the way they appear in Excel 4.0. The major difference between the versions is that Excel 4.0 uses separate Formula, Data, and Macro menus whose items are located on other menus in Excel 5.0. Don't put an X in this check box and then expect to make sense out of the instructions and steps in this book — this option is intended for old Excel 4.0 hands who just can't make (or *think* they just can't make) the transition to the new menu system.

- *Ignore Other Applications.* When this check box contains an X, Excel ignores requests made from other programs using DDE (which stands for Dynamic Data Exchange — as if you care). This option is of interest only if you are using data created in other programs in Excel. If this is the case, you definitely want to leave this check box deselected.
- *Reset TipWizard.* Normally, the TipWizard — the tool with the light bulb that glows yellow when it's got a hot tip for you — shows you a particular tip only once during a work session and does not redisplay that tip in subsequent work sessions unless you perform the tip-related action three more times. Select this check box when you want to reset the TipWizard to clear its memory of which tips it has already shown you. An X in the check box enables Excel to once again display tips you've already seen immediately after you perform the related action once.
- *Prompt for Summary Info.* Normally, Excel displays a Summary Info dialog box where you can enter information about the subject of the workbook and key words that you later use when searching for the file. If you're tired of Excel putting this Summary Info dialog box in your face every time you save a new workbook (if you routinely ignore this dialog box anyway), deselect this check box. Note that, should you have a change of heart and decide that you want to add a summary to your workbook, you can still do so, even after turning off this option. Simply choose the Summary Info command on the File menu when the workbook is active.
- *Sheets in New Workbook.* As stated earlier, Excel normally puts 16 blank worksheets in each new workbook you open. If you're never in a million years gonna use that many worksheets, you can select this option and reduce the number. Or you can use this option to increase the number of worksheets in a new workbook if you find that you're routinely using *more* than 16 sheets and you're getting tired of having to use the Worksheet command on the Insert menu. However, I don't think many Excel users will want to use the maximum number of 255 worksheets in a single workbook. (See Chapter 9 for more information on manually inserting and removing worksheets from a workbook.)
- *Standard Font and Size.* Use these options to change the font and font size that Excel automatically assigns to all the cells in a new workbook. If you have a favorite font that you want to use in most of the worksheets you create (and Chicago ain't it), this option is the way to change it. By using this option, you don't have to call on the Font tool on the Formatting toolbar all the time.
- *Default File Location.* If you don't specify a folder for this option, when you first start Excel, the program tries to find each workbook that you open or put each new workbook that you save in the same folder where all the Excel program files are located in most cases (Macintosh HD:EXCEL), which is seldom if ever the place you want your workbooks. Use this option to override Excel's tendency to use the program folder as the repository of your precious documents. Simply enter the path name of the

folders (directory) where you do most of your work (**Macintosh HD:Simple Simon's Pie Shoppe:COOLJUNK**, for example). Note that this folder must exist before you can use this option. It can't be a folder that you meant to create but just haven't gotten around to yet. If you don't know how to create a new folder for your work, get your hands on a copy of *Macs For Dummies*.

- *Alternate Startup File Location.* Normally, Excel opens any document that you put in the special startup folder whenever you start Excel. On the Mac, it's known more simply as the STARTUP folder; it's an alternative place to have Excel store your files. If you don't feel that one startup folder is enough, you can use this option to specify another startup folder. Again, this folder must already exist before you can designate it as your alternate startup location.
- *User Name.* This is usually *Greg Harvey* — unless I'm using my nom de plume, *I. M. Shakes Peer* — in my version of Excel but will differ in your version, unless you happen to go by the same name or alias. If you want to change your user name to *Greg Harvey* or *I. M. Shakes Peer* or some other name, this where you do it.

Colors for every palette

If you're fortunate enough to have a color monitor on your computer, you can spruce up the on-screen appearance of your documents by applying various colors to different parts of worksheets or charts. Excel lets you choose from a palette of 56 predefined colors. You can apply these colors to specific cells, cell borders, fonts, or graphics objects (such as a particular data series in a chart or a text box or an arrow):

Excel 5 introduces three floating pull-down menus that transform into floating boxes, allowing users to use and edit cell selections and worksheet colors — it's cool. The three *tear-off* menus are Borders, Color, and Font Color (see Figure 10-7). To tear off one of these menus, click your mouse on the menu as you would any pull-down menu, drag the menu down to the bottom, and then keep dragging until the menu tears off. Then you can place it like a floating menu, anywhere you want it.

- To apply a new color to a cell selection or a selected graphics object, click on the Color tool on the Formatting toolbar (the one with the paint bucket) and select the color you want to apply from the pop-up palette of 56 colors.
- To change the color of the font used in a cell selection or for a selected graphics object, such as a chart title or text box, choose the Font Color tool on the Formatting toolbar (the one with a T and a red square) and

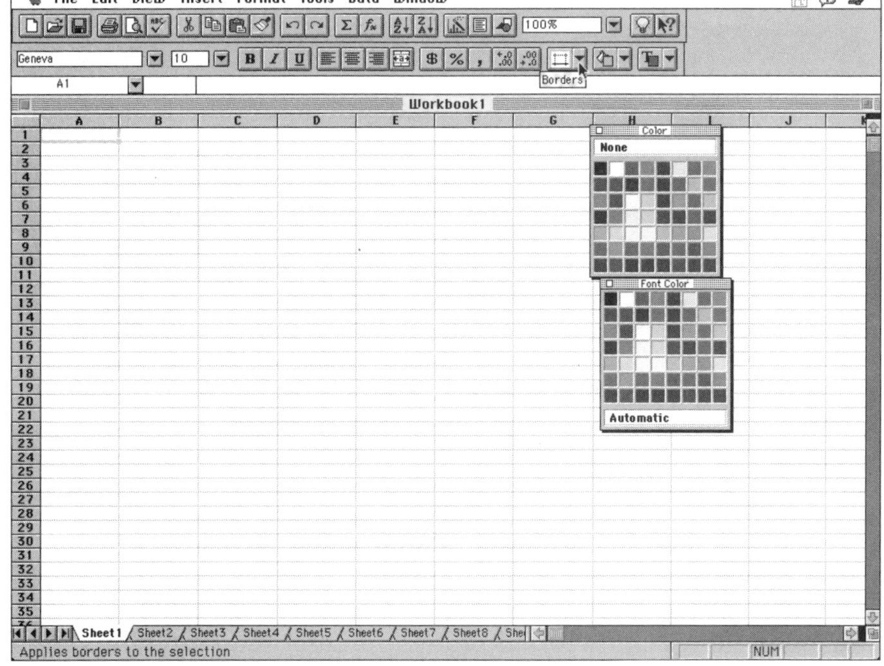

Figure 10-7: The new tear-off menus on the far right side of the Formatting toolbar: Borders, Color, and Font Color.

select the color you want to apply from the pop-up palette of 56 colors. Remember, the Font Color can be torn off the Formatting toolbar for editing made easy.

- To change the color of the borders of a cell or cell selection, open the Format Cells dialog box (⌘+1), select the Border tab, and choose the Color option or click its pull-down menu button to display the palette of 56 colors. From this palette, you can select the color you want to assign to the selected cells' borders. Remember, the Borders pull-down menu tears off to become the Border floating menu. Go figure.

If the 56 predefined colors don't exactly suit your artistic tastes, you can customize colors on the palette. Although you cannot place additional colors on the palette, you can change any or all the predefined colors, depending on how ambitious you want to get.

To customize a color on the palette, choose the Color tab in the Options dialog box, shown in Figure 10-8, and select the color you want to modify in Standard Colors, Chart Fills, Chart Lines, or Other Colors. Finally, select the Modify button.

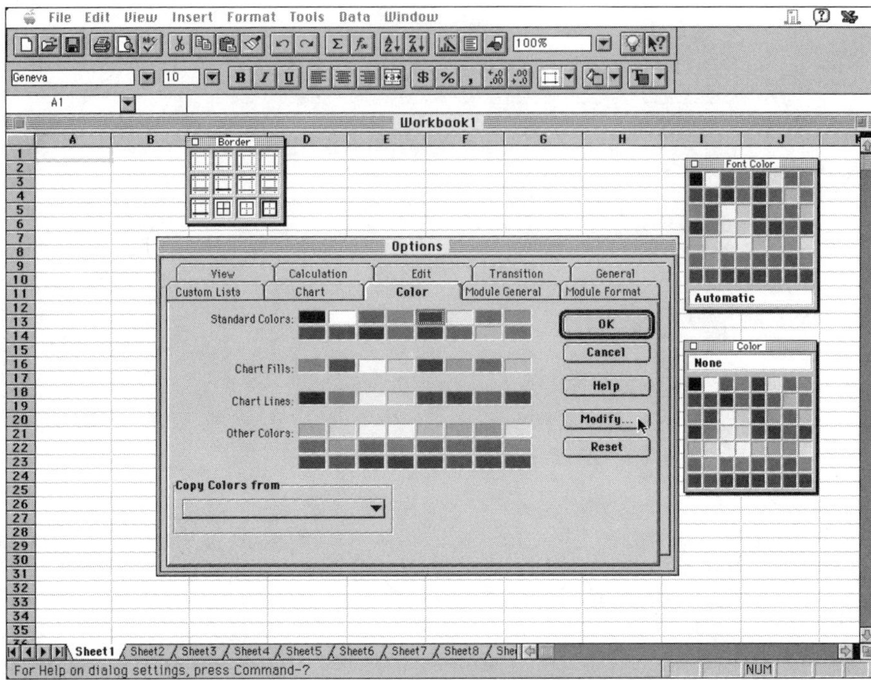

Figure 10-8: The Color tab in the Options dialog box.

When you choose Modify, Excel opens the Color Wheel dialog box, where you can modify the selected color (see Figure 10-9). If you know something about color theory, you can modify the color by adjusting its Hue, Saturation, and Brightness, or its Red, Green, and Blue content. Don't you wish this book were printed in color?

If you're like me and you don't have the foggiest idea of what to do with these individual settings, you can still customize the color by dragging the circle crosshair around the color wheel or by dragging the scroll box or by clicking on the scroll arrows in the accompanying scroll bar on the right:

- When you drag the circle crosshair, you change the color's hue and saturation.
- When you drag the scroll box or click on the scroll arrows in the accompanying scroll bar, you change the color's brightness as well as its mixture of red, green, and blue.

As you change the color settings, check to see how the color will appear by looking at the Color/Solid rectangle in the Color Wheel dialog box. When you've got the color just the way you want it, click OK or press Return to close the Color Wheel dialog box and return to the Color Palette dialog box. The custom color now appears in this dialog box.

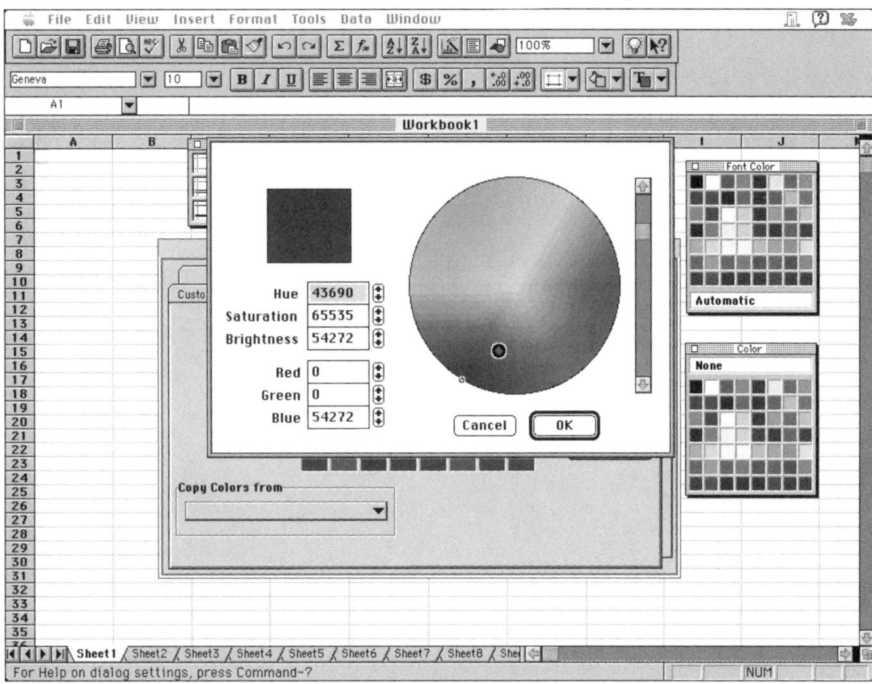

Figure 10-9: The Color Wheel dialog box.

To customize other colors in the palette, select them and repeat this modification process. To restore the predefined colors to Excel, click on the Reset button in the Color tab.

After you customize the colors for a particular workbook, you can copy these colors to another workbook, which saves you all the time and effort of modifying each color individually again. To copy the colors to another workbook, open the workbook with the customized palette and, using the Window pull-down menu, switch to the workbook document to which you want to copy the palette. In the second workbook, choose Options from the Tools menu, open the Color tab, and select the first document in the Copy Colors From pull-down menu.

Excel modifies the colors in the Color tab of the Options dialog box to match the ones in the workbook you selected. You can use these colors in the new workbook as soon as you close the Options dialog box by clicking OK or pressing Return.

Chapter 11

Tooling Around

In This Chapter

- How to customize the built-in toolbars in Excel
- How to create new toolbars
- How to assign macros to blank tools
- How to assign your own pictures to tools

Up until now, you've used the tools on the various built-in toolbars that come with Excel exactly as they were configured. Now it's time to learn how to customize the toolbars so that they contain only the tools you need, as well as learn how to create toolbars of your own.

As you will soon discover, the tools found on the built-in toolbars represent just a small part of the total number of tools supplied with Excel. You can add unused tools to any of the existing toolbars or use them to create new toolbars of your own design.

Not only can you customize Excel toolbars by creating new combinations using various built-in tools, but you also can customize toolbars by assigning the macros you've recorded — see Chapter 10 for details — to any of the unassigned tools that come with Excel. Further, if none of the pictures used on the unassigned tools suits the function of the macro you're adding to a toolbar, you can put a graphic created in another program (such as a clip-art image or one that you create yourself with another graphics program) on your tool.

The Right Tool for the Job

As you learned in previous chapters, Excel comes with a set of several built-in toolbars. Each toolbar consists of a group of tools that the program designers thought would be most helpful in getting particular tasks done. As you know, the Standard and Formatting toolbars, which are automatically displayed at the top of the screen when you start Excel, contain a wide variety of tools useful for creating, formatting, and printing documents.

Although the arrangements on most of the built-in toolbars may satisfy your needs, modifying the arrangement of any of them is easy. If there are tools you seldom or never use, for example, replace them with ones that are more useful for the type of work you do. If you use a tool quite often but are not happy with its position in the toolbar — or even the toolbar it's on — move the tool to a more convenient position.

You determine which toolbars are displayed on the screen and modify their contents from the Toolbars dialog box (see Figure 11-1). To display the Toolbars dialog box, choose Toolbars from the View menu or choose the Toolbars command from the toolbar shortcut menus, which you open by pressing the Control key (or ⌘+Option) and clicking on any of the toolbars (see Figure 11-2).

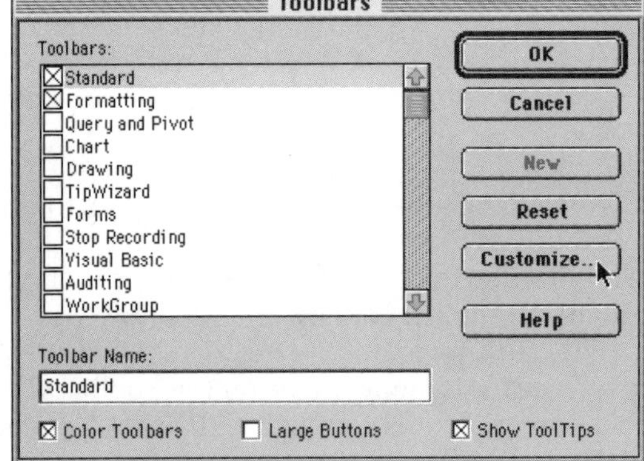

Figure 11-1: The Toolbars dialog box.

To display a toolbar in the Excel program window from the Toolbars dialog box (remember that you can also do this task by choosing the toolbar's name on a toolbar shortcut menu), click on the toolbar's particular check box in the Toolbars list box. Likewise, you can hide any of the displayed toolbars by removing the X from its check box.

Across the bottom of the Toolbars dialog box are three check boxes; their settings affect all the toolbars displayed in Excel:

- *Color Toolbars.* Remove the X from this check box when you're using Excel on a monochrome monitor, such as a monochrome laptop or Macintosh.
- *Large Buttons.* Normally, Excel uses small buttons to display the tools on the toolbars. Select this check box to increase the size of the buttons. (This feature is especially helpful when you're running Excel on a computer with a really small screen — on a laptop or Mac with a built-in 9-inch screen, for example.)

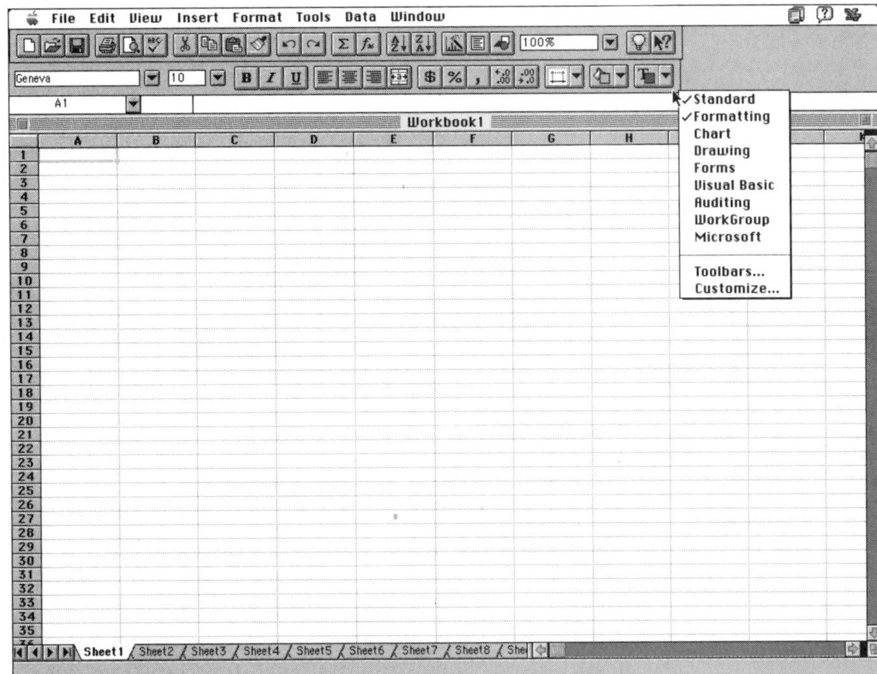

Figure 11-2: The toolbar shortcut menu

- *Show ToolTips.* Normally, Excel shows you the name of each tool on a toolbar when you position the mouse pointer on the tool's button without clicking the mouse button. (Microsoft refers to these names as *ToolTips.*) If you no longer need to see the name of each tool, you can remove the ToolTips display by deselecting this check box.

For you to modify the contents of a particular toolbar from the Toolbars dialog box, the toolbar must already be displayed, or you must select it in the Toolbars dialog box. You can select a toolbar in that dialog box by clicking on either its check box or its name in the Toolbars list box. Remember that you can select as many toolbars as you want in this list box if you feel up to modifying more than one toolbar at a time.

After selecting the toolbars that aren't already displayed on-screen, choose the Customize button to display the Customize dialog box (see Figure 11-3).

If the toolbar you want to edit is already displayed on the screen, you can open the Customize dialog box directly without first having to open the Toolbars dialog box: Click on the toolbar while pressing the Control key (or ⌘+Option), and then choose the Customize command on the toolbar's shortcut menu.

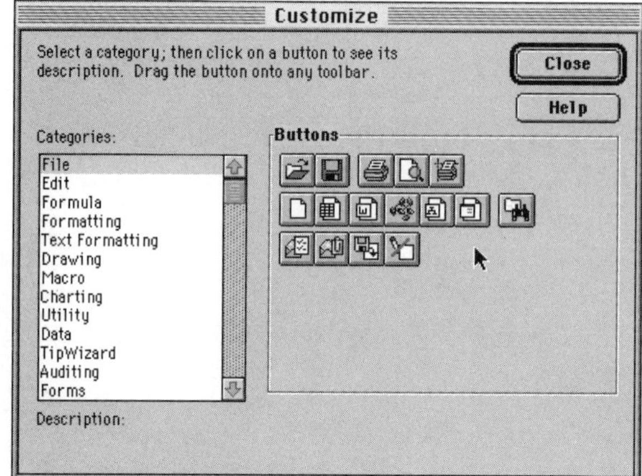

Figure 11-3: The Customize dialog box.

Musical toolbars

When you open the Customize dialog box, Excel displays all the toolbars that you selected in the Toolbars dialog box (these toolbars are added to the list of those that were already shown on the screen). You can select individual tools on any of the displayed toolbars just as you do any graphics object in a worksheet window.

- To remove a tool after selecting it, simply drag the tool off the toolbar and release the mouse button.
- To reposition a tool on the same toolbar, drag the tool until it is positioned slightly in front of the tool it is to precede and release the mouse button.
- To move a tool to a different toolbar, drag the tool to the desired position on the new toolbar.
- To copy a tool to a different toolbar, hold down the Control key as you drag the tool (you see a small plus sign next to the arrowhead pointer, just as you do when copying a cell selection with the drag-and-drop feature).

Figure 11-4 shows the Standard toolbar with its Function Wizard (`fx`) tool being removed. (Remember that the Function Wizard tool automatically appears on the formula bar anytime you type = to start a formula.) After you drag this tool off the toolbar, Excel removes the tool when you release the mouse button. Figure 11-5 shows the Standard toolbar right after the mouse button was released.

Figure 11-4: Removing the Function Wizard tool from the Standard toolbar.

Figure 11-5: The Standard toolbar after the Function Wizard tool was deleted.

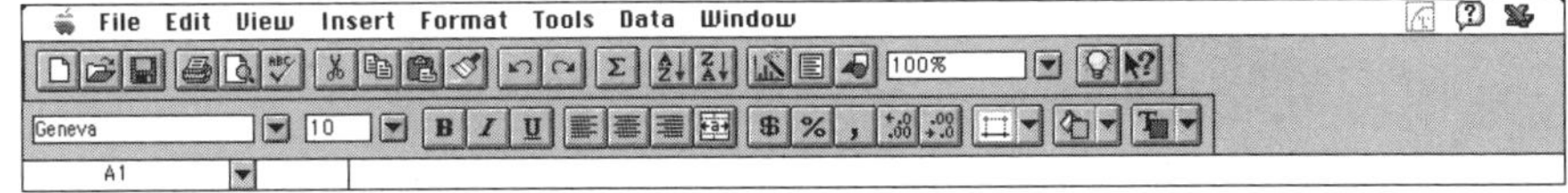

New tools for old jobs

Removing and moving tools are just a small part of the story of customizing the built-in toolbars. You'll find the capacity to add new tools to the toolbars even more important. The new tools I'm talking about are tools that come with Excel but for some reason or other didn't make it to the built-in toolbars.

All the Excel tools are grouped into the following categories: File, Edit, Formula, Formatting, Text Formatting, Drawing, Macro, Charting, Utility, Data, TipWizard, Auditing, Forms, and Custom. All tools — with the exception of those in the Custom category — perform specific tasks. Custom tools are blank so that you can assign macros to them (see "A Blank Tool Is a Terrible Thing to Waste," later in this chapter).

Where's that toolbar?

Whenever you exit Excel, the program saves the current toolbar layout and display shown in the Excel window in a special file named EXCEL TOOLBARS (5). This file is located in the Preferences folder in the System folder. If you're using a System 6 version of the Finder, this file is located in the System folder.

- To display the tools for a particular category in the Buttons area of the Customize dialog box, select the name of the category in the Categories list box.
- To find out what a particular tool does, click on the tool in the Buttons area. Excel displays a short description of the tool's function in the Description area at the bottom of the dialog box.
- To add a tool to a toolbar, drag the tool from the Buttons area to the desired position on the toolbar and release the mouse button.

Figure 11-6 shows the process of adding a new tool to the Standard toolbar. In this figure, the Set Print Area tool, from the File category, is being added to the Standard toolbar (right in between the Print and Print Preview tools). Figure 11-7 shows the tool being dragged into position. The Set Print Area tool allows whatever cells are currently selected to be printed whenever you click on the tool.

Spaced-out tools

You may have noticed how tools on various built-in toolbars are grouped together with little spaces before and after the group of tools. You, too, can group various tools when customizing a toolbar.

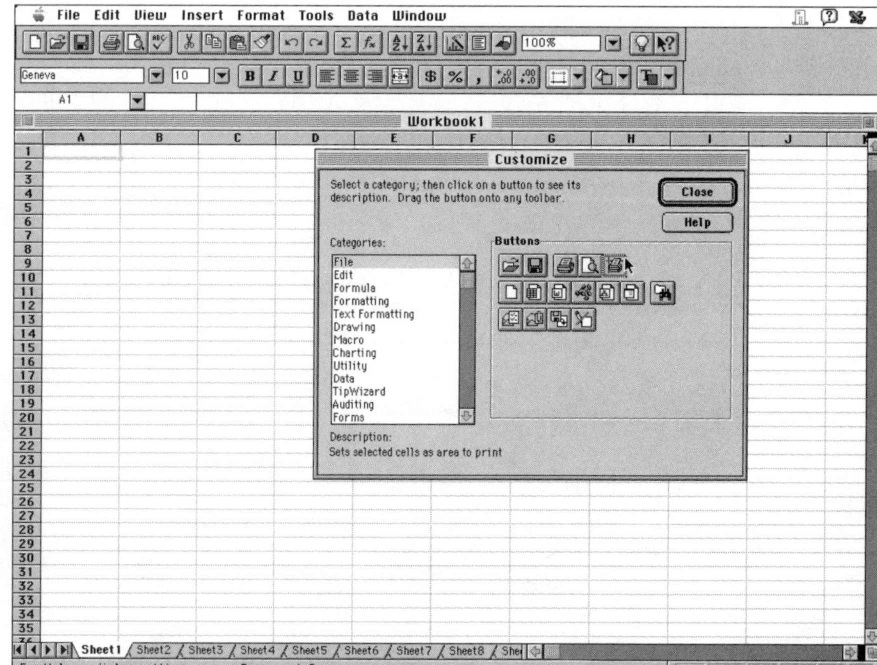

Figure 11-6: Adding the Set Print Area tool to the Standard toolbar.

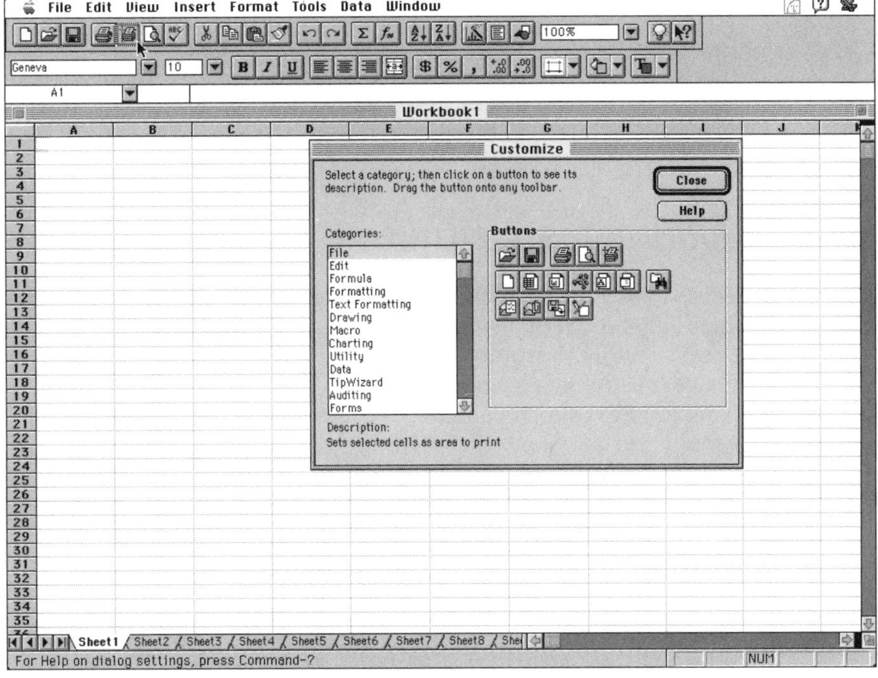

Figure 11-7: The Standard toolbar while adding the Set Print Area tool.

You can insert a space on the left or right side of a tool to separate it from other tools. To do so, open the Customize toolbars dialog box, drag the tool slightly in the opposite direction of where you want the space to appear (to the right to insert a space on the tool's left side, to the left to insert a space on its right side), and release the mouse button. Excel inserts a space before or after the tool you just dragged.

Why is that Customize toolbars dialog box open all the time?

To edit or copy toolbars, you first must open the Customize toolbars dialog box. Then you can access the special shortcut menu by pressing the Control key (or ⌘+Option) and clicking on a toolbar. The Customize toolbars dialog box must be open to move buttons around or to delete them. When this dialog box is open, the buttons are treated as objects that can be edited; however, if the Customize toolbar dialog box is not open, there is no way to select the buttons without activating their respective functions (see Figure 11-3).

To delete a space in front of or after a tool so that the tool abuts (that means *touches*) the tool next to it, drag the tool in the appropriate direction until it touches or slightly overlaps the neighboring tool and then release the mouse button. Excel redraws the toolbar to remove the space from the tool you just dragged.

Toolbar restoration

Sometimes you may make changes to a built-in toolbar that you don't want to keep. No matter what wild changes you make to a built-in toolbar, you can always restore the toolbar to its original form. Open the Toolbars dialog box by choosing Toolbars from the View menu or choosing the Toolbars command from a toolbar shortcut menu; then select the toolbar's name in the Toolbars list box and choose the Reset button.

Toolbar for Every Occasion

You are by no means limited to the built-in toolbars that come with Excel. You can create your own toolbars to combine any of the available tools, those that are used in the built-in toolbars as well as those that are not.

To create a toolbar of your very own, follow these steps:

1. **Open the Toolbars dialog box by choosing Toolbars from the View menu or selecting the Toolbars command from a toolbar shortcut menu.**
2. **Enter a name for the new toolbar in the Toolbar Name text box.**
3. **Select the New command button.**

   The Customize dialog box opens, and a small toolbar dialog box appears in the upper left-hand corner of the document window. Use the Customize dialog box to add the tools to the new toolbar.
4. **Choose the category containing the first tool you want to add to the new toolbar from the Categories list box.**
5. **Drag the tool from the Buttons area in the Customize dialog box to the tiny toolbar dialog box in the upper left-hand corner of the document window. Release the mouse button.**
6. **Repeat Steps 4 and 5 until you have added all the tools you want to the new toolbar.**

   After the tools are in the toolbar, you can rearrange and space them as you want.
7. **Select the Close button or press Return to close the Customize dialog box.**

As you add tools to the new toolbar, Excel automatically widens the toolbar dialog box. When the dialog box is wide enough, the name you assigned to the toolbar appears in the title bar. If the toolbar dialog box starts running into the Customize dialog box, just drag the new toolbar down by its title until it's entirely clear of the Customize dialog box.

You also can create a new toolbar simply by dragging a tool from the Customize dialog box to somewhere in the document window and releasing the mouse button. Excel creates a new toolbar dialog box for the tool and assigns a name (like Toolbar1) to the toolbar. You then can add more tools to the new toolbar. Unfortunately, when you create a toolbar in this manner, you can't rename the toolbar later to give it a more descriptive title.

Figures 11-8, 11-9, and 11-10 show the process of creating a new toolbar called, modestly enough, Greg's Cool Tools. Figure 11-8 shows the Toolbars dialog box after entering the catchy name for the new toolbar. Figure 11-9 shows the new toolbar after clicking on the New button on the Toolbars dialog box. This action adds a blank toolbar dialog box and activates the Customize dialog box. Figure 11-10 shows Greg's Cool Tools toolbar with tools for copying stuff to the Clipboard, pasting just the formats or values, erasing just the formulas and values or just the formats from the cells, and inserting various symbols routinely used in setting up new formulas.

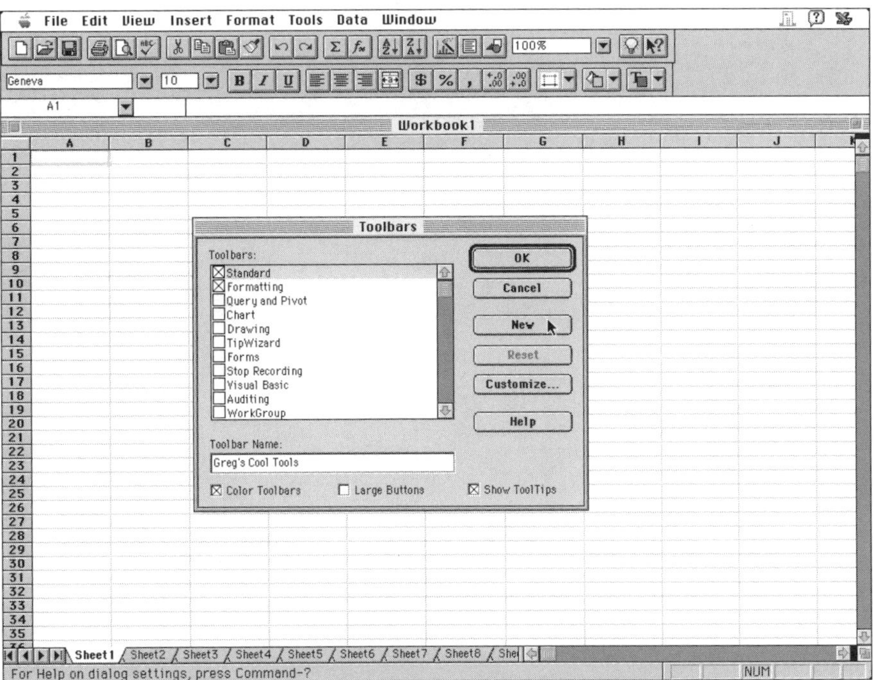

Figure 11-8: Naming the new Greg's Cool Tools toolbar.

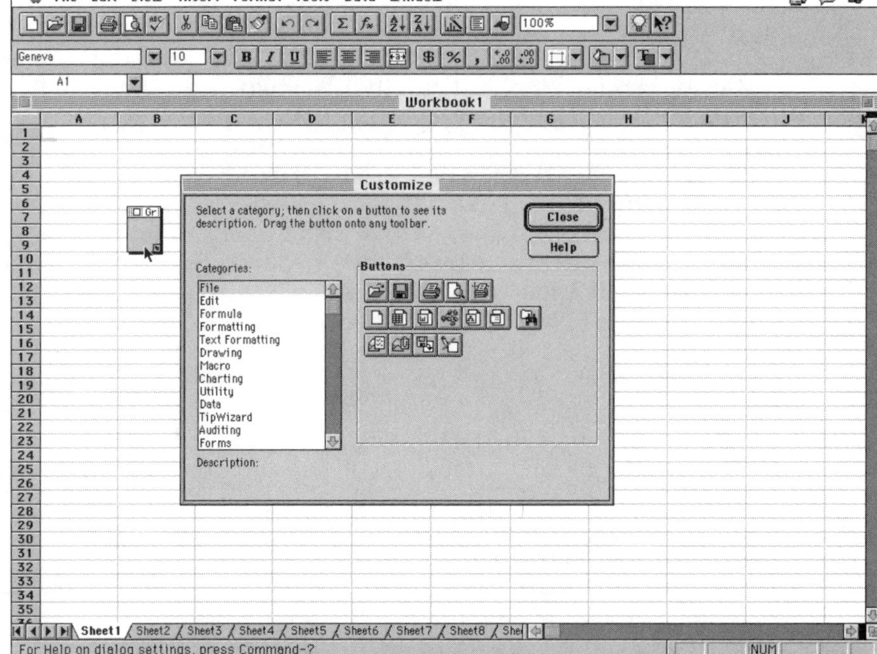

Figure 11-9: The new Greg's Cool Tools toolbar before adding the cool toois.

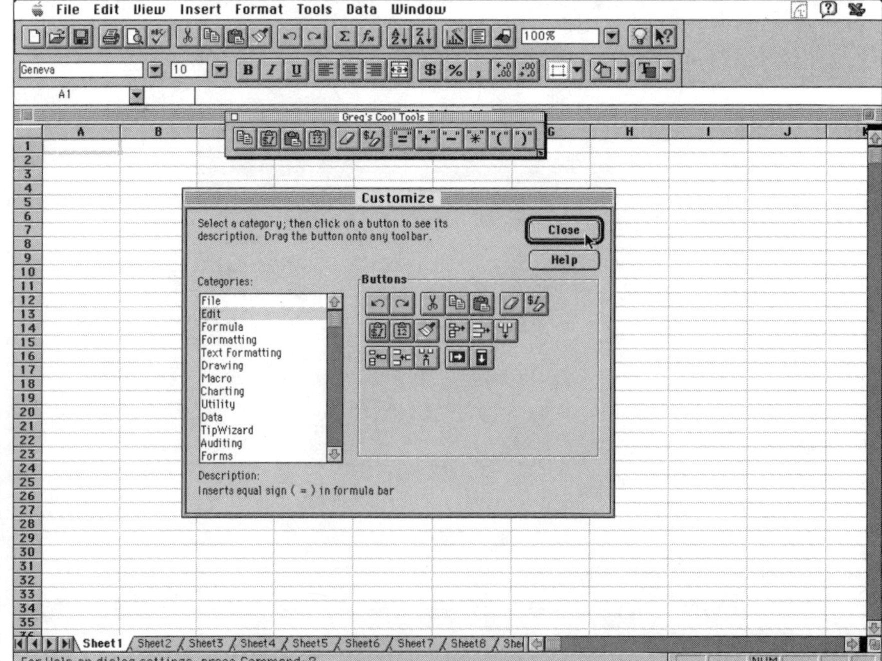

Figure 11-10: The completed Greg's Cool Tools toolbar.

After creating a new toolbar, you can display, hide, move, resize, and dock it just like you do any of the built-in toolbars. If you don't want to keep a toolbar you've created, delete it by opening the Toolbars dialog box and selecting the toolbar in the Toolbars list box. As soon as you select the name of a toolbar you created, Excel replaces the Reset button with a Delete button (the program won't let you delete any built-in toolbar). When you click on Delete, Excel displays an alert dialog box, in which you confirm the deletion by choosing OK or pressing Return.

A Blank Tool Is a Terrible Thing to Waste

As hinted at earlier, you can assign macros you've recorded (covered back in Chapter 10) to tools and then place these tools on toolbars (either on one of the built-in toolbars or on one of your own creations). That way, you can play back a macro by clicking on its tool. This feature is particularly helpful when you've assigned all 26 letters (A through Z) and 10 numbers (0 through 9) as shortcut keystrokes in a particular macro sheet.

Excel has a variety of blank tools in the Custom category to which you can assign macros (see Figure 11-11). Unfortunately, these tools use a mixed bag of pictures, many of which you will be hard put to associate with the function of a macro. I mean, come on — what's a Happy Face macro supposed to do?!

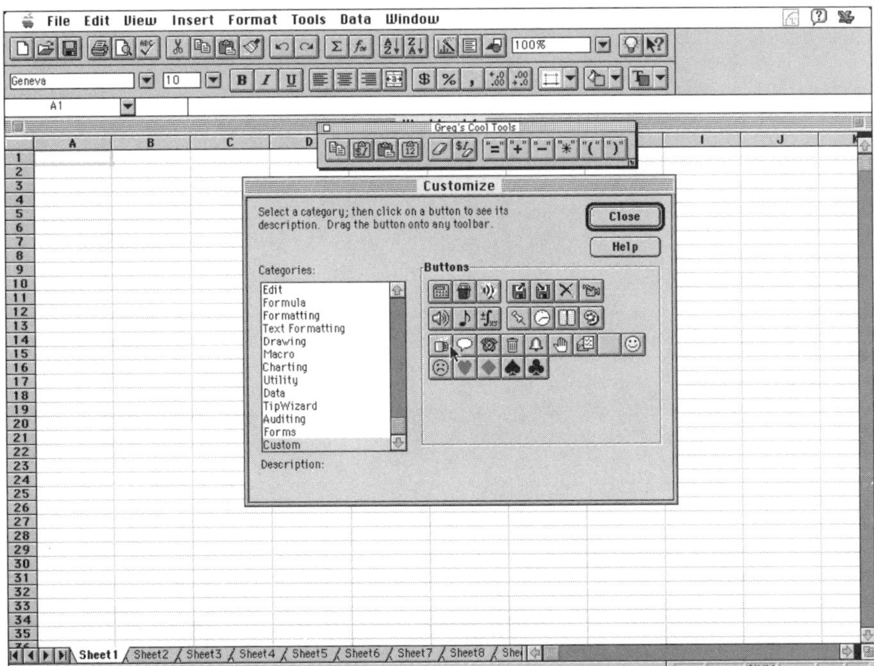

Figure 11-11: The Customize dialog box with the Custom tools.

To assign a macro to a tool, follow these steps:

1. **If the macro you want to assign to a tool is attached to a particular workbook rather than to your personal macro workbook, make sure that the particular workbook is open. If it is not open, you need to open it with the Open tool on the Standard toolbar or the Open command on the File menu.**

   Remember, Excel opens the personal macro workbook each time you start the program, making that workbook's macros available anywhere and anytime in the program. Macros saved as part of a particular workbook, however, are only available when that workbook is open.

2. **If necessary, display the toolbar to which you want to add the macro.**

3. **Open the Customize dialog box by choosing the Customize command from a toolbar shortcut menu.**

4. **Select the Custom category in the Categories list box.**

   Excel displays the Custom buttons shown in Figure 11-11.

5. **Drag one of the Custom buttons in the Buttons area to the desired position on your toolbar. Release the mouse button.**

   Excel opens the Assign Macro dialog box (see Figure 11-12). From this dialog box, select or record the macro you want to assign to the tool.

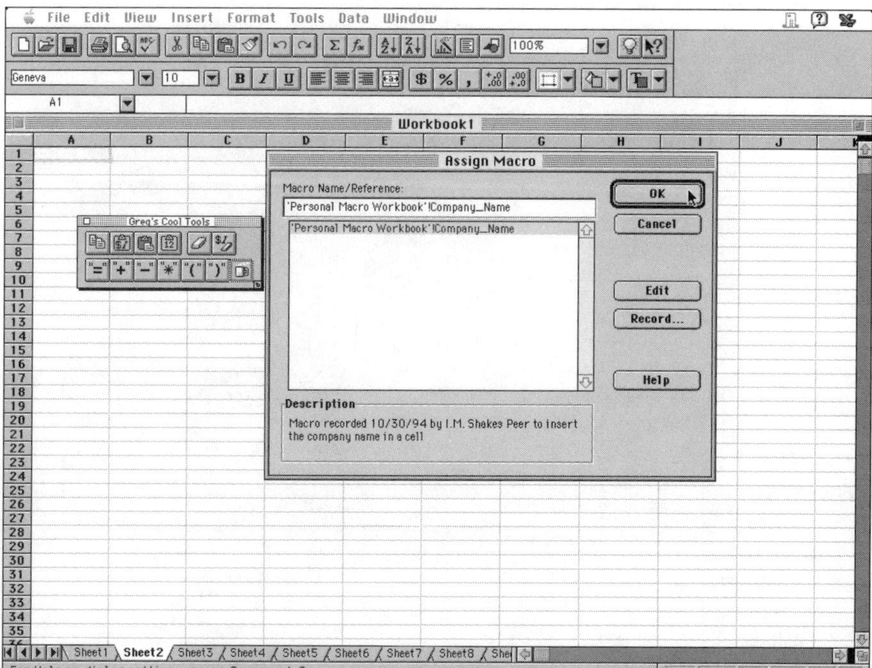

Figure 11-12: The Assign Macro dialog box.

6. **Select or record the macro to be assigned to the tool.**

   To assign an existing macro to the selected tool, double-click on the macro name in the Macro Name/Reference list box or select the macro and choose OK or press Return.

   To record a new macro for the tool, click on the Record button and record a macro just like you record any other (see Chapter 10).

7. **Repeat steps 5 and 6 for every macro you want to assign to a tool.**
8. **Click on the Close button or press Return to close the Customize dialog box.**

Cute as a Button

Fortunately, you aren't stuck with customized tools that have pictures of smiley faces, hearts, and coffee mugs. You can copy an image from another button, or, if you're an *artiste,* you can use the Button Editor to create your image.

To paste a picture from one button to another, follow these steps:

1. **Open the Customize dialog box by choosing the Customize command from a toolbar shortcut menu.**
2. **Select the button you want to copy in the Buttons area of the Customize dialog box; then choose Copy Button Image from the Edit pull-down menu.**
3. **Select the custom tool in the toolbar whose image you want to replace with the one you just copied; then choose Paste Button Image from the Edit menu or the Paste Button Image command from the toolbar shortcut menu.**

That's all there is to it. Excel replaces the face of the selected tool with the picture stored in the Clipboard.

If you prefer to create your own masterpiece rather than steal one of the other existing button images (which may already be associated with a particular action if the image appears on another toolbar that you use), you can do so by editing an image with the new Button Editor. To open the Button Editor, open the Customize dialog box. Then choose the tool whose image you want to edit on the toolbar and select the Edit Button Image command from the toolbar's shortcut menu.

Part VI

Excel Function Reference (for Real People)

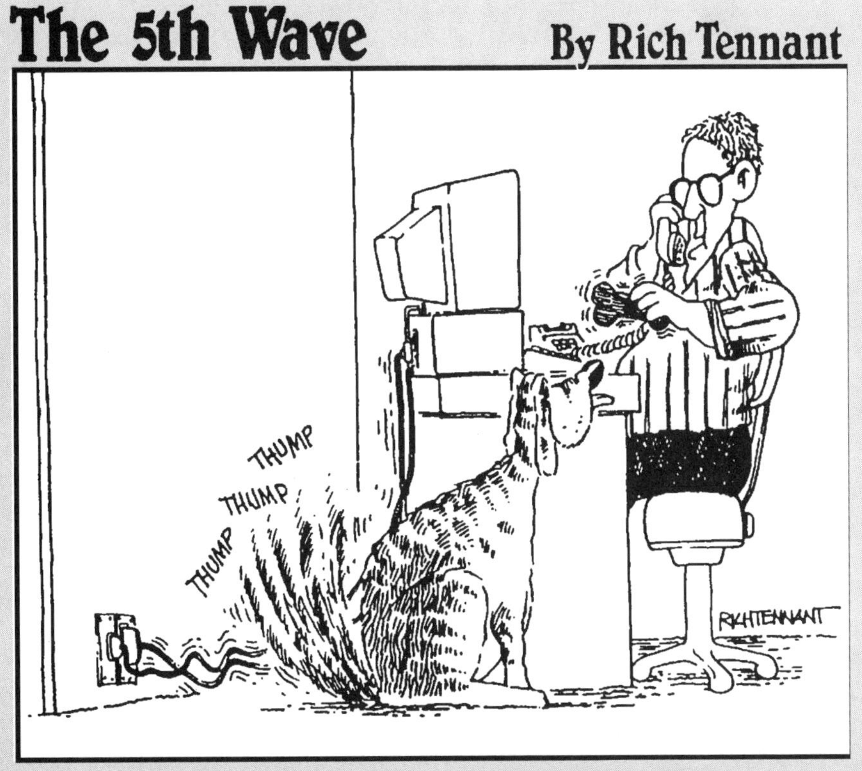

"I TELL YA I'M STILL GETTING INTERFERENCE—
- COOKIE, RAGS? RAGS WANNA COOKIE? -
THERE IT GOES AGAIN."

The part in which . . .

You learn how to use an array of Excel worksheet functions. You start with the most common functions, such as SUM, AVERAGE, and MIN, and then you progress to the more specialized functions, such as the financial functions PV and PMT. This part takes you all the way to the functions IF, VLOOKUP, and HLOOKUP!

Chapter 12

I Love Everyday Functions

In This Chapter

- How to use the SUM, PRODUCT, and SUMPRODUCT functions to total figures
- How to use the AVERAGE function to find the average of the values in a list
- How to use the COUNT function to find the number of items in a list
- How to use the MAX and MIN functions to find the highest and lowest values in a list
- How to use the ROUND function to round values up or down
- How to use the NOW function to stamp a worksheet with the date and time

Let's face it: If you do a great deal of work with formulas, you need to become as familiar as possible with the built-in worksheet functions. As you undoubtedly recall, functions perform specific, predefined calculations based on the type of information (called, for the sake of argument, *arguments*) you supply. To use an Excel function, all you have to know are the arguments the function takes.

This chapter looks at the more common, everyday functions that you use most often. It should come as no surprise that the bulk of these functions are statistical in nature. After all, bean counting is what most worksheets are all about.

When fooling around with Excel functions, don't overlook your good ol' buddy Mr. TipWizard — the tool with the `fx` on the Standard toolbar and that also appears on the formula bar when you type = to start your formula. You can use the TipWizard in conjunction with information in this and the following chapter to make short work of specifying the necessary parameters for these babies to work.

To SUM Up

You are already familiar with the SUM function, at least as it's applied with the AutoSum tool on the Standard toolbar. Being the most commonly used function in the world of spreadsheets, it's only fitting that this chapter start with a brief discussion of the way you can use the SUM function (in addition to AutoSum).

Take a look at your *Excel Function Reference* (part of the documentation provided with your program). You will see the following form, which they insist on calling *syntax,* of the SUM function:

```
SUM(number1,number2,...)
```

As is standard practice, the arguments of the function (remember that the arguments are the text between the parentheses) are shown in italics, signifying that they are *variables*. Because you have variables in the form, you can substitute such things as the cell reference **B5**, the value **100**, or even a simple calculation like **100*B5** in place of the *number1* argument.

In the *Excel Function Reference,* the arguments shown in ***bold italics*** are required to get the function to work at all. All arguments shown in regular *italics* are optional ones that you can use when you need them but are not required to get the blasted function to work.

In terms of the SUM function, all this bold/italic/variable lingo simply means that you must substitute something for the ***number1*** argument but that the *number2* argument is purely optional. The three periods — **...** (aka ellipsis) — after the *number2* argument just mean that you can add more number-type arguments to the SUM function (up to 30 total).

The concept that's most confusing about the way the *Excel Function Reference* presents the arguments of the SUM function is that you easily can misinterpret ***number1,*** *number2,* and so on as representing only individual values whether they are in the cells referenced, the numbers you enter, or the numbers calculated by formulas. If you remember how you total a row or column of numbers with the AutoSum tool, you realize that this is clearly not the case. The ***number1*** and *number2* arguments can just as well refer to ranges of cells that contain numbers or formulas.

Suppose that you need to figure the grand total of the values in three different columns of a worksheet, say in the ranges C3:C15, G3:G19, and H2:H25. To calculate these values with the SUM function, replace the ***number1*** argument with the first cell range, C3:C15; the *number2* argument with the second cell range, G3:G19; and the *number3* argument with the third range, H2:H25. Enter the following formula in the cell where you want the total of all the numbers in these cells to appear:

```
=SUM(C3:C15,G3:G19,H2:H25)
```

When creating formulas like this, keep in mind that you must separate each argument with a comma and no space. After you type the comma, remember that Excel allows you to select the individual cell ranges with the mouse or keyboard so that you don't have to type cell references unless you want to.

I'm Just a PRODUCT of My Times

You use the SUM function when you want to add values together. When you want to multiply them together, you use the PRODUCT function. The PRODUCT function otherwise works just like the SUM function; it follows the same form with the same kind of arguments:

```
PRODUCT(number1,number2,...)
```

Again, the *number* arguments can be cell ranges, individual cell references, or numbers that you enter or Excel calculates. You can include up to 30 such arguments in the function.

For example, if you want to know the product of a value in cell D4 and the value in cell E4, you can use the following PRODUCT function:

```
=PRODUCT(D4,E4)
```

Alternatively, you can create the following formula, which returns the very same result:

```
=D4*E4
```

You can use the PRODUCT function to multiply all the values in a range by each other. If you want to find the product of all the values in the cell range B23:F23, for example, enter the following function in the cell where you want the product:

```
=PRODUCT(B23:F23)
```

The SUMPRODUCT

The SUMPRODUCT function combines multiplication and addition. You can use this function to add two columns of figures that are first multiplied together. For example, the Simple Simon Pie Shoppe might put the number of pies ordered by the Mother Goose Inn in column C, multiply the number of pies by the pie price in column D, and then place the results (the products) in column F.

The total due for this invoice would be the sum of the products in column F. Cell F11 would contain the formula with the SUMPRODUCT function. The function calculates the amount due by multiplying the cells in column C with their counterparts in column D and then summing these products. The actual formula reads as follows:

```
=SUMPRODUCT(C7:C10,D7:D10)
```

I'm Just Your AVERAGE Joe

The AVERAGE function calculates what's technically known as the *arithmetic mean.* The AVERAGE function follows the same form as the SUM function:

```
AVERAGE(number1,number2,...)
```

Excel calculates the average by adding up all the values specified by the number arguments, counting how many values there are, and dividing the total by the result of this tally (just as you were taught in grade-school math class).

The only catch with using the AVERAGE function is how Excel counts (or miscounts, depending on how you look at it) the number of entries. The easiest way to explain this little quirk is by way of an illustration.

Figure 12-1 shows two ranges of figures in separate columns. The numbers are identical except that the fourth cell of the first range (C5) is empty and the fourth cell in the second range (E5) has a 0 in it.

Although the addition of 0 to the second range makes no difference in the sum of these two ranges, it *does* change the count (zeros in cells are counted but blank cells are not). The different count is the reason Excel calculates a different average for the second range. What a difference a zero makes!

File Edit View Insert Format Tools Data Window

C7 =AVERAGE(C2:C6)

Function Examples

	A	B	C	D	E
1					
2			12		12
3			45		45
4			30		30
5					0
6			19		19
7		Average	26.5		21.2
8		Sum	106		106
9		Count	4		5

Average / Sheet2 / Sheet3 / Sheet4 / Sheet5 / Sheet6 / Sheet7 / Sheet8

Ready NUM

Figure 12-1: Averaging, summing, and counting two ranges that are identical except for a zero.

COUNT Me In!

The COUNT function is useful when you are dealing with a really large cell range and need to know how many items it contains. For example, you can use the COUNT function to get an accurate count of the number of records in a database.

The COUNT function, like the AVERAGE function, counts cells that contain a zero; it does not count blank cells. If you designate a range that has blank cells, the COUNT function doesn't include them in the tally. When you are counting records in a database, make sure that you don't select a field (or column) that is missing many entries, because the result will be skewed. Excel tells you that you have fewer records than you actually have because it fails to count the records that are missing entries in that particular field. For this reason, always choose a field that has an entry in each and every record, and select its cell range as the argument for COUNT.

The MEDIAN Strip

Sometimes, instead of knowing the average value in a series of numbers, you want to know the *median value,* that is, the value truly smack dab in the middle of the series. For a median value, you have just as many values higher than the median as you have values lower. The MEDIAN function is set up just like the AVERAGE function (which in turn is set up just like the SUM function).

How To Get the MAXimum in the MINimum Time

Whereas the MEDIAN function gives you the value in the middle of those in a list of arguments, the MAX function returns the highest value and the MIN function returns the lowest value. Like COUNT, these two functions are most useful when dealing with a large range of values (especially when they haven't been sorted) and you need to find out quickly which one is highest or lowest. The MAX and MIN functions take the same argument series as do the SUM or AVERAGE functions.

Going ROUND About

In Chapter 3, I made a big deal about how formatting values in a worksheet affects only their display on-screen and not how they are stored in the cell. Back then, I recommended clicking on the Precision as Displayed check box in the Calculations Options dialog box to have Excel round off all the values to the number of decimal places allowed by their number formats. The only trouble with this solution is that it is universal (it applies to all values in the entire worksheet).

For those situations where you only want to round off *some* of the values in a worksheet, use the ROUND function instead. The ROUND function has two required arguments (see, they're shown here in ***bold italic*** type) that are entered according to the following pattern:

```
ROUND(number,num_digits)
```

The first argument, ***number,*** indicates the value (or its cell reference) you want rounded. The second argument, ***num_digits,*** indicates the number of decimal places you want in the rounded number.

To round a value to a specific number of decimal places, enter a positive value for the ***num_digits*** argument that represents the number of decimal places to round to the right of the decimal point. To round a decimal value to the nearest whole number (integer), enter **0** as the ***num_digits*** argument. To round off a whole number, enter a negative value for the ***num_digits*** argument that represents the number of places to round to the left of the decimal point.

Figure 12-2 shows the effect of changing the ***num_digits*** argument when rounding two values; one a large whole number with seven digits and the other a small decimal value with six decimal places.

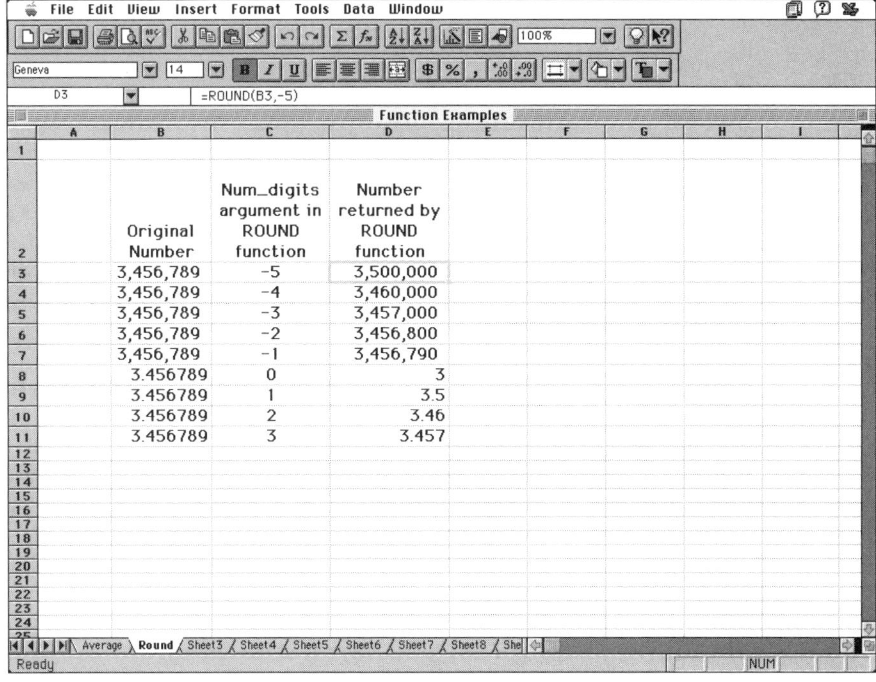

Figure 12-2: Using the ROUND function with positive and negative values.

I Want It NOW!

The last function you learn about in this chapter is the date function NOW, which returns the current date and time to the worksheet. Because this function gets its date and time information directly from your computer's clock/calendar, the NOW function doesn't require any arguments; you simply enter (or paste) the following in a cell when you want to stamp the worksheet with the current date and time:

```
=NOW()
```

When you first enter the NOW function, Excel returns both the date and time and selects a date/time format that displays them both. If today were November 9, 1995, and you entered the NOW function in a cell exactly at 3:45 PM, the following entry would appear in the worksheet:

```
11/9/95 15:45
```

You can modify what the NOW function displays in the cell by selecting a new date or time format. If you aren't concerned with the time and only want to see the date, open the Format Cells dialog box (⌘+1), choose the Number tab, and then choose a format code in the Date format category. On the other hand, if you don't care about the date and only want to see the time, choose one of the format codes available for the Time format category.

When using the NOW function, keep in mind that Excel enters the date and time in a dynamic fashion. Each time the program recalculates the worksheet, it updates the date and time. To test this out, enter the NOW function in a blank cell of a worksheet, wait a minute, and then press F9 or ⌘+= (the Calculate Now key). Or open the Options dialog box, choose the Calculation tab, and then click on the Calc Now button or the Calc Sheet button. When Excel recalculates the worksheet, the program updates the time in the cell with the NOW function, adding a minute to it.

This automatic updating is useful when you have formulas you need to keep up-to-date (or up-to-the-minute, as the case may be). For example, you can use the NOW function to calculate the age of various equipment purchases by subtracting the date of purchase from the current date supplied by the NOW function. This calculation gives you the number of days. Then divide by 365.25 to convert this figure into years. Every time you open the worksheet with these formulas, Excel updates them, advancing the ages by the number of days that elapsed between now and the last time you worked with the document.

But what if you don't want the date or time to change? What if your purpose is to record a sale or a purchase in a worksheet that you made today? In such a case, you freeze the date/time entry made with the NOW function so that it is never again subject to being updated. To freeze an entry or formula on the Mac, press ⌘+U to activate edit mode (in the cell or formula bar) and then press ⌘+= (or F9 if you have the extended keyboard) to calculate the formula. Then press Return.

Chapter 13

Functions for the More Adventurous

In This Chapter

- How to use financial functions such as PV and PMT
- How to use text functions such as PROPER
- How to use lookup and reference functions such as VLOOKUP
- How to use logical functions such as IF

Beyond the pale of run-of-the-mill functions like SUM, AVERAGE, and NOW lies a whole world of specialized Excel functions. This chapter exposes you to a few of these functions in the financial, text, lookup and reference, and logical categories. Although some of these worksheet functions are full of arguments that, at first glance, may look like so much gobbledygook, you don't have to be a spreadsheet guru to comprehend and use them. Believe me, you are ready for them, even if you have limited experience with formulas and functions.

When learning a more complex function, concentrate mostly on what arguments the function uses and their order of appearance in the function. Then look at which arguments are required and which are optional. By mastering the few functions covered in this chapter and learning how their calculations can help you create more effective worksheets, you will be in great shape to learn on your own any other functions you may need.

High Finance (or, "I Want My PMT")

As you would expect from any good spreadsheet program, Excel offers many sophisticated financial functions. This section takes a look at just two of the most common financial functions: PV (Present Value) and PMT (Payment).

You use the PV function to calculate the current worth of a series of future payments (the very definition of the term *present value*). You can use this function to determine whether the return on a particular investment is a sound one, considering the initial cost to you. The PV function follows this pattern:

```
PV(rate,nper,pmt,fv,type)
```

Notice that the arguments ***rate*** (the interest rate per period), ***nper*** (the total number of payment periods), and ***pmt*** (the payment made each period) are all required. (Any required argument to a command is formatted in ***bold italic*** type.)

The arguments *fv* (future value or cash balance you want to realize after the last payment) and *type* (0 if the payment is made at the end of the period, 1 if made at the beginning) are optional. These optional arguments are formatted in plain *italic* type. If you omit the *fv* argument, Excel assumes that the future value is 0 (as would be the case when paying off a loan). If you omit the *type* argument, Excel assumes that you make the payment at the end of each period.

When using other financial functions similar to PV (such as PMT, FV, and the like), first make sure that you're dealing with a true *annuity,* which in English just means an investment where all the payments are the same and made at regular intervals (monthly, quarterly, or yearly—you get the picture). The best example of an annuity is a fixed-rate mortgage where you pay a set amount each month for a continuous fixed period. An adjustable-rate mortgage, however, where the interest rate is adjusted annually or semiannually, is not a true annuity.

The most common mistake when working with annuity functions is not expressing the ***rate*** argument in the same time units as the ***nper*** argument. Most interest rates are quoted as annual rates, but payment periods are monthly. When this is the case, divide the annual interest rate by 12 to get a monthly interest rate to go with the monthly payments. Likewise, if you make payments on a monthly basis, but the payment period is in years (as in 30 for a standard 30-year mortgage), convert this payment-period value into equivalent monthly periods by multiplying the value by 12.

With annuities, keep in mind that the money you pay out is always expressed as a negative number (hey, it comes out of your account); money you earn (for example, a dividend you put in your account) is expressed as a positive number. For example, if you make an initial investment of $5,000 for a term-life insurance policy, it shows up as -5000 on your worksheet but as 5000 on the insurance company's worksheet.

Figure 13-1 shows an example of the PV function used to determine the advisability of an annuity by comparing its present value against the initial cash outlay. Here you evaluate the present value of an annuity that pays $150.00 at the end of each month for the next 10 years at an annual interest rate of 7 percent. Assume an initial investment of $10,000. The PV function calculates the present value for this annuity at $12,918.95. Because you're only required to invest $10,000, it's not such a bad deal at all.

For the sake of argument

If you were paying attention in Chapter 12, you know this already. If not, here's a refresher on functions and arguments.

Functions perform specific predefined calculations based on the type of information (called *arguments*) you supply. To use an Excel function, all you have to know are the arguments the function takes. When you put together the function itself and the arguments it takes, you have what is called the *syntax* of the function.

Remember the SUM function? Here's the syntax:

SUM(***number1***,*number2*,...)

The arguments (the text between the parentheses) of the function are considered *variables*, and they are shown in italic type. In computer lingo, a *variable* is something you replace with your own thing. So in place of the ***number1*** argument, you can put in cell references like **B5**, values like **100**, or even a calculation like **100*B5**.

When an argument is shown in ***bold italics***, this means that you *must* use something for that argument or the function won't work at all. All the arguments in regular *italics* are optional ones that you can use when you need them, but they are not required to get the function to work.

The three periods (a.k.a. ellipsis) after the *number2* argument just mean that you can add more number-type arguments to the SUM function (up to 30 total).

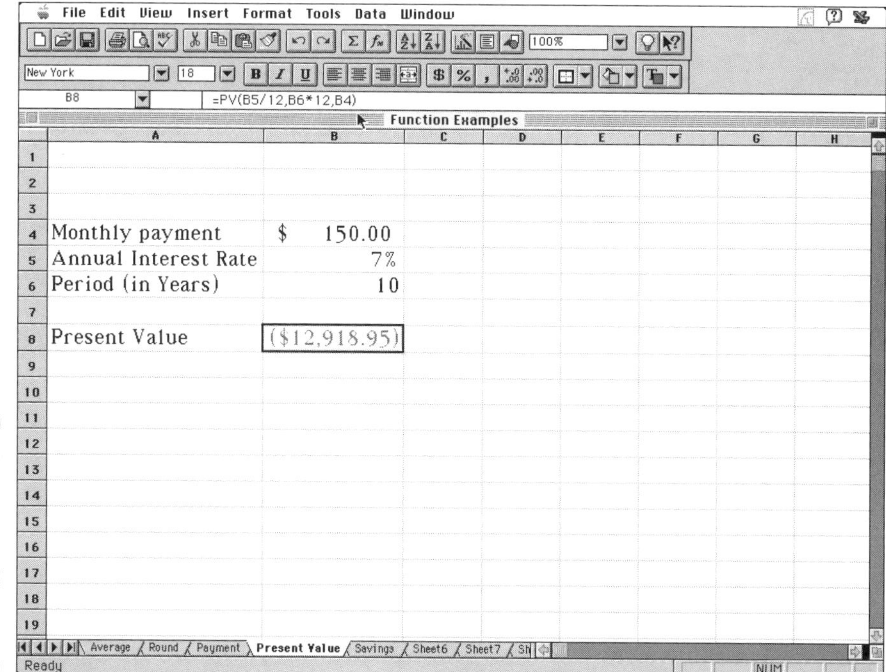

Figure 13-1: Using the PV function to determine the present value of an annuity.

The PMT function is another commonly used annuity function. It uses almost the same arguments as the PV function except that instead of a ***pmt*** argument (which is what the function finds), it requires a ***pv*** (present value) argument, as follows:

```
PMT(rate,nper,pv,fv,type)
```

The PMT function is most often used to calculate loan payments. To do so, you enter the interest rate as the ***rate*** argument, the period as the ***nper,*** and the amount of the loan as the ***pv*** argument. Again make sure that the ***rate*** and ***nper*** arguments are expressed in the same time units (monthly interest rate and a number of monthly payments if you want to calculate the amount of a monthly payment).

Figure 13-2 shows an example of the PMT function used to calculate a monthly mortgage payment. Here the amount of the loan is $150,000, the annual interest is 8.75%, and the period is a standard 30 years. To calculate a monthly mortgage payment, you must divide the annual interest in cell B5 by 12 and multiply the period in years in cell B6 by 12.

You also can use the PMT function to determine how much you need to save to realize a certain return. Suppose that you just had a baby and you want to start a college savings account for her. To find out how much to put away each month, assuming a tuition for a four-year state school of $80,000 (this may not

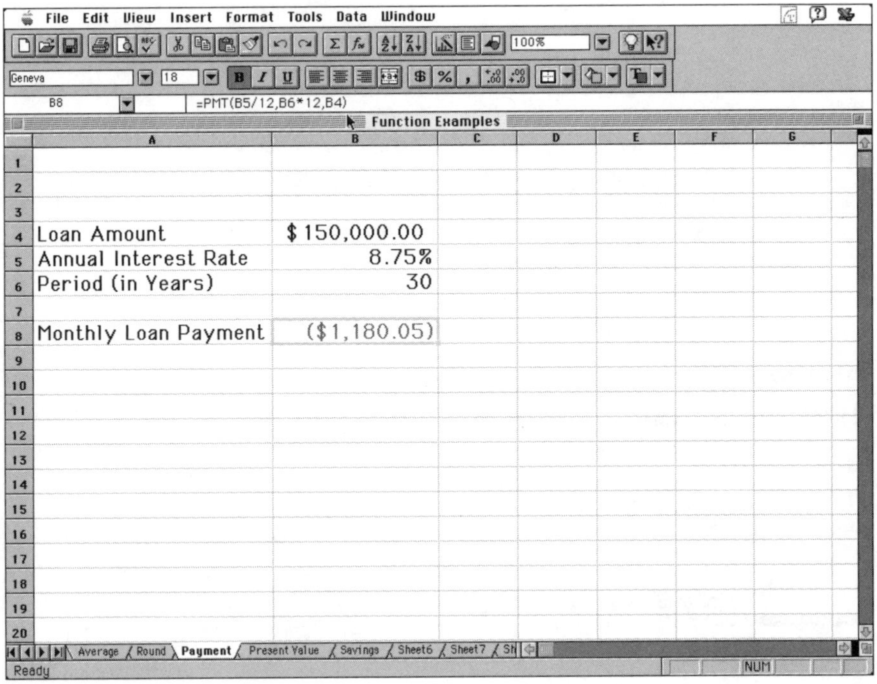

Figure 13-2: Using the PMT function to calculate the monthly loan payment.

be enough in 2010 dollars!) and assuming that you have 18 years to save, you can use the PMT function as shown in Figure 13-3. If the bank pays you 5 percent interest on your savings account (which, as of this writing, may be a bit optimistic), you have to cough up a mere $229.09 a month. (Does she *really* have to go to a four-year school?)

In the example that uses the PMT function to determine how much to save to reach a target amount, you enter **0** as the required ***pv*** (present value) argument; the target amount ($80,000) is entered as the optional *fv* (future value) argument.

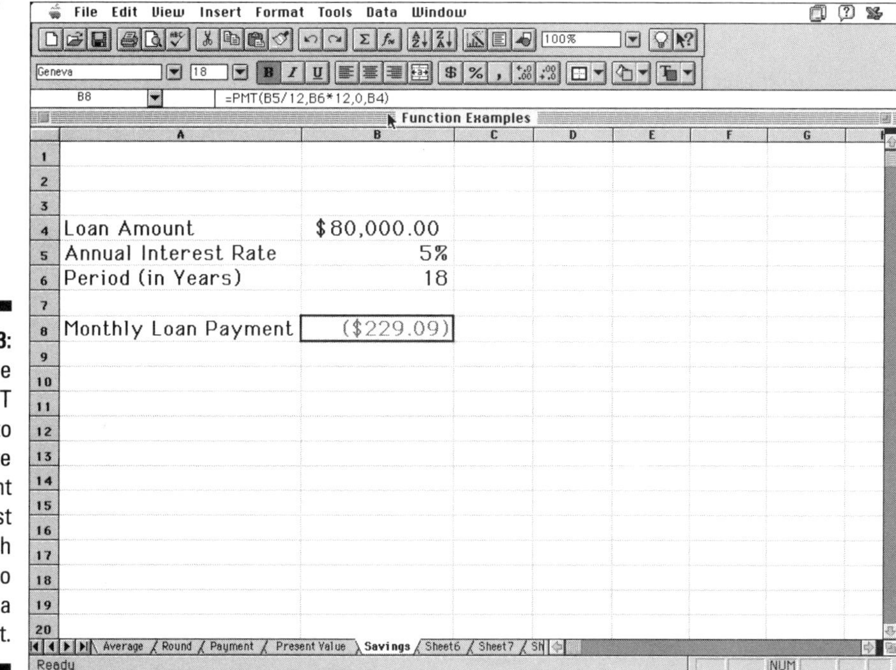

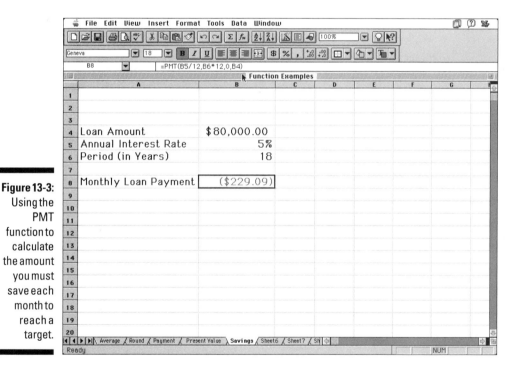

Figure 13-3: Using the PMT function to calculate the amount you must save each month to reach a target.

Just for the Text of It

It may come as a bit of a surprise to learn that you can construct formulas to perform various operations on text, because you associate calculations quite naturally with numbers. Well, believe it or not, Excel includes a wide variety of text functions that work exclusively with text arguments. Admittedly, you may not find too many uses for the text functions unless you routinely import information into worksheets from other sources — perhaps from on-line services, such as Dow Jones — where you don't have any control over how the information is formatted.

For example, you may find that the text you take into the worksheet is in all uppercase or all lowercase letters. (When you purchase lists on disk, it's not unusual to find the text in all uppercase letters). Instead of wasting time retyping the information with the proper capitalization (say, for mailing labels), you can use the PROPER function to convert the text for you.

Figure 13-4 shows how you can use the PROPER function to take a list of names entered in all uppercase letters and convert the list to proper capitalization. To convert the list, enter the following formula in cell B2:

```
=PROPER(A2)
```

Then use the AutoFill feature to copy this formula down to the cell range B3:B7. The PROPER function capitalizes all the entries correctly — with the exception of Jack'N'Jill Cafe, where the function mistakenly capitalizes the N between the two apostrophes. (The PROPER function uppercases the first letter of each word as well as any letter that does not follow another letter.) You must fix this by editing this particular entry either in its cell or on the formula bar.

If you want to do any more processing to the entries (such as sorting or spell-checking them), you must convert the formulas to their calculated values (in this case, that means converting them to text). If you don't convert the formulas

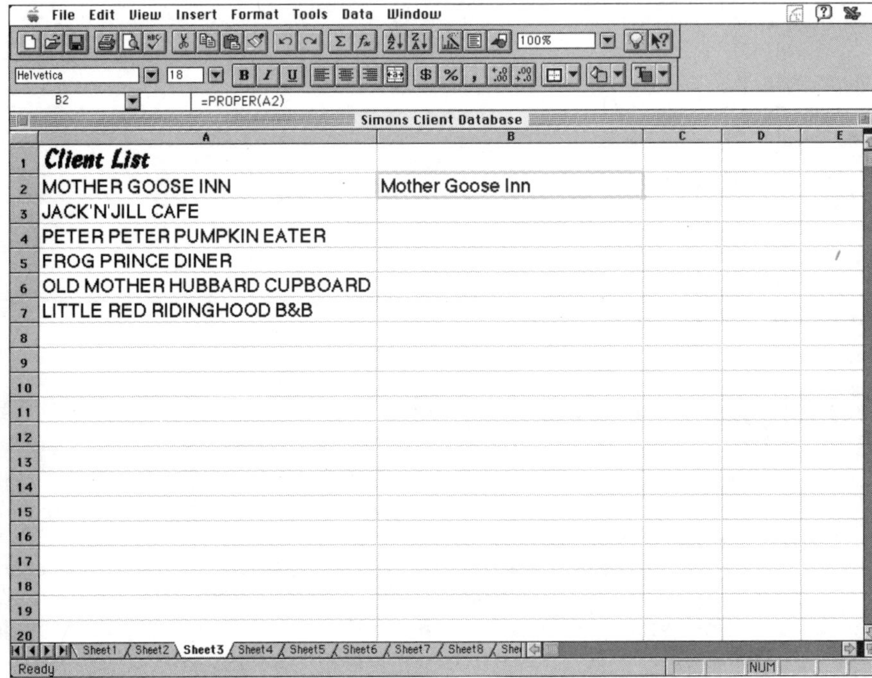

Figure 13-4: Using the PROPER function to change to proper capitalization.

to their text values, Excel sorts or spell-checks the formulas in the cells (*=PROPER(A2)* in cell B2 of the example) rather than the text (*Mother Goose Inn*).

To convert the formulas to their text values, first select the cell range containing the PROPER functions: B2:B7. Then choose the Copy command from the Edit menu. In this example, you can replace the original all-uppercase range with the properly capitalized text by pasting the values in range B2:B7 over the original entries in range A2:A7. (Remember that Excel always replaces existing entries with new ones.)

To replace the uppercase range with the properly capitalized range and convert the PROPER formulas to their text values, select the first cell, A2, in response to the prompt: `Select the destination and press RETURN or choose Paste`. Then choose the Paste Special command from the Edit menu and click on the Values radio button. Finally, choose OK or press Return (see Figure 13-5).

Figure 13-6 shows the results of pasting the values in the cell range A2:A7. Notice the contents of cell A2 on the formula bar: It reads *Mother Goose Inn* just as though you typed it rather than calculated it with an Excel function! After you copy the values to the range A2:A7, delete the formulas in B2:B7, edit the entry in cell A3, and save the worksheet.

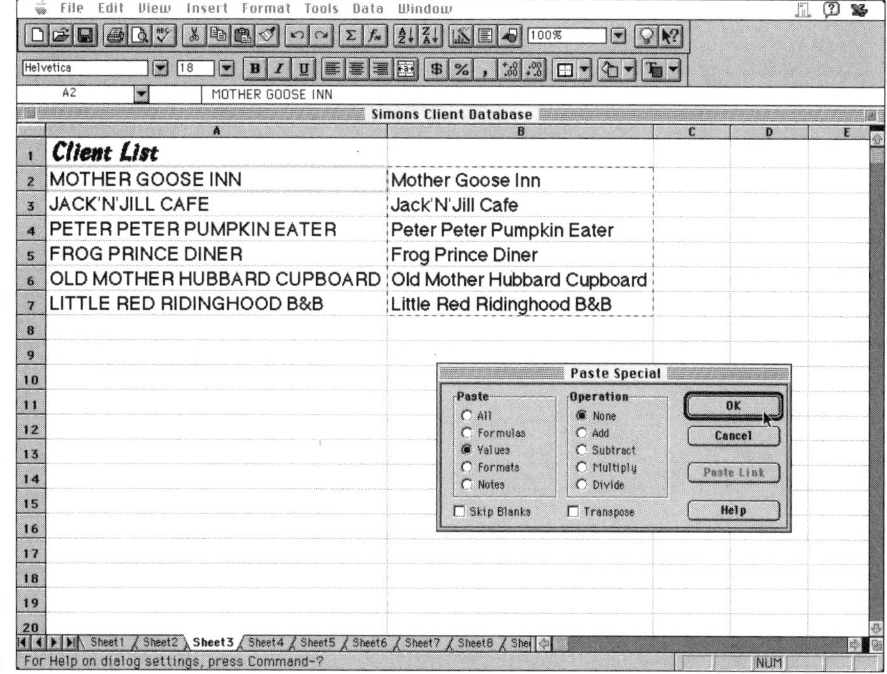

Figure 13-5: Using the Paste Special dialog box to convert to text the formulas with the PROPER function.

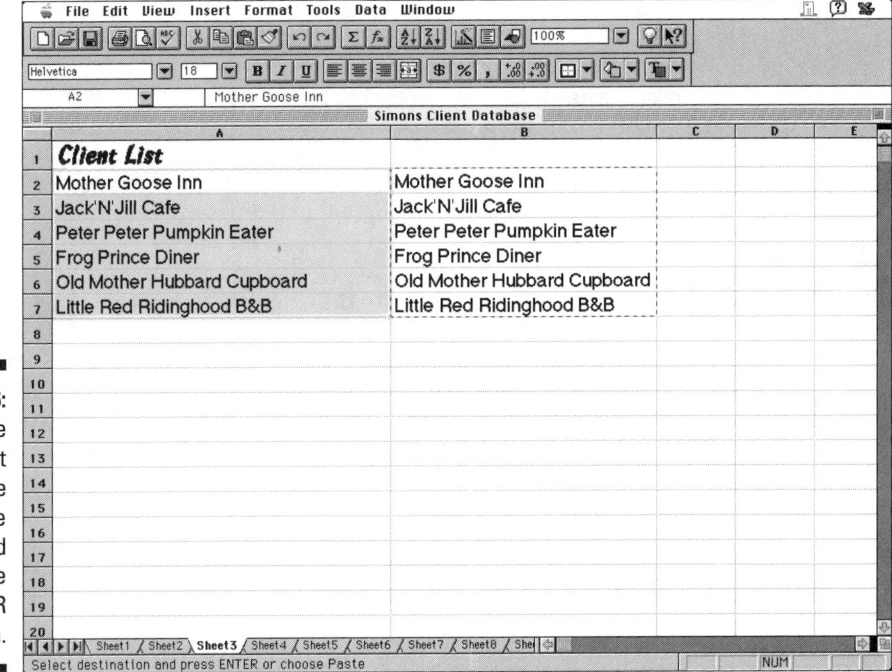

Figure 13-6: The worksheet after the formulas are converted with the PROPER function.

In addition to the PROPER function, Excel includes UPPER and LOWER functions:

- Use the UPPER function to convert the text in a cell to all uppercase letters.
- Use the LOWER function to convert the text to all lowercase letters.

Just as with the PROPER function, remember to convert UPPER or LOWER formulas to their resulting text if you want to perform further text-based operations, such as sorting on these cells.

Hey, Look Me Over!

The functions in the lookup and reference category offer a rather mixed bag of tricks. The reference-type functions return various kinds of information about your current whereabouts in a worksheet. (These functions are primarily used in complex macros that process worksheet data. The functions keep track of the current cell position during the processing.) The lookup-type functions can return particular information from a series or a table of data and, therefore, have more practical uses for the average spreadsheet user.

The most common lookup functions are VLOOKUP (for vertical lookup) and HLOOKUP (for horizontal lookup). Both these functions look up a particular value or text entry in a table and return related information from the table. They differ simply in the way they do their work:

- The VLOOKUP function moves vertically down the rows of the lookup table, looking for matching information in the first column of the table.
- The HLOOKUP function moves horizontally across the columns of the lookup table, looking for matching information in the top row of the table.

To get an idea of how handy these lookup functions can be, I'll tell you how you would go about using the VLOOKUP function to return specific information from a table in one worksheet to a form in another worksheet.

Figure 13-7 shows a workbook with two worksheets arranged in horizontal windows. The top window shows the Price worksheet that contains the price lookup table, and the bottom window contains the Invoice worksheet with an invoice form. The price lookup table in the Price worksheet relates the item numbers assigned to the various Simple Simon pies in the first column to their description, cost, and price in the columns to the right. This information is then fed to the invoice form in the Invoice worksheet with the help of some VLOOKUP functions.

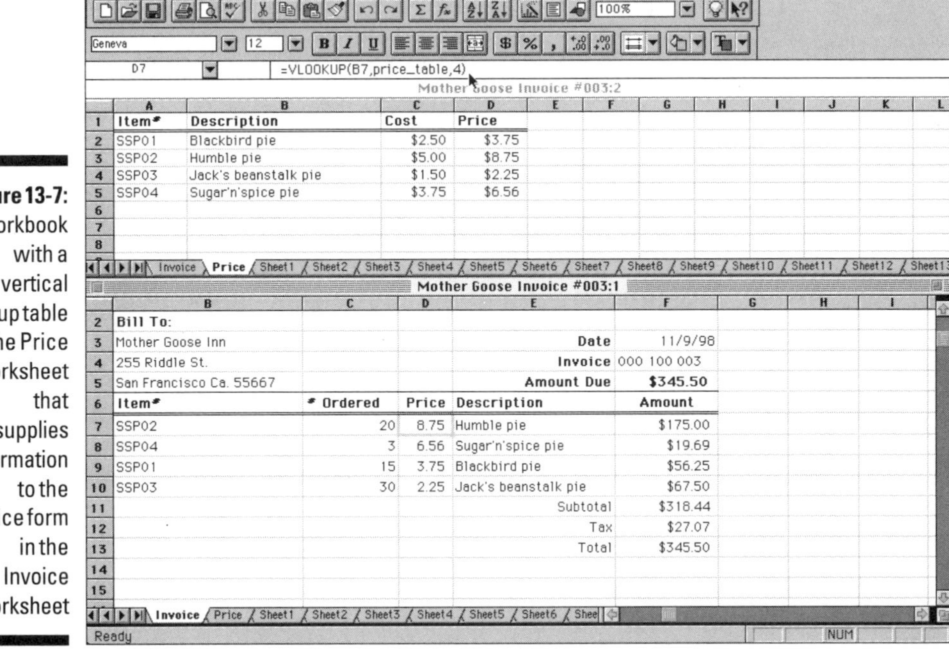

Figure 13-7: Workbook with a vertical lookup table in the Price worksheet that supplies information to the invoice form in the Invoice worksheet

When setting up a vertical lookup table like the one shown in the Price worksheet in Figure 13-7, you always place the information you will use to look up other information in the first (leftmost) column. In this case, because you want to look up the description and cost of an item by its item number, you make the column contain the item numbers in the first column.

Further, after entering all the information in a lookup table, you must sort its data in ascending order, using the first column of the table as the sorting key (see Chapter 8 for a complete rundown on sorting with keys). Notice how the lookup table in Figure 13-7 is sorted in ascending order by item number.

After you create and sort the information in a vertical lookup table, you can use the VLOOKUP function in the invoice form in the Invoice worksheet to return any of the information in the lookup table in the Price worksheet that you need.

The arguments for the VLOOKUP function are as follows:

```
VLOOKUP(lookup_value,table_array,col_index_num)
```

The ***lookup_value*** argument in this example is the cell in the form in the Invoice worksheet that contains the item number you want looked up in the lookup table in the Price worksheet in Figure 13-7.

The ***table_array*** argument is the cell range that contains the lookup table itself (excluding column headings). In this example, the lookup table occupies the cell range A2:D5 in the Price worksheet. To make things simpler, I gave the cell range A2:D5, range the name ***price_table***. That way, I could paste this range name into the ***table_array*** argument of the VLOOKUP function rather than having to select the actual cell references.

The ***col_index_num*** argument is the number of the column in the lookup table whose information you want returned by the VLOOKUP function. To derive this number, count the columns in the lookup table from left to right, starting with 1. For example, if you want the VLOOKUP function to return the description of the pie when you enter its item number, enter **2** as the ***col_index_num*** argument. To return the cost of the pie instead of its description, you need to enter **3** as the ***col_index_num*** argument. To return the price of the pie, you enter **4** as the ***col_index_num*** argument.

The bottom window with the Invoice worksheet in Figure 13-7 shows how you can use the VLOOKUP function to get both the description and the cost of a pie from the table in the Price worksheet by entering just its item-number code in the form of the Invoice worksheet.

Cell B7 contains the following formula:

```
=VLOOKUP(B7,price_table,4)
```

This formula takes the item-number code entered in cell B7 (item number SSP02 in the form in the Invoice worksheet shown in Figure 13-7), looks it up in the first column of the vertical lookup table named ***price_table*** (cell range A2:D5 in the Price worksheet) by moving vertically down the rows in the first column of the table. When Excel locates the item number in the lookup table, the VLOOKUP function returns the price entered in column 4 (a/k/a column D) of this table (8.75 for item number SSP02 in cell D3 of the Price worksheet) to cell D7 in the Invoice worksheet, the one containing the VLOOKUP function.

The description of the pie sold is returned to cell E7 in the Invoice worksheet from the lookup table on the Price worksheet with a similar formula that uses the following VLOOKUP function:

```
=VLOOKUP(B7,price_table,2)
```

The only difference between the formula in cell E7 and the one in cell D7 is that this second formula uses **2** as the ***col_index_num*** argument; therefore, this lookup formula returns the description (Humble pie for item number SSP02) instead of its price.

By copying the formulas entered in cells D7 and E7 down their columns, you can continue to use the lookup table to find the description and cost for whatever item-number code you enter in column B.

Is That Logical? (or, IF I Were a Rich Man)

The logical-functions category is a small group, consisting of just six functions in all. These functions are noted for their black-or-white result. A logical function can return only one of two possible results: TRUE or FALSE.

The most common and powerful of the logical functions is the IF function. This function is particularly powerful because it can test for a particular condition in the worksheet and use one value if the condition is true and another value if the condition is false.

To use the IF function, you use the following arguments:

```
IF(logical_test,value_if_true,value_if_false)
```

The ***logical_test*** argument can be any expression that, when evaluated, returns either a TRUE or FALSE response. For example, you can test whether a value in one cell is greater than or equal to a particular value by entering this formula:

```
=IF(B2>=1000)
```

In this example, the IF condition is TRUE when B2 contains a value of 1000 or larger; the condition is FALSE when the value in cell B2 is anything less than 1000.

To indicate what value should be used when the ***logical_test*** argument is TRUE, enter the *value_if_true* argument right after the ***logical_test*** argument. To indicate what value should be used when the ***logical_test*** argument is FALSE, enter the *value_if_false* argument right after the *value_if_true* argument.

For example, if you want Excel to put the value 100 in the cell when B2 contains a value greater than or equal to 1000, but you want 50 in the cell when B2 is less than 1000, enter the following formula:

```
=IF(B2>=1000,100,50)
```

If you want Excel to put 10% of the value in B2 in the cell when B2 contains a value greater than or equal to 1000, but only 5% of the value when B2 is less than 1000, enter the following formula:

```
=IF(B2>=1000,B2*10%,B2*5%)
```

Although you usually want an IF function to enter or calculate a particular value when the ***logical_test*** argument returns TRUE or FALSE, you also can have the IF function enter text. Do this by entering the different text alternatives as the *value_if_true* and *value_if_false* arguments of the IF function. Suppose that you want Excel to enter the text **A grand or better** when B2 contains a value greater than or equal to 1000, but the text **Less than a grand** when B2 contains any lesser value. To do this, enter the following formula:

```
=IF(B2>=1000,"A grand or better","Less than a grand")
```

When you use text as the *value_if_true* or *value_if_false* argument, you must enclose the text in a pair of double quotation marks (“”).

Figure 13-8 shows a typical use for the IF function. Here the IF function calculates the price of a particular pie based on what it costs to bake it. If the pie costs more than 3 bucks, the markup is a reasonable 75%. If the item costs less than 3 bucks, the markup is a piddling 50%.

You enter the IF function that determines which markup percentage to use in calculating the price in cell D2 as follows:

```
=IF(C2>3,C2*1.75,C2*1.5)
```

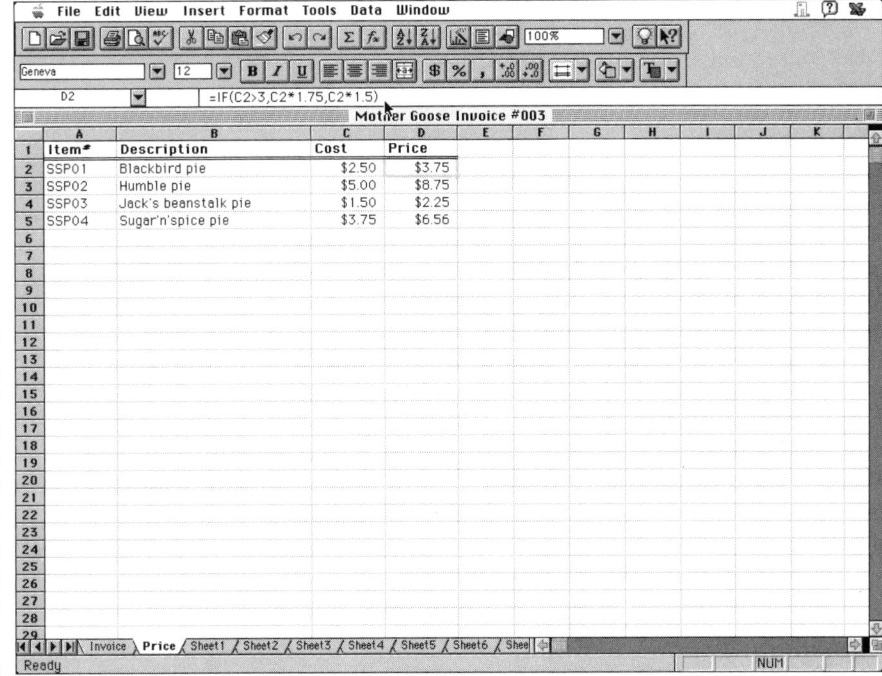

Figure 13-8: Using the IF function to determine the price of each pie based on what it costs to bake it.

In this formula, the ***logical_test*** argument, C2>3, tests whether the cost entered in cell C2 is greater than $3.00.

- If the value is greater than $3.00, Excel uses the *value_if_true* argument, C2*1.75 (it's 1.75 because the resulting price is the total cost plus a markup of 75% of that cost) and returns the calculated value to cell D2.
- If the value is less than $3.00, Excel uses the *value_if_false* argument, C2*1.50 (total cost plus a markup of 50% of that cost) and returns the calculated value to cell D2.

In this particular example, the IF function calculates the price in cell D2 according to the *value_if_false* argument because the cost in cell C2 is $2.50 (50 cents less than our $3.00 cutoff).

After creating the IF formula in cell D2, you can copy it down column D to calculate the prices for the other pies in the Price worksheet based solely on the cost. Figure 13-8 shows the worksheet after copying the original formula entered in cell D2 down to cell D5.

Part VII
The Part of Tens

"COMPATABILITY? NO PROBLEM. THIS BABY COMES IN OVER A DOZEN DESIGNER COLORS."

The part in which . . .

You learn the ten basics every beginner needs, the ten Excel commandments, ten printing pointers, ten clever ways to customize Excel, ten welcome warnings to save you heartache, ten tips for working smarter — not harder — in Excel, ten amazing tricks in Excel 5 and Word 6, and, as a special bonus, the final chapter includes 10,000 (more or less) keystroke shortcuts that are guaranteed to save you time or drive you crazy — perhaps both!

Chapter 14

Ten Beginner Basics

If these ten items are all you really master in Excel, you'll *still* be way ahead of the competition. When all is said and done, this list of ten lays out all the fundamental skills required to successfully use Excel — with the exception of printing, which is so important that it rates its own chapter (Chapter 16). Here they are:

- To start Excel from the Macintosh Finder, double-click on the Microsoft Excel program icon in the Microsoft Excel folder.
- To open a workbook at the same time you start Excel, locate the workbook document in your Excel workbook folder (remember when I advised you to save your workbook files in their own folder?) and double-click on the file. To open a workbook from within Excel, choose the Open tool on the Standard toolbar or choose File ⇨ Open or press ⌘+O.
- To locate a part of a worksheet that you cannot see on-screen, use the frame that labels the columns and rows. Columns are assigned letters of the alphabet from A through IV; rows are assigned numbers from 1 through 16,384. Use the scroll bars at the right and bottom of the workbook window to bring new parts of the worksheet into view.
- To start a new workbook (containing 16 blank worksheets), choose the New Workbook tool on the Standard toolbar or choose File ⇨ New or press ⌘+N. To insert a new worksheet in a workbook, if you should need more than 16, choose Insert ⇨ Worksheet or press Shift+F11.
- To activate an open workbook and display it on-screen in front of any others that you have open, open the Window pull-down menu and select the workbook's name. To locate a particular worksheet in the active workbook, click on its sheet tab at the bottom of the workbook document window. To display more sheet tabs, click on the sheet-scrolling arrows on the left side of the bottom of the workbook window.
- To enter stuff in a worksheet, select the cell where the information should appear and then begin typing. After you're finished, click on the Return box on the formula bar or press Tab, Return, or one of the arrow keys.
- To edit the stuff you've already entered into a cell, double-click on the cell or put the cell pointer in the cell and press ⌘+U. Excel then locates the insertion point at the end of the cell entry. After you've finished correcting the entry, click on the Return box on the formula bar or press Tab or Return.

- To choose one of the many commands on the pull-down menus, click on the menu name on the menu bar to open the menu and drag down while pressing the mouse button to highlight the command name on the pull-down menu. To choose a command on a shortcut menu, while pressing the Control key, click on the object (cell, sheet tab, toolbar, chart, and so on) and hold down the mouse button to open the menu. Then drag down to select the command.
- To save a copy of your workbook on disk the first time out, choose File ⇨ Save As. Designate the drive (or Desktop) and folder where the file should be located and replace the temporary Workbook1 filename with your own up-to-32-character filename. To save changes to the workbook thereafter, click on the Save tool on the Standard toolbar or choose File ⇨ Save or press ⌘+S.
- To quit Excel, choose File ⇨ Quit or press ⌘+Q. If the workbook you have open contains unsaved changes, Excel asks whether you want to save the workbook document before closing and returning to the Finder or another open program (System 7 or later).

Chapter 15

Ten Excel Commandments

In working with Excel, you will find certain *dos* and *don'ts* that, if followed religiously, can make using this program just *heavenly*. Lo and behold! The following ten Excel commandments contain just such precepts for eternal Excel bliss:

- Thou shalt commit thy work to disk by saving thy changes often (File ➪ Save or ⌘+S). If thou findest that thou tendest to be lax in the saving of thy work, then shalt thou engage thy AutoSave add-in (Tools ➪ Add-Ins ➪ AutoSave) and have thy program automatically save thy work for thee at a set time interval.
- Thou shalt name thy workbooks when saving them for the first time with filenames of no more than 32 characters (Windows users are stuck with 8 characters and no spaces). So too shalt thou mark well which folder thou savest thy file in, lest thou thinkest in error that thy workbook be lost when next thou hast need of it. If, however, thou be of the blessed Macintosh tribe, the filenames of thy Excel workbooks shall suffer under no such limitations and can be set down so that they are fathomable by all (unlike this phony King James dialect).
- Thou shalt not spread wide the data in thy worksheet, but rather shalt thou gather together thy tables and avoid skipping columns and rows unless this be necessary to make thy data intelligible. All this shalt thou do in order that thou mayest conserve the memory of thy computer.
- Thou shalt begin all thy Excel formulas with the = sign as the Sign of Computation. If, however, thou be formerly of the Lotus 1-2-3 tribe, thou shalt have special dispensation and may commence thy formulas with the + sign and thy functions with an @ sign.
- Thou shalt select thy cells before thou bringest to bear upon them any Excel command, just as surely as thou dost sow before thou reapest.
- Thou shalt straightaway use the Undo feature (Edit ➪ Undo or ⌘+Z) immediately upon committing any transgression in thy worksheet so that thou mayest clean up thy mess. In no wise shalt thou choose another command in Excel before thou hast called upon Undo to restore thy worksheet to its former state.

- Thou shalt not delete — neither shalt thou insert — columns and rows in a worksheet lest thou hast first verified that no part as yet uncovered of thy worksheet will thereby be wiped out or otherwise displaced.
- Thou shalt not print thy worksheet lest thou hast first previewed the printing (File ➪ Print Preview) and art satisfied that all thy pages are righteous in the sight of the printer.
- Thou shalt change the manner of the recalculation of thy workbooks from automatic to manual (Tools ➪ Options ➪ Calculation tab ➪ Manual) when thy workbook groweth so great in size that Excel sloweth down even unto a camel crawl whenever thou dost do anything in any one of its worksheets. Woe unto thee, however, shouldst thou also remove the X from the Recalculate before Save check box when thou settest up manual calculation or shouldst thou ignore the Calculate message on the status bar and not press the Calculate Now key (⌘+=) before such time as thou mayest print any of thy workbook data.
- Thou shalt protect thy completed workbooks and all their worksheets from corruption and inequities at the hands of others (Tools ➪ Protection ➪ Protect Sheet or Protect Workbook). And if thou be brazen enough to add a password to thy workbook protection, beware lest thou forget thy password in any part. Verily, I say unto thee, on the day that thou knowest not thy password, that day shalt be the last upon which thou canst look upon thy workbook in any wise.

Chapter 16

Ten Printing Pointers

Being able to print out the work just the way you want it in Excel is so important that I decided to give the subject its own list of ten:

- Preview the coming attractions at a printer near you (File ➪ Print Preview): Take a good look at what you've created with the Zoom feature, check the header and footer, change margins and column widths, take care of certain setup items, and print the thing from the Print Preview window. Do your editing, however, back in the document window.
- When the big moment finally arrives for you to send your sheet to the printer for real, click on the Print tool on the Standard toolbar to print everything not hidden in the current worksheet.
- To print everything in every worksheet in the whole workbook — in other words, the whole shebang — open the Print dialog box (File ➪ Print or ⌘+P) and select the Entire Workbook radio button before you choose OK.
- To print only the cells that you have selected in the current worksheet, make your cell selections, open the Print dialog box (File ➪ Print or ⌘+P), and select the Selection radio button before you choose OK.
- When you're printing a worksheet that extends many columns over — in other words, a worksheet that is every bit as wide as or wider than it is tall — change the orientation of the printer from the normal *portrait* setting to the *landscape* setting (File ➪ Page Setup ➪ Page tab ➪ Landscape).
- To squeeze all the data you're printing in a particular worksheet onto a single printed page, open the Page Setup dialog box (File ➪ Page Setup), choose the Page tab, and then select the Fit To radio button under Scaling. Excel reduces the printing size as required to get everything on one page, although Excel doesn't guarantee that anyone will be able to read the page without a magnifying glass.
- Use headers and footers in multipage reports to print running heads in the top or bottom margin of each page, which can contain information such as page number, date and time of printing, and document name (File ➪ Page Setup ➪ Header/Footer tab).
- Designate headings in rows and columns of the worksheet as print titles to appear at the top or left edge of each page in multipage reports (File ➪ Page Setup ➪ Sheet tab ➪ Rows to Repeat at Top or Columns to Repeat at Left).

- Normally, Excel prints gridlines in light gray that show the column and row boundaries. Remember to remove these gridlines before printing any report that uses borders around cell ranges or other graphics elements with which the gridlines may conflict (File ⇨ Page Setup ⇨ Sheet tab ⇨ Gridlines).
- To keep Excel from splitting up information that should always appear together on the same page, position the cell pointer in the place where the page should break and insert a manual page break (Insert ⇨ Page Break).

Chapter 17

Ten Clever Customizers

In keeping with that old adage "Man does not compute by data alone," this chapter provides ten ways that you can spice up your Excel worksheets with charts, graphics, and custom toolbars. The chapter also reminds you of some of the common ways to customize the old Excel screen:

- To chart a table of data, select the cells in the range (including the first column of row headings and the top row of column headings), click on the ChartWizard tool, wave your ChartWizard wand over the area in the worksheet where the chart should appear, and follow the yellow brick road through the five steps. You soon will have the chart of your choosing.
- When you select a chart in a worksheet, you have instant access to tools on the Chart toolbar. You can use the tools on the Chart toolbar to change the chart type at any point and to add or remove gridlines or a legend.
- After you double-click on a chart, you can edit its objects to your heart's content. You can add or edit the chart titles, format the values on the x- or y-axis, move the legend, or — in the case of a 3-D chart — rotate and manipulate the perspective from which you view the chart.
- Call up the Drawing toolbar and use its tools to add more graphics to your charts and worksheets, including text boxes with arrows that contain all sorts of witty comments.
- You can customize any of Excel's built-in toolbars by removing tools, adding new tools, or rearranging the buttons. To customize a toolbar, display the toolbar and then choose Customize on its toolbar shortcut menu.
- To create a new toolbar, open the Toolbars dialog box (View ⇨ Toolbars), enter the name for the new toolbar in the Toolbar Name text box, and click on the New button. Drag the tools that you want to appear on your new toolbar from the Customize dialog box to the appropriate position on the new toolbar and then choose OK to close the Customize dialog box.
- To assign a macro to a tool, open the Customize dialog box (View ⇨ Toolbars ⇨ Customize) and then choose Custom from the Categories list box. Drag the Custom button to the toolbar to which you want to hitch the macro. Finally, double-click on the name of the macro in the Assign Macro dialog box.

- Remember that you can draw your own picture and put it on a button by using the Button Editor. To customize your own button, you must open the Customize dialog box by selecting View ➪ Toolbars ➪ Customize and then the toolbar button you want to edit. Then choose the Edit Button Image on the toolbar's shortcut menu.
- Keep in mind that the View tab in the Options dialog box (choose Tools ➪ Options) gives you ultimate control over what elements show up in the Excel program window and each worksheet in your workbook. For example, you can use the Show options to remove the formula bar and the status bar from the Excel program window, or you can use the Window options to remove the automatic page breaks or gridlines from the current worksheet.
- To customize the colors in a document's color palette for use on a cell, cell text, cell border, or a particular graphics object, select the color you want to customize and choose the Modify button in the Color tab of the Options dialog box (Tools ➪ Options ➪ Color tab ➪ Modify). Then you can create your custom color with the Color Wheel.

Chapter 18

Ten Welcome Warnings

The following "welcome warnings" point out the most common pitfalls that lie in wait for beginning Excel users. Avoid these pitfalls like the plague — I pro-mise, you'll be much happier using Excel:

- *If you introduce a space into an otherwise completely numeric entry, Excel categorizes the entry as text, indicated by its alignment at the left edge of the cell.* If you feed that entry into a formula, the text classification completely throws off the answer because a text entry is treated as a 0 (zero) in a formula.
- *When nesting parentheses in a formula, pair them properly so that you have a right parenthesis for every left parenthesis in the formula.* If you do not include a right parenthesis for every left one, Excel displays an alert dialog box with the message `Parentheses do not match` when you try to enter the formula. After you close this dialog box, Excel goes right back to the formula bar, where you can insert the missing parenthesis and press Return to correct the unbalanced condition. By the way, Excel always highlights matched parentheses.
- *You can reenter edited cell contents by clicking on the Return box on the formula bar or by pressing Tab or Return, but you can't use the arrow keys.* While you are editing a cell entry, the arrow keys move only the insertion point through the entry.
- *Be sure that you don't press one of the arrow keys to complete a cell entry within a preselected cell range.* Instead, you should click on the Return box or press Return. Pressing an arrow key deselects the range of cells when Excel moves the cell pointer.
- *The Undo command on the Edit menu changes in response to whatever action you have just taken.* Because the Undo command keeps changing after each action, you have to remember to strike while the iron is hot: Use the Undo feature to restore the worksheet to its previous state before you choose another command.
- *Deleting entire columns and rows from a worksheet is risky business unless you are sure that the columns and rows in question contain nothing of value.* Remember: When you delete an entire row from the worksheet, you delete all information from column A through column IV in that row, even though you can see only a very few columns in the row. Likewise, when you delete

an entire column from the worksheet, you delete all information from row 1 through row 16,384 in that column.

- *Be careful with global search-and-replace operations.* They really can mess up a worksheet in a hurry if you inadvertently replace values, parts of formulas, or characters in titles and headings that you hadn't intended to change. As a precaution, never undertake a global search-and-replace operation on an unsaved worksheet. Also, verify that the Find Entire Cells Only check box is selected before you begin. You can end up with a great many unwanted replacements if you leave this check box unselected when you really only want to replace entire cell entries (rather than matching parts in cell entries). If you *do* make a mess, choose the Undo Replace command on the Edit menu (⌘+Z) to restore the worksheet. If you don't discover the problem in time to use Undo, close the messed-up worksheet without saving the changes and open the unreplaced version you saved.
- *Be very careful with passwords.* To make it impossible to remove protection from one worksheet or an entire workbook unless you know the password, enter a password in the Password (Optional) text box of the Protect Sheet or Protect Workbook dialog box (Tools ⇨ Protection ⇨ Protect Sheet or Protect Workbook). Excel masks with an asterisk each character you type in this text box. After you choose OK, Excel makes you reenter the password before protecting the worksheet or workbook. From then on, you can remove protection from the sheet or workbook only if you can reproduce the password *exactly* as you assigned it — including case. If you forget the password, you cannot change any locked cells and you cannot unlock any more cells in the worksheet (or in the case of a workbook, any of its worksheets)!
- *You cannot use the Undo feature to bring back a database record you removed with the Delete button in the data form!* Excel is definitely *not* kidding when it uses words like `deleted permanently`. As a precaution, always save a backup version of the worksheet with the database before you start removing old records.
- ***This is a bogus, Windows-only warning* that doesn't apply to Mac users.** *Remember that you can have no spaces in the filenames you assign to your Excel workbooks and that these filenames can have no more than eight characters.* Excel automatically adds the file extension XLS to the main filename you assign to your workbook document, indicating that the file contains Excel worksheets. When you edit a filename (rather than replace it), be careful to leave the XLS extension intact.

  Don't you feel sorry for DOS/Windows users, when we have 32-character filenames and we can even use spaces in them? However, you should learn to abbreviate filenames so that you don't waste too much time reading long filenames, which some programs and the Finder may abbreviate in various text boxes.

Chapter 19

Ten Ways to Work Smarter, Faster, and Get That Promotion!

The little tips contained in this chapter are worth their weight in Power PC chips. Please keep them in mind as you work with Excel. After all, who wants computing to be any harder than it has to be?

- Watch the TipWizard tool on the Standard toolbar. When the lightbulb turns yellow, that means Excel has some tidbits of wisdom to dispense to you based on the things you were just doing in the workbook. Click on the TipWizard to display a box of tips above the formula bar, complete with scroll arrows enabling you to peruse the list at your leisure. When you've taken in as many tips as you can stand, click on the TipWizard tool a second time to make the box of tips disappear.
- Give a name to any cell range that you use often in a worksheet by choosing Insert ➪ Name ➪ Define. Then use that name to move to the range, select its cells, or print it. Remember that you can press the Go To key, ⌘+L, and then select the range name in the Go To dialog box. After you choose OK, Excel not only moves you to the first cell in that range but selects all its cells as well.
- Don't waste all day scrolling through a seemingly endless table of data. Instead, use ⌘+arrow key (or End, arrow key) to jump from one edge of the table to another or to jump from the edge of one table to the other.
- If you find yourself continually entering the same list of items over and over again in new worksheets that you create, make a custom list of items. That way, you can enter the entire list by typing just the first item in the series and then dragging out the rest of the series with the AutoFill handle. See "Designer Series" in Chapter 2 for a refresher course on how to create a custom series.
- Lose the graphics in a worksheet by replacing their display with placeholders when you find that Excel just can't keep up with your movements: Choose Tools ➪ Options ➪ View tab ➪ Show Placeholders. Screen response time is greatly improved by this trick. Just don't forget to put the graphics back before you print the worksheet, or you'll end up with shaded rectangles where the pictures ought to be!

- When editing and formatting, don't overlook the shortcut menus attached to the things that need fixing. Open shortcut menus by first holding down the Control key and then clicking the mouse button. Shortcut menus can save a lot of time that you would otherwise waste searching the menus on the menu bar to find the editing or formatting command you need. Also, don't forget how much time you can save by using the tools on the Standard and Formatting toolbars to get things done.
- Before making changes to an unfamiliar worksheet, use the Zoom control button on the Standard toolbar to zoom out to 50 percent or 25 percent so that you can get a good idea of how the information is laid out. When inserting or deleting cells in an unfamiliar worksheet, resist the temptation to insert or remove entire columns and rows, because you can damage unseen tables of data. Instead, just insert or cut out the cell ranges in the region you're working in — you know: Think globally, act locally.
- To maximize the number of worksheet cells displayed on-screen at one time without having to resort to changing the magnification with the Zoom feature, choose View ⇨ Full Screen. Full Screen makes the formula bar, the Standard and Formatting toolbars, and the status bar all go away, leaving only the pull-down menus, scroll bars, and the cells in the current worksheet — giving you a view of 25 full rows instead of the normal 18. When you're ready to return to the normal, rather cramped screen display, click on the tool in the floating Full toolbar (which automatically appears whenever you choose View ⇨ Full Screen). If this toolbar is hidden, choose View ⇨ Full Screen a second time.
- Give yourself a break and record a macro for doing those little tasks that you end up doing over and over and over again (Tools ⇨ Record Macro ⇨ Record New Macro). Using macros to get repetitive things done not only alleviates boredom but also frees you up to do truly important things, such as playing another game of Puzzle.
- Name each worksheet with some intelligible English name, such as Invoice or Price List, by double-clicking on the sheet tab and entering a new name in the Rename Sheet dialog box. This is much better than leaving the worksheets with their normally indistinguishable names, such as Sheet1 and Sheet2. By renaming the worksheets, you not only know which sheets have been used in your workbook but you also have a fair idea of what the worksheets contain and when you should select them.

Chapter 20

Ten Amazing Word 6 and Excel 5 Tricks

If you have Word 6.0 for Macintosh and Excel 5.0, count yourself among the fortunate few! Thanks to the bundling of these two products in Microsoft Office and Microsoft Office Pro, Microsoft has made great strides in the two programs' capabilities to communicate with each other. Key among them is something called *in-place activation,* which is a fancy way of saying that editing stuff you bring from Excel 5.0 (like worksheet data or charts) into Word 6.0 causes the Word toolbars and pull-down menus to change to the Excel 5.0 toolbars and pull-down menus that you've come to know and love. After you finish editing the Excel object and deselect it, the Word 6.0 toolbars and pull-down menus come right back, and you can go about your business creating the rest of the document.

- To go from Excel 5.0 to Word 6.0, display the Microsoft toolbar by clicking on Microsoft in the toolbar shortcut menu, which you open with the secondary mouse button. Click on the Microsoft Word tool (the first one with the W on it). If Word for Macintosh 6.0 is not running at the time, clicking on this button starts the program. If Word 6.0 is already fired up, clicking on this button displays Word 6.0 for Macintosh with the current document.
- To go from Word 6.0 to Excel 5.0, display the Microsoft toolbar by clicking on Microsoft in the toolbar shortcut menu, which you open with the secondary mouse button. Click on the Microsoft Excel tool (the first one with the XL on it, of course). If Excel 5.0 is not running at the time, clicking on this button starts the program. If Excel 5.0 is already running, clicking on this button displays Excel 5.0 with the current workbook.
- To switch back and forth between Word 6.0 and Excel 5.0 after you have them both open, you can either click on the appropriate button in the Microsoft toolbar or change programs from the Application menu pull-down menu.
- To display both the Word 6.0 program window and the Excel 5.0 program window on the same screen (assuming they're both full-size windows), you must manually resize and move the two program windows until you have the program windows arranged in such a way that you can see the data you want to compare or exchange on the screen (see the next trick).

- To put a table of Excel 5.0 data into a Word 6.0 document, switch to Excel 5.0, open the workbook containing the table of data, and then select its sheet tab. Next, select all the cells of the table in that worksheet. To copy the selected table to the Word document, you can use the Clipboard (⌘+C). Then switch to Word 6.0 (trick 3), position the insertion point at the beginning of the new line in the Word document where the Excel table of data is to be inserted, and press ⌘+V.

  If both the Word 6.0 and Excel 5.0 program windows are displayed on the same screen (see trick 4), you can use drag-and-drop to move or copy the selected table of worksheet data to the Word 6.0 document, as follows (note that the table is copied as a picture element):

  1. **Position the Word 6.0 program window above the Excel 5.0 program window, click on the Excel window, and then open the workbook and select the worksheet that contains the table of worksheet data to be moved or copied.**
  2. **Select the table (range) of worksheet cells you want to move or copy to Word and then, if necessary, scroll the worksheet up until you can position the mouse pointer on the bottom edge of the selection (the mouse pointer should assume the arrowhead shape).**
  3. **To copy the worksheet's cells to the Word document, press and hold down Ô as you drag the mouse pointer up to the Word document.**

     To move the worksheet cells out of the Excel worksheet and into the Word document, just drag the mouse pointer up to the Word document.
  4. **Position the I-beam pointer at the place in the document where the table of worksheet data is to appear and then release the mouse button.**

- To edit a table of Excel 5.0 worksheet data that's been imported into a Word 6.0 document, double-click somewhere on the table in the Word document. Double-clicking selects the entire table, indicated by the appearance of a heavy border with crosshatching containing selection handles along with the workbook frame (with the cell column letters and row numbers), sheet tabs, and horizontal and vertical scroll bars around the table. In addition, the pull-down menus and Standard and Formatting toolbars change from those used by Word 6.0 to those used by Excel 5.0.

  Make your changes to the worksheet cells, using the Excel commands on its toolbars, pull-down menus, and shortcut menus. You also can edit the contents of cells just as you do in Excel. After you are finished making changes to the Excel data, click outside the table somewhere else in the Word document to deselect the table of worksheet data.

- To create a brand new Excel 5.0 worksheet in a Word 6.0 document, switch to Word 6.0 and then click on the Insert Microsoft Excel Worksheet button on the Word 6.0 Standard toolbar (the tool with the tiny table and the XL on it, to the immediate left of the Columns button). Drag downward and to the right to select the number of columns and rows you want in the Excel table in the pop-up menu that appears.

  When you release the mouse button, Excel draws a new worksheet table, complete with a frame showing column letters, row numbers, Excel toolbars, and pull-down menus. You can create your new worksheet in this table just as you would in Excel 5.0 itself. After you've finished creating the new worksheet table, click outside it somewhere else in the Word document to deselect the table of worksheet data.

- To copy an Excel 5.0 chart into a Word 6.0 document, create the chart in its own window by selecting the range of worksheet data to be charted, pressing F11, and then selecting the entire chart. After the chart is selected — you should see a *marquee* of ants marching around it — press ⌘+C to copy the chart to the Clipboard. Then switch to Word 6.0 (see trick 3), position the I-beam pointer at the beginning of the line in the document where the chart is to be inserted, and press ⌘+V.

  If the imported chart is too large for the current margin settings in the document, which is often the case, simply edit the chart (see the next trick). During editing, Word for the Macintosh automatically resizes the chart to fit within the current document margin settings. When you click outside the chart to deselect it (you don't have to make any changes to the imported chart unless you see something that needs revising), the chart remains within the current margin settings.

- To edit an Excel chart that's been imported into a Word 6.0 document, double-click somewhere on the chart. Not only does Word select the chart and change the pull-down menus to the Excel 5.0 variety, but the Chart toolbar appears in the Word 6.0 document. You then can use that toolbar or the Excel pull-down or shortcut menus to make your changes to the chart. After you've finished editing, click outside the chart in the Word 6.0 document to deselect the chart and bring back the Word 6.0 toolbars and pull-down menus.

- Word 6.0 contains a bunch of great graphics images that you may want to use in an Excel worksheet. To bring a Word 6.0 graphics image into an Excel 5.0 workbook, switch to Word 6.0 (trick 3) and open the graphic image in a new Word document (Insert ➪ Picture) that you want to use in your Excel worksheet. With the graphic still selected in Word, press ⌘+X to cut from Word and copy it to the Clipboard. Then switch to Excel 5.0, open the workbook, select the worksheet and cell where you want the Word graphic to appear, and then press ⌘+V. After pasting the Word graphic image in your Excel worksheet, you can move and resize it if you want. Click on a cell outside the graphic image to deselect it.

Chapter 21

Ten Thousand (More or Less) Useful Keystroke Shortcuts

When You Need Help	
Press	***To***
⌘+/	Open the Excel Help window
⌘+Shift+?	Get context-sensitive Excel Help

When You Want to Move through the Worksheet	
Press	***To***
Arrow keys	Move up, down, left, right one cell
Home	Move to the beginning of the row
Page Up	Move up one screenful
Page Down	Move down one screenful
⌘+Home	Move to the first cell in the worksheet (A1)
⌘+End	Move to the last active cell of the worksheet
⌘+Arrow key	Move to the edge of a data block

When You Need to Select Cells in the Worksheet	
Press	***To***
Shift+Spacebar	Select the entire row
⌘+Spacebar	Select the entire column
⌘+A or ⌘+Shift+Spacebar	Select the entire worksheet
Shift+Home	Extend the selection to the beginning of the current row

When You Want to Move around a Cell Selection	
Press	***To***
Return	Move the cell pointer down one cell in the selection when there's more than one row, or move one cell to the right when the selection has only one row
Shift+Return	Move the cell pointer up one cell in the selection when there's more than one row, or move one cell to the left when the selection has only one row
Tab	Move the cell pointer one cell to the right in the selection when there's more than one column, or move one cell down when the selection has only one column
Shift+Tab	Move the cell pointer one cell to the left in the selection when there's more than one column, or move one cell up when the selection has only one column
⌘+Shift+A	Move to the next corner of the current cell range
Shift+Delete	Collapse the cell selection to just the active cell

When You Need to Size or Move through the Worksheets in a Workbook	
Press	***To***
Arrow key	Scroll one row up or down or one column left or right
Page Up	Scroll up one screenful
Page Down	Scroll down one screenful
⌘+Page Up	Move to previous sheet in workbook
⌘+Page Down	Move to next sheet in workbook
⌘+F10	Toggle key that maximizes or minimizes the workbook

When You Need to Format a Cell Selection	
Press	***To***
Control+Shift+~	Apply the General number format to the cell selection
Control+Shift+$	Apply the Currency format with two decimal places to the cell selection
Control+Shift+%	Apply the Percentage format with no decimal places to the cell selection

(continued)

Press	To
Control+Shift+^	Apply the Scientific (exponential) number format with two decimal places to the cell selection
Control+Shift+#	Apply the Date format with the day, month, and year to the cell selection, as in 27-Oct-94
Control+Shift+@	Apply the Time format with the hour and minute, indicating AM or PM, to the cell selection, as in 12:05 PM
⌘+Option+0 (zero)	Apply an outline border to the cell selection
⌘+Option+-	Get rid of all borders in the cell selection
⌘+1	Display the Format Cells dialog box
Control+B or ⌘+Shift+B	Apply or get rid of bold in the cell selection
Control+I or ⌘+Shift+I	Apply or get rid of italics in the cell selection
Control+U or ⌘+Shift+U	Apply or get rid of underlining in the cell selection
⌘+Shift+_	Apply or get rid of strikethrough in the cell selection
Control+9	Hide selected rows
Control+Shift+9	Unhide all hidden rows
Control+0 (zero)	Hide selected columns
Control+Shift+0 (zero)	Unhide all hidden columns

When You're Editing the Worksheet

Press	To
Enter	Carry out your action
⌘+. (period)	Cancel a command or close the displayed dialog box
⌘+Y	Repeat your last action
⌘+Z	Undo your last command or action
⌘+I	Display the Insert dialog box to insert new cells, columns, or rows in the worksheet
⌘+K	Display the Delete dialog box to delete cells, columns, or rows from the worksheet
Delete	Display the Clear dialog box to clear the contents or formatting from your cell selection
⌘+B	Clear the entries in your cell selection
⌘+X or F2	Cut the selection to the Clipboard

(continued)

(continued)	
Press	***To***
⌘+C or F3	Copy the selection to the Clipboard
⌘+V or F4	Paste the contents of the Clipboard
⌘+Shift+N	Display the Cell Note dialog box
⌘+F2	Switch between the Info window with information about the active cell and the active document window
Shift+F3	Display the Paste Function dialog box so that you can paste a function and its arguments into a formula
⌘+L	Display the Define Name dialog box so that you can assign a range name to the cell selection
⌘+= or F9	Recalculate the formulas in all open worksheets
⌘+Shift+=	Recalculate the formulas in just the active worksheet
⌘+Shift+T	Create a sum formula (same as clicking on the AutoSum tool on the Standard toolbar)
⌘+T	Toggle on and off the outline symbols or, if no outline exists, display an alert dialog box prompting you to create an outline
⌘+Shift+Z	Select only the visible cells in the cell selection (same as clicking on the Visible Cells Only tool in the Utility toolbar)
F7	Check spelling
⌘+F	Find
⌘+H	Replace

When You're Editing an Entry in the Cell	
Press	***To***
⌘+U	Edit the entry in the current cell by positioning the insertion point at the end of the entry
⌘+-	Insert the current date in the current cell
⌘+;	Insert the current time in the current cell
⌘+'	Copy the formula from the cell above the active cell
⌘+Shift+'	Copy the value from the cell above the active cell

(continued)

Press	*To*
Option+Enter	Enter the contents of the current cell in all cells in the cell selection
Arrow keys	Move the insertion point one character up, down, left, or right in edited entry
Home	Move the insertion point to the beginning of the edited entry
⌘+Option+Return	Insert a new line in the cell entry
⌘+Option+Tab	Insert a tab in the cell entry
Delete	Delete the preceding character in the edited entry or activate and clear the entry in the selected cell

When You Need to Print, Open, or Save Excel Documents

Press	*To*
⌘+P	Display the Print dialog box
F11	Insert a new chart sheet in the workbook
⌘+F11	Insert a new macro sheet in the workbook
⌘+Shift+S	Display the Save As dialog box
⌘+S	Save the workbook
⌘+O	Display the Open dialog box

Appendix

How to Install Excel 5.0 on Your Mac without Going Crazy

This book assumes that you've already conned someone into installing Excel 5.0 on your computer (maybe your dealer, systems administrator, landlord, best friend, or someone you just met or think you would like to). If this is not the case, then you'll have to bite the bullet and go through the steps in this appendix. Just look at this way: By going through this little installation exercise, you'll be able to help other people install their copies of Excel 5.0 — not what exactly you had in mind, eh?

Ahoy, potential pirates! Shiver me timbers — you must be *licensed* to install Excel 5.0 on your computer legally. Keep in mind that your license only entitles you to make *one* backup copy of the original Excel diskettes and to install it on *one* computer. If you are about to installed a "borrowed" copy of Excel that you got from someone else in the office or from a friend of yours, then you are contemplating hauling up the electronic Jolly Roger. *Don't do it!* Software piracy is neither condoned nor appreciated in the civilized world.

What It Takes to Run This Baby

It's no use going through a long installation process (it's copying of all those blasted backup disks that takes so long) only to find out that you can't even run the program. So just glance over the following to make sure that you have what it takes to get Excel 5.0 up and running before you install the program:

To run Excel 5.0 for the Macintosh, you need the following:

- A working Macintosh computer equipped with Macintosh System 6.02 or higher (including System 7 or later); Finder version 6.1 or later.
- A single 800KB floppy drive or a 1440KB drive.
- A hard disk with lots of free disk space (we're talking lots of room if you want to install the entire program — 10MB or so, plus more for the files you'll create). If your computer is tight on space, you may want to remove

unused documents or programs from the disk. (Please be sure to back up any documents that you created or any of your coworkers created before you trash them.)

- A minimum of 2MB of memory — 4MB if you're using Multifinder under System 6, and a minimum of 4MB under Macintosh System 7.0 or later.

Getting the "Little Sweetheart" Installed

Before you install Excel 5.0, exit any application programs you may have open. If your computer uses a virus-protection program, you should turn it off before you start the installation. If you are upgrading to Excel 5.0 from a previous version of the program, you can either replace the previous Excel version with Excel 5.0 or you can install Excel 5.0 in another location (if you happen to have enough free disk space on your hard disk for both versions of Excel) and keep the previous version installed until you've had a chance to use this book and become comfortable with the new version.

To install Excel 5.0 for the Macintosh, take a deep breath and follow these steps:

1. **If necessary, start your computer. You may want to hold down the Shift key to prevent extensions (System 7) or INITs (System 6) from loading.**

   You start your computer by pressing a button (it's probably on your keyboard if you have a newer Mac, or on the front or in the back of your computer). I said that you may want to hold down the Shift key when starting your computer, because some extensions may interfere with the installation program — it happens once in a while, but not frequently.

2. **Insert the disk labeled Install Disk 1 into your floppy drive.**

   The floppy disk should have automatically opened after you inserted it; if it didn't, open the disk to reveal the Microsoft Excel startup icon.

3. **Double-click on the Microsoft Excel startup icon.**

   In Figure A-1, you see the first of a series of screens or windows known as the Microsoft Excel 5.0 Setup dialog box. This screen gives you the warning about the copyright notice. I've already warned potential pirates, so the rest of us can click the OK button.

4. **Follow the setup instructions in this automated setup program.**

   We discuss some of the choices in this appendix — but it's not so bad. The main concern is whether you have enough room on your hard drive and whether you have a previous version of Excel installed.

   If someone has previously installed Excel 5, then you see the dialog box shown in Figure A-2, the "Welcome to the Microsoft Excel 5.0 installation maintenance program" dialog box. It has three options — Add/Remove,

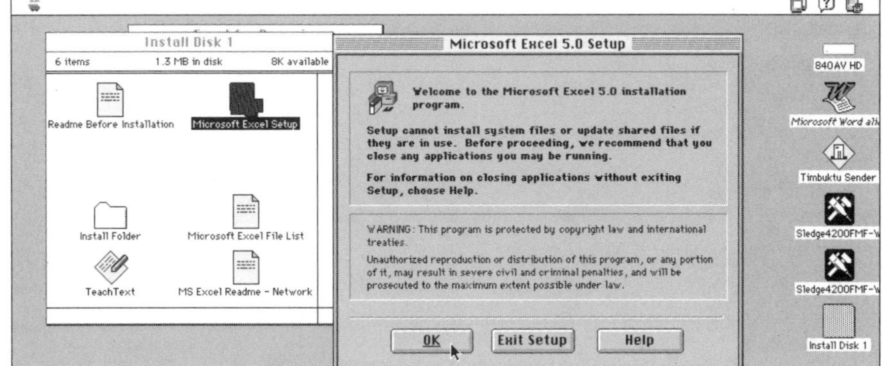

Figure A-1: The Microsoft Excel 5.0 Setup dialog box.

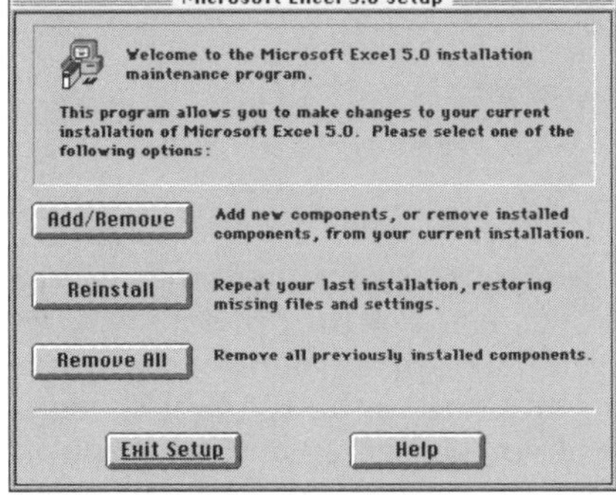

Figure A-2: The "Welcome to the Microsoft Excel 5.0 installation maintenance program" dialog box.

Reinstall, and Remove All. These options are useful for changing the items installed if you need more room on your hard disk or you want to reinstall entirely.

5. **If this is a *new* installation, when the Microsoft Excel Setup screen appears, follow the setup instructions, inserting new disks into your floppy drive when prompted to do so.**

Here are some of the things you'll be asked to accept as-is or change during the installation:

- You may be asked to verify the serial number if Excel 5.0 has already been installed. Otherwise, you must enter your name and organization, as shown in Figure A-3. After typing your name, press the Tab key or use the mouse to go to the next line and then enter your organization's name. Figure A-4 shows you the screen that gives you a chance to change or confirm your entries.

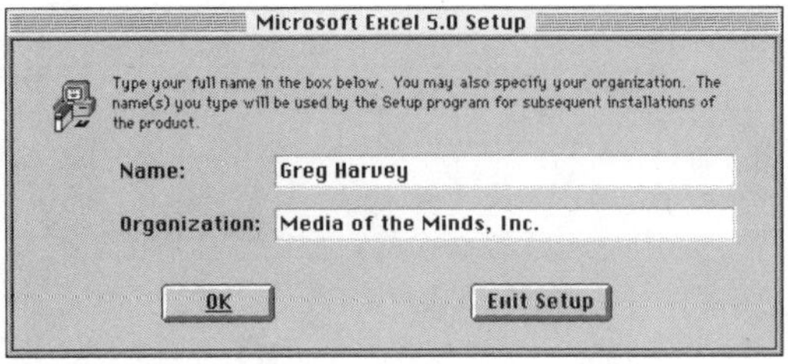

Microsoft Excel 5.0 Setup

Type your full name in the box below. You may also specify your organization. The name(s) you type will be used by the Setup program for subsequent installations of the product.

Name: Greg Harvey

Organization: Media of the Minds, Inc.

OK Exit Setup

Figure A-3: The Name and Organization screen.

Confirm Name and Organization Information

Please confirm that the information you have typed is correct. If it is correct, choose the OK button. Choose the Change button to retype any of the information.

Name: Greg Harvey

Organization: Media of the Minds, Inc.

OK Change

Figure A-4: The Confirm Name and Organization Information dialog box.

- If you're upgrading from a previous version, the Setup program performs an upgrade check on your system to find the previous version. If you've already removed the old version (to make room for the new version), you may need to keep choosing the Continue button even though the Setup program starts displaying all sorts of screens accusing you of not being worthy of upgrading. If you don't need to press a Continue button — or even if you did — you'll see a screen similar to Figure A-5, which I call the "Please select a destination folder for your new software" dialog box.
- By default, the Setup program suggests that you install Excel 5.0 in the same folder you may have used for a previous version of Excel. If you want to retain a previous version of Excel or if you need to install Excel 5.0 on a different hard disk (one that has more free space), you need to change the folder/hard disk designation when you're prompted to verify the default folder for installation. If you want to retain an older version of Excel or if you like your own names for your folders, then press the New Folder button, as I did in Figure A-5. Figure A-6 shows the New Folder Name dialog box; I chose to call my folder Microsoft Excel 5. Original, isn't it?

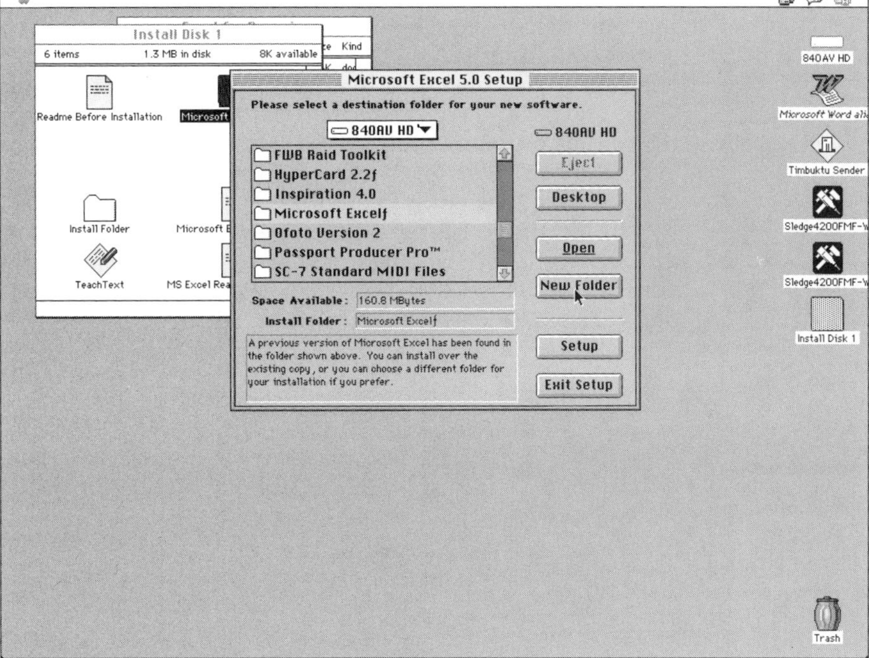

Figure A-5: The "Please select a destination folder for your new software" dialog box of the Microsoft Excel 5.0 Setup process.

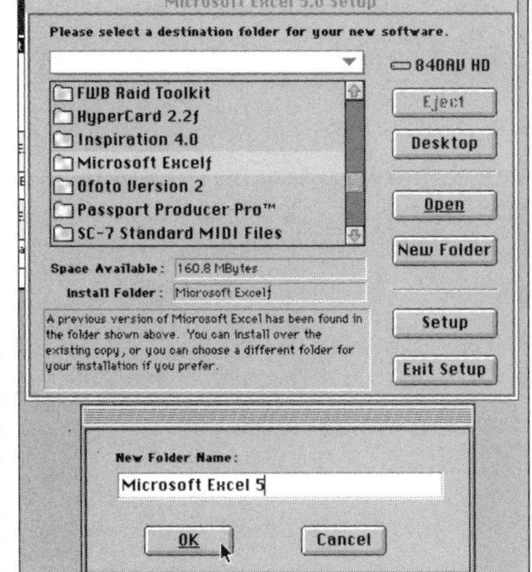

Figure A-6: The New Folder Name dialog box.

- There are three types of installations that you can perform: Typical, Custom (includes complete), or Minimum (laptop). Please refer to the last screen of the Microsoft Excel 5.0 Setup dialog box, shown in Figure A-7. If you have something like 10 or 11MB of free space on your hard disk, go ahead and click on the Typical button (that big box that says `Typical` is really a button you can click on!). If you are *really* pressed for disk space and only have something like 5 or 6MB free, select the Minimum (laptop) button instead. Leave the Custom (complete) button to installations that require just the core program files along with specific auxiliary files, or to install everything, including stuff that isn't in the Typical installation (if you choose Custom, you'll have to help the Setup program select which parts to install and which to leave out).

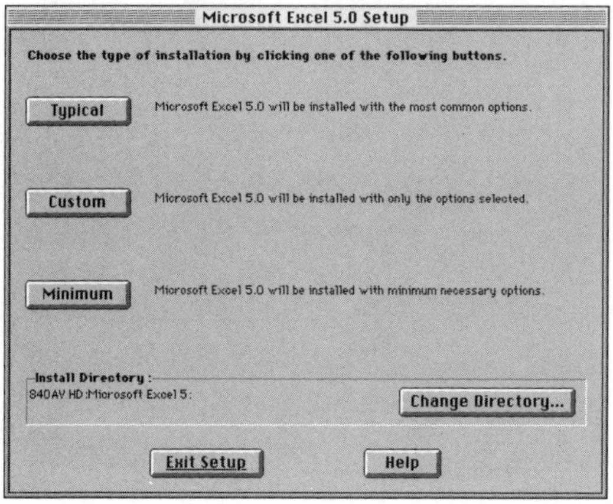

Figure A-7: The Typical, Custom, and Minimum screen of the Microsoft Excel 5.0 Setup process.

When the installation is finished, you see a dialog box informing you that your ordeal is over with and that Excel 5.0 has been successfully installed.

Congratulations! You've now graduated and are ready to start reading how to use Excel in Chapter 1.

Glossary

absolute cell reference

A cell reference that Excel cannot automatically adjust. If you're about to copy a formula and you want to prevent Excel from adjusting one or more of the cell references (the program has a tendency to change the column and row reference in copies), make the cell references absolute. Absolute cell references are indicated by a dollar sign (yes, a *$*) in front of the column letter and the row number — $K$11, for example. You can convert a relative reference to an absolute reference with the F4 key. See also ***relative cell reference.***

active

The program window, workbook window, worksheet window, or dialog box currently in use. The color of the title bar of an active window or dialog box is different from the color of inactive window title bars. When several document windows are displayed, you can activate an inactive window by clicking on it.

arguments

Not what you have with your spouse, but rather the values you give to a worksheet function to compute. Arguments are enclosed in parentheses and separated from one another by commas. See also ***function.***

borders

The different types of lines Excel can draw around the edges of each cell or the outside edge of a bunch of cells. Excel offers a wide variety of line styles and colors for this purpose.

cell

The basic building block of plant and animal life and also of the Excel worksheet. The *worksheet cell* is a block formed by the intersections of column and row gridlines displayed in the sheet. Cells are where all worksheet data is stored. Each cell is identified by the letter of its column and the number of its row, the so-called *cell reference.*

cell pointer

A heavy outline that indicates which cell in the worksheet is currently selected. You must move the cell pointer to a particular cell before you can enter or edit information in that cell.

cell range

A bunch of cells that are all right next to each other. To select a range of cells with the mouse, you simply point at the beginning of the range, click the mouse button, and drag through the cells.

cell reference

Identifies the location of a cell in the worksheet. Normally, the cell reference consists of the column letter followed by the row number. For example, B3 indicates the cell in the second column and third row of the worksheet. When you place the cell pointer in a cell, Excel displays its cell reference at the beginning of the formula bar. See also ***relative cell reference*** and ***absolute cell reference.***

chart

Also known as a *graph.* This is a graphic representation of a set of values stored in a worksheet. You can create a chart right in a worksheet, where it is saved and printed along with the worksheet data. You also can display a chart in its own chart window, where you can edit its contents or print it independently of the worksheet data. (Such as chart is called, appropriately enough, a *chart sheet.*) See also ***workbook.***

check box

Turns an option on or off in a dialog box. If the check box contains an X (sorry, not a check mark), the option is turned on. If the check box is blank, the option is turned off. The nice thing about check boxes is that you can select more than one of the multiple options presented as a group. See also ***radio button.***

click

The simplest mouse technique. You press and immediately release the mouse button. See also ***double-click.***

Clipboard

The Macintosh equivalent of a hand-held Clipboard to which you attach papers and information you need to work with. The Clipboard is a special area of memory, a holding place where text and graphics can be stored to await further action. You can paste the contents of the Clipboard into any open Excel document. The contents of the Clipboard are automatically replaced as soon as you place new information there (whether in Excel or some other program).

command button

A dialog-box button that initiates an action. The default command button is indicated by a dotted rectangle and a darker border. A button with an ellipsis (. . .) opens another dialog box or window. Frequently, after you choose options in the dialog box, you click on the OK or Cancel command button.

database

A tool for organizing, managing, and retrieving large amounts of information. A database is created right on a worksheet. The first row of the database contains column headings called *field names,* which identify each item of information you are tracking (like First Name, Last Name, City, and the like). Below the field names you enter the information you want to store for each field (column) of each record. See also ***field*** and ***record.***

default

Don't be alarmed, I'm not talking blame here. A *default* is a setting, value, or response that Excel automatically provides unless you choose something else. Some defaults can be changed and rearranged. If you like controlling everything, see Chapter 10.

dialog box

A box containing various options that appears when you select Excel commands followed by an ellipsis (. . .). The options in a dialog box are presented in groups of buttons and boxes (oh boy!). Many dialog boxes in Excel 5.0 contain different tabs (see ***tab***) that you click on to bring up a different set of options. A dialog box also can display warnings and messages. Each dialog box contains a title bar and a Control menu but has no menu bar. You can move a dialog box around the active document window by dragging its title bar.

docking

Has nothing at all to do with the space shuttle. Docking in Excel refers to dragging one of the toolbars to a stationary position along the perimeter of the Excel window with the mouse. See also ***toolbar.***

document

A file where you store the information you generate in Excel. In Excel, a workbook is equivalent to a document (or file). To save the information in an Excel file, you must name the file with the generous Mac naming conventions of up to 32 characters. To retrieve a document so that you can do more work on it or print it, you must remember the name you gave it. See also ***file*** and ***workbook.***

double-click

To click the mouse button twice in rapid succession. Double-clicking opens things: a program or a document. You can double-click to close things, too. See also ***click.***

drag-and-drop

A really direct way to move stuff around in a worksheet. Select the cell or range (bunch) of cells you want to move, position the mouse pointer on one of its edges, and then press and hold down the mouse button. The pointer assumes the shape of an arrowhead pointing up toward the left. Hold the mouse button as you move the mouse and drag the outline of the selection to the new location. When you get where you're going, let it all go (See also the section in Chapter 4 called "Drag until You Drop").

error value

A value Excel displays in a cell when it cannot calculate the formula for that cell. Error values start with # and end with ! and they have various capitalized informative words in the middle. An example is #DIV/0!, which appears when you try to divide by zero. Error values look like they have been censored.

field

A column in an Excel database that tracks just one type of item, such as a city, state, ZIP code, and so on. See also ***database*** and ***record.***

file

Any workbook document saved to a computer disk. See also ***document*** *and* ***workbook.***

font

Shapes for characters — the typeface. Fonts have a point size, weight, and style, such as Helvetica Modern 20-point Bold Italic. You can choose fonts used to display information in an Excel worksheet and change their settings at any time.

footer

Information you specify to be printed in the bottom margin of each page of a printed report. See also ***header.***

formula

Ready for some math anxiety? A sequence of values, cell references, names, functions, or operators that is contained in a cell and produces a new value from existing values. In other words, a mathematical expression. Formulas in Excel always begin with an equal sign (=).

formula bar

Sounds like a high-energy treat. Well, it is — sort of. Located at the top of the Excel window under the menu bar, the formula bar displays the contents of the current cell (in the case of formulas, this means you see the formula rather than the calculated result, which shows up in the cell itself). You also can use the formula bar for entering or editing values and formulas in a cell or chart. When activated, the formula bar displays a Return box, Cancel box, and Function Wizard button between the current cell reference on the left and the place where the cell contents appear on the right. Click on the Return box or press Enter to complete an entry or edit. Click on the Cancel box or press Esc to leave the contents of the formula bar unchanged.

function

(Let's see, I know what *dysfunction* is . . .) A function simplifies and shortens lengthy calculations. Functions have built-in formulas that use a series of values called *arguments* to perform the specified operations and return the results. The easiest way to enter a function in a cell is with the Function Wizard, which walks you through the entry of the function's arguments. The Function Wizard tool is the one with the `fx` on it, appearing on both the Standard toolbar and the formula bar.See also ***arguments.***

graphics object

Any of the various shapes or graphics images you can bring into any of the sheets in your workbook document (including charts). All graphics objects remain in a separate layer on top of the cells in the sheet so that they can be selected, moved, resized, and formatted independently of the other information stored in the sheet.

header

Information you specify to be printed in the top margin of each page of a printed report. See also ***footer.***

I-beam cursor

The I-beam shape, which looks like the end of a girder or a capital I, is what the mouse pointer assumes when you position it somewhere on the screen where you can enter or edit text. Click the I-beam cursor in the formula bar or a text box in a dialog box, for example, to place the insertion point where you want to add or delete text. When you double-click on a cell or press ⌘+U, Excel positions the insertion point (see next glossary entry) at the end of the entry in that cell — you then can click the I-beam cursor in the cell entry to reposition the insertion point for editing.

insertion point

The blinking vertical bar that indicates your current location in the text. The insertion point shows where the next character you type will appear or where the next one you delete will disappear. When you double-click on a cell or press ⌘+U on the Mac, Excel positions the insertion point at the end of the entry in that cell; you then can move the insertion point through the characters as required to edit the cell entry.

list box

A boxed area in a dialog box that displays a list of choices you can choose from. When a list is too long for all the choices to be displayed, the list box has a scroll bar you can use to bring new options into view. Most list boxes are already open and have the list on display. Those that you must open by clicking on an arrow button are called *pull-down* (or *pop-up*) *menus.*

macro

A sequence of frequently performed, repetitive tasks and calculations that you record. From then on, at the touch of a couple keystrokes, you can have Excel play back the steps in the macro much faster than is humanly possible.

marquee

The moving lights around the movie stars' names, right? Well, a marquee exists in Excel in a slightly toned-down version. It's the moving dotted line around a selection that shows what information is selected when you move or copy data with the Cut, Copy, and Paste commands on the Edit menu. Looks sort of like marching ants.

menu

A vertical list of commands that can be applied to the active window or application. Also known as a *pull-down menu* because the menu opens down from the menu bar when you select the menu name. When an option is currently unavailable on a pull-down menu, the option is dimmed, or *disabled.* See also ***shortcut menus.***

menu bar

The row at the top of a program window that contains the names of the menus available for the active document window.

message box

Also known as an *alert box.* This is a type of dialog box that appears when Excel gives you information, a warning, or an error message, or when it asks for confirmation before carrying out a command.

mode indicators

The information on the right side of the status bar (the row at the bottom of the screen) that tells you what keyboard modes are currently active. Some examples are ADD, NUM, and CAPS.

mouse pointer

Indicates your position on-screen as you move the mouse on the desk. It assumes various forms to indicate a change in the action when you use different features: the arrowhead when you point, select, or drag; the I-beam when you place the insertion point in text; the double-headed arrow when you drag to adjust row height or column width; and the hourglass when you need to wait. The most common shapes of the mouse pointer are revealed in Chapter 1.

nonadjacent selection

Also called a *discontinuous selection* (is that any better?). A nonadjacent selection is one composed of various cells and cell ranges that don't all touch each other. To accomplish this feat, click on the first cell or click and drag through the first range. Then hold down ⌘ as you click on or drag through the remaining cells or ranges you want to select.

notes (text and sound)

Comments that you attach to a particular worksheet cell to remind yourself of something important (or trivial) about the cell's contents. Text notes can be displayed in a separate dialog box or printed with the worksheet. If your computer is wired for sound, you can record sound notes to be played back directly through your computer's speaker for all the world to hear.

pane

A part of a divided worksheet window. You can display different parts of the same worksheet together on one window in different panes. Horizontal and vertical split bars are involved with creating and sizing.

paste

Yum, yum. Remember kindergarten? Alas, in the computer age, *paste* means to transfer the cut or copied contents of the Clipboard into a document, either into the cell with the cell pointer or into a line of text at the location of the insertion point.

pointing

Babies do it, politicians do it, and so can you. *Pointing* also means selecting a cell or cell range as you enter a formula in the formula bar to automatically record cell references.

program icon

Not the idol for our new cult, but a graphical representation of an application, such as Excel, that appears in the Microsoft Excel folder on the desktop. To start a program in Excel, you double-click on the program icon.

pull-down menu

A text box that displays the currently selected option accompanied by an arrow button. When you click on the associated text arrow button, a menu with other options that you can choose from drops down (or sometimes pops up) from the text box. To select a new option from this menu, click and drag the mouse down (or sideways or even up) while continuing to hold down the mouse button until the desired option is highlighted.

radio button

A radio button in a dialog box works like an old-fashioned pushbutton radio when it's selected (shown by a dot in the middle). Radio buttons are used for dialog box items that contain mutually exclusive options. This means that you can select only one of the options at a time (only one can have the dot in the middle). See also ***check box.***

range

Also called a *cell range.* A range is a bunch of neighboring cells that form some type of solid block when selected with the mouse or the keyboard.

record

A single row in a database that defines one entity (such as an employee, a client, or a sales transaction). See also ***database*** and ***field.***

relative cell reference

The normal cell reference (like A2) that is automatically adjusted when you copy formulas that refer to the cell. Row references are adjusted when you copy up or down, column references when you copy left or right. See also ***absolute cell reference*** and ***cell reference.***

scroll bar

The vertical or horizontal bar in the active document window and in some list boxes. Use a scroll bar to move rapidly through a document or list by clicking on the scroll arrows or dragging the scroll box.

selection

The chosen element, such as a cell, cell range, nonadjacent selection, file, directory, dialog box option, graphics object, or text. To make a selection, highlight it by clicking (and possibly dragging) the mouse or pressing keystroke shortcuts. You normally select an element before choosing the actions you want to apply to that element.

sheet tabs

The tabs that appear at the bottom of each workbook window in Excel 5.0. To select a new sheet (worksheet, chart, and so on) in your workbook, you click on its sheet tab. To display new sheet tabs, you use the tab scrolling buttons. Excel indicates which sheet is the active one by displaying the sheet name in bold on its tab. To rename a sheet tab (which are normally given boring names such as Sheet1, Sheet2, and so on), double-click on the tab and enter the new name in the Rename Sheet dialog box, then select OK or press Enter. See also ***tab.***

shortcut menus

Nutritious meals for the whole family in 30 minutes or less. No, not really — *these* menus are attached to certain things on the screen, namely the toolbar, worksheet cell, or parts of a chart open in a chart window. They contain a quick list of command options related to the object they're attached to. You must use the mouse to open a shortcut menu and choose its commands. You press ⌘+Option as you click on the object (or, if you have a Control key on your menu, hold *it* down as you click). See also ***menu.***

spreadsheet

A type of computer program that enables you to develop and perform all sorts of calculations between the text and values stored in a document. Most spreadsheet programs like Excel also include charting and database capabilities. *Spreadsheet* is also commonly used as alternate term for *worksheet* — so see also ***worksheet.***

status bar

The bar at the bottom of the Excel window. The status bar displays messages, such as `Ready`, or a short description of the menu option you have chosen, and indicates any active modes, such as `CAPS` or `NUM` when you press Caps Lock or Num Lock.

style

If you've got it, flaunt it. Also known to some of us as a group of formatting instructions, all combined, that you can apply to the cells in a worksheet. Use styles to save time and keep things consistent. Styles can deal with the number format, font, alignment, border, patterns, and protection of the cells.

tab

You find tabs in two places in Excel 5.0: in some larger dialog boxes, such as the Format Cells or Options dialog boxes, and attached to the bottom of each worksheet in a workbook. In the case of dialog box tabs, you simply click on a tab to display its set of options on the top of all the others in the dialog box. In the case of sheet tabs, you click on a tab to display its sheet on top of all the others in the workbook. See also ***dialog box*** and ***sheet tabs***.

table

This is often used to refer to contiguous blocks of data that are organized within a single worksheet.

tear-off menus

These are the three special pull-down menus that can be moved and placed elsewhere off the Formatting toolbar. The Borders, Color, and Text Color menus are the only menus that float above the worksheet. The "Borders" menu loses its "s" when it is ripped-off the Formatting toolbar and is transformed into the "Border" floating menu. Go figure.

text box

The area in a dialog box where you type a new selection or edit the current one.

title bar

The top bar of a program window, workbook window, or dialog box that contains its title. You can move an active window or dialog box around the screen by dragging its title bar.

toolbar

A series of related tools (buttons with icons) that you simply click on to perform common tasks like opening, saving, or printing a document. Excel comes with several built-in toolbars you can use as-is or customize. You can create toolbars of your own design, using predefined tools or blank tools to which you assign macros. Toolbars can be displayed in their own little dialog boxes that float around the active document window. They also can dock along the perimeter of the screen. See also ***docking.***

workbook

The Excel file that contains multiple related sheets such as worksheets, charts, and macro sheets. When you start a new workbook, Excel automatically puts 16 blank worksheets in it (named Sheet1 through Sheet16) and gives the workbook a temporary name (such as Workbook1, Workbook2, and so on). You then can add or remove worksheets as needed, as well as add chart or module/macro sheets as needed. When you save the workbook, you then can give the workbook a permanent filename. See also ***chart***, ***document***, ***file***, and ***worksheet***.

worksheet

Also called a *spreadsheet.* This is the primary document for recording, analyzing, and calculating data. The Excel worksheet is organized in a series of 256 columns and 16,384 rows, making for a heck of a lot of cells. Each new workbook you open contains 16 blank worksheets. See also ***workbook*** and ***spreadsheet.***

Index

• Symbols •

• A •

• B •

• D •

• G •

• J •

• K •

• L •

• M •

• N •

• O •

• P •

• S •

• T •

• U •

• V •

• W •

Notes

Notes

Notes

Notes

Notes

Notes

IDG BOOKS' ...FOR DUMMIES QUICK REFERENCE SERIES

IDG's bestselling ...For Dummies Quick Reference Series provides a quick and simple way to remember software commands and functions, written in our down-to-earth, plain English style that guides beginners and experts alike through important commands and hidden troublespots.

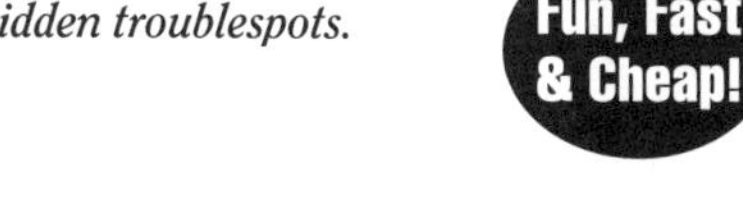

"Thanks for coming up with the simplest idea ever, a reference that you really can use and understand."
Allison J. O'Neill, Edison, NJ

ILLUSTRATED COMPUTER DICTIONARY FOR DUMMIES™
by Dan Gookin, Wally Wang, & Chris Van Buren

This plain English guide to computer jargon helps with even the most techie terms.

ISBN: 1-56884-004-7
$12.95 USA/$16.95 Canada
£11.99 UK & Eire

WINDOWS FOR DUMMIES™ QUICK REFERENCE
by Greg Harvey

The quick and friendly way to remember Windows tasks & features.

ISBN: 1-56884-008-X
$8.95 USA/$11.95 Canada
£7.99 UK & Eire

DOS FOR DUMMIES™ QUICK REFERENCE
by Greg Harvey

A fast, fun, and cheap way to remember DOS commands.

ISBN: 1-56884-007-1
$8.95 USA/$11.95 Canada
£7.99 UK & Eire

WORDPERFECT FOR DOS FOR DUMMIES™ QUICK REFERENCE
by Greg Harvey

With this guide you'll never have to worry about deciphering cryptic WordPerfect commands again!

ISBN: 1-56884-009-8
$8.95 USA/$11.95 Canada
£7.99 UK & Eire

WORD FOR WINDOWS FOR DUMMIES™ QUICK REFERENCE
by George Lynch

End your stress over style sheets, mail merge, and other pesky Word features with this quick reference. Covers Word 2.

ISBN: 1-56884-029-2
$8.95 USA/$11.95 Canada

1-2-3 FOR DUMMIES™ QUICK REFERENCE
by John Walkenbach

Keep this quick and easy reference by your desk and you'll never have to worry about forgetting tricky 1-2-3 commands again!

ISBN: 1-56884-027-6
$8.95 USA/$11.95 Canada
£7.99 UK & Eire

EXCEL FOR DUMMIES™ QUICK REFERENCE
by John Walkenbach

A fast, fun and cheap way to remember bothersome Excel commands.

ISBN: 1-56884-028-4
$8.95 USA/$11.95 Canada
£7.99 UK & Eire

WORDPERFECT FOR WINDOWS FOR DUMMIES™ QUICK REFERENCE
by Greg Harvey

The quick and friendly "look-it-up" guide to the leading Windows word processor.

ISBN: 1-56884-039-X
$8.95 USA/$11.95 Canada/£7.99 UK & Eire

For more information or to order by mail, call 1-800-762-2974. Call for a free catalog! For volume discounts and special orders, please call Tony Real, Special Sales, at 415-312-0644. For International sales and distribution information, please call our authorized distributors:

CANADA Macmillan Canada 416-293-8141 | UNITED KINGDOM Transworld 44-81-231-6661 | AUSTRALIA Woodslane Pty Ltd. 61-2-979-5944

IDG BOOKS' PC WORLD SERIES

"I rely on your publication extensively to help me over stumbling blocks that are created by my lack of experience."

Fred Carney, Louisville, KY on
PC World DOS 6 Handbook

IDG BOOKS PC WORLD

PC WORLD MICROSOFT ACCESS BIBLE

by Cary N. Prague & Michael R. Irwin

Easy-to-understand reference that covers the ins and outs of Access features and provides hundreds of tips, secrets and shortcuts for fast database development. Complete with disk of Access templates. Covers versions 1.0 & 1.1

ISBN: 1-878058-81-9
$39.95 USA/$52.95 Canada
£35.99 incl. VAT UK & Eire

PC WORLD WORD FOR WINDOWS 6 HANDBOOK

by Brent Heslop & David Angell

Details all the features of Word for Windows 6, from formatting to desktop publishing and graphics. A 3-in-1 value (tutorial, reference, and software) for users of all levels.

ISBN: 1-56884-054-3
$34.95 USA/$44.95 Canada
£29.99 incl. VAT UK & Eire

PC WORLD DOS 6 COMMAND REFERENCE AND PROBLEM SOLVER

by John Socha & Devra Hall

The only book that combines a DOS 6 Command Reference with a comprehensive Problem Solving Guide. Shows when, why and how to use the key features of DOS 6/6.2

ISBN: 1-56884-055-1
$24.95 USA/$32.95 Canada
£22.99 UK & Eire

QUARKXPRESS FOR WINDOWS DESIGNER HANDBOOK

by Barbara Assadi & Galen Gruman

ISBN: 1-878058-45-2
$29.95 USA/$39.95 Canada/£26.99 UK & Eire

PC WORLD WORDPERFECT 6 HANDBOOK

by Greg Harvey, author of IDG's bestselling 1-2-3 For Dummies

Here's the ultimate WordPerfect 6 tutorial and reference. Complete with handy templates, macros, and tools.

ISBN: 1-878058-80-0
$34.95 USA/$44.95 Canada
£29.99 incl. VAT UK & Eire

PC WORLD EXCEL 5 FOR WINDOWS HANDBOOK, 2nd EDITION

by John Walkenbach & Dave Maguiness

Covers all the latest Excel features, plus contains disk with examples of the spreadsheets referenced in the book, custom ToolBars, hot macros, and demos.

ISBN: 1-56884-056-X
$34.95 USA/$44.95 Canada /£29.99 incl. VAT UK & Eire

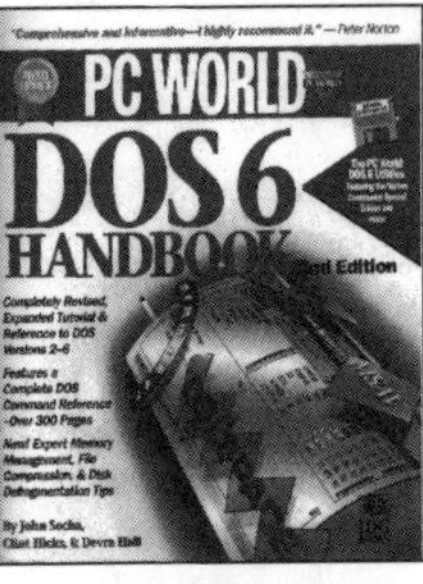

PC WORLD DOS 6 HANDBOOK, 2nd EDITION

by John Socha, Clint Hicks & Devra Hall

Includes the exciting new features of DOS 6, a 300+ page DOS command reference, plus a bonus disk of the Norton Commander Special Edition, and over a dozen DOS utilities.

ISBN: 1-878058-79-7
$34.95 USA/$44.95 Canada/£29.99 incl. VAT UK & Eire

OFFICIAL XTREE COMPANION, 3RD EDITION

by Beth Slick

ISBN: 1-878058-57-6
$19.95 USA/$26.95 Canada/£17.99 UK & Eire

For more information or to order by mail, call 1-800-762-2974. Call for a free catalog! For volume discounts and special orders, please call Tony Real, Special Sales, at 415-312-0644. For International sales and distribution information, please call our authorized distributors:

CANADA Macmillan Canada 416-293-8141 — UNITED KINGDOM Transworld 44-81-231-6661 — AUSTRALIA Woodslane Pty Ltd. 61-2-979-5944

...SECRETS

"Livingston is a Windows consultant, and it is hard to imagine any tricks or tips he has ommitted from these 990 pages. True to the name, there are lots of undocumented hints that can make life easier for the intermediate and advanced user."

Peter H. Lewis, New York Times *on Brian Livingston's* Windows 3.1 SECRETS

"Brian Livingston has worked his magic once again. *More Windows 3.1 SECRETS* is well worth any serious Windows user's time and money."

Stewart Alsop, Editor in Chief, InfoWorld

"...Probably the most valuable book on computers I've ever seen, and I work in a library."

Jacques Bourgeios, Longueuil, Quebec, on Brian Livingston's Windows 3.1 SECRETS

MORE WINDOWS 3.1 SECRETS™

by Brian Livingston

BESTSELLER!

IDG's Windows guru, Brian Livingston, reveals a host of valuable, previously undocumented, and hard-to-find Windows features in this sequel to the #1 bestseller.

ISBN: 1-56884-019-5
$39.95 USA/$52.95 Canada
£ 35.99 incl. VAT UK & Eire

WINDOWS 3.1 SECRETS™

BESTSELLER!

by Brian Livingston

The #1 bestselling Windows book/ disk by the renowned *InfoWorld* and *Windows Magazine* columnist. Over 250,000 in print! A must-have!

ISBN: 1-878058-43-6
$39.95 USA/$52.95 Canada
£35.99 incl. VAT UK & Eire

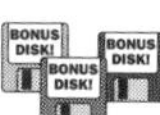

WINDOWS GIZMOS™

by Brian Livingston and Margie Livingston

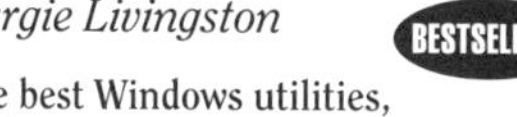

BESTSELLER!

The best Windows utilities, applications, and games—over 30 programs on 4 disks!

ISBN: 1-878058-66-5
$39.95 USA/$52.95 Canada
£35.99 incl. VAT UK & Eire

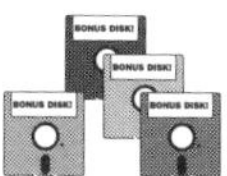

"David Vaskevitch knows where client/ server is going and he tells it all."

Dr. Robert Metcalfe, Publisher/CEO, InfoWorld *on David Vaskevitch's* Client/Server Strategies

Over 750,000 SECRETS Books In Prints

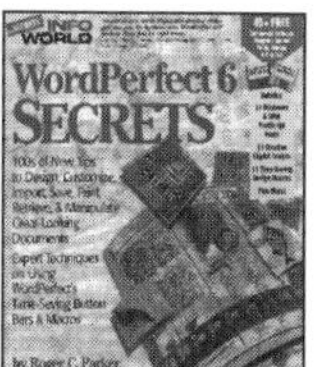

WORDPERFECT 6 SECRETS™

by Roger C. Parker and David A. Holzgang

Bestselling desktop publishing wizard Roger C. Parker shows how to create great-looking documents with WordPerfect 6. Includes 2 disks with Bitstream fonts, clip art, and custom macros.

ISBN: 1-56884-040-3; $39.95 USA/
$52.95 Canada/£ 35.99 incl. VAT UK & Eire

DOS 6 SECRETS™

by Robert D. Ainsbury

Unleash the power of DOS 6 with secret work- arounds and hands-on solutions. Features "Bob's Better Than DOS" shareware Collection with over 25 programs.

ISBN: 1-878058-70-3; $39.95 USA/
$52.95 Canada/£ 35.99 incl. VAT UK & Eire

PC SECRETS™

by Caroline M. Halliday

BESTSELLER!

IDG's technical support expert shows you how to optimize your PC's performance. Includes two disks full of valuable utilities.

ISBN: 1-878058-49-5; $39.95 USA/
$52.95 Canada/£ 35.99 incl. VAT UK & Eire

HARD DISK SECRETS™

by John M. Goodman, Ph.D.

Prevent hard disk problems altogether with the insider's guide. Covers DOS 6 and SpinRite 3.1. Includes a disk of hard disk tune-up software.

ISBN: 1-878058-64-9; $39.95 USA/
$52.95 Canada/£ 37.99 incl. VAT UK & Eire

NETWORK SECURITY SECRETS™

by David Stang & Sylvia Moon

Top computer security experts show today's network administrators how to protect their valuable data from theft and destruction by hackers, viruses, corporate spies, and more!

ISBN: 1-56884-021-7;
$49.95 USA/$64.95 Canada
£ 44.99 incl. VAT UK & Eire

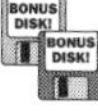

CLIENT/SERVER STRATEGIES: A SURVIVAL GUIDE FOR CORPORATE REENGINEERS

by David Vaskevitch

An essential read for anyone trying to understand the data highways that will drive successful businesses through the '90s and beyond.

ISBN: 1-56884-064-0; $29.95 USA/$39.95 Canada
£ 26.99 incl. VAT UK & Eire

For more information or to order by mail, call 1-800-762-2974. Call for a free catalog! For volume discounts and special orders, please call Tony Real, Special Sales, at 415-312-0644. For International sales and distribution information, please call our authorized distributors:

CANADA Macmillan Canada 416-293-8141

UNITED KINGDOM Transworld 44-81-231-6661

AUSTRALIA Woodslane Pty Ltd. 61-2-979-5944

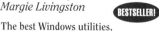

Order Form

Order Center: (800) 762-2974 (8 a.m.-5 p.m., PST, weekdays) or (415) 312-0650

For Fastest Service: Photocopy This Order Form and FAX it to: (415) 358-1260

Quantity	ISBN	Title	Price	Total

Shipping & Handling Charges

Subtotal	U.S.	Canada & International	International Air Mail
Up to $20.00	Add $3.00	Add $4.00	Add $10.00
$20.01-40.00	$4.00	$5.00	$20.00
$40.01-60.00	$5.00	$6.00	$25.00
$60.01-80.00	$6.00	$8.00	$35.00
Over $80.00	$7.00	$10.00	$50.00

In U.S. and Canada, shipping is UPS ground or equivalent.
For Rush shipping call (800) 762-2974.

Subtotal __________

CA residents add applicable sales tax __________

IN and MA residents add 5% sales tax __________

IL residents add 6.25% sales tax __________

RI residents add 7% sales tax __________

Shipping __________

Total __________

Ship to:

Name __________

Company __________

Address __________

City/State/Zip __________

Daytime Phone __________

Payment: ❑ Check to IDG Books (US Funds Only) ❑ Visa ❑ Mastercard ❑ American Express

Card# __________ Exp. __________ Signature __________

Please send this order form to: IDG Books, 155 Bovet Road, Suite 310, San Mateo, CA 94402.

Allow up to 3 weeks for delivery. Thank you!

IDG BOOKS WORLDWIDE REGISTRATION CARD

RETURN THIS
REGISTRATION CARD
FOR FREE CATALOG

Title of this book: **EXCEL 5 FOR MACS FOR DUMMIES**

My overall rating of this book: ❑ Very good [1] ❑ Good [2] ❑ Satisfactory [3] ❑ Fair [4] ❑ Poor [5]

How I first heard about this book:

❑ Found in bookstore; name: [6] ❑ Book review: [7]

❑ Advertisement: [8] ❑ Catalog: [9]

❑ Word of mouth; heard about book from friend, co-worker, etc.: [10] ❑ Other: [11]

What I liked most about this book:

What I would change, add, delete, etc., in future editions of this book:

Other comments:

Number of computer books I purchase in a year: ❑ 1 [12] ❑ 2-5 [13] ❑ 6-10 [14] ❑ More than 10 [15]

I would characterize my computer skills as: ❑ Beginner [16] ❑ Intermediate [17] ❑ Advanced [18] ❑ Professional [19]

I use ❑ DOS [20] ❑ Windows [21] ❑ OS/2 [22] ❑ Unix [23] ❑ Macintosh [24] ❑ Other: [25] ________ (please specify)

I would be interested in new books on the following subjects:
(please check all that apply, and use the spaces provided to identify specific software)

❑ Word processing: [26] ❑ Spreadsheets: [27]

❑ Data bases: [28] ❑ Desktop publishing: [29]

❑ File Utilities: [30] ❑ Money management: [31]

❑ Networking: [32] ❑ Programming languages: [33]

❑ Other: [34]

I use a PC at (please check all that apply): ❑ home [35] ❑ work [36] ❑ school [37] ❑ other: [38] ________

The disks I prefer to use are ❑ 5.25 [39] ❑ 3.5 [40] ❑ other: [41] ________

I have a CD ROM: ❑ yes [42] ❑ no [43]

I plan to buy or upgrade computer hardware this year: ❑ yes [44] ❑ no [45]

I plan to buy or upgrade computer software this year: ❑ yes [46] ❑ no [47]

Name: Business title: [48] Type of Business: [49]

Address (❑ home [50] ❑ work [51]/Company name:)

Street/Suite#

City [52]/State [53]/Zipcode [54]: Country [55]

❑ **I liked this book!** You may quote me by name in future IDG Books Worldwide promotional materials.

My daytime phone number is ________

IDG BOOKS
THE WORLD OF COMPUTER KNOWLEDGE